my psychedelic explorations

"A remarkable collection of Claudio Naranjo's writings on psychedelics and their role in spirituality and psychotherapy—what he considers two sides of the same coin. Of special value are his plentiful case reports in which we see on display the humanity and wisdom of this wise and humane psychedelic guide and trainer. Naranjo's unwavering commitment to the centrality of actual experience to personal growth provides a unique perspective on understanding and utilizing the psychedelic drug state. A timely and most valuable contribution to the field."

RICK STRASSMAN, M.D., AUTHOR OF
DMT: THE SPIRIT MOLECULE

"Today's psychedelic culture is a hotchpotch of conflicting and harmonious factors bubbling together in a multicolored cauldron of potential. With such a long history of seemingly miraculous successes and well-known epic controversies, it takes a scholar of epic proportions to guide us through the maelstrom. Claudio's years—decades in fact—of frontline immersion in the multidisciplinary field of psychedelics has now produced the go-to text to navigate this fascinating space. This book is a cutting-edge examination of contemporary science with an essential focus on the story of humanity's oldest philosophy. What better captain to steer us than the man who has been there since the beginning, always alert and vigilant to the emerging psychedelic tides and their place in our lives. Read this book; carry it with you on your journey. There can be no better map."

BEN SESSA, M.D., MRCPSYCH, PSYCHIATRIST, RESEARCHER,
COFOUNDER AND COCHAIR OF BREAKING CONVENTION,
AND AUTHOR OF *THE PSYCHEDELIC RENAISSANCE*

"Imagine a life that brings together the shamanic and the scientific side, of the psychedelic renaissance, the spiritual and the therapeutic, North and South, East and West. Imagine a writer who describes, with clarity and grace, the ineffable nature of the altered state. Imagine a psychedelic pioneer who is not afraid to call out the hedonism, grandiosity, and foolishness that sometimes darken this 'enlightened' community. Imagine Claudio Naranjo."

DON LATTIN, AUTHOR OF *THE HARVARD*
PSYCHEDELIC CLUB AND *CHANGING OUR MINDS*

"I first met Dr. Claudio Naranjo 50 years ago when we both studied at the Esalen Institute with Dr. Fritz Perls, the founder of Gestalt Therapy. Claudio was already a psychotherapy pioneer at that time. He has continued to lead us toward new and important information on healing, now including this magnum opus that contributes significantly to the present worldwide renaissance in psychedelic psychotherapy."

DR. RICHARD LOUIS MILLER, PH.D.,
AUTHOR OF *PSYCHEDELIC MEDICINE*

"Claudio Naranjo is the most shaman of the scholars and the most learned of the shamans."

LUIS WEINSTEIN, PHOTOJOURNALIST, AUTHOR,
AND FORMER PRESIDENT OF THE AMERICAN FILM INSTITUTE

"Dr. Claudio Naranjo, pioneer of consciousness, has written the fundamental work for the psychotherapist who wants to not only experience but understand the world of known meditation techniques."

RABBI ZALMAN SCHACHTER-SHALOMI "REB ZALMAN,"
ONE OF THE FOUNDERS OF THE JEWISH RENEWAL MOVEMENT

"I knew Claudio for many years. He is someone who immersed himself in a great variety of teachings and practices in order to help others heal their pain and find the way to the development of consciousness."

TARTHANG TULKU RINPOCHE, TIBETAN TEACHER

my psychedelic
explorations

THE HEALING POWER AND TRANSFORMATIONAL POTENTIAL OF PSYCHOACTIVE SUBSTANCES

Claudio Naranjo, M.D.

Translated by Tania Mollart Rogerson

Park Street Press
Rochester, Vermont

Park Street Press
One Park Street
Rochester, Vermont 05767
www.ParkStPress.com

Text stock is SFI certified

Park Street Press is a division of Inner Traditions International

Originally published in Spanish under the title *Exploraciones psicodélicas: Para la transformación colectiva de la conciencia* by Ediciones La Llave
First U.S. edition published in 2020 by Park Street Press
Published by arrangement with International Editors' Co.

Cataloging-in-Publication Data for this title is available from the Library of Congress

ISBN 978-1-64411-058-4 (print)
ISBN 978-1-64411-059-1 (ebook)

Printed and bound in the United States by Lake Book Manufacturing, Inc. The text stock is SFI certified. The Sustainable Forestry Initiative® program promotes sustainable forest management.

10 9 8 7 6 5 4 3 2 1

Text design by Debbie Glogover and layout by Virginia Scott Bowman
This book was typeset in Garamond Premier Pro, Gill Sans, and Legacy Sans with Acherus Grotesque used as the display typeface

Contents

APPENDICES

Foreword

By Jose Maria Fàbregas, M.D.

Philosopher, psychiatrist, teacher of therapists, seeker and finder of deep meanings of life, gestalt world reference, integrator of the psycho-spiritual legacy of East and West, militant and inspirer of transformative education, teacher of the healing of love as a tool for personal, social, and transpersonal change . . . Dr. Claudio Naranjo's facets are as numerous as the thousand faces of the hero that Joseph Campbell spoke to us of (who, by the way, was his friend: one of the many remarkably interesting friends of this remarkably interesting man). However, I shall never tire of insisting on one of the lesser-known facets of this exceptional researcher with his long white beard, tender heart, and strong character: that of pioneer in psychopharmacology research from the early sixties, as well as a figure of fundamental importance in the development of psychedelic therapies, not only in the golden era of the Revolution of Consciousness in the prodigious decade, but also later, in the troubled seventies of prohibition, in the dismal eighties of the "war on drugs," in the bleak nineties of conformism . . . and in the resurgence, forty years later, already in the twenty-first century, of the medical and humanistic interest in psychotropic substances as bearers of a new revolution, this time of psychiatry (that, unlike other fields of medicine, came to a standstill forty years ago in Haloperidol and Prozac), as well in the search for consciousness.

Let us see to what extent Claudio's work has been that of a pioneer. In the midsixties, when he had already visited the Amazon to experiment firsthand with ayahuasca and already had extensive experience as a therapist, Claudio joined forces with Alexander Shulgin and Tony Sargent to research and develop a whole panoply of previously unimaginable psychotropics. It was an association of ten years with astounding results. Together, they developed over one hundred psychoactive substances. Not only that, they also rediscovered MDMA, or ecstasy, overlooked by the Merck laboratories after discovering it in 1912, believing it to be an unusable substance.

The merit of these "cheerful lads" of psychedelic chemistry is vast. Nowadays, researching visionary substances, psychedelics, or psychodysleptics requires great courage, but if we take this to the era when Shulgin, Naranjo, and Sargent started, we find something of great merit, at a time when there was no demand for it, neither was there a generalized sensitization about the need to open the doors of the mind to the unknown. That in the early sixties somebody should intuit and suggest the possibility of using new psychedelic substances, beyond LSD, for therapeutic uses, is most surprising. The catalog of what was created was gathered partly by Shulgin, the eldest of the three and head of the team, in his books *PiKHAL* (*Phenethylamines I Have Known and Loved*) and *TiKHAL* (*Tryptamines I Have Known and Loved*). The catalog includes substances such as TMA, DMMDA, TeMA, DOM, 2C-B, 2C-T-7, U4E . . . among dozens of others.

Although among the psychedelic community of the United States there has been a tendency to not sufficiently remember or value Claudio's role, the invaluable results of his collaboration with Shulgin during the sixties remain, nevertheless, strongly rooted among us, and I believe that the fact that Shulgin ended up being recognized as "the father of ecstasy," implies some kind of injustice in the face of team research work where Naranjo was also instrumental because of his clinical trials, both regarding MDMA and the case of so many phenethylamines.

Since we are discussing clinical trials, one of the most striking features of that team is that not only did it carry out research, but it was also first in testing the results, above all as a way of protecting future users, which I find to be of astonishing ethical nobility. Many scientists experiment on animals, but one who experiments on himself, and who is able to take on that risk and that responsibility, and share that personal experience with the public in order that it can rely on trustworthy information and previous trials, inevitably becomes a key reference for the creation and right guidance of a critical mass of conscious "psychedelic warriors" capable of helping many other people in their quest. For my part, I must admit that I would not be capable of lending myself as a human guinea pig to my own experiments. I do not know whether these pioneers were sure about which substances could fry their brains and which could not. Either way, they did it and they survived it.

In my work as a psychiatrist specialized in the treatment of drug addictions, seekers of sensations who open their mouths and close their eyes make up for a large cohort. It is fundamental, therefore, to develop means of social protection and precaution, generating information and research—never forms of repression, prohibition, or concealment that, as we have already seen, bring with them the restriction of freedom and terrible social and public health consequences. It is curious that the group of researchers that generate books, synthesize substances, and pave the way to improve the world, and the group of candidates to be admitted to a detoxification clinic share a common trait: disdain for the risk they are exposed to by experimenting on their own bodies. Some are close, as demonstrated, I believe, by the example of Howard Lotsof, initially a junkie on the streets of New York who, when discovering ibogaine and recovering, became a vital researcher—later, by the way, he was to establish a relationship with the discoverer of the effects of ibogaine, who is none other than Claudio.* However, beyond apparent

---

*Dr. Naranjo was the first to describe the hallucinogenic effects of ibogaine and to become involved in clinical experiments with *tabernanthe iboga* extract. Moreover, in the early sixties he conducted forty ibogaine sessions with volunteers in Chile, and he was the first to describe the experience scientifically. (*Note from the editor of the Spanish edition.*)

similarities, it would seem that the wisdom of the researcher, the pioneer, has an invaluable protective effect: after hundreds or perhaps thousands of psychedelic "trips," Shulgin died aged almost 90 and with his composure as a gentleman intact. I am unaware of Sargent's fate. However, Naranjo's life and work are well known: at the time of his death at eighty-six years old, his was one of the most privileged minds of the intellectual, psychotherapeutic, transpersonal, and humanistic panorama of the Anglo-Saxon and Latin American world, if not of the entire world. He is surely among the most important references in the field of psychedelic explorations.

More recently, as Shulgin already did with phenethylamines, Claudio compiled his research as a pioneer in therapeutic use of yagé in the book *Ayahuasca, the Vine of the Celestial River* (in Spanish). Now he presents us with *Psychedelic Explorations*—fifty years of therapeutic work with consciousness catalyzers that will truly surprise readers. But . . . has research with drugs been carried out all this time? Was it not illegal? How is it that we have not come to know about the enormous therapeutic potential of the substances described in this book before? Is the end of prohibition and the "war on drugs" just around the corner? Will we have, in brief, ecstasy on prescription, as Rick Doblin, from MAPS (Multidisciplinary Association for Psychedelic Studies) says? What will a future society where psychedelics are used with common sense and administered not by experts, but by wise people, as Naranjo proposes, be like? So many questions . . . I believe all of them are answered, whether implicitly or explicitly, in the pages of this powerful book.

In the time of the pioneers, there were psychopharmacologists like Shulgin, psychonauts like Huxley, and psychiatrists like Osmond. However, Naranjo was these three things all at once. This sum of roles brought about a shift in the research and practical applications of psychedelic substances: nobody had ventured so far, nobody had progressed so much in their therapeutic application as Claudio. Half a century later, he stands as the psychotherapist with the most clinical experience in individual and group treatment with psychedelics. He must be recognized and valued for his ability to intuit a path that, in that time, did not have full meaning.

Let us briefly discuss the return to research with psychedelics, forty years later. A research that, as evidenced by this book, never ceased, but adopted discreet forms, beyond institutional channels, to avoid the dark shadow of prohibitionism. The sixties was a crucial time in the history of the search for consciousness: working in that decade were Albert Hofmann, Shulgin, Naranjo, and Sargent, Humphrey Osmond, Ken Kesey, and Timothy Leary, Alan Watts, Richard Alpert, Stanislav Grof, Jonathan Ott, Antonio Escohotado, Richard Jensen, and many other researchers, alive at the same time as Ernst Jünger, Aldous Huxley, Robert Graves, Gregory Bateson, Arthur Koestler, Henri Michaux, Anaïs Nin, Allen Ginsberg, Jack Kerouac, William Burroughs, and many other famous psychonauts. It was a truly prodigious generation. However, the Nixon and Reagan administrations' "war on drugs" nipped the psychotropics revolution in the bud. Today we are confronted with the official demise of that detrimental war: if ten years ago, when setting its goals for the decade, the United Nations instituted the eradication of illegal substances, today we can say that battle is lost—there are more drugs, cheaper, purer, and more affordable. Although, unfortunately, the black market does not offer any guarantee to users. We are also facing a new public debate that is attempting to rectify the strayed course of prohibitionism, and negotiating stances of responsibility is already being openly discussed with users. It would be very interesting to reach new social agreements concerning the use of psychotropic substances, for, in spite of the efforts of prohibitionism, today we are facing new problems, such as the lack of perception of risk among adolescents. Cannabis abusers have multiplied and are initiated earlier than a few years ago, which combined with a genetically modified marijuana and psychosocial vulnerability and risk factors, is causing an increase in learning, behavioral, and psychiatric disorders, directly associated with this consumption.

A new awareness and understanding of psychotropics in general seems therefore paramount to me. I found one of the theses of Naranjo's book very relevant in that sense: the need to train professionals that can work as specialists in administering psychedelic substances, that can infuse new energy into the groups of users of these substances, that know how to select participants to avoid the greedy ones and alert vulnerable people about unnecessary risks, that can add to the use of substances an extensive pyschotherapeutic and consciousness training. This should be accompanied by a policy of transparent and responsible public information, as well as certain restrictions: if one needs to be eighteen to drive a car, then to consume drugs, one should also need to be eighteen, and perhaps older, as a psychedelics user should have completed the neural network biological maturation process and be old enough to know how to weigh the risks. The result of all of this could place us before a much healthier panorama (in terms of public health) than the present one. I wish to stress something, more so in the current environment of illegality and trafficking not subject to quality controls: the so-called drugs have therapeutic, medical, and psychological indications that for the most part are yet to be discovered; but they also have contraindications, like any other pharmacological substance. It is an error, for example, to think that the "natural" cannot do any harm. If an ayahuasca consumption facilitator has not trained conscientiously in the prevention of risks associated with this sacred brew, he or she will be putting many people's health at risk. The pharmacological oversight services have protocols that serve to identify problems and contraindications in the interest of the consumer's health; I am not saying it is a perfect system, but it works, and it prevents undesirable effects. In this sense, the right to carry out research becomes fundamental: to evaluate the effects of psychedelic substances is to ensure the well-being of millions of users throughout the world. An anonymous database that would collect secondary effects described by users all over the world would be of great help, and what to say about Energy Control, the international service whose confidential analyses have avoided many overdoses. There is, moreover, a novel and very promising field of research that we are already implementing in the clinic where I carry out my professional role: the analysis of genetic codes to foresee, amongst other things, the secondary effects of some medications.

We have realized that, genetically, each person metabolizes medicine in a different way. A slow metabolizer will need, therefore, a much smaller dose than a fast metabolizer. Here, surely, lies the reason why certain medicines cause secondary effects to a few among thousands of people, or why a same dose of a drug can affect one person negatively while it may have no effect on another. Was it a draw? No: it is the physical conditions and the personal genetic code that determine such effects, and this will lead us to refine with great precision the administering of medicine doses in the future.

Neither are the psychological vulnerability factors inconsiderable. There are people with more stable psychological structures that tolerate experimentation without any problems. There are others, on the contrary, who are shaken by the slightest push. One of the most desirable and formative effects of psychedelics is the experience of death and rebirth, as well as the de-identification of the self. The flexibility of the structure of the self is fundamental here. When the self has been deconstructed and reorganized through a psychedelic experience, what remains afterward tends to be more stable, more joyful, and safer than any other structure that lives with the fear of being deconstructed or confronted.

Beyond that, as I have already mentioned, every medical substance has indications and contraindications. Even aspirin, which some people use for life as a cardiac protector, has them (and many). MDMA really has some very clear therapeutic uses: in post-traumatic stress disorder it acts by unlocking emotions. In extremely vulnerable people, very rarely, it could produce self-referencing, psychotic profiles. However, used in the correct doses, with a safety distance in time between each intake, in the right place, with the appropriate companions, we find ourselves facing a substance safe enough that it would be absurd not to tap into its therapeutic benefits. If we are speaking of ayahuasca, whose neurotoxicity and hepatoxicity simply don't exist, we find ourselves facing a substance with an even greater capacity to evoke memories, relive them with the intensity with which they were created, rearrange them; we might not be able to change the reality of the traumas experienced, but we can reconcile ourselves with the past, no matter how traumatic it may have been. In Brazil, a Chilean torturer came to take ayahuasca in a session that I witnessed. Unaware of it, in that group there was another man who had been a victim of tortures during the Argentinian dictatorship. Both had the opportunity to contact the immense pain that those life situations had meant for them. They both were able to purge and harmonize that past.

In *Psychedelic Explorations,* Claudio talks about his own experience with substances that seem to be, on the one hand, safe enough, and on the other hand, very suitable for undertaking psychedelic therapy with them. These are MMDA, MDMA, ayahuasca, ibogaine, psilocybin, and more. One cannot ignore that the personal experiences described by Claudio, those wonderful sessions transcribed from his psychedelic groups, where marvelous insights and existential gifts of an overwhelming magnitude occur, represent one of the great gifts that this book contributes to the advancement of knowledge. This represents the most luminous aspect of research with psychotropics.

On the other hand, there are substances such as cocaine or heroin that it seems do not present that potential to help. I would find a group dynamic supported by beer or vodka very strange, although Gurdjieff used it with his disciples. In my opinion, the main difference between them is that the first are consciousness expanders, while cocaine is a focalizer of attention and heroin, as benzodiazepines and alcohol, is a depressor of the central nervous system.

Following two decades in which unsound research teams of suspiciously biased financing dedicated themselves to scaring the community describing catastrophic effects of the consumption of almost any known psychedelic substance, today we find a revival of scientific interest in the therapeutic potentialities of psychedelics, and every year more studies appear in specialized journals; with ample guarantees, the beneficial potentialities of these substances are evaluated. Researcher Teri Krebs and clinical psychologist Pål-Ørjan Johansen, of the Neurosciences Department of the Norwegian University of Science and Technology, used data from a United States national health survey with 130,000 people to see if there was a correlation between the use of psychedelic drugs and mental health problems. The authors did not find any links; however, they did find some significant associations between the use of psychedelic drugs and a lesser prevalence of mental health problems. A couple of studies on ritual ayahuasca users in which I have participated reveal similar data. We carried them out, with authorization from the government of Brazil, together with scientists, doctors, and researchers such as José Carlos Bouso, Débora González, Sabela Fontdevila, Marta Cutchet, Xavier Fernández, Paulo César Ribeiro Barbosa, Miguel Ángel Alcázar-Córcoles, Wladimyr Sena Araujo, Manel J. Barbanoj, and Jordi Riba. The studies, "Evaluation of the Severity of Addiction among Ritual Users of Ayahuasca" and "Personality, Psychopathology, Life Attitudes and Neuropsychological Performance among Ritual Users of Ayahuasca: Longitudinal Study," published respectively in *Drug and Alcohol Dependency* and in *PLoS ONE,* revealed that ritual use of ayahuasca does not induce the psychosocial alterations that the abuse of other substances typically causes, and that all the ayahuasca users studied (with fifteen years of consumption twice a week) scored better in resolution ability tests and did not present a higher incidence of psychopathological problems or cognitive deterioration.

Nevertheless, these studies present methodological limitations, such as the self-selection phenomenon, which is that we are unaware of how many individuals have given up consumption due to presenting harmful effects, or the fact that we do not have previous evaluations from before these groups started consuming ayahuasca. Nonetheless, we discover that long-term ayahuasca users obtained much higher scores in matters relating to the meaning of life, personal satisfaction, humanism, intrapsychic life, capacity for empathy, and the like.

Another important methodological limitation for the scientific analyses of the benefits and contraindications of psychedelics is the importance of the setting: it is not the same to take ayahuasca connected to sensors in a hospital, as at a ceremony in the middle of nature, therefore evaluation in a laboratory becomes a complicated procedure.

Moreover, the world of psychedelics is not and cannot be solely in the hands of the medical, scientific, or psychotherapeutic community. Only in the very diverse world of ayahuasca do traditional shamanic lineages, the religious world of the Brazilian ayuasquera churches like the Santo Daime, and the Western representatives of the research and psychotherapy world coexist. The Brazilian government brought together these three lines in a symposium some years ago: the aim was to tell the world that ayahuasca was not a drug, and neither should it be prohibited. Getting these three lines to agree was a real feat, for each group defended itself as the genuine bearer of knowledge.

As I have previously mentioned, Claudio Naranjo is someone who has many merits, and I believe because of this he is someone who should be at the forefront of the fight to make the world understand the importance of research and psychotherapy with psychedelics. Claudio is a shaman recognized by the world of Amazon indigenous Taitas as an equal; likewise, he is someone who has been invested with authority to officiate the ritual reserved for the *padrinhos* of the Santo Daime; lastly, his rise and referentiality as a researcher from universities such as Berkeley, and professor of the University of California in Santa Cruz, psychiatric doctor, and pioneer researcher in psychopharmacology, is already more than accredited.

I still think that his idea of creating a psychedelic therapy facilitator training school goes beyond the visionary. Such an approach represents an overcoming of the disparities between the three lines described, for such a school would invariably integrate them all. Moreover, it would be the opportunity to rescue from anonymity many psychiatrists, psychotherapists, and other daring people who, today, continue to discretely practice psychedelic therapy, as they did back in the sixties when psychiatrists could still provide their patients with psychedelics freely in many parts of the world without it generating criticism or legal problems. It is high time this open secret is made public.

The school that Claudio Naranjo advocates would avoid, moreover, another of the evils that I believe stems from prohibitionism: shamanic amateurism, weekend "training" courses, and feather and maraca commercialism. Who has the right to decide that another is authorized or not to administer sacred plants or psychedelic substances? There is merit, there is greatness and perseverance, and Claudio has all of these, as he has the traits needed to be a reference in the subtle territory of psychedelia: being a shaman, an experimenter scientist, and a humanist teacher simultaneously.

A new chapter in the history of psychedelia is beginning. We are facing a very promising future. We know already that LSD helps patients that suffer from debilitating headaches, according to a study. That microdoses of LSD, it is being reported, are extremely beneficial for the development of creativity. That psilocybin helps to alleviate the anxiety of patients with advanced cancer, that it reconfigures the brains of people with depression, and eliminates the loop of negative thoughts—there are already studies that suggest it. That ketamine is promising as a fast-acting antidepressant, as another scientific study argues. That ibogaine is extremely useful to detoxify recalcitrant addicts. We have already referred to the many benefits (without forgetting, of course, that there will always be contraindications) of MDMA or ayahuasca. A revolution, then, is drawing close. One that will probably overtake Prozac, Haloperidol, and Valium—and that will finally deal with the root of psychiatric and psychological ills, instead of persisting in the error of treating only the symptoms. Psychedelics act on the root of problems. They are direct, clear, inspiring, and although the contraindications are not negligible and therefore they are not a panacea, it is evident that we can no longer prohibit or ignore them: the health of our civilization needs this opportunity for knowledge.

Claudio Naranjo has written, regarding all this, an essential book.

In it is traced a pathway to a future where society disposes of what Claudio has come to call the "psychic dynamite" that we need to avoid the perilous and grim future that is on the horizon if we do nothing to raise the level of our consciousness as a civilization. In that sense, Claudio can be likened to a prophet who restores our hope that an awakened, loving, and pacific world is possible. For just this (and for much more), *My Psychedelic Explorations* is a journey worth initiating. I believe that, for its value, our children and our children's children will continue to find inspiration in these pages.

Jose Maria Fàbregas, M.D., is a psychiatrist specializing in substance abuse treatment. An advocate of the transformational power of ayahuasca in overcoming addiction, in 1981 he created his own clinic, the Center for Research and Treatment of Addictions (CITA), with the objective to develop a therapeutic community.

PROLOGUE
Psychedelics as a Transformational Resource

I feel that it is the right moment to return to a subject I have said relatively little about since the sixties, when providentially I became the discoverer or first researcher of the therapeutic effects of a number of substances (such as ayahuasca, the "empathogens," and ibogaine) of which much has been said recently and that, since then, have affected the consciousness of multitudes.

Lately I am often asked to share my experience as a witness of my experimental or therapeutic use of such substances, especially after I accepted some years ago the invitation of the publisher La Llave to finish a book on ayahuasca written in the sixties. Thus, for example, its publication led to me being invited to deliver the keynote address at the first international conference on ayahuasca, which took place this year (2014) in Ibiza, and to Italian publishers in turn becoming interested in publishing both this new book and my old book *The Healing Journey,* written in the sixties.

However, being asked for interviews and conferences is not the only reason I have decided to now write a new book about psychedelics, but also because it is no longer reasonable to think that at eighty-two years of age one can leave things pending for the indefinite future, and I soon ought to do what I think is important

enough to do. In addition to these there is an even more important reason, which is that I think it is *the opportune moment to do
so;* it is evident that the authorities are beginning to question the
staunch prohibitionism they have embraced so far regarding the use
of these substances, and I sense that my voice can serve to proceed
most appropriately among the alternatives that have been discussed
for decades. For similarly to the situation of the long-standing cold
war between the United States and the Soviet Union, it seems to me
that the impasse between the repressive spirit and libertarianism has
not been overcome—more precisely the conflict between the war on
drugs and the call to freedom and autonomy regarding the exploration of one's own consciousness.

Feminism has already weakened the patriarchal culture that has
dominated throughout the history of all current civilizations, taking us to the threshold of what has been glimpsed as a new era, but it
is also obvious that our crumbling patriarchal order defends itself by
way of intensifying its violent, exploitative, and dehumanizing nature,
and therefore we are witnessing an increasingly critical situation. On
account of this, for the past fifteen years I have been preaching the need
for a change of consciousness through education; however, lately I have
begun to feel that both the fossilization of our educational institutions
and the negligence of most governments concerning the need to reform
the current education for mediocrity has reached such an extent that
it is possible that the necessary change of consciousness that may put
an end to the multifaceted crisis of our corrupt and dying society will
make the wise application of the healing potential of so-called hallucinogens imperative.

Apropos of this term, I will explain from the outset that I have
chosen for the title of this book the word *psychedelic,* the etymology
of which refers to the "expansion" (*delos*) of consciousness, instead of
the more common and formal medical term *hallucinogen,* which is
literally incorrect (as the images that are typically visualized under its
effect are not true hallucinations, which by definition are confused

with reality*). Moreover, I do not share the prejudice of those who want to avoid the alleged vilification of the association of the more appropriate term (*psychedelic*) with the time of half a century ago when, in the midsixties, the youths around the universities of Harvard and California (and then all over the United States and even beyond) felt that the perversion of the usual ways of life and existing institutions justified a counterculture.

Certainly, a "New Era" (which we are still awaiting) was spoken of prematurely then, not only the concept, born at that time, of a "revolution of consciousness" seems valid to me, but also the countless fruits of that fertile period that the authorities tried so hard to combat and discredit seem to have been validated by history: the new therapies, the interest in the spiritual traditions of the East, pacifism, ecology, a new phase in the development of feminism, solidarity with the civil rights movement, and so on. And while the authorities' fear of the voice of youth led to the intensification of repressive and conservative tendencies (that have prevailed in the world since), I think we should not fall into the deception of condemning something that, rather, we ought to be able to appreciate; because the psychedelic consciousness that inspired that time may be what works best today for the sociocultural and political-economic transformation that we are already entering to flow in consonance with a wisdom that our science would barely be able to comprehend, and that only our matured consciousness will know how to navigate as it awakens. For, as Einstein said and as is often repeated: "No problem can be solved from the same level of consciousness that created it."

Nietzsche famously said that only the Dionysian spirit can free us of the repressive spirit of a fossilized Western Christian society, and Alain Denielou has argued eloquently about the identities of the god the Greeks knew as Dionysius and the god the Hindus called Shiva, from

---

*It seems equally inappropriate to me to speak of "entheogens," since regarding the "mystical-mimetic" potential, only their psychotomimetic effects or intensifiers of psychopathological states are most commonly manifested, and insistence on such use suffers from a dishonest propagandistic intention.

whom the Hindus have awaited the transition of our dark Kali Yuga to a new golden age. So, the Dionysian spirit that characterized the libertarian spirit of the counterculture in California during the sixties (as commemorated in the book *To a Dancing God* by the theologian Sam Keen) is closely related to the dissolution of the ego under the influence of psychedelics. Not only is it revealed by the phenomenology of relevant experiences, but also by the history of the oldest of the Western religions, which informs us that the wine that was used in the mysteries of Eleusis contained more than fermented grape juice.

It is understandable, then, that for one who intuits that both Nietzsche and the Hindu prophecy were right, and one who has seen also the deeply transformative effect of a single psychedelic experience in many people, to account for such experiences constitutes not only another book, but one written with a special sense of social responsibility. What is more, I write in the hope that just as in the sixties life made me the discoverer of important psychotropic drugs, it may be giving me the opportunity to contribute now to the knowledge of psychedelics becoming appreciated and recognized as a necessary resource to the collective evolution of consciousness that we have so problematically been resisting.

I have begun this book with a "psychedelic autobiography" that, as an implicit overview of my activities, will serve as a framework for the following chapters, and also for a series of scientific papers or press articles that I have relegated to a section of appendices, or inserted as illustrations.

Then, it seemed appropriate to reproduce the chapter on "Pharmacologically Induced Altered States of Consciousness" that I was requested to write in the eighties by Benjamin Wolman (editor also of the largest encyclopedias of psychology), for a manual on altered states of consciousness.*

Thirdly, I address the issue of "interpersonal psychedelics" that I had the privilege to discover and that I baptized as *feeling-enhancers*

---

*Benjamin Wolman, ed., *Handbook of States of Consciousness* (New York: Van Nostrand Reinhold, 1986).

(or affective optimizers) although they are better known today as *empathogens;* and I start to do so with the transcript of a lecture I delivered at the Unitarian Church of San Francisco in response to the invitation from the Multidisciplinary Association for Psychedelic Studies (MAPS) on the fiftieth anniversary of the discovery of LSD-25. This transcript already appeared in Julie Holland's book about ecstasy.*

Furthermore, provided in the section of the book dedicated to interpersonal psychedelics, I have included and discussed the transcription of a group session with MDMA (3,4-methylenedioxymethamphetamine), and also some advice for the use of MDMA in individual psychotherapy. In an appendix I have selected some passages from a never-published book about the therapeutic use of MMDA (3-methoxy-4,5-methylenedioxyamphetamine), which seems to me the most appropriate psychedelic for potentiating Gestalt therapy.

Fourthly, I dedicate some words to *oneirophrenic* substances—that is to say, beta-carbolines and ibogaine. Although regarding the first I have already written enough in my book on ayahuasca, I include in this volume some new texts. I also include as new chapters on ayahuasca the transcription of what was said at the roundtable on ayahuasca and human development at the international conference on ayahuasca in 2014 and the conference on ayahuasca and psychotherapy given online under the auspices of the Open University of Catalonia, which took the unplanned form of a conversation with Mia Fàbregas, who introduced me. I have also included a brief synopsis by Asunta de Hormaechea about her experience taking ayahuasca more than a hundred times with the "Union of the Plant."

Concerning ibogaine, regretfully, I mislaid the article I wrote in preparing my visit to the University of California conference on LSD in 1967, but it seemed to me appropriate to reproduce here a conference given in a California hospital during 1968 (later published by the

---

*Julie Holland, *Ecstasy: The Complete Guide; A Comprehensive Look at the Risks and Benefits of MDMA* (Rochester, Vt.: Park Street Press, 2001).

Journal of Toxicology) that contains the first written description of a session with ibogaine.

The next chapter about the use of ibogaine in small doses in a context of meditation, self-knowledge, and liberation, is a recent work that I wrote as the closing speech for the first international conference on ibogaine that was held in March 2016 in Tepoztlán.

The next section of the book contains a couple of articles on a classic hallucinogen: the psilocybin mushroom, in which I have emphasized different aspects of this experience of immense potential for transformation when it is done in a group setting and following a few days preparation through meditation, self-knowledge, and expressive activities.

I turn next to the theme of the spiritual, and after making a few general remarks about the theme I present an essay on how the psychedelic experience is often an awakener of the psycho-physiological process that Hindu spirituality describes as "the awakening of the kundalini."

Next, I include an essay on the interpretation of the psychedelic experience in the light of the psychology of meditation, which was originally written as a contribution to the *Festschrift* in honor of Albert Hofmann* and then included in the *Yearbook of Cross-Cultural Medicine and Psychotherapy*.†

Also, I have included in this section of the book devoted to the spiritual aspects of psychedelic trips the particularly lucid account of a transformation process written by Monica Udler, a professor of philosophy and a Sufi, who through several sessions with MDMA and ayahuasca realized a stable connection to her fundamental consciousness.

Finally, this book ends with a chapter I have entitled "The Role of Psychedelics in a Policy of Consciousness," in which I argue that the debate between prohibitionism and libertarianism can only be

---

*Christian Ratsch, ed., *Gateway to Inner Space: A Festschrift in Honor of Albert Hofmann* (Bridport, Dorset: Prism Press, 1989).

†Michael Winkelman and Walter Andritzky, eds., *Yearbook of Cross-Cultural Medicine and Psychotherapy: Sacred Plants, Consciousness, and Healing; Cross-Cultural and Interdisciplinary Perspectives* (Berlin: Verlag für Wissenschaft und Bildung, 1995), 75–90.

addressed from the perspective of a consideration that has never been explicitly raised, about the alternative between control policy and the policy of promoting human development, which has been systematically but unconsciously postponed in our patriarchal culture in favor of earnings or profit utility.

I conclude my book proposing that if one wanted to finally realize the potential of psychedelics for mental health and social evolution, it would not suffice to end the problematic criminalization of drugs, but it would be essential to train expert psychonaut guides who, like the shamans of ancient cultures, would be able to provide the community with the highly sought after and rewarding experiences of expansion of consciousness; experiences that certainly are not of interest to all, but are to the seekers who (also like the shamans of ancient cultures) constitute something like a fermentation agent of healing transformation. This, of course, would require that in addition to establishing training centers for psychedelics therapists (or whatever they may be called), they be allowed to practice in the future, so that regardless of the restrictions that may continue in effect with respect to the distribution or free use of drugs, at least a channel of legitimate use may be opened to the community through these licensed professionals.

One of the reasons for my long silence about psychedelics has been a move away from the psychedelic community; I was encouraged to revisit the issue, however, by the idea that my voice can break the impasse between a tragicomic prohibitionism and anarchical libertarianism—and this by promoting initiatives that result in the establishment of vocational training centers for specialists and in the review of the laws or regulations necessary for the community to access psychedelics with maximum benefit and minimal complications.

I hope, then, that all the comments, information, and ideas presented here provide a stimulus for a social shift that promises as much as feminism and the sexual revolution have meant for us, and that in turn allows us to leave behind the patriarchal paradigm to enter the much-heralded "New Era."

POST SCRIPTUM

Lastly, a note about the title of this work that I originally entitled *Psychedelic Explorations,* for *explorations* is the term that best describes the spirit in which I have addressed the personal experiences, scientific experiments, clinical sessions, and intellectual essays that I give account of in these pages.

My editor, David Barba, tells me that a better title would be *The Pathway of Psychedelics,* but although one can certainly talk about "the pathway of yagé" or "the pathway of peyote," I do not think one can talk about a "pathway of MDMA," which is a great help for those who ingest it but only for a few sessions, or the "pathway of ibogaine," which constitutes an experience of initiation in the original culture of the Bwiti-Feng, and not one that is intended to be repeated throughout one's life path.

Indeed, in my own use of psychedelics I never proposed them as a pathway, but rather, I have insisted that their best use is the special and occasional stimuli along a path defined by ideas and practices whose effectiveness is independent of such stimuli—and that I have developed as a novel integration of elements of Buddhism, the Fourth Way, psychotherapy, and music.

I understand, however, my editor's feeling that what I am offering in my book is more than a series of explorations, and that the title should announce something of great importance to the world. Did I not write it precisely because doing so seemed very important to me?

Searching for an alternative, then—or rather a main title that allows me to keep "explorations" in the title—I have accepted my editor's suggestion to add a subtitle acknowledging the potential of psychoactive substances for a collective transformation of consciousness, from the belief that the intelligent integration of psychedelics into our culture of psychological and spiritual ignorance may be the salvation that we can barely imagine now to the critical state of our agonizing and destructive patriarchal society.

1

A Psychedelic Autobiography

LSD-25 IN THE DARK CHAMBER

My first step toward what later came to be a long exploration of the psychedelic field was accepting the invitation to be an experimental subject for research on the effects of LSD in conditions of sensory deprivation. It was headed by Dr. Marconi of the psychiatric clinic of the University of Chile where I was doing my internship at that time, and I think that I had already read the now-famous book by Aldous Huxley entitled *The Doors of Perception,* in which he narrates his experience under the influence of mescaline and perceives a world not only of beauty but of *Being—Istigkeit,* he calls it, using a term of Meister Eckhart.

Marconi had surely been encouraged to conceive this experiment by reading a publication of John Lilly, who had written something about his first experiments of sensory deprivation and cited as relevant material things such as the experiences of solitary isolation of Eskimos, sailors, and hermits.

The conditions of the experiment were not suitable for use with humans, as the only facilities deprived of light and isolated from sound in the psychiatric clinic had been built for dogs. There was, however, enough room for a person to lie down in the chamber, which I entered once they had injected 40 micrograms of LSD intramuscularly in my left arm. I was about twenty-nine years old.

Once in this dark chamber, the experience began like any other of simply being in the dark, and I awaited with great expectation the first signs of an altered state of consciousness. When the effects finally came, I knew it through the appearance of a sharp image in front of my eyes that might have been one imprinted on the ceiling of the place where I lay—if it were not for the complete darkness. It seemed to me to be a translucent paper, with the word *Sandoz* repeated in greenish letters.

Later I recognized the image on the paper accompanying the vials of LSD that Sandoz offered to doctors for experimental use, but I do not remember being shown the wrapping of the capsule that they administered to me via injection, so I would say that my first "hallucination" was a phenomenon of clairvoyance; I am still struck by the humor of my first introduction to the hallucinatory state having the laboratory mark on it, as if an expert propagandist had arranged it this way. Beyond this initial symptom, I cannot say that the experience of the next few hours was of any great interest.

At first, I saw a light behind my left shoulder, or I felt a luminosity rather than saw it, and then I saw many spirals. All there was were a few images, and I cannot say that my awareness or my identity, or my emotional state had changed. I did, however, feel a philosophical curiosity about what those lights and those spirals might mean.

Then, however, I had something that seemed more like a hallucination for its realism. A lizard came in, apparently through a hole in the wall just beyond my feet and in the right corner of where I lay. I think it was then that I first wanted to communicate with the outside world, as I had been told to do. Or perhaps I had already given notice of Sandoz's sign, the light, and the spirals? I no longer remember, but I am sure that until that moment, to report such experiences would have seemed very ordinary, and only when I tried to talk about the lizard did I realize that I could not reach the end of a thought without forgetting what I was talking about. When, after the experiment, I mentioned it to the experimenters—Marconi and my colleague Wilma Armengol—

they seemed content that this episode was proof of the famous *psychoto-mimetic* (psychosis inducer) effect of the drug.

Apparently, I could not remember what I was trying to communicate because as soon as I tried to, I was offered countless associations that distracted me. I would let it go, and only then remembered what I had meant, or rather I rediscovered it, wanting once again to mention it, and so my explanation started over, only to find myself once more with the same difficulty of saying no more than a few words—and continued in this way many times in succession.

Yet, was this disturbed thinking a psychotic symptom? It seems too rough an analogy. Mainly, I would say that my problem throughout those hours in the dark chamber was that while I waited lucidly to be presented with something new, nothing happened. Something seemed to happen only when something distracted me from my alertness; only, my alertness seemed necessary to speak, and it was so incompatible with the dream world I had peered into that whatever I came to glimpse seemed destined to remain unconscious, for in wanting to communicate it, again it became secret to me.

Everything I have described was relatively indifferent to me, however, apart from moments of aesthetic interest, and something of greater emotional depth was made present to me only fleetingly. I felt like one sailing in a small boat alongside a steamboat on which, opposite me, were the experimentalists who I was speaking to, and I felt at times that they might forget me, and I would get lost in the ocean. Or that the bond between us might break. . . . While I was talking to people beyond a dark glass invisible to me, it seemed to me that I was on a lifeboat following the larger ship they were sailing on, but I feared the bond might break, so that they would forget me, or I them, and in this there was something akin to a hint of panic of desolation or the possibility of rescue, and a feeling of helplessness. Thus, a feeling of insecurity in how I experienced my relationship with others became manifest, and also a fear of abandonment that I had known little in my conscious life except for an episode in childhood when I got lost in a forest, which had no doubt resonated with a much more ancient anguish.

However, I found the experiences I recorded after returning home even richer. Some effect lingered in me, and once back in my usual environment and with eyes open, I noticed new things. The ornamental creeper in the corner of my home (an agapanthus of very fine leaves and more or less spiral formation, danced very pleasantly, and also other things seemed to breathe as if everything had a life of its own).

I also began to hear voices in my mind, and when I started writing, the prevailing voice was one similar to that of Pablo Neruda, whom I knew closely, as a friend of my father's and as a neighbor, and whose poetry was very familiar to me, but in whose voice I had never perceived as now a quality that at this moment seemed "oceanic." It was as if a great oceanic space had a voice of its own, or a cadence that also evoked in me the cadence of Shakespeare and the vastness of the inner world of this prodigious mind that could contain within it both the footman, the murderer, the courtier, the king himself, and his jester.

At other times, I heard a woman's voice with a Spanish accent, and this was not something I remembered from my immediate environment, unless perhaps during my childhood I had heard Spaniards when visiting my father's family. By then, however, I had already traveled to Europe, and I had felt very attracted to the way the Spanish spoke, so I wonder if perhaps such a way of talking, which I associated with my father's environment, revealed an implicit love toward aspects of my family's cultural heritage that I became distanced from; as I later realized, this was due to my mother's decision and aristocratic prejudice. I cannot say I understand what those voices were saying, but I could interpret them as a manifestation in my consciousness of something dear and rather forgotten, according to the etymological sense of the term *psychedelic* that is explained as "amplifier of consciousness."

Another image that I remember seemed to me, as soon it started to appear, an intuition of something beyond my ordinary consciousness for having avoided or suppressed it. It was a scene from the opera

Carmen, that I had been greatly impressed by in its American musical version: a film called *Carmen Jones* in which the role of the leading man was not represented by a bullfighter, as in the original opera, but by a black boxer. The scene I saw before my eyes as if it were continually recurring, was the one in which Carmen is about to be strangled by her spurned lover. My thoughts on this image that must have lasted at least an hour, while I thought of a thousand other things and I moved about the house, was that it confronted me with a tragic sense of life that I had always felt removed from, in an implicitly optimistic, but superficial indifference, as a result of a lack of contact with my emotional world. The image left me feeling that one day it would be my turn to experience that tragic sense of life, so unfamiliar to me in my almost autistic isolation.

A SMALL DOSE OF PSILOCYBIN

The second episode in my psychedelic life was after ingesting a small amount of psilocybin. The story is as follows: I had visited Harvard in '61 or '62, and my trip was due to my mother, suffering from a rare disease that was destroying her retina and already making her a little blind, who needed me to accompany her to consult an ophthalmologist in Baltimore. A philanthropist named Gildemeister, widower of a friend of my mother, had created a foundation to support the development of thoracic surgery and thus honor the memory of his wife, complying with her wish after being saved by this emerging specialty. My mother, who had trained as a lawyer and was, along with her friend, the first woman lawyer in Chile, had never felt competent to practice her profession because due to a very scrupulous character she had never felt assured that one of the litigating parties was more in the right than the other. So, she had offered her services to the foundation of the husband of her friend Gabriela Gildemeister, well known for being a lover of the arts, as she herself was, and for her musical salon. It is not surprising, then, that as an expression of gratitude for her many years of volunteering, this philanthropist offered my mother, now that she was losing her sight, the tickets so that she could travel in my company to the United States to consult the specialist she had been recommended as the most knowledgeable about her condition.

For me, probably the most important part of that trip to the United States was visiting Harvard, where on one of my walks around the campus I met Frank Barron. I had gone into the "center for studies of personality" in search of Henry Murray (the famous creator of the Thematic Apperception Test and a great motivation theorist), and while the secretary in the lobby informed me that Murray was no longer working in that building but in another building nearby, my eyes fell on the list of people in the building and I was pleased to find the name Barron, whose works I had been reading for some years since I came across his now-famous article on creative people's preference for complex images in the *Scientific American.*

That article had interested me enough to look up other publications cited in it, and so reading about the research of this psychologist who was especially interested in the study of creative people had been a learning experience for me. Barron was working in Berkeley at a center that had invited many notable people from the fields of literature, architecture, and other activities to be subjected to interviews and an original battery of tests, but Frank Barron was at that time standing in for the famous Gordon Allport during his sabbatical year, and knowing he was so close to where I was myself, I could not resist asking him for an audience.

He received me without knowing my name, and within minutes we felt like friends. We had several ideas in common, including an interest in psychedelics and an appreciation of Aldous Huxley—and, of course, creativity. He had little time on that occasion, due to an expected visit, but he proposed that meanwhile I visit an exhibition on William Blake in the neighborhood and that we meet at dinnertime.

Shortly after we were gathered at his home with his wife, who reminded me much of my own wife then, and during this dinner, when I explained that I was traveling with my mother (at that time hospitalized in the nearby Massachusetts hospital), they wished to meet her. And they did, and so after my return to Chile, when she chose to stay longer in the United States to visit her brother in New York, the Barrons' appreciation of my mother led to her being invited to one of the early experimental sessions that took place in Harvard with psilocybin.

At the meeting, naturally, were the researchers that included Frank, Tim Leary, and Dick Alpert, but there were also among the experimental subjects most remarkable people, like Alan Watts, who was trying a psychedelic for the first time and would thereafter write *The Joyous Cosmology,* and Dizzy Gillespie, the famous jazz trumpeter, who spent hours lying like a baby on my mother's lap.

Perhaps Frank's friendship with my mother further strengthened the bond of great appreciation that he had established with me and led him to make an exception in his usual research, in which he had only given psilocybin to people physically present: he sent me a dose to take for myself and asked me to send him an account of the results.

What I did, however, was divide that dose into three parts, so as to share it with two friends: Rolando Toro and Ludwig Zeller, a surrealist artist and great admirer of André Breton who because of this had had some contact with my mother. Rolando Toro, my partner at the School of Medicine, is today remembered as the creator of Biodanza.

I do not remember in what order we did the three experiments, neither do I remember anything about the experiences of my friends. All I recall now is that for a long time we were in a place near the base of Santa Lucia Hill opposite the small apartment where I was staying in central Santiago, and that there we spent at least half an hour talking about what I saw in a flower. It was a "thought," and I did not tire of looking, for in what I looked at I discovered not only meanings, but also harmonious relations, just as an expert who teaches others to look at a work of art might do.

At another point in the session I was contemplating the expressive qualities of phonemes and syllables: the sibilant *S,* the wonderful *M,* and how the *M* and the *S* together evoked for me something like an elephant, with its soft shape and benign character and its sinuous trunk; and then the syllable *mat,* that I later had in mind in naming my son Matías: *mat* as in mathematics, the science of sciences, which seemed to me a sound that exuded wisdom. Later these reflections inspired an investigation into the expressive qualities of shapes and sounds, which I carried out when a psychology student asked me for inspiration and supervision for her doctoral thesis.

LEO ZEFF: MY FIRST
THERAPEUTIC SESSION WITH LSD

These two glimpses of the psychedelic world, first with a small dose of LSD, then with a very small dose of psilocybin, was what my experience amounted to when in the year 1962, in Berkeley, I had the opportunity of a first therapeutic experience with LSD in the company of an expert. Leo Zeff was a psychologist who had worked at the Menninger clinic before settling in Berkeley, a person of predominantly spiritual interests who had just completed his doctoral thesis on self-realization. He had also trained in Judaism, which might not be the training of a rabbi, but which was deep enough for him to feel one of those paterfamilias who, as he once explained to me, should take over the transmission of Judaism since the priesthood ceased to exist in the temple of Jerusalem.

Years after I met him—after receiving from me a session with what I at that time called "yagé" but that was more precisely a combination of harmaline with a small dose of LSD—he wished to repay that experience with five gifts, which felt like the material support of an act of transmission: the Torah (that is to say, the parchment with the five books of the Pentateuch), the Kiddush cup, the Mantle, the Kippah (the skullcap), and a small book: the Pirkei Avot (Chapters of the Fathers).

However, having taken a great leap forward in the chronology of my story I must go back to the time when my friends Tony Sargent and his wife Vicky, after learning of my wish to have a therapeutic experience with LSD, invited Leo and myself for dinner in order that we meet. On this occasion Leo already accepted my request for a therapeutic session before my imminent return to Chile, and the session took place on the day before my departure.

In the morning, when I went to Leo's office and we had a brief preliminary discussion, he asked me what experience I had with psychedelics, and I spoke very briefly of my minor experiences with LSD and psilocybin. He then asked me if I had experienced a "bad trip," and I asked him what that was. He told me it was a psychotic state, like a state of paranoia. "Could it happen to me?" I asked, and his response was that anything could happen. "The important thing is to not identify with it," he added. He advised me to take the experience as the tunnel of terror in Disneyland: no matter how many ghosts and skeletons or corpses appeared, the thing was to not forget that they are only projections of one's own mind.

In retrospect, I was very grateful to him for preparing me for a possible descent into hell, for I think it was acceptance of that possibility that allowed me to reach, beyond the usual promised lands, a place beyond time and space that I have never again come into contact with except, in a sense, through Buddhist meditation in recent years.

When during the session itself Leo asked me if I liked the music that was playing, I was able to appreciate that where I was, there was no music or anything that could be named, only a current, flow, or continuous emanation of something that could be called "being" and that was accompanied by a vision of golden rays that, with the music, emerged from nothingness or from something comparable to a mother's breast.

At some point, however, the experience became abominable, first while still listening to the music, and then during hours of contact with Leo, who later told me that he had left me in silence for at least four hours, and that it had seemed to him that I was emotionally dead. I was disappointed by such a comment from him because I had experienced the deepest of ecstasies and the deepest plenitude conceivable, in spite of my face not showing any emotion and my emotional-expressive system remaining still.

During the abominable period, when Leo and I were sitting face to face, his face became a mountain that was also something like an amusement park, and when I tried to speak I found myself silenced from the first word due to a deep sense of shame. This feeling made what I pretended to communicate to Leo over and over so unspeakable that I forgot it as soon as I started to enunciate a sentence, just as during my experience in the camera obscura, only then I forgot what I was saying without being aware that an emotion was preventing me from speaking. This feeling now was more than a guilty feeling, as it implied, rather, something monstrous, but what kind of monster I cannot specify, other than to say that at the center of this experience was self-shame.

Finally, after a couple of hours, the experience progressed to a third phase. The abominable state gave way to one in which I felt that I was back in the world and with the great satisfaction of serene well-being where everything was fine. Sitting beside Leo during this part of the session, I spoke at length about what looking at the back of my hand brought to my mind; however, I do not remember now what I said except when I compared my state to that of Brahms the moment just before he died, when, moved, he thanked the landlady where he was staying for the care received by her. The contrast between this state of grateful plenitude of Brahms's and Beethoven's attitude in the face of death, with his compelling question *Muss es sein?* (Must it be so?) was something that Tótila had called my attention to apropos a passage from the poem he had written while listening to the slow movement of Brahms's double concerto for violin and cello.

In this part of the session, also significant was something that Leo told me and that nobody had told me before: that I was a very special person, and he was sure that one day I would be recognized as such in the world. It is true that my friend and teacher Bogumil Jasinowsky had considered me the greatest of the talents he had known, but Leo's impression mattered more to me because it did not refer to talent but (implicitly at least) to a fruitful life.

Only very briefly will I add that the effect of this session was such that it marked a before and after in my life. I might describe it by saying that now, for the first time, I was on my path, and that if I had previously felt unable to help others therapeutically, I knew now that I could be helpful to others in spite of not knowing how I would do it. I simply trusted that, moment by moment, I would know what I should do, and that was enough. I trusted in life, or in myself, and that was new for me, for I would now say that until then I had never had faith in myself. Now it was as if I had freed myself of a deep implicit doubt or invalidation that had prevented me from functioning properly up until now.

AN EXPEDITION TO THE PUTUMAYO

Instead of dedicating myself to the incubation of this experience, however, I kept to my fixed schedule that would now take me to Chile through Colombia for the purpose of a short expedition to the Putumayo in search of yagé and developments about its uses. During the first night in Bogotá (before taking the bus that would take me overland to Sibundoy and then to the land of the Cofán Indians), I had an experience that, like the one with LSD, I have not experienced again in my life: I was conscious throughout the whole night, although I was not aware of dreams or the external world or of anything corporeal or imaginary. I know that the sixteenth Karmapa, whom I had the opportunity to be close to for a while some years later, only lost consciousness briefly the moment he fell asleep, regaining lucidity during the rest of the night, and that this achievement is well known among Tibetan teachers. Beyond this first night, however, I would say that the many things I had to attend to during the trip, including visits to indigenous people or anthropologists, were somewhat comparable to an intensive film session, not very conducive to experiencing something deeper that required being with myself; even so, I would say that I left Berkeley in a state of spiritual insufflation, which lasted until I was faced with a thwarted love affair shortly after arriving in Santiago. My partner at the time had tired of waiting for me and was leaving the country, and I succumbed to the temptation of becoming enraged. Although the intensity of my pain and anger persuaded her to give up a scholarship to remain with me, I had fallen from heaven to such a state of emotional disturbance that it was no longer compatible with our living together.

Naturally, I thought that nothing could rescue me from my fall but to again turn to Leo, and it was not long before the opportunity arose when the Guggenheim Foundation allowed me to return to Berkeley for a further season. Moreover, not only did I have the opportunity to have a second individual session with Leo, but also, I now started LSD-assisted group therapy, which I attended (monthly, I think) for approximately one and a half years.

COMPARATIVE RESEARCH ON THE EFFECTS OF HARMALINE AND MESCALINE

I will not speak here of my trip to Putumayo, about which I have already written in my book on ayahuasca and during which I only collected plants (that are now in the botanical museums of Harvard and Bogotá) and stories. Rather, I shall jump forward a little to the time after my return to Santiago, when I took it upon myself to start the research on the effects of the plants collected during my visit to the Sibundoy and the Cofán.

As I have already explained in my book on ayahuasca, I ended up focusing on comparative research of two alkaloids rather than on the corresponding plants: harmaline and mescaline. Later, I had the opportunity to present the results of these at the conference on psychoactive substances that took place in San Francisco (with the support of the Karolinska Institute in Sweden and the Health and Welfare Service of the United States).*

Four things drew my attention more than anything during this

---

*Daniel H. Efron, ed., *Ethnopharmacologic Search for Psychoactive Drugs: Proceedings of a Symposium held in San Francisco, California, January 28–30, 1967* (Washington, D.C.: U.S. Government Print Office, 1967).

experiment, and one of them was a certain similarity between the images described by my volunteers (particularly the animal images described by these Chileans who had not been informed that they had ingested a substance related to a plant from the Amazon). The fact that 30 percent of them saw snakes and many others saw tigers, and also that many eagles appeared (as well as all kinds of animals) answered a question that I had posed myself at Harvard: was the similarity between the experiences of indigenous people recorded by travelers or anthropologists explicable as a result of expectations passed on by their culture? I could no longer think that it was so, and as my volunteers in Chile had not harbored the expectation of seeing such images, one might consider that the drug was activating archetypal images.

A second thing, which interested me even more, was the idea that all these animal images, as well as the frequent images of indigenous or black people, constituted symbolic translations of a greater presence of the instinctual in the minds of those under the effect of yagé. In this case it could be said that it was acting as a *liberator of the reptilian brain*.

In addition, I noticed that the experiences of my subjects revealed not only a concurrence with the instinctual, but also stimulation of intuitive thinking and of the philosophical spirit. Today I might ask myself whether the approach to the instinctual is related to the activation of intuition, but I think it appropriate to bear in mind that these two effects are related to two neurologically distinguishable phenomena: activation of the primitive brain in the case of the instinctual, and activation of the right hemisphere in the case of intuition (a capacity phenomenologically conceivable as a receptivity to an implicit inspiration, like when a poet invokes his muse). My subsequent experiences throughout many years make me feel that in the experience of ayahuasca, not only is openness to instinct important, but also an opening to something akin to an inner guide that teaches (sometimes through angels, gods, guides, a mere voice, or through an intuition of a deep self that is like a teacher).

Lastly, this preliminary exploration of the effects of harmaline confirmed its therapeutic effect, and hence I subsequently experimented with its use in the context of group therapy. Could it be that the healing effect of ayahuasca was due, as the Freudian psychotherapy of psychoanalysis claims, to a reintegration of the instinctual? Very likely; however, sometimes the therapeutic effect could be understood rather as a result of stimulation of the intuitive mind, and therefore we can say that ayahuasca therapy is an implicit "therapy for the spirit," in which "the spirit" guides us from within and rescues us. Following this interpretation, the role of the person administering the ayahuasca perhaps should not be "therapeutic" in the habitual sense of the word, which usually refers to a repertoire of interventions that in this specific altered state of consciousness tend to be, rather, interruptions or distractions.

MDA, FIRST OF THE EMPATHOGENS

I met Sasha Shulgin through Tony Sargent shortly before I met Leo Zeff, and I met several times with him during my first brief visit to Berkeley. He was at that time very interested in the various alkaloids of peyote, and at one of these meetings, while I was preparing for the trip to Putumayo that Shultes had recommended, he told me of the experiment Gordon Alles (known for the discovery of the effects of amphetamine) had carried out on himself to ascertain whether MDA might be useful as a vasodilator.

During this experiment, Alles was struck by how he became very talkative, and also by how, for a moment, he thought he saw smoke rings even though no one was smoking. Sasha thought that the chemical similarity of MDA to mescaline (as well as that fleeting hallucination) suggested that MDA could be a hallucinogen, and he provided me with a small amount to investigate. I proceeded to do so, starting with myself, accompanied by Lee Sanella.

I have already described my experience in an autobiographical book as yet unfinished, and I will just mention here briefly that as the dose that I tentatively calculated started having its effect, I was telling

Lee about the history of my relationships, which I continued explaining throughout the hours that followed, but with a very different attitude to my habitual one; because throughout my life I had felt very guilty regarding women, and now for the first time I felt innocent, as one who simply did what he could in view of his previous experiences and circumstances. I remember mentioning that for the first time I felt I was "the hero of my life," and today I would say that for the first time I was contemplating myself with self-love. Moreover, it was not only a temporary effect, lasting the duration of the drug's effect; it was as if I had left a great burden of guilt behind, and I was feeling happier and lighter.

The effect of MDA was apparently very different from that of LSD and in no way could it be called a hallucinogen; however, it was definitely a drug of great therapeutic promise, as I found soon after, first through a joint session with my partner that left me feeling how much it could facilitate communication, and then through therapeutic sessions with acquaintances. I later referred to these sessions in an article published by *Medical Pharmacology* in collaboration with Shulgin and Sargent, in 1967.*

Back in Chile, I suggested to my boss at the CEAM† that I conduct more systematic research of MDA, to which I invited not only acquaintances but also patients of my colleagues in the psychiatric clinic. Among them I was able to observe the remarkable regression experiences that I described years later in my book *The Healing Journey* and that later also came to draw the attention of those who have published their work with the amino derivative of MDA—MDMA or ecstasy—similar in its effects but without the occasional toxicity of the first.

---

*A. Shulgin, C. Naranjo, and T. Sargent, "Evaluation of 3,4-methylenedioxyamphetamine (MDA) as an Adjunct to Psychotherapy," *Medicina et Pharmacologia experimentalis* 17, no. 4 (1967): 359–64.
†Center for Studies in Medical Anthropology at the School of Medicine, University of Chile.

SHULGIN'S PHENYLISOPROPYLAMINES

Meanwhile, Sasha had become interested in the study of the relationship between the molecular structures of amphetamine derivatives, and suggested that I investigate the effects of a series that he had already succeeded in synthesizing in humans. We assembled an informal team with Tony Sargent, with whom we had already published the first reports about the effects of MDA, and we then published an article in *Science* on these relationships between structure and effect (followed by further articles about new compounds such as 4-bromo-phenylisopropylamine). We also published a study of the physiological effects of MMDA in animals, as befitted before proceeding to the study of the psychological effects on volunteers—which constituted the next research project in Chile, and the results of which I gave a rather impressionistic account of in another chapter of *The Healing Journey*.

I explained in this that unlike MDA, which led people to regressive experiences and did not lend itself, to the extent I had imagined, to working with Gestalt therapy, MMDA did admirably allow the concentration of attention on the present moment and dream work. So much so that I thought to publish a book, which I tentatively considered entitling *Gestalt Therapy Revisited*—and that I could have entitled, echoing Susan Langer, rather than Huxley, *Gestalt Therapy in Another Key*. Although I never got to publish it, that book project influenced my life, because Fritz Perls,* who until then had enjoyed my work, became so enraged over the proposed title (interpreting it as an expression of a competitive attitude on my part), that this led to the breakdown of our friendship.

When I returned to Chile at the end of my time as a research associate at the University of California under the auspices of the Guggenheim Foundation, I had already researched another of the substances synthe-

---

*Born Frederick Perls and sometimes referred to as such in this book. (*Note from the editor of the English edition.*)

sized by Sasha, TMA-2, which after a personal experiment of his, had left him with the impression that it induced paranoia. I had the chance to carry out a group experiment by invitation of a therapist in Los Angeles who was conducting group therapy with LSD (that had been one of the premises in Leo Zeff's training), in which approximately fifteen people sampled TMA-2 in a dose that I must have previously determined on an individual experience, although I no longer remember. The expectation of paranoid reactions was not confirmed, but neither was it a good group experience, and I think the reason for this has been that I also ingested the drug (something I had never done before and that I did not do again except many years later with ayahuasca, by adopting in my sessions the model of the Santo Daime Church in Brazil).

The problem with having ingested TMA-2 myself was that, as I found the next day, instead of perceiving the pathology in others, I found all of them too admirable and therefore perceived myself as inadequate to help them. Furthermore, although one might think that if the therapist treats everyone affectionately it favors the establishment of a positive transference, I imagine they must have perceived that my admiring attitude had revealed too great a need for affection, and I was not treated as a therapist. However, it was too long ago to be able to analyze something as complex as a group dynamic in which I also allowed myself great sincerity about my little esteem of one of the people with whom I was in a small group for part of the time, and though I only take into account this episode now after forty odd years, it seems plausible to me that my seemingly arbitrary lack of sympathy toward that person may have had an impact on the judgment of others.

Back in Chile, however, I experimented with the whole series of the six isomers of TMA (trimethoxyamphetamine or trimethoxy-phenyl-isopropylamine) but given that I did not get to publish the results of such tests, I can only say that I did not find any of them particularly important in terms of novel therapeutic properties. I think perhaps the one that best served my patients was TMA-1, similar to mescaline, only more active.

I also tested the entire series of six MMDA and DMMDA and

cannot remember so far back in time the doses that I found useful or the clinical cases. I do remember, however, that the substance that struck me as the most interesting was MMDA-3a, and my own experience with it was unique in two respects. Firstly, it is the only time I have suffered intense episodes of cold and heat (alternating), which were most unpleasant. Secondly, the focus of my experience was one that has never been repeated in another psychedelic experience, although it led me to what I thought was important work on one aspect of my psyche: a limitation in my ability to attend to what was in front of me, which now led me to perceive a kind of veil that had always covered my visual experience, robbing it of vivacity. It was as if the act of seeing was complicated in me by a will to not see; as if a certain negativism distanced me from the world, preventing me from a real encounter with it. I looked at the palm of my hand insisting on seeing it completely, and apparently, I could only do so for fleeting moments, for it required intense attention.

I would say that this experience was rewarding, because the next day, in the company of Michael Murphy and some friends at the Esalen Institute, someone suggested that we interrupt our conversation and resume it after meditating for a while, and I had the most profound mystical experience that I had hitherto known; one in which I strongly felt to be nothing in the presence of God, and for the first time I understood the mystics who had said the same thing and whom I had misconstrued as masochists. Tears of gratitude ran down my cheeks and when I came out of the trance they were all gone from the room.

To what extent was this experience due to my desire of the previous day to see, a desire that had been like wanting to leave a cocoon through the force of looking? I do not know. . . . However, despite the favorable outcome attributed to my ingesting MMDA-3a, I did not try it again until many years later, in 1984, this time in combination with ibogaine—and I found it an excellent combination.

Although already in the late sixties I patented (in association with M. Bocher, the owner of the laboratory at Ivry-la-Bataille) the association of ibogaine with MDA, over time and with the report of accidents I came to understand that the occasional toxicity of MDA necessitated a preliminary check to ensure that this drug was not toxic to the patient prior to the administration of the usual dose, and it was not recommended for general use. However, ibogaine always seemed to me an alkaloid that, like harmine, works best with a complement, and today I would say the best complement I have known is MMDA-3a.

PSYCHEDELIC GROUP THERAPY

When I migrated to California in 1967 my experiences and experiments with psychedelics were interrupted, so I never got to publish more than what is written in *The Healing Journey*—in part due to turning my attention to my work at the Institute of Personality Assessment and Research (IPAR) of the University of Berkeley, and in part due to my workshops at Esalen and the work on my first books (*The One Quest, The Psychology of Meditation, Gestalt Therapy, The Healing Journey,* and *The Divine Child and the Hero*). Neither did I get to include in *The Healing Journey* anything about my therapeutic explorations in groups, so I will say something about them here.

The first psychedelic therapy group I brought together took place with the people who had already had an individual session with me (either during the brief period when I offered some of them individual sessions with LSD, or during the therapeutic experiments with MDA or MMDA, harmaline, or mescaline). Naturally, the recounting of these individual experiences was a very significant form of presentation, and the whole was of great interest, since the communication of psychedelic experiences is not always easy, and to share these experiences with others who have gone through something similar is, however, something intrinsically interesting—for something like a common framework to always different and unique individual experiences can be intuited—something that favors the establishment of emotional bonds and also a "learning by contagion," so it was a good preparation for the group sessions that followed. During these I adhered to what had been my experience with Leo Zeff, who on my recommendation had already adopted the use of MDA and harmaline in addition to LSD in his groups, and in whose sessions as a participant I was able to appreciate that integrative learning seemed to take place when people were in different states of consciousness under the effect of different drugs. Thus, for example, in the meeting of those who were journeying in the archetypal world of harmaline with others under the effect of MDA who shared their feelings concerning their difficulties in relationships, the latter were stimulated to a certain archetypal consciousness while the former seemed to be encouraged to translate their experience into words.

The decor that Leo used in his sessions always seemed important to me; he would prepare the space for these sessions with many candles, flowers, and beautiful objects, and I continued taking care of this seemingly aesthetic appearance only with an implicit conviction that it contributed something to the spiritual quality of the sessions, creating something akin to a temple or a place of purity. I also adopted Leo's rule that invited people to be spontaneous but also to be careful not to be invasive, and that included renunciation of sexual relations with and violence toward other participants in the session.

Unlike Leo Zeff's groups, however, the first group session with psychedelics I facilitated took place in the context of a program that included gestalt sessions, meditation, and various interpersonal exercises, fencing, expressive movement, and the practice of "surrendering" that I had come to appreciate through my contact with Subud.*

Over time, this program that came to be called Esalen in Chile and was mentioned in successive Esalen catalogs, received support from the Senate, and would have developed further as the "Institute for Human Development" had I not decided to travel to California again, this time as a resident.

---

*Subud is an international spiritual movement that was founded in the decade of 1920 by Muhammad Subuh in Indonesia. It is based on a spiritual practice called *latihan,* an exercise in surrendering to God or the great life-force existing in each human being.

The series of sessions I led with the group I have described, and which more of my volunteers joined for the trials with experimental substances, was not only a confirmation of the therapeutic value of the various drugs used, but also a learning experience for me. In the beginning, I anticipated greater therapeutic intervention, but then I intervened only minimally, just as Leo had done, as good results seemed to depend more on the attitude of the participants and on their preparation than on my interventions in the course of the meeting. I also developed the confidence to trust that a group of people could be led to deep waters without fear of catastrophes occurring, for it would seem that when people surrender control over their own psyche, an intelligence that goes beyond the ordinary mind of each operates in the groups. Things happened as if a greater intelligence orchestrated the group situation in such a way that those with certain needs found what they needed interacting with other significant coparticipants, synchronously and seemingly magically. Something that I found particularly miraculous was that those who were experiencing states of regression in which they needed a safe haven that I would not have known how to provide for more than one at a time, found others who at that time were feeling as if they had just finished flowering spontaneously and were willing to give their attention to whoever needed it.

I never got to publish anything about these meetings, although I did mention something about my groups with MDA and MDMA in a conference organized by Hanscarl Leuner in Hirshhorn, in Germany; as a result, I was invited by Akos Tatar to lead a group in Berlin that was announced in the newspapers (for MDA had not been banned yet) and was attended by several people close to Osho.

IBOGA

It is now time to talk about my exploration of ibogaine, which I became interested in following a meeting with a French missionary named Ireneo Rosier, who had by then published a book about the presence of god in the coalmines of France, where the workers lived in particularly miserable conditions. I was introduced to him at a dinner party by some friends in Santiago, and when at the request of my hosts I told him about some of my research on yagé and harmaline and I mentioned the identification of shamans with jaguars, he remarked that it reminded him of the closeness between lions and the African sorcerers whom he had lived among in recent years.

In the same way that under the effect of yagé Colombian shamans seemed to turn into jaguars in full sight of those present, also African shamans, Rosier explained to me, seemed to turn into lions, and it is even said that after shooting a lion the bullet has been found in the sorcerer's body.

I wondered if this did not suggest that a hallucinogen was used also in African culture, and my suspicion fell on ibogaine, which was used then as a tonic in cases of convalescence and was sold in pharmacies in France under the name Lambarène. Could it be the case, I wondered, that what Westerners have thought was a mere stimulant used by the natives in their dances was actually a hallucinogen? The information from anthropologists that later confirmed my suspicion had not yet come into my hands, and all I came across in the literature were reports of the use of ibogaine in the vagina of rats and the intestines of rabbits. Since I found nothing on experiments on humans, I took it upon myself, as on previous occasions, to use myself as an experimental subject. I have already recounted this experience in more than one interview, but I will repeat here the essential details, which were a lesson for me and can be one also for those who read me.

Shortly after feeling the first dizziness that announced to me the effect of the drug (I think 300 mg of pure ibogaine), the entire universe seemed to revolve around the place where I lay, and although I cannot say exactly that it was a hallucination, I simply felt (as I lay with my eyes closed) as if the entire universe was revolving, that each celestial body had an orbit, and that all these orbits were synchronized in something like a great cosmic celebration, a dance orchestrated by a mysterious will.

Only I, myself, in the midst of this great dancing universe, remained oblivious to this universal liturgy. Would it not be better that I join it all? Is this not what I had always aspired to, instead of living a kind of ghostly existence? It seemed very simple to say "yes," which was like saying "be it according to your will"; and it seemed to me as if my finger was already on a switch: Yes? Or no? However, the problem was that if I surrendered to divine will could it not be that in such a divine will I was not meant to be anything significant?

If I surrendered—I felt—I would have to renounce a special importance I always wished to have. Was I prepared for the eventuality that in the cosmic order corresponding to me, I was to be but something akin to dust? It seemed that a decision was expected from me, and I was not risking losing control. First, seconds went by and then a few minutes, but not many. Perhaps I was given around three minutes, after which it was clear that my opportunity had passed, and the rest of the experience was like a Walt Disney cartoon; or, rather, a chaotic succession of images, of which I only remember now the first: a rabbit hiding in a tree trunk.

The experience left me feeling that I had been tested by a higher intelligence, and it was evident that I had a long way to go yet. The respect that ibogaine instilled in me, however, might have indirectly served the volunteers I invited to participate in the series of individual sessions through which I would explore its possible therapeutic effects.

I remember my first subject was a dancer whose talent had greatly impressed me. In his session, his talent seemed to be revealed again, and I never witnessed an experience like it among those to whom I administered this new drug.

At the center of this experience was a blue ray: a wonderful blue light, as I have described in the last chapter of my book *The Healing Journey*. Another of my subjects, my collaborator at the Center for Anthropology, saw turtles and lions, and that reminded me of the jaguars of ayahuasca, as well as how joyfully my volunteer danced to the melody of Stravinsky's *The Rite of Spring*. It appeared to be a drug of similar effects to the beta-carbolines of South American shamanism: images appeared, insights were gained about life itself, but there were no distortions of time, neither the paradises or infernos of LSD, nor the contemplation of personal relations of MDA.

I had just completed my series of thirty experiences when I was invited to the conference on LSD organized by the University of California in 1966, and when I asked the organizer (now known as Baker Roshi, for he shortly after became Suzuki Roshi's successor in California's first Zen monastery) if rather than speak about LSD I could talk about ibogaine, which I had just discovered, he agreed.

I then wrote an article that attracted a lot of attention, not only at the conference but also from the wider public, as a news item of my perspective appeared in the *San Francisco Examiner*.* Unfortunately, however, I lost it, and I doubt that I can find a copy to include in this book. All that I have left now, in addition to the final chapter of *The Healing Journey,* is a lecture I was invited to give in a hospital in California that later appeared in the journal *Clinical Toxicology* with the title "Psychotherapeutic possibilities of the new fantasy enhancing drugs."†

It seems appropriate to mention at this point in my narrative that the article I sent to the journal *Experientia* describing the effects of ibogaine and its apparent therapeutic effect was rejected, and in view of the numerous treatment centers now offering sessions with ibogaine to combat states of chemical dependency to other addictive drugs, I find it ironic that this magazine underestimated its therapeutic potential.

Two statements especially caught my interest when ending my presentation at the famous conference organized by the University of California: one by someone, Howard Lotsof, who had been cured of an addiction to heroin by ingesting ibogaine, and would subsequently set up the first clinic for this purpose; the other was a letter from the

---

*Willam Boquist, "African Drug Aid to Insight, UC Panel Told," *San Francisco Examiner,* June 16, 1966.
†The full conference can be read at the end of chapter 4.

wife of a celebrated chemist who had been one of the idols of my youth, Linus Pauling, the well-known Nobel Prize winner whose interest represented for me a particularly significant sign of recognition. In those days, however, the time of my move from Chile to Berkeley as a resident was approaching, and I barely experimented with ibogaine again except in a couple of therapeutic group sessions, in which I also tested this substance in association with various phenethylamines. I have only recently used ibogaine again, and I will give account of my new findings in two of the chapters of this book.

10-METHOXY-HARMALAN

During my time at the CEAM, I used to spend periods in the library of the medical school, where I leafed through magazines looking for the latest developments regarding biochemistry or possibly psychoactive alkaloids, and this is how one day I came across the formula of the so-called 10-methoxy-harmalan, a relative of harmine that I had not heard about before. The article featuring the formula reported that this compound could be obtained *in vitro* from bovine pituitary via transformation of melatonin, and this suggested that it might also occur *in vivo*. Could this 10-methoxy-harmalan be a hallucinogen that our pineal gland produces in trace amounts, and could it explain hallucinatory states triggered by spiritual practices?

Naturally, it was of interest to begin by researching the psychological effects of the substance in question, and for that the first step would be to find out if it appeared in the catalog of any of the commercial chemical laboratories.

I was very pleased to find that indeed it was on the market, and I proceeded one day to ingest what I calculated (from the effects of other substances in that chemical family) to be a small dose.

I took it upon myself, pencil in hand and blank paper in front of me, to observe my own mind as one who records the protocol of an experiment. Then, letting my mind engage in free association of ideas,

I wrote down the word *wing*, for it was the first thing that came to my mind.

Then I noticed that the sensation of a flapping wing was the memory of an image that I had during one of the LSD sessions in which Leo was listening to Japanese music, the title of which referred to ducks taking flight from a lagoon.

I will not include here the poem that resulted when I consigned this first image to paper in the attitude of one guiding the protocol of a scientific experiment, but when the literary journal *Maguey* in Berkeley requested a contribution from me, I offered them this poem and this fact, together with the praise it attracted, could be considered arguments in favor of the conclusion that the ingested substance stimulated in me a latent poetic talent, rarely expressed. Could one generalize, saying that 10-methoxy-harmalan is a stimulant of intuitive thinking? It seemed so to me after administering it to two experimental subjects, but since I have lost the notes of that time, and I do not even remember who the people that had had the relevant experiences were, I think this is an investigation that merits being continued.

5-METHOXY-DIMETHYLTRYPTAMINE

Another investigation I carried out on myself and the results of which I confirmed on some friends, was that of a substance whose formula I found among the chemical analysis carried out on the initiative of the Swedish anthropologist Wassen, whom I met with Bo Holmstet at the conference Ethnopharmacologic Search for Psychoactive Drugs. Wassen gave me one of his articles on plant products inhaled by South American Indians. On the list of compounds that Wassen had published in a journal, I found 5-methoxy-dimethyltryptamine especially interesting for its formula, and also in this case I was pleased that it could be procured from one of the commercial laboratories.

The effects of inhaling the vapors was perhaps the most indescribable of all the psychedelic states I have known, inasmuch as it involved a dissolution of thought and also of the imagination—this annihilation of the ordinary mind was extremely attractive to me. When I gave it to my friend Armando Molina to try on one of his visits from Spain, his description seemed very accurate to me. "A delightful dissolving of the mind into nothingness." Then I shared it with another friend, Peter Gruber, whose verdict was that this was "the H-bomb."

I smoked this "H-bomb" on many occasions and sometimes it seemed to me, on returning to ordinary consciousness, that under the effect I had moved about without any awareness of doing so, rearranging objects around the meditation cushion I was sitting on. It seemed to me the expression of an impulse to reach beyond, even though it was a deeper dissolving into nothingness. However, not many days passed before I became alarmed by the addictive potential that this substance was presenting to me, and that it could well end up damaging my brain. And I even wonder whether it did not do me some harm, for this experiment coincided with a seemingly barren time in my life during which I felt not only minimally creative but also inwardly impoverished, although I would not be able to say how far this had been the natural result of a process of meeting with my original pathology, or whether an element of toxicity had been added to this natural process.

I gave this "H-bomb" to two others to try: José Matsua, a Huichol Indian who smoked it at one of his ceremonies and stopped singing for the rest of the night; and Sri Harish Johari, a Hindu tantric master, whose repertoire of experiences included cobra venom, and who guessed correctly that it was a tryptamine. Through him, the secret was revealed, and this compound began circulating among connoisseurs of the psychedelic world in my entourage, but I persisted in not talking about it in view of my fear that it might lead to some damage.

KETAMINE

I met the Mexican psychedelics pioneer Salvador Roquet following an annual meeting of the U.S. Association of Humanistic Psychology, which took place in Berkeley. I invited him home for dinner, and this led me to subsequently have a session with LSD and ketamine with him. I suppose that the ketamine dose was too much for me because I was not moved by Beethoven's Ninth Symphony, and it scared me to feel psychologically dead. Fortunately, a little while later I received a visit from Joan Halifax, and she offered me the opportunity to experience ketamine in combination with marijuana, which I found most interesting—although of doubtful transformative value. I repeated the experience several times in the course of subsequent years, confirming the sense that the ordinary mind, seen from the "ketaminic consciousness," seemed to me a rather trivial dream.

MARÍA SABINA'S LITTLE MUSHROOMS

Another definer in my psychedelic autobiography was a visit, also at the invitation of Salvador Roquet, to the famous María Sabina. I went with him on this occasion to Oaxaca accompanied by the minister of health of a Central American country and a senior mental health official in the United States, and we reached Huautla on a roofless bus when it was already dark, and she was already asleep beside her husband, but the legendary priestess rose and accepted to see us.

I was intrigued by the fact that she offered the mushrooms to each member of our group in a fine banana leaf except to me; I was served in newspaper. I asked Roquet if he thought this was significant, and he suggested that I ask her directly. So, I did, and the answer I received was: "you will write about it," which I have not done until now, but this did not lead me to invalidate her explanation, since she seems to have perceived correctly in me someone given to writing.

María Sabina assigned us our places in a row on the floor, with Roquet to the extreme right, myself beside him, and the two officials to my left, and she sat in front of me, her back turned to us all, as if she was in front of us on a boat or leading us in a procession. She sang or prayed continually, and she recommended that we pray also, especially in response to the officials when they cried out at the beauty of their visions.

For myself, who spent the entire session thinking about Quetzalcoatl, her special advice was to not forget about Jesus Christ—especially for the sake of others. I suppose this meeting was the main incentive for a couple of group sessions with *Psilocybe* that I conducted in Chile, which I will discuss later, so I will limit myself to saying here that they led me to feel a gratitude to the mushrooms comparable to that felt by the indigenous people, who named them *teonanacatl,* or "flesh of god."

RESEARCH WITH MDMA IN CHILE

I was distanced from psychological research and pharmacologically assisted therapy for several years, but one exception was working with the so-called ecstasy, MDMA, which was provided to me by Sasha Shulgin during the '80s and that I was able to use during my trips to Chile, since the military dictatorship, in spite of its repression of the local hippie culture, allowed doctors to practice pharmacologically assisted therapy, which was even detailed in the fees.

Once again, I did individual sessions, and in synthesis I would say that my priority, at that stage of my life, was to use the therapeutic context for working on character and personality, which was a field I had specialized in for many years. I sent a written report about my experience in response to the request of the psychedelic community, which at that time wanted to bring the issue of the therapeutic use of MDMA to court, but unfortunately that document was never returned, and I lost my own copy. I can say, however, that these sessions helped me to deepen my own understanding of the twenty-seven characters that result from the application of the Enneagram to personality, and that they confirmed my impression (concordant with David Shapiro's*) that the greatest contribution to the profound transformation of people is

---

*David Shapiro, *Psychotherapy of Neurotic Character* (New York: Basic Books, 1989).

overcoming the characterological patterns, which should not be conceived as an aspect of the symptoms of neuroses, but as their true skeleton.

THE SANTO DAIME

Another phase of my psychedelic autobiography began when Graciela Figueroa, a collaborator of mine in the first SAT program in Spain, told me about the Santo Daime Church in Brazil and offered to introduce me to its leader (or *padrinho*) in Rio de Janeiro. I had not taken any psychedelics for some years, since I had separated from a woman whom I had only lived with for a few years but whom I had also felt was the love of my life. I had met her at the same period that my mother died, and she, who had lived in Ibiza, was very fond of both psychedelics and marijuana. Although I joined her on a few MDMA "trips" that seemed to help us speak openly about our conflicts, her addictive personality ended up being a serious problem for our relationship, and no doubt in response to what my body considered an excess, one day I felt that I no longer wanted to take any drugs at all. Rather than a reasoned decision, it was as if my body suddenly said "no" to me, and this preference persisted over the years following our separation.

However, there was an exception to this in 1988, after Graciela Figueroa, who was working with me at that time in Spain, told me about the Brazilian Santo Daime Church. We were working then in an extraordinary place that had been built for us in Almeria by a philanthropist named Ignacio Martin Pollo, who felt that after successfully working in the field of marketing for many years, he owed something to the world. When I was in Rio some time later, for a workshop, not only did I want to make the most of my trip to have a session with this excellent friend who over time has trained many body therapists in Europe and the Americas, but also to meet the padrinho Paolo Roberto.

In my conversation with him I told him about my adventure in the Putumayo, and what most impressed him was how a coral cobra had been just inches from my ankle, so I would not be there telling the story if not for the shaman guiding me who threw his machete from a few meters away and split it in two before I had even seen it. Taita Anselmo, who was guiding me, then made an invocation to the sun, and he explained that the snake was the guardian of the plant. On hearing the story, Paolo Roberto took it as a sign to invite me to a meeting to be held the same day, after our encounter, at the Centro Ceu do Mar where we were having our conversation. I happily accepted, of course, as it was already my wish to be able to experience the "Daime" in the context of one of the ayahuasca religions in Brazil, whose guides were said to act as shamans and who, unlike those working with altered states of consciousness in other parts of the world, in Brazil enjoy governmental protection for the practice of their service that can be described as a combination of therapeutic and priestly.

Like in the meetings of the Santo Daime in general, much singing was going on in this one, and as I did not understand the hymns in Portuguese I decided that I would use them as inspiration to practice my own form of devotion, which was repeating the mantra of Padmasambhava, which in turn reminded me of trying to always see everything that was happening as a dream. The experience of devotion from a perspective of de-identification with everything was enriching for a while, but Paolo Roberto served me one tall glass of ayahuasca after another, as if he wanted to test me, and I have the impression that, past a certain point, its stimulating effect became an overdose that robbed my energy; I listened to the fervor of the strange songs with a feeling that my own fervor was not up to what it had been just before, and as time went by, after the fourth glass, just the effort to stand became too much for me. To my surprise, however, I did not vomit, in spite of the exceptional amount I had taken, but this lasted only while we were in the room. When we left, about four hours later, when the effect seemed to be over, I felt the nausea—perhaps because, distracted with the atmosphere and the encounter with others, I had stopped paying attention to my subtler experience.

The next day, I went back to see Paolo Roberto, this time to invite him to Spain. With the generous help of Ignacio, our host in Babia, who paid for the tickets, Paolo Roberto arrived at the end of the next SAT program in Babia accompanied by his wife (daughter of the famous Padrinho Sebastiao, who founded the church), and of a team of singers and guitarists.

The session was announced as an addition to the third year of the SAT program, which was then the last, and curiously I do not remember anything in particular of it, except dancing in the square of the castle with the full moon over our heads, and where Graciela and I, at the beginning of the row of women and men, respectively, looked at each other, caught up in a continuous interchange of surrender and devotion.

The next morning, we said goodbye to Paolo Roberto before I was to proceed to a retrospective meeting, but we agreed that he would return the following year. However, the next meeting that was held was not related to the SAT program, as it was Ignacio's wish to have the opportunity to share his experience with a wider Spanish audience, so the Santo Daime Church came into being during those days in Madrid. However, regarding my psychedelic autobiography, this turned out to be one of the important sessions of my life, even though my intention was to not drink the sacramental plant, excusing myself to Paolo Roberto as people received their potions of Daime, explaining that it was my responsibility to preserve my energy for the following day, when the final session would be held. Paolo Roberto listened to me politely, but he suggested that perhaps it would be good to drink a small amount before I went to sleep, and I accepted his offer. I cannot remember now whether or not I did sleep at all that night, but I remember the continuous ecstasy of the songs of those who danced for hours under my window.

The following morning, I was filled with a new joy I had never known before, except perhaps fleetingly. This session gave rise to a new stage in my life that I have sometimes called of "milk and honey" but also of "milk, honey, and war," but I reserve the explanation of it for an autobiography, and I will just say, to close this brief narrative about

Paolo Roberto, that despite having granted me the star that symbolically authorized me to conduct Santo Daime sessions, I later had conflicts with him and did not see him again.

I was of course still interested in being able to offer ayahuasca sessions to my followers while legal circumstances allowed it, and I envisaged the next opportunity in the invitation of one of the successors of Padrinho Sebastiao, who had gone to live in a wonderful country called Aiuruoca, where it is said by local people that alien spacecraft landed before his arrival. My partner at the time, Suzy, and I were visiting this wonderful territory, and attended a session conducted, not by Guilherme, as the Daime friend was called, but by an associate of his from the União do Vegetal, Paolo Maya, who spoke a great deal during the session, and it seemed to me that he wanted to take advantage of the effect of the ayahuasca to impress his audience. Guilherme had promised me a certain amount of ayahuasca, and complied with his offer in spite of the disagreements we had with his partner, and as a result I was able to use it on several occasions over the years, until one of the people who earned a living from my ideas wrote to me threatening to report me to the Ministry of Health, and this seemed to me a sign to interrupt this work.

Guilherme's ayahuasca was used for some new experiments. In one of them, I wanted to use mythological material, so I read to the group the Homeric hymn that tells the story of the abduction of Proserpine and her rescue by Demeter, and it was a group confirmation of the observation I made at the beginning of my exploration of ayahuasca on how it facilitates, not just intuition, but specifically the understanding of mythical thinking.

On another occasion I conducted work that was focused on reflection about relationships, which together with the work for couples in the light of the Enneagram that I had presented in Brazil in response to an invitation from Suzy Stroke, turned out to be an inspiration for the excellent work she developed later, and thus an indirect gift from ayahuasca to a whole generation.

Eventually, however, it was the success of my own SAT work in Brasilia that attracted people from both the Santo Daime and the União do Vegetal church in that city and having them as disciples led to me receiving invitations from both centers, first to participate, then to guide sessions. Ultimately, the appreciation of the Daime community prompted the possibility of having my own center, which does not carry the name of church but which for the community of Brazilians is another group within the "Brazilian ayahuasca religions." I will not speak here of my work with ayahuasca, as I have done this in my book on the subject, but to complete my psychedelic autobiography, I must say that for a long time, ayahuasca led me to a loving and devotional ecstasy, and I seemed to function as one touched by holiness, but I lost that state in a specific session in which I wanted to do without any structure. I invited people to spontaneity and I felt paranoidly mocked. I came out of this session feeling utterly crushed, with less authority, less dignity and validity, and I have never since regained the plenitude of the loving ecstasy that for me was the effect of the drink, in contrast to the contents of the many descriptions I have heard about the experiences of others. I remember that Paolo Quatrini once asked me what I felt and saw, and my answer was that I felt one thing, not a thousand things, and that thing was not something I could talk about other than to say that it was simply a state of happiness. However, to say it was a happy state does not say as much as to explain that it was a happiness derived from a state of holiness, which in turn, had something to do with the divine; a kind of friendship with God.

For some years now, I have been conducting ayahuasca sessions twice a year in Brazil, first under the auspices of leaders of the Santo Daime Church, and then by the independent organization of which I am the spiritual guide. I drink the ayahuasca with the groups that I lead just as is done in the Santo Daime Church and the União do Vegetal, for I feel that doing so allows me to be more in tune with the group and lend more valuable service.

MARIJUANA

I have not yet said anything about marijuana, which I discovered in the midsixties, the early experiences of which I have described in my autobiography (*Up and Down the Holy Mountain*). I would say that the effect it had on me at that time was similar to the one that has always been so appreciated by musicians; it heightened my sense of rhythm, my wish to improvise, and it made me loquacious. However, over time I saw that it also intensified any devotional act, and more broadly, it seemed to facilitate all kinds of meditations; it was this that led me to use it at a time in my life that followed years of abstinence from all types of psychedelics, which started when I became interested in joining a group work dynamic led by the great Afghan Sufi Idries Shah. The prerequisite for this was to abandon all types of psychotherapy and also all kinds of drugs, and I accepted—although later I wrote to Shah to ask him if I was authorized to make an exception during a visit to Don Juan that Carlos Castaneda had proposed at that time. (He gave his consent, but due to bureaucratic circumstances the trip in question did not materialize.)

Regarding marijuana, I felt freer to experiment with it years later, when I no longer felt so close to Idries Shah and I used to visit the Hindu tantric Sri Harish Johari, in whose house smoking was the custom every evening, and also when I entered that period of barrenness on the inner journey that is often described as "the dark night of the soul." I wanted to compensate for my inner impoverishment and the poor results of my spiritual practices with the stimulus of marijuana; and I would say that while it helped me a little at the beginning, afterward it only contributed to my troubled state, and finding myself becoming increasingly dependent on it during the eighties, I decided to discipline myself, and only after being able to do so was I able to truly understand how much it had been contributing to my lack of progress in meditation.

THE PSYCHEDELIC COMMUNITY

It seems appropriate to me that before concluding this psychedelic auto-biography, in addition to giving an account of my personal experiences and my therapeutic explorations with patients, I mention at least briefly something about my relationship with the North American psychedelic community, in which I was considered a pioneer, but for which I ended up becoming (as in the case of the community of Enneagram dissem-inators and the East Coast community of Gestaltists) a not openly declared, but blatantly ignored enemy. I will also leave the details of this for my autobiography, but I will say that through my encounters with the psychedelic community over the years, I have been able to appreciate not only their competitive envy, but also the same arrogance and blind-ness found in other professional associations, and this has led me to a rather critical view of a movement that originally seemed very promis-ing to me. I do not consider that the psychedelic culture has done what it seemed to promise back in the sixties, despite having inspired major initiatives during that fleeting "new era." So I think that, despite psy-chedelic drugs constituting a great potential for healing and even for the salvation of the world, it is of fundamental importance that this potential is properly channeled; for this reason, in recent years I have been arguing that regardless of how important it is to decriminalize drugs, to end prohibitionism will not suffice, and with the understand-ing that their abuse has mainly derived from their misuse, it is time a suitable channel be established for their good use.

I believe that an appropriate channel would be something like what we see in shamanic cultures, where the special competence of shamans is not questioned in terms of sacred plants and the democratic right of all to make use of them was never called on (at least before the interest of seekers in the "developed" world encouraged the development of a pseudo-shamanism for tourists). But I will come back to this issue at the end of this book.

2

Pharmacologically Induced
Altered States of Consciousness

Many years ago, in 1985, Benjamin B. Wolman—famous for his extensive encyclopedia on psychology—commissioned me to write a chapter for his manual of altered states of consciousness. Next, I reproduce the full article.*

DRUG INDUCED STATES

EFFECTS OF THE LSD-LIKE PSYCHEDELICS
OR HALLUCINOGENS

A case may be made for calling this group that of the "hallucinogens," for it was in view of their effect that this word came into use—though not in its literal meaning (which would be the property of eliciting true hallucinations), but in that of bringing about hallucination-related or *hallucinoid* phenomena. If I sometimes call them the "LSD-like psychedelics" rather than "hallucinogens," it is only to avoid confusion in the mind of readers unfamiliar with my suggested nomenclature, for

---

*Claudio Naranjo, "Drug Induced States," chap. 12 in *Handbook of States of Consciousness,* ed. Benjamin B. Wolman and Montague Ullman (New York: Van Nostrand Reinhold, 1986), 365–94.

the term *hallucinogen*—unless specifically defined as I am proposing— might be considered applicable to the fantasy-enhancers as well and is generally (though somewhat inappropriately) regarded as a synonym for "psychedelic."

The group comprises lysergic acid diethylamide and related compounds, mescaline, dimethyltryptamine (DMT) and related compounds, psilocybin and psilocin, and some phenylisopropylamines, in addition to plants containing some of the above. The drugs in this group differ in the duration of their effect and in subtle characteristics (mescaline, for instance, produces more visual phenomena than psilocybin, the effect of which tends to be more cognitive, while the experiential quality of LSD has been characterized as more "electric" than others); yet they all differ from the feeling- and fantasy-enhancers in that they elicit characteristic perceptual phenomena, may bring about psychotic experiences (including depersonalization, delusions of damnation, messianic ideas, gross misinterpretations of the ongoing situation, etc.), and have the potential to bring about the "psychedelic experience" par excellence—characterized by a combination of contemplative experience, ecstasy, and varying degrees of spiritual insight.

The variety of psycho-spiritual states that may be evoked by the hallucinogens has surely been apparent to those familiar with the domain. In the *Varieties of Psychedelic Experience,* Masters and Houston (1967) distinguish aesthetic, recollective-analytic, archetypal or symbolic, and integral or mystical experiences. Grof (1975), in *Realms of the Human Unconscious,* speaks of a psychodynamic or "Freudian" domain, a perinatal or "Rankian" domain, and transpersonal experiences (some of which correspond to the archetypal and thus "Jungian" domain). Following Huxley (1964), I proposed in the *Healing Journey* (1973) a classification of psychedelic states in general into "heavenly" ones, characterized by the apprehension of intrinsic values (and frequently accompanied by rapture), and "hellish" states, characterized by a near-psychotic intensification of psychopathology. I proposed, too, a further subdivision of the positive feeling states according to the quality of value characterizing the experience; and, influenced in this by the thinking of Scheler and Spranger, I proposed a gamut of value leading from the sensate (pleasure) through aesthetic (beauty) and the social and interpersonal (love) to the religious (holiness associated with the apprehension of Being).

This classification would have been more complete had I included, along with the heavens and hells, "purgatory" states, neither wholly positive nor wholly negative in terms of satisfaction and dissatisfaction, which may be simultaneous, and characterized by striving and the sense of moving along, working through obstructions.

In spite of the validity of such distinctions, expressions such as "archetypal experience," "psychodynamic experience," and "heavenly state of the religious kind" fail to convey the specificity of archetypal, psycho-dynamic, or religious states brought about by the action of LSD-like psychedelics, which reside, not in the core phenomenon (archetypal-mythical, self-insight, or mystical experience proper) but in the context of physical, perceptual, affective, and cognitive phenomena in which it appears embedded. In what follows I will describe the effects of hallucinogens (sensu strictu) in greater detail in regard to behavior, the emotions, perception, thinking, and the spiritual realm proper.

By far the most common effect on behavior after a full dosage of LSD or similar hallucinogen is a surrender to what Barber (1970) has labeled "dreamy-detached" feelings, and which might appropriately be called a spontaneous contemplative attitude and state. Words such as *dreamy* or *reverie,* I think, fail to do justice to the psychedelic state, which, while involving a rich visual component (either with eyes closed or with eyes open) is in other ways a hyperalert state rather than one of obnubilation (the effects of the LSD-like hallucinogens in this regard differ from those of *Amanita muscaria,* the fly-agaric mushroom, which causes a desire to sleep).

The connotation of the word *contemplative* in the spiritual traditions derives in part from the fact that it exists as part of a word pair, designating a polarity: contemplative/active. Contemplative experience arises in the practice of meditation, which in turn entails a moving away from the world of action and the senses. Aside from its implication of passivity, the word *contemplation* makes reference, in its traditional use, to a spiritual experience; that is, one in which the individual has access to spiritual riches. Also, it is a state in which the habitual duality of subject and object is reduced or may disappear, so that the contemplator is absorbed in the object of his contemplation. In the "hallucinogenic trance," as we may also call this particular effect of the LSD-like psychedelics, the individual feels inclined to lie down and usually to close his eyes, relinquishing every intention aside from that of mere experiencing while the characteristic perceptual and spiritual effects to be described unfold.

When the eyes are kept open, objects become more interesting, as they are regarded in a way different from the habitual—in a "contemplative" manner in the sense of its being gratuitous rather than motivated by the ordinary utilitarian outlook; one in which seeing is its own satisfaction. There is a tendency to linger on things, which either undergo transformations in terms of formal or aesthetic attributes, significance, or, as Huxley (1954) puts it, is-ness.

On the affective side, the experience of the body may range from one of "oceanic bliss" on the positive side, to malaise, localized pains, suffocation, and other painful symptoms on the negative. On the whole, we may say that the body reflects, just as visual perception does, the experiential qualities of heavenly, hellish, and intermediate states— or, to say it in Grof's terms, physical experience reflects the "perinatal matrices." According to him, these experiences of physical distress sometimes suggest the reexperiencing of birth trauma, while the experience of relaxed plenitude suggests life in the womb before the onset of labor and the experience of "purgatory" that lies between these extremes of superabundant well-being and of distress may also be described in reference to the metaphor of birth, for we may attribute it to the fetus as it progresses along the birth canal.

Grof (1975, 1980) suggests that the perinatal matrices (that is to say, modes of experience related to the experiences surrounding birth) are memories or replays of the past—a hypothesis in line with convincing examples of hallucinogenically induced age regression yet in conflict with the fact that by the time of birth, myelinization of the peripheral nerves is not complete. Alternatively, we may conceive that these distinct states are not in essence memories but "mental landscapes" *analogous* to those surrounding birth—which, precisely by virtue of this analogy, are *associated* with memories and fantasized reconstructions of the past. Hallucinogen-elicited death/rebirth experiences are, I think, experiences pertaining to the temporary "death" of what spiritual traditions have called "ego" (our ordinary identity and what it entails) and the "birth" of deeper layers of one's nature. Yet it is not to be wondered that these experiences that correspond to the perception of a psycho-spiritual death/rebirth process and which echo those of physical birth at a higher octave, so to speak, may become symbolized in these earlier experiences and memories—in the way all experiences under the influence of the hallucinogens tend to become symbolized.

A symbol both expresses and has the potential to conceal—and it is my impression that this is particularly the case in regard to the painful experiences of the body, which may include, aside from those suggestive of birth trauma, all sorts of psychosomatic symptoms and seemingly individual aches and muscle tensions. It is a common finding of those involved in psychotherapy with hallucinogens that these ailments constitute a projection upon the body of affective experiences that have not yet been confronted, and that they disappear along with the undoing of repression. Striking examples of this may be found in the first-person account *Myself and I,* by Constance Newland (1963), who discovered, for instance, that her painfully full bladder was an equivalent of sexual arousal, that her excessive sensitivity to pain in the teeth was connected to fantasies of biting, and that her chronic tensional aches in the arms, amplified under LSD into a sensation that she described as the buzzing of an electric saw, disappeared after a therapeutically guided session in which she was able to remember a traumatic event that occurred when she was two and a half. On that occasion her nurse had tied her arms to give her an enema, the water of which was too hot, and which made her feel as if she were to burst. In addition to retrieving this memory, she was also able to discover that she experienced this painful event as punishment for masturbation.

We may note that any feeling possible to our human nervous system may be aroused in the psychedelic state, and this applies not only to the ordinary feelings but also to very early preverbal feeling states, for among the effects of the hallucinogens is that of age regression. The passivity itself that characterizes the hallucinogenic state at its peak, a non-goal-directed state that may be characterized as a de-differentiation of the mind, can be regarded as regressive, for it is tempting to regard it as analogous to what may have been the state of mind of a fetus. This state and the reliving of early experiences are related, in that de-differentiation is the basis for the psychological permeability that allows the accessing of remote mental contents or their "manifesting" to the conscious mind.

Very characteristic under the influence of hallucinogens are, of course, the ecstatic states and the counter-ecstatic states, which are to grief what ecstasy is to ordinary happiness and pleasure. The most profound among the ecstatic states is that associated with the physical states that I have described as "oceanic," by virtue of the seeming dissolution of boundaries between the individual and the world, the inner and the outer, self and other, and even subject and object. It is a supremely impersonal or transpersonal domain of experience in which even the visionary content is abstract rather than figurative. Individuals sometimes spontaneously use the word *cosmic* in reference, not only to experienced boundlessness, but to the sense of superabundant plenitude. Though individuals with religious or philosophical sophistication may translate this ineffable experience into terms such as "the clear light of the void" as Huxley did, or Sat-ChitAnanda, Brahman, "The Absolute," and so forth, I will not undertake to engage in any such conceptualizations here—aside from distinguishing this "mystical" experience from religious experiences proper, which lie in a domain where thought is not altogether absent and images or concepts of an exalted, "superhuman," or mythical quality are manifest in the visions. In reference to them I will speak of "religious-archetypal" experiences, being of the opinion that the religious and the mythical can be only artificially separated— archetypes being essentially symbols imbued with numinosity, sacred symbols that arise from an experience of sacredness. (Thus, experiences of an "otherness" perceived as a "heavenly father" or a "cosmic mother," usually regarded as "religious," may also be considered to be implicitly archetypal.)

Some reports of profound ecstatic states could be used to illustrate either religious ecstasy or the ecstatic feelings associated with deeply felt love; in other instances, an arousal of love may be manifest without an explicit religious content. One may wonder in these cases, however, whether there is not a factor of spiritual awareness that underlies what nonreligious individuals perceive only at the interpersonal end of the feeling spectrum. At least the association between both is frequent, and particularly in the context of group therapy facilitated by LSD. One comes across episodes where individuals engage in a silent communication of a depth uncommon in ordinary life; these may be simply interpreted as experiences of deep empathy, in the sense of seeing the common humanness between self and other; or may be articulated as experiences of which the outer manifestation is love but which arise from a glimpse of that transcendent self that is the essence of both self and other.

Just as a transcendent background of experience may manifest itself in the interpersonal realm as feelings of love, it is also possible that the same spiritual factor projects itself in aesthetic experience, in a way that some individuals may acknowledge as such while others, not open to the spiritual dimension (perhaps by virtue of an antireligious bias), fail to acknowledge or articulate. It seems quaint to me that in so many of the early reports on the effects of psychedelics only the aesthetic aspect stands out, and references to love and mystical insights are absent. (Klüver, 1966, on the last page of his essay on mescal, disdainfully puts in quotation marks the expression "cosmic significance," which some individuals report in connection to their visions.) Perhaps the spirit of the times was not sufficiently receptive to the transcendent dimension of hallucinogenic experiences, and thus it was revealing to read Huxley's (1954) report in the *Doors of Perception,* in which he describes a no lesser degree of aesthetic ecstasy than his predecessors but is able to trace the beauty of the perceived world back to an underlying enhancement of *Istigkeit,* the sense of Being.

Another source of ecstasy is connected to something akin to pleasure. I say "akin to" pleasure in order to point out the peculiar kind of bliss that some individuals interpret or express in reference to body feelings or sensations rather than religious interpersonal or aesthetic emotions, for it differs in quality from the pleasure of instinctual gratification. It is to a considerable extent pleasure associated with seeing and with hearing, a delight not in the aesthetic qualities of particular music works, but in sound itself, and not in aesthetic form but in colors and textures—a pleasure residing in the affective tone of sensations themselves. Part of it comes from proprioceptive sensing—as in a state of free-flowing "body energies"—and may be described simply as intense well-being. Just as in the above instances, however, we may have reason to think that such "pleasure" is not unrelated to the core factor in psychedelic peak experiences: the mystical or spiritual factor that spills over the different domains of experience including that of sensing. In the same way that the beauty of Huxley's carnation and iris owes its intensity to a felt meaningfulness that is projected upon them from the field of experience of Huxley, who contemplates them, all sensory experience partakes of increased meaningfulness in the awareness of one immersed in the expanded hallucinogenic state. This "translates" itself into apparent intensification, but we know that this sensory intensification is a subjective phenomenon, not verified by experiments on tactile discrimination or visual acuity. It constitutes, rather, like visual distortions, a symbolic projection of luminosity, enhanced significance.

Another state that I want to mention among the peak experiences elicited by the hallucinogens (along with the paradises and states of inspiration, culminating in trances of divine possession) is one characterized by an intense feeling of all-rightness in the face of the concrete, undistorted here and now and one's individual circumstances. This state (usually accompanied by a feeling of gratefulness, as has been described by Aldous Huxley in *Island*) best corresponds in the perinatal domain to the state of the newborn—who has emerged from the beyond and comes into the world of persons and objects as a ripe fruit. In the language of religious symbolism, we may call this state an "earthly paradise."

The super-negative or "hellish" states may be understood not only as intensifications of psychopathology (as I put it in *The Healing Journey*) but as states of intense value deficiency. Accordingly, for each state of enhanced value we may distinguish the corresponding state of valuelessness, or negative value. To pleasure, there corresponds, on the sensory level, a state of distress that is an indescribable agony of a vague sort, in which an individual probably somatizes a psycho-spiritual distress to such a degree that it sometimes requires the interruption of the experience. To the aesthetic level and the perception of beauty on the positive end of the feeling range, there corresponds an intensified perception of ugliness, where any particular object or the world as a whole becomes something flat, caricature-like, grotesque, in bad taste, artificial, hideous, and so forth. To love there corresponds, on the negative end, a lovelessness that can be the background of a state of forlornness and depression or of a paranoid state, in which the world or others are perceived as hateful, malevolent, demonic. In a special class among paranoid states are states of possession by demonic or malevolent entities, in which the individual may either engage in destructive behavior (frequently described as a reaction to *Amanita*) or feel that his mental processes are forced upon him—as during part of Albert Hofmann's (and the world's) first LSD self-experiment (Hofmann 1983). To the highest level of value—the sense of the holy—there corresponds, as a counterpart, a complete desacralization of life, an absence of being, a sense of unreality, insubstantiality, or emptiness of self and of the world.

A rarer affective state that may be brought about by the hallucinogens is neither positive nor negative (nor both), but of intensified indifference—as in the catatonic syndrome. It is neither "heavenly" nor "hellish" (in appearance), but to borrow another word from religion, one of "limbo." In psychiatric terminology I think most would agree to call these states, as in the first case reported in Sydney Cohen's *The Beyond Within* (1967, 113–14), catatonic reactions.

Though "heavens" and "hells"—peak and nadir experiences—may be regarded as the most typical states induced by the hallucinogens, they are perhaps not the most frequent, particularly if we consider their duration in the course of a specific session. I think that if a statistical calculation were made of the time spent on different experiential realms across subjects, this would show that the most frequent state is neither one of unalloyed bliss nor despair, but one in which positive and negative feelings are present side by side. It is essentially a *seeking state,* a state that is half abundance, half deficiency, and is characterized by the striving for abundance and a pursuit of optimization.

It is this feeling state, I believe, that explains those visions that Klüver (1966, 31) has called *presque vu* experiences:

> events in the visual field . . . suggest an end which is not quite reached, or they lack the proper completion; they do not—to use a Gestalt psychological term—call forth a "closure" experience.

That these experiences reflect not only the structure of neurological events, but an affective state is suggested by less abstract embodiments of near perfection, such as a vision of innumerable snail shells, each with a little piece missing.

This seeking state, echoing the situation of "wanting to be born" that we may emphatically attribute to the child as it advances through the birth canal, is frequently associated with psychotherapeutic inquiry or with what may be described as spontaneous spiritual work—such as that of seeking to surrender more deeply, to accept the pain of the moment less defensively, or to experience ever more fully one's aspiring, perhaps prayerful attitude. This is the state that religious symbolism has projected into the afterworld as *purgatory*—a place of purification—and I do not think that it should be explained as a mere reliving of a perinatal situation any more than the impulse to progress psycho-spiritually in life should.

The seeking impulse, which I see as the core phenomenon in "purification" states, is a longing that, detaching itself from habitual objects (such as romantic love or the affirmations of one's idealized self-image), comes to interpret itself as a thirst for what may be variously interpreted as plenitude, wholeness, higher consciousness, God, Enlightenment. The spontaneous aspiration to escape the prison of internal limitations and to attain an intuited possibility of higher consciousness and greater satisfaction is, I think, objectively justified by the perception of these limitations and potential in the present. Its foundation need not be sought in early experience, therefore, but in the condition of the organism at the moment: a condition of dysfunction and pain that the hallucinogens (and also the feeling-enhancers) characteristically bring into awareness—along with glimpses of an alternative.

It has been one of Grof's merits to point out the hallucinogenic syndrome that he calls "volcanic"—and which he describes in terms of its association with the moment immediately preceding birth, when passage along the birth canal is fastest and suffocation has reached its maximum. In it a volcanic type of ecstasy is manifest simultaneously with an intensification of suffering to cosmic proportions. It may be accompanied by sexual feelings, experiences of dying and being reborn, and intense physical manifestations ("pressures and pain, suffocation, muscular tension and discharge, nausea and vomiting, hot flushes and chills, sweating, cardiac distress, problems of sphincter control, ringing in the ears"; Grof 1980, 82). Among the visions typically accompanying these experiences he includes titanic battles, archetypal feats, explosions of atomic bombs, launching of missiles and spaceships, exploding volcanoes, earthquakes, tornadoes and other natural catastrophes, bloody revolutions, dangerous hunts for wild animals, discoveries and conquests of new continents.

Volcanic states may be regarded as intensified states of emptiness-fullness and are those that may most properly be spoken of as death-rebirth processes, for there is in them at the same time a crumbling down of the habitual personality (with the consequent fear) and an ecstatic emergence of new energies and a new sense of self. They may be regarded as a greatly accelerated or amplified form of the ongoing dying and being born that are part of human evolution.

To end this survey of affective states, I will mention the frequent occurrence of hypomanic or manic states. These can be of two kinds: (1) narcissistic excitement about the wonders of one's experience, corresponding to the phenomenon of inflation (pride in spiritual experience, most common toward the end of sessions); and (2) the irresistible humor associated with otherwise shallow experiences, as a facet of a defensive reaction.

Writing of the affective aspect of hallucinogen-induced states would not be complete without discussion of something implicit in all of them: a variable measure of detachment. Out of detachment grows the contemplative experience; it is out of abandon that visions arise. When "getting out of the way" is thorough, mystical experiences manifest; when the eruption of the mind-depth is resisted, it is hells that arise. These hells not only are resisted but are created through an inward act of jumping into the void; they constitute an otherworld of the mind that has been arrived at through a measure of death, an incomplete yet real though temporal dissolution of the "little" I, the ordinary self.

All affective states, from terror to bliss, arise, I think, from this background of detachment—ranging from "dreamy-detached" feelings (to borrow Barber's expression) to ego-death.

It is the perceptual effects of the hallucinogens that have suggested their name; they are intense and unfamiliar and echo the range of affective states. Thus, it is not only with respect to feelings but in visual terms that we encounter hells, purgatories, heavens—and an enriched earth.

For the earthly paradise of the hallucinogens, unlike the one brought about by feeling-enhancers, is linked with a special mode of perception in which the world of persons and objects is neither distorted nor left behind (along with the body itself and one's sense of identity), nor is it hidden behind a screen of half-materialized fantasies; it becomes more of itself, we might say. Everything becomes clearer, sharper, not only appearing to be more "present" than usual, but with a density of formal relationships that creates the impression that each thing is a miracle of perfection even in its imperfections.

No less remarkable are the distortions in visual perception (dismorphopsia), which, like illusory movement, are of an expressive nature.

We may speak of varying degrees in which a projection of the inner world is effected upon the outer. The intensification of light and perception of expressive qualities stand at the lower end of this range; illusory movements and perceptual distortions constitute an intermediate stage; a further step in this direction is the creation of hallucinations proper (which are rare) or pseudo-hallucinations (in which the individual knows the perceived form to be the materialization of a fantasy).

According to Masters and Houston (1967), every category of myth may spontaneously arise: creation myths, myths of death-rebirth, of questing and transformation. Yet more common than mythological sequences proper (which are more common with the fantasy-enhancers) is the emergence of symbolic scenes and the stimulation of mythical understanding—linking the content of visions with universal themes.

Most characteristic of the hallucinogens are abstract visionary experiences, or ones in which realistic elements are embedded in an abstract pattern. It is such visions that Klüver (1966) studied in his classic study of mescal in 1928. In that work he points out the existence of "forms and form elements which must be considered typical for mescal visions," and which he proposes to call form-constants. He describes three of these. One of these form-constants, for example, is always referred to by terms such as *grating, lattice, network, filigree, honeycomb,* or *chessboard* design. Closely related to this is another that he calls the cobweb figure;

for instance, "colored threads running together in a revolving center, the whole similar to a cobweb." The cobweb may be regarded, I think, as a combination of lattice and circularity or (to echo Jung's generalization of the Oriental word) mandala. Related to the latter are also kaleidoscopic images.

Klüver suggests that such images may have a neurological basis. Without discarding such a thought, we may also regard them as remarkable projections of the state of affairs in the individual's psyche, which is one of increased associations between mental contents—felt as an interconnected and coherent multiplicity.

A second form-constant singled out by Klüver (1966) is one "designated by terms such as tunnel, funnel, alley cone, or vessel." Here are some of his illustrations:

> Sometimes I seemed to be gazing into a vast hollow revolving vessel, on whose polished concave mother-of-pearl surface the hues were swiftly changing; the field of vision is similar to the interior of a cone, the vertex of which is lying in the center of the field directly before my eyes; . . . upon pressure of the closed eyes I first saw an alley in very deep perspective; deep beautiful perspectives . . . going to the infinite. (23)

Here, too, we may understand the formal pattern as a visual representation of an experience: that of moving along an *experiential path*. A tunnel may be regarded as the mandalic structure of a field of experience (with the self at the center) unfolding in time. When such visions occur as a response to music, the sense of onward movement echoes not only the felt progression of a physical and psychological process but the perception of music as an unfolding in time.

A third form-constant mentioned by Klüver (1966) is the *spiral*.

> There appears a brown spiral, a wide band, revolving madly around its vertical axis. The band spiral opens and closes on a concertina

according to the rhythm of the whistling . . . a procession, coming from the lower right, moved slowly in spiral turns to the upper left. . . . At the same time one of my legs assumes spiral form the luminous spiral and the haptic spiral blend psychologically. . . . A physician, a subject of Beringer, reports: "Before me I see the lower part of my body from the hips down as a large green varnished object which has about the shape of a truncated cone with spiral windings." (23–24)

At the time when Klüver was writing his pioneering report, there was not in his environment something that has come into ours that echoes the style of psychedelic abstractions better than words and even human painting can do: certain computer graphics. And they do this, I think, because they convey the same combination of mathematical regularity and organic complexity that is perhaps the fundamental aspect of these visions. Among computer graphics and, more generally, bidimensional geometric displays, it is particularly moiré patterns involving the superimposition of "reverberating" conic sections (ellipses, etc.) that are most expressive of the visionary realm. If we want to convey harmonious complexity with a single line, however, in no way could we do it better than with the spiral—which for this and other reasons may be the most appropriate graphic symbol of psychedelic consciousness. Containing in itself a radial pattern, a sense of advancing toward a goal never reached, and plural reverberation, in addition to the felt harmonious complexity of its equation, by its serpentine form it evokes the snake, universal symbol of the life-force, kundalini, or cosmic orgone.

True as may be the description by Havelock Ellis (De Ropp 1957, 36) of his mescaline experience as "an orgy of vision," listening to music is at least as significant as attending to the visual world and is generally regarded as the best doorway to ecstatic experience.

At best, the experience of musical audition may lead the individual to echo the statement of classical India: "*Sabda Brahman*: sound is God." Just as the visual world may convey (beyond the particulars of form, color, objects, and meanings) Beingness or *Istigkeit,* so sound in itself, beyond musical forms and psychological content, becomes suffused with Being, a Being with which the listener identifies as he dissolves in the music, becoming nothing and the music all at once.

While in the depths of oceanic dissolution music ceases to be perceived as such, at a more differentiated level of consciousness audition becomes musical audition proper, though an intensified musical audition. This is a transpersonal realm equivalent to that of visual archetypes, and distinct from the state of musical audition in still another state of consciousness characterized by the presence of personal contents. In the latter, the music becomes the mirror of the ordinary psyche, rather than the spirit: an acoustical projective device. According to the context of the experience projected upon it, music then will be (at either level) heavenly, hellish, or anything in between.

Broadly speaking, the cognitive aspect of hallucinogen-induced states may be discussed in regard to an interference with rational, linear, discursive, and goal-directed thinking; a stimulation of unusual forms of cognition (an "expansion of consciousness" by virtue of which it is possible to grasp "other realities"), and the possible presence of delusional thinking. These three seem to be interrelated in such a manner that the suspension of rational thought allows for the emergence of nonrational, intuitive, analogical, and magical thinking—which in turn can be manifest in a productive or an aberrated manner.

It is my impression that delusional phenomena constitute an intuitive potential gone askew, and that psychotic thinking in general may be viewed as a distorted approximation of reality. It is as if the psychotic came into contact with too much truth—more than he could bear—and evaded such an excess of perception through the escape valves of projection, displacement, distortion, and so on. This is suggested, for instance, by Laing and Esterson's (1964) investigation of schizophrenics and their families, in which they invite us to consider madness as a step in the direction of healing. All the same, it is a step in the direction of a truth (about the love of parents, for instance) that cannot be handled, and because it cannot be handled it is transformed into an approximation—usually a symbolic equivalent of the truth that is in equal measure a truth that rises above the common world of lies and an absurdity that falls below the standards of reason.

In connection with the interference of rational thinking, I will omit laboratory data (summary of which may be found in Barber 1970) and stay at the phenomenologic level. When interference is profound, this may be subjectively experienced as a "nothingness," skillfully described by Michaux (1974) in his essay on "What Is 'Coming to Oneself'?" His answer to the question is, accordingly, being "restored to thought."

Not everyone will agree in regard to the total suspension of thought under the effect of a hallucinogen. Huxley (1954), for instance, in *The Doors of Perception*, remarked that he could think clearly and conceptualize throughout the experience. However, besides being the expression of one particular kind of experience—an extreme one—it is possible that suspension of thought may have been a state particularly available to Michaux, since there is a tendency for hallucinogenically induced states to counterbalance in some regards the salient features of one's personality; and Michaux—who described such nonthinking (1974) throughout his writings—appears to be the epitome of a "thinking type."

In another passage, Michaux (1974, 27–28) described trying to write under the effects of a hallucinogen. Here thought was not totally silenced but was in a process of disintegration. The passage shows an abundance of thought leading to an interference of goal-directed thinking. While the writer aims at the expression of a thought, an overwhelming increase in the density of associations causes the emergence of other thoughts that compete with the first as objects of expression— and so on. Yet this is a phenomenon that can be experienced in two different attitudes. The subject may either, like Michaux, insist on thinking in a linear way and be distressed to realize that his thinking is disturbed; or he may, alternatively, give up the attempt—or rather *intent*—to think and discover himself immersed in a different cognitive medium, so to speak; for it is precisely this silencing of thought that traditional spirituality has recognized as the point of departure for contemplative experience. St. Gregory says contemplation is "to rest from exterior motion and to cleave only to the desire of the Maker." We might expand this description inasmuch as the passivity of the contemplative state entails the relinquishment, not only of external action, but of the thinker, the computing, analyzing mind.

The astounding abundance of detail of hallucinogen-induced visions seems to reflect admirably the wealth of elements simultaneously present in the individual's field at any moment. The state of increased permeability characteristic of this state allows for easy access to memories, to new connections, and to constellations of experience such as those that Jung has called complexes and Grof (1980) proposes to call systems of condensed experience (COEX systems). Such constellations of reciprocally associated mnemonic traces and their corresponding affect may be said to exist in our psychological structure, where they are, in the first place, buried because of repression and amnesia, and are not grasped as wholes, but sequentially, through the linear and one-dimensional progression of discursive thought.

The condition of increased interconnectedness and accessibility of mental contents may not only lead to the lifting of childhood amnesia and the arising of personal insights but is likely to be the basis for the potential of hallucinogens to stimulate creativity (Harman and Fadiman 1970), and, most typically, it constitutes the basis for the gift of contemplation. This manifests itself not only in regard to external objects, but in regard to internal or mental objects as well. Any subject matter that motivates the individual (and these emerge spontaneously in the course of any hallucinogenic experience) is invested with a great wealth of associations drawn out of the "oceanic" depth of the mind and experienced not merely as a thought construction but as inseparable—by virtue of associative links—from the whole of one's inner life. I believe that the experiences that Grof (1975) classifies as temporal and spatial expansions of consciousness (ancestral experiences; collective and racial experiences; identification with other persons, with animals, plants, planetary consciousness, etc.) constitute, in essence, expressions of contemplative experience—inasmuch as the individual not only mobilizes an unusual degree of creative imagination in them, but (as is usual in contemplation) identifies himself with his mental creation. It is no wonder that—by virtue of this movement—the products of contemplative experience may be taken literally as a tapping by the human mind of a "group consciousness," a consciousness inherent in inorganic matter, extraplanetary consciousness, and so on. The question remains, however, of whether the sense of certainty that accompanies these experiences reflects literal truth or is instead a phenomenological trait associated with an "inner" truth comparable to that of a poem or a myth.

Peyote-consuming Indians and researchers alike (Grof 1975; Kripner 1974) have noted that the hallucinogens may elicit experiences of extrasensory perception.

If the hallucinogens indeed stimulate clairvoyance and clairaudience, that should not be wondered at, since it should be expected from increased access to "the other side of the mind" and would naturally arise from increased receptivity.

Contemplative experience may find support in any object, symbol, or concept, and leads (when contemplation is most successful) to an apprehension of the "mysteries": eternal truths concerning existence that cannot be grasped by thought alone, and at most can be expressed gropingly in art and philosophical discourse.

That the sense of time may expand is easy to understand as a result of the acceleration of thought; yet time may also shrink, and this seems a natural consequence of the silencing of discursive thinking at the hallucinogenic peak. The apparent suspension of time is usually associated with the mystical experience and a sense of the eternal, in which the experience of time-arrest is compounded with a sense of infinite time.

In connection with delusional thinking, my view is that it corresponds to a superposition of higher cognition and defensive distortion. Through rejection of an experience that, when accepted, may be called divine, there thus arises a sense of the demonic, of paranoia, and a sense of a remote, indifferent, or inaccessible cosmos or self in depression.

I have already touched upon the spiritual effects of hallucinogens in speaking of the experiences of the body, perceptual and cognitive phenomena, emotional and behavioral effects; for the domains of the psyche cannot be wholly separated, and spiritual experience has a physical correlate (the movement of "energy" in the body or, to speak in Indian terms, the activation of the kundalini and the circulation of prana through the chakras and nadis) and is also related with the emotional sphere (with its polarity of deficiency/abundance, craving versus love) and with the cognitive domain. The fact that many cognitive experiences have been classified by Grof (1980) as "transpersonal" is an indication of how difficult it may be to separate the transpersonal or spiritual factor proper from its cognitive and perceptual "envelope" or echo. Indeed, though the mystical experience, as the word itself reveals, is ineffable (the Greek root *mus* meaning "mute") it is typically articulated through the medium of symbolism.

If we want to move on from such projections of spirituality to the domains of cognition, emotion, action, and the experienced body, seeking to penetrate to the spiritual sphere itself, transcendent to these components of the "person," we might do best by not saying anything. Such is sometimes the Buddhist attitude, as an expression of its "theology" of nothingness (if we can continue to use this word for a nontheistic articulation of transcendence). For spirit, in this view (consonant with the *ein Soph* doctrine of the Kabbalah and the Chinese concept of the Tao), is something that cannot be pointed at, and lies in an altogether different domain from that of articulate consciousness with its awareness of body, feelings, qualities, things, logical classes, and persons. To speak of it as "voidness," as Mahayana scriptures do, does more than express its ineffability: it points to a sphere of experience (or nonexperience?) that is like the matrix in which the articulate contents of the mind unfold, the "space" in which thoughts and images arise and mental states occur—a field that, according to Vajrayana Buddhism, may possess increasing degrees of permeability or openness according to stages of spiritual development and meditational depth.

Along with the interpretation of the transpersonal factor as nothingness—which invites us to interpret the spiritual element in psychedelic experiences as a factor of self-annihilation and surrender—spiritual traditions have also spoken of spirit as the *ultimate something,* an "invisible" sphere endowed with a degree of reality of which the reality of manifest existence seems but a shadow or reflection (as in Plato's myth of the cave). Whether it is spoken of as Absolute, ultimate Truth, Being, Mind, God, or Self, it is declared to be—inasmuch as it is all that—everywhere, pervading everything. However, one who experiences himself as *Self* (rather than isolated and limited self) experiences himself as the Self of all; he whose identity has shifted from an individual personality to Being feels unified with the infinity of all that is. Thus, we may say that becoming nothing is the other side of becoming everything; nothingness is the other side of totality.

In figure 1 (page 66) I attempt to summarize the relation between some LSD states graphically. The solid arrows point out that the "death experience" is the gateway to nothingness, the "birth experience," the gateway to Being. The dotted arrows indicate transition from one "perinatal domain" to another, transition through which nothingness becomes a context for birth, and the experience of Being permits the extinction of the "ego." Double arrows linking the center of the diagram with the periphery suggest the arising of the transpersonal experiences out of "madness" as surrender of control becomes more complete than in psychotic states where it is resisted and incomplete. It will be noted that in this diagram the horizontal axis (voidness-plenitude) is the static one, while the vertical (Birth-Death) is dynamic (dying is a process *oriented* to nothingness; birth the process *oriented* to Being). The volcanic vertical axis and the serene horizontal one may be also regarded in light of the "enstatic" versus "ecstatic" polarity that has been the subject of Roland Fischer's discussions.

A common misunderstanding that has arisen in regard to the death-rebirth and voidness-plenitude experiences under the effects of

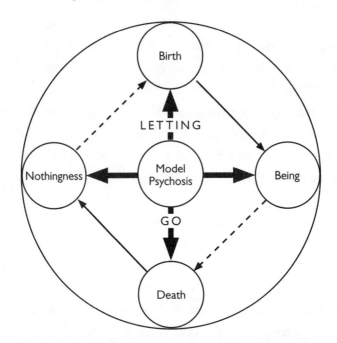

Figure 1. Graphical representation of spiritual effects of LSD

hallucinogens is that of failing to draw a distinction between states and stages of consciousness, transient experiencing, and phases of spiritual growth. While the "annihilating illumination" (Andrews 1963) may occur rather easily in the course of a psychedelic experience, this cannot be equated to the death-in-God of Christian mystics who have attained permanent mystical union or sanctity, or to *nirvana* (annihilation) of the Buddhist who attains the happiness of that "other shore," where the passions are transcended. The death and rebirth of the Greek myths, of the Egyptian teachings concerning Osiris, and of the Christian myth are formulations of a life process involving a death-in-life—death to "oneself" and "the world"—and the initiation and birth of a higher life. Psychedelic experiences are, I think, only glimpses of the great transformation that lies within our potential, archetypal anticipations and, at best, steps along the way.

While access to the transcendent or spiritual factor in human life has been often sought in the spiritual traditions through the acceptance of nothingness and death, only in shamanism was the acceptance of madness recognized as a pathway, and in the Dionysian religion of the Greek mysteries. (In the figure of the god of drunkenness, human genius expressed an appreciation of surrender to the point of divinization.) The hallucinogenic experience—known to the Greeks through the use of *Amanita muscaria* according to Graves (1982), or *Psilocybe* according to others—is, I think, a spiritual experience of an eminently Dionysian kind. This Dionysian element in it may account in part for the reluctance of some Christians to equate it with the mystical experience of their saints; for, even if we allow for a common core of spiritual experience beyond the characteristics of each religious path, the utter abandonment of the individual under the effects of a hallucinogen is sharply in contrast with the austerity and discipline of the desert fathers or the Theravada monks. A strong anti-Dionysian spirit may be perceived, for instance, in the attitude of Zaehner (1961)—best known and most learned among those denying (in his *Mysticism: Sacred and Profane*) the spiritual significance of "psychedelics."

Though Alan Watts (1962) is possibly the best-known religious thinker who has endorsed the validity of psychedelically induced mystical experiences, it is to Pahnke that we owe the most satisfactory attempt at experimental validation of this contention (1963 and 1967). Nine universal psychological characteristics were derived from the literature of spontaneous mystical experience reported throughout world history from almost all cultures and religions. They are unity (consciousness and memory are not lost; instead the person becomes very much aware of being part of a dimension much vaster and greater than himself); transcendence of time and space; deeply felt positive mood; sense of sacredness; noetic quality ("a feeling of insight or illumination with a tremendous force of certainty"); paradoxical; alleged ineffability; transiency; and persisting positive changes in attitudes and behavior. On a memorable double-blind experiment carried out with ten theology students and professors in Boston on a Good Friday (Pahnke 1970, 152ff) these characteristics proved to be identical for spontaneous and psyche-delically induced mystical experiences.

I think that the most important question is not whether hallucinogen-induced experiences are similar or identical to those elicited by means of austerities, meditation, and prayer, but whether both are of comparable value for an individual's life. It may be surmised that an experience obtained through spiritual discipline is one that the individual has earned, having developed the necessary aptitude to induce it; an artificial experience, on the other hand, is one in which the individual has not brought about in himself the inner conditions necessary to elicit it. Inasmuch as the experience requires an outer stimulus, the person depends upon it as on a crutch, and we may wonder whether such a crutch can interfere with the progress of meditative depth rather than assist it. Since it is well known that the depth of hallucinogenic experiences diminishes after some time, the peak experiences that lie within their potential to elicit may be regarded, perhaps, more as initiatory experiences than as a *path,* and thus an alternative to spiritual methodologies.

THE FEELING-ENHANCERS

I have proposed (1973) the name *feeling-enhancers* for drugs such as MDA and MMDA, which share with the LSD-like psychedelics the effect of eliciting "spontaneous self-analytic experiences," and yet differ from them in that they do not bring about the characteristic perceptual phenomena of the hallucinogens, do not stimulate mythical thinking, and do not bring a person to angelic or demonic realms—but do elicit peak or nadir experiences that remain within the bounds of the familiar human domain. To this category of drugs belong, along with MDA and MMDA, a number of other less known ones such as TMD-2 and MDMA. The psychedelic effect of many such amphetamine-related compounds was reported by Shulgin et al. (1961) without reference to qualitative differences, which may be conceptualized in terms of varying degrees of amphetaminic activity and hallucinogenic effects. MMDA, for instance, is of little activity as a stimulant (subjects report drowsiness) and is slightly hallucinogenic (in that imagery may be present when the eyes are closed). The nature of this imagery, however, reflects the typical inner atmosphere of the feeling-enhancers, for it is neither abstract nor mythical but realistic, and related to persons more than animals or objects. MDA, on the other hand, may be regarded as the prototype of this group, for it is mostly a feeling-enhancer, with rare and negligible hallucinogenic effect.

On the behavioral level the effects of the feeling-enhancers differ from those of the hallucinogens in that there is less of an inclination to become absorbed in a trance. The person under the effects of MDA usually feels like lying down during the first hours of the experience, but this impulse is not so compelling as with LSD and related compounds. The individual remains in greater contact with the environment and with the body. This is probably not unrelated to the characteristic talkativeness of people under the effect of feeling-enhancers. Such talking is not only motivated by the communication of the experience but is frequently the expression of an exploration of one's life—its contents being that of one's relationships, personality, and projects.

At the cognitive level, one characteristic of the feeling-enhancers is a relative lack of disruption of thought as found with hallucinogens. Yet perhaps the subtle "relaxation" of discursive thought that takes place under their effects is related to a facilitation of cognition in another regard, for as remarkable as feeling-enhancement itself is the facilitation of insight that they bring about in regard to one's personality and one's relationships. Under the effect of the MDA-like drugs it is easier to feel what one feels, to see things as they are. The insights, which may sometimes profoundly affect the individual's life, are not usually discoveries of anything remote but are the outcome of a willingness to see what is obvious—such as, "I have been afraid all my life," or "I have never allowed myself to be who I am with my lovers," or "I am feeling guilty." They constitute a discovery of what has always been the case but has not been acknowledged, out of a fear of not being able to face the consequences of such perception.

Another cognitive effect, which, like the above, may be understood in the light of a deactivation of repression, is the lifting of amnesia concerning painful events—usually in one's early history. It would seem that the same capacity to see the obvious in the present also allows the individual to see what has happened to him in the past that he has "forgotten."

Feeling-enhancement is not something irrelevant to this cognitive effect of undoing repression. It is hard to say whether we are in the presence of a quasi-physiological affective amplification of the emotions or simply a more direct experience of the emotions—usually veiled from our awareness because of our unwillingness to cope with our true situation (or fear we will not be able to). The enhancement of feelings that this group of psychedelics characteristically bring about applies to positive and negative feelings as well, and just as the hallucinogens have their heavens and their hells, we can say that there also is something like heavens and hells in the MDA or MDMA experience—only these archetypal terms do not seem so evocative in regard to the MDA domain of the psyche, which is not the mythical-magical domain or the domain of symbolization at all, but a domain of memory (i.e., that of the facts of life as they are stored in our experience). The peak experience of MDA, for instance, is one that may justify the popular talk of it as a "love drug," for it is an experience characterized by warmth. The negative end is characterized by the intensification of psychological pain, and may involve sadness, guilt, shame, and less commonly, anger.

THE FANTASY-ENHANCERS

In *The Healing Journey* (1973) I proposed to call harmaline and ibogaine "fantasy-enhancers" to emphasize the property that led William Turner (1964) to coin the term *oneirophrenic* for yagé, after his pioneering self-experiment with a plant extract. This special term seemed justified in view of the fact that, while these substances may in a broad sense be called psychedelic, their effect is different enough from those of the LSD-like psychedelics and feeling-enhancers to distinguish them. Together with other harmala and iboga alkaloids, they constitute a group of "dream-inducing" drugs, as we might also call them if we were to adopt the language of South American Indians (who use the word *dream* in an extended sense, also applicable to dreams in the absence of sleep).

The main differences between these alkaloids and the hallucinogens, aside from the prominence of dreamlike sequences with archetypal content, is the absence of perceptual distortions, scant stimulation of the emotions, and absence of psychotomimetic potential of these drugs. Such is the case of the drink variously known as yagé, ayahuasca, and so on, prepared by medicine men of the South American montaña from a combination of at least two plants, which usually contains DMT in addition to harmala alkaloids. The difference between the state elicited by this mixture and the one induced by LSD and similar hallucinogens lies in the prominence of the oneirophrenic effect, the typical content of the visions, and, as I propose below, the prominence of instinct-related ideation rather than emotion or cognitive involvement.

The characteristics of the harmaline and yagé experiences led me in the sixties to think that it was *Peganum harmala* rather than *Amanita muscaria* that had been the source of the Iranian haoma and Indian soma—central to the early Aryan sacrifices and religion. This hypothesis has recently received convincing support from research by David Flattery (Flattery and Schwartz 1985).

The psychedelic property of the harmala alkaloids is also of interest in view of the demonstrated transformation of serotonin into melatonin and (psychoactive [see Naranjo 1967, for further references]) 6-methoxy-harmalan in pineal tissue.

Before carrying out the human experiments with ibogaine reported at the LSD conference organized by the University of California in 1966 and in a subsequent paper (Naranjo 1968), I had only been able to find literature about the effects of the drug on the intestine of the rat, the vagina of the rabbit, and the brain cortex of the cat (upon which it elicited the electrical response of a stimulant)—the last being in accord with anthropological reports suggesting that a stimulant based on the iboga roots was used in ceremonies. In accordance with such notion, a preparation from iboga root was introduced in the French pharmacopoeia early in the twentieth century. The effects that I was able to observe on volunteers (Naranjo 1968) and later on patients (Naranjo 1973) are now confirmed by other psychotherapists and may be said to be very close to those of harmaline. This is not surprising in view of some chemical similarity between ibogaine and the beta-carbolines. The differences between both are subtle and consist in a more archetypal and less personal content in harmala experiences, a greater prominence of telluric and "primordial goo" visions (along with the animal and solar visions common to them and the yagé experiences), less death imagery, and a tendency for the iboga experience to be more "malleable" (that is to say, subject to control or guidance). Rather than lumping the harmala alkaloids and ibogaine together in this exposition, however, I will concentrate on the effects of harmaline and of harmaline associations. I will use the term *yagé* for the latter, extending the use of the Indian designation to the combinations of harmaline not only with DMT but with other hallucinogens or feeling-enhancers.

At the time when I conducted the experiment with Chilean volunteers in 1967 (Naranjo 1967) the content of yagé visions was generally regarded by anthropologists as the result of indoctrination and expectations, for the natives reporting them usually partook of the infusion in the context of specific traditions and instructions. The finding that some of the motifs reported in a shamanistic context, such as the visions of animals (snakes, felines, and birds of prey in particular), are spontaneously elicited by harmaline in individuals who have no such expectations not only seems to provide an impressive demonstration of a collective unconscious but shows that this alkaloid stimulates a specific province of the archetypal mind.

The imagery-complex of the yagé experience is, above all else, suggestive of animality, primitiveness, and the sense of the body as flesh—perishable flesh that survives through eating. It may be understood as the symbolic projection of an experiential atmosphere that might be described as the experience of oneself as animal—and which, I believe, arises from the stimulation of the instinctive reptilian brain. (Suggestive of this are the experiments performed at the University of Chile on clinically decerebrated cats, which showed a primary stimulating effect of harmaline on the reticular formation at the pons.)

Though the South American Indians take yagé in their ritual dances and, in smaller amounts, to increase proficiency in hunting, most non-Indians could hardly conceive such a thing under the effect of the drug, for they feel very dizzy and are compelled to lie down and "dream." Visionary trance is, anyhow, the common behavior of Indians and non-Indians alike at the peak of effects.

The content of visions is partly abstract and mostly realistic or surrealistic (that is to say, realistic-archetypal) and rarely personal. Animal imagery stands out (all kinds of animals, insects and spiders included), and imagery related to death and to flying. Among animal images the most prominent are, by far, those of big cats, snakes, and birds of prey.

If aggression were not evident in the frequent visions of tigers and snakes, it would be apparent from the content analysis of visions as a whole; war scenes, weapons, crashing automobiles, the action of cutting, burns, and so on, abound. "Not only teeth are prominent in harmaline visions—teeth of cats, sharks, or monsters—but bayonets, scissors, broken glass" (Naranjo, unpublished book). Sexuality is somewhat less prominent than aggression in the content of visions; yet when present it is most striking—sometimes in the form of orgiastic sexual activity, other times elevated to an archetypal-religious level of expression.

More characteristic than the fact that instinct is conveyed by the images in harmaline experiences is the form of relationship in which the individual stands to his or her instinctual reality, when not one of terror or disgust, as in yagé nightmares; this relationship is, especially in peak experiences, what may be regarded as contemplative experience of instinct. Thus, rather than sexual stimulation, the alkaloid elicits a contemplation of sexuality; more than stimulating aggression, it presents aggression to the inner eye as a force of nature that inspires awe and reverence. The "heavens" of harmaline, thus, are not so much celestial as netherworld paradises of self-satisfied sexuality and aggression perceived as a divine force.

The symbolic complex of death, aggression, and sexuality that the South American Indians articulate with the image of jungle animals suggests that a single experience contains the qualities of dying and bursting forth, of detachment and of letting go to life impulses. It is interesting to note that the snake, feline, and bird have been compounded by the human mind in that most archetypal of archetypes: the dragon—which, like yagé visions, fluctuates between the divine and the demonic. In it we witness a synthesis of the facets of an experience that—as experience with yagé shows—contains them all. (The same symbolic complex, of detachment, recurs in the figure of Shiva, lord of yogis, who is at the same time worshipped in the form of the generative organs and regarded as the destructive aspect of the godhead.)

The mythologem of death as fountain of life, dramatized in the death-rebirth rituals in the ancient world, is the expression of an inner experience easy to understand by one under the influence of harmaline: that of an inner death that is the fountain of life; a detachment from oneself that leads, not to indifference, but to leaving one's organism alone; a letting go not only *of* but *to* organismic function. Images of flying, which are frequent in yagé experiences, seem to convey this convergence of detachment and flowing, freedom and vitality.

Though much more could be said about yagé visions, I will only add that the name *telepathine* was once proposed for the main alkaloid in yagé because the South American Indians (who are the world experts in its use) have employed it as a means to the development of parapsychological abilities. Anecdotes collected from Indians in the Putamayo and visits among them leave me with the impression that their claim deserves to be investigated. In addition to clairvoyance and clairaudience, hunting people are particularly interested in learning about nature, and use the drug in order to become acquainted with the behavior of animals and the properties of plants. In this, their experience echoes the representation of Zoroaster as learning about plants from drinking haoma in early Iranian sources (Flattery and Schwartz 1985).

While discursive thinking is put to rest rather than disrupted under the effect of the harmala alkaloids, not only is oneiric activity stimulated, but also, more generally, is symbolic thinking. Some people thus may become involved in allegorical or mythical (or distinct from abstract-conceptual) speculation, such as I have illustrated in an unpublished book. One of the subjects in it, for instance, began in this way his retrospective account of the experience: "Is humanity in the process of uniting into a single individual? Is the devil—defined as a conscious entity—real and trying to prevent this, or is he a figment of our imagination?"

It is the stimulation of intuitive thinking that South American Indians may have in mind when they speak of taking yagé in order to "learn medicine"; for their concept of learning medicine includes, as an important aspect, the ability to understand dreams and visions. Reichel-Dolmatoff has reported (1971) how through periodic ingestion of yagé the Desana Indians penetrate into the meaning of the creation myth recited once every year under the influence of the drink. Whereas in the normal state of consciousness it might not be understood beyond its literal meaning, yagé opens the door to the experiences behind the symbols and thus might be regarded as a stimulant of a hermeneutic ability. When visionary experience is spoken of (in this manner), we may well bear in mind that it entails not only the facility for internal visual representation but an implicit faculty of encoding-decoding, an awakening of analogical thought.

In regard to the affective domain, I will say that there are peak and nadir experiences with yagé, but these are of a very different experiential quality from those of feeling-enhancers or hallucinogens. Peak experiences convey the expression of free and unobstructed instinct, as is manifest in visions of animals, and not so much experiences of warmth but of freedom and power. One could well use the terms applied in connection with haoma intoxication in the Avesta: "shining," "vivid," "energetic," "accompanied by joy-making truth" (Flattery and Schwartz 1985). So, while one can speak of heavens and hells in connection with yagé experiences, these are not so much heavens of beatitude and hells of damnation, but, rather, positive experiences closely related to the visions of jungle animals in the form of allies (or as images with which an individual identifies) and "hells" in which snake, tiger, and so on, become aggressors. This suggests strongly (in line with the interpretation of these images as projections of one's instinctive nature) that the essence of these heavens and hells is, in the first case, free-flowing instinct, and in the latter, instinct rejected through vilification or "demonization." Just as in traditional mythology snakes, tigers, and lions have positive and negative connotations, and dragons may be embodiments of supreme evil or the power of heaven, it is the same "energy" that manifests at opposite ends of the affective continuum, depending on individual attitudes of acceptance or rejection of the spontaneity that they involve. At times a transition may take place from the contracted to the expanded state, as on the occasion of my giving a mixture of harmaline-LSD to a colleague. A huge snake that seemed the embodiment of all evil appeared before him, and in the presence of this apparition he was distressed (and suffered from a migraine headache). The confrontation of the image led, however, to his allowing himself to be eaten by the snake and swallowed, and when he was able to surrender in this way to the spontaneous course of the experience (in which he seemed to be annihilated), he felt himself in the belly of the snake. There, digested, he finally dissolved into its otherness until he and the snake were one— "and behold! The snake was God."

Just as at the positive end of the feeling continuum it is not exactly emotions that characterize the experience but a sense of spontaneity and pleasure in which there seem to converge mostly spiritual and sensory ingredients, also at the negative end of the spectrum it is not negative "emotions" that stand out, except for the possible appearance of terror; it is rather the case that emotions are *symbolized* as "terrifying visions" (which may not be frightening at all, but perceived with detachment). Alternatively, these emotions may be somatized in the form of physical discomfort verging on collapse. That the hell of harmaline is a *physical* hell (rather than one characterized by *emotions* of separation, emptiness, guilt, shame, etc.) reinforces the notion that it involves (or makes manifest?) a dysfunction at the instinctual level; we observe in these cases an intensification of the desire to sleep, general malaise, and vomiting.

In regard to the spiritual effects, I have proposed to call the contemplative states elicited by yagé "illuminative" rather than mystical, applying here a distinction introduced by St. Ignatius: whereas in the mystical experience there is rapture and a plunging into an ineffable realm, difficult to articulate in thought, this illuminative experience is one characterized by clarity and the joy of understanding (an understanding usually inseparable from the symbolic content of the visions). Another aspect of yagé spirituality, is, as has been implicit in discussion above, the fact that it is a spirituality of the belly or a spirituality of the body, the gist of which is a sacralization or a resacralization of instinct.

A deeper peak experience than any of those mentioned thus far, a near imageless experience comparable to the oceanic experience of LSD but of a different "flavor," is one that I call the "molten gold" experience because in it the sense of fluidity is coupled to a fiery component and an experience akin to orgasm but neither genital nor even clearly located in the body—a sexuality on a higher sphere, one could say.

Finally, it should be borne in mind that all these mind-manifesting experiences of wrathful, orgiastic, or "golden" content occur in a background of implicit death—that is, of an implicit detachment and letting go that is frequently arrived at through a process of encounter with death in the visionary realm. Appropriately, the word *ayahuasca* with which the Peruvian Indians call their sacred plant means "vine of death" as well as "vine of the soul."

The spiritual effects of yagé are taken for granted by South American Indians. Those of harmaline, containing *Peganum harmala* as was mentioned, seem to have been recognized in ancient Iran. The experience elicited by the harmala alkaloids seems cognate with the heroic spirituality of our Indo-European ancestors, with its cultivation of the willingness to die for life.

CANNABIS

I will use the word *cannabis* here to signify the leaves, flowering tops, derivatives, and active ingredients of *Cannabis sativa,* one of the oldest cultivated nonfood plants of humankind (Julien 1981, 169).

From the point of view of the states of consciousness that it may elicit, cannabis is remarkable for its versatility. Unlike the feeling-enhancers that mostly activate interpersonal awareness present and past, and unlike the fantasy-enhancers that are typically avenues to the symbolic domain, cannabis can stimulate these and other states as well, approximating the range of the LSD-like hallucinogens: the oceanic state, religious-archetypic or artistic-contemplative states, possession states. In regard to the spectrum of consciousness that it activates, the main difference from the hallucinogens is the infrequency of psychotic reactions and "volcanic" episodes. It would seem as if cannabis acted as an all-purpose lubricant of the psyche rather than an explosive. Whatever facilitation it brings about can be controlled and channeled in alternative directions, and, while facilitating the suspension of the ego, it does not visit the individual with an "annihilating illumination" coming from outside—much less with a terrifying one.

In small or moderate amounts marijuana is said to have the effect of a "euphoriant," yet in saying this we should point out that the euphoria it brings about is very different from that elicited by cocaine. Writing of the marijuana experience in the *American Handbook of Psychiatry,* Balis

(1974, 407) appropriately comments that "the term 'euphoria' is loosely used in the literature to describe a variety of affective states," and "does not seem to represent a distinct affect or to be associated with a specific stimulus or a specific psychological state." He points out that it is an over-inclusive term "that encompasses such qualitatively different feelings as those induced by narcotics (opiates), inebriants and intoxicants (ethanol, ether), stimulants (amphetamines), or moods experienced by manic patients," and that "the euphoric experience of 'high' induced by marijuana . . . is a complex psychological response characteristic of this drug."

The euphoria arising from the effect of cannabis is, to a considerable extent, the outcome of a spontaneous detachment of the user from ordinary cares and is usually better described as well-being than joy or excitement. Thus, we are in the presence of something more akin to a tranquilizer, though one differing from ordinary tranquilizers in its effect of sharpening sensory (and, I will propose, pattern) awareness. In greater dosages the effect of cannabis is that of a fantasy-enhancer, and sometimes that of a feeling-enhancer. Hallucinogenic effects may be present with high doses (see, for instance, McGlothlin 1968), but in our culture a full-blown psychedelic effect is rare, just as paranoid and anxiety states are rare.

Curiously, reports of cannabis experiences from the nineteenth century show a much more hallucinogenic effect than those in recent times. When we consider Ludlow's (1858) descriptions and Baudelaire's (1860) "artificial paradises," we may wonder whether the hallucinogenic effect that they report was just a matter of dosage or the result of there being a greater distance between the average personality of Victorian man and the psychedelic state than between the latter and our relatively liberated contemporary psyche. I suspect that the model personality of some generations ago was more explosive than today's, as is also suggested by the disappearance of classical hysteria with its fits of fainting and seizures. There was no door or avenue of expression for spontaneity, and when drugs (or hypnosis) provided an outlet, the result was dramatic.

The most remarkable effect of cannabis on feelings is the well-being arising from "selective inhibition" of worry and pugnacity, and from the relaxation of the impulse to sustain an image of oneself, as well as increased naturalness and a temporary inhibition of the "passions," which no doubt inspired the Chinese appellation of "liberator of sin" for it (Taylor 1966, 20). Also (mostly on the first occasions), everything seems very funny; perhaps a "cosmic joke." At other times there is the excitement of grandiosity (as in Baudelaire's report): a grandiosity arising from fantasized narcissistic gratification. There is usually a greater openness in the expression of feelings, and spontaneity in behavior. With eyes open, the effects of cannabis are not very remarkable: an increased appreciation of form and sensory experience, mostly. More intense is the effect on the perception of music, which may be greatly enhanced in regard to texture and expressiveness. With eyes closed, the effects are those of a fantasy-enhancer—but one without the content-specificity of the harmala alkaloids and ibogaine.

In the cognitive sphere, as in the case of other psychedelics, there is a slight impairment of reasoning and a facilitation of intuitive-aesthetic understanding (McGlothlin 1968). In regard to thinking impairment, what stands out is perturbation in short-term memory and an increased distractibility. As for the stimulation of intuition, I think that a case may be made for the hypothesis that cannabis use involves a facilitation of nonlinear thinking. This facilitation, I believe, is not merely the outcome of an interference with linear thinking, but of a more specific potential of cannabis as a stimulant of "higher cognition": an effect of sharpening pattern perception. For while the perception of novel patterns arises in the case of other hallucinogens through an abundance of material to be connected and associated, there is at play in the cannabis experience, rather, something like the activation of a patterning function, an increased ability to organize chaos into form. It is thus not just a matter of the (Bergson-Huxley) "reducing valve" of the brain being opened and of consciousness being flooded, but of consciousness pursuing a definite track—which happens to be unusual.

The spiritual effects of hashish were well known to the Sufis, who are said to have introduced "the wine of the poor" in the Muslim world in the twelfth century (Rosenthal 1971, 45 ff.). Yet they must have been well aware, as the doctors of law and contemporary writers were, of the adverse aftereffects of hashish, and the "deterioration of personality" caused by hashish addiction. Hashish—also called, significantly, "the killer"—was claimed to help the pious in their religious devotions and to "allow the human mind to go beyond the limitations of reality" (Rosenthal 1971, 45 ff.). Al-Is'irdi speaks of the "secret" of the drug that permits "the spirit to ascend to the highest points in a heavenly ascension (miraj) of disembodied understanding" (Rosenthal 1971, 93; 163, verse 8). It may not have taken them long to realize that the potential of hashish to stimulate some aspects of the person's growth is offset by retarding effects in other regards, and that the net result of continuous use is probably harmful, as is suggested by literary and legal reference throughout Muslim history (Rosenthal 1971).

It is in the Hindu tantric tradition and in African shamanism, however, that cannabis has been employed as a sacrament—just as soma, peyote, teonanacatl, fly agaric, yagé, and iboga have been in other cultures.

In Indian Tantrism the most characteristic use of the plant is for devotional exercises employing visualization along with the chanting of mantras and attention to the chakras (subtle energy centers) and nadis (subtle pathways) in the body. These exercises are typically embedded in a context of ritual, which may include (in the secret ritual) sexual union. In the latter, cannabis serves as an enhancer of many aspects of the experience, ranging from the sensory level to the spiritual, which involves regarding self and other as male and female personifications of the divine (Woodroffe 1965, 590–648).

REFERENCES

Andrews, G. "Annihilating Illumination." *Psychedelic Review* 1 (1963): 66–68.

Balis, G. U. "Psychotomimetic and Consciousness-Altering Drugs." In *American Handbook of Psychiatry,* edited by S. Arieti and E. Brody, 404–48. New York: Basic Books, 1974.

Barber, T. S. *LSD, Marijuana, Yoga and Hypnosis.* Chicago: Aldine, 1970.

Baudelaire, P. C. *Les paradis artificiels.* Paris: Ponlet-Malessis, 1860.

Cohen, S. *The Beyond Within: The LSD Story.* 2nd ed. New York: Atheneum, 1967.

De Ropp, R. S. *Drugs and the Mind.* New York: St. Martin's Press, 1957.

Flattery, D. S., and M. Schwartz. *Haoma and Harmaline: The Botanical Identification of the Intoxicating "Soma" of Ancient Indo-Iranian Religions.* Near Eastern Studies 21. Berkeley: University of California Publications, 1985.

Graves, R. *The Greek Myths.* Garden City, N.Y.: Viking Press, 1982.

Grof, S. *LSD Psychotherapy.* Pomona, Calif.: Hunter House, 1980.

———. *Realms of the Human Unconscious: Observations from LSD Research.* New York: Viking Press, 1975.

Harman, W. W., and J. Fadiman. "Selective Enhancement of Specific Capacities through Psychedelic Training." In *Psychedelics: The Uses and Implications of Hallucinogenic Drugs,* edited by B. Aaronson and H. Osmond. New York: Anchor Books, 1970.

Hofmann, A. *LSD: My Problem Child; Reflections on Sacred Drugs, Mysticism, and Science.* Los Angeles: J. P. Tarcher, 1983.

Huxley, A. *The Doors of Perception.* New York: Harper Brothers, 1954.

Julien, R. M. *A Primer of Drug Action.* 3rd. ed. San Francisco: Freeman, 1981.

Klüver, H. *Mescal: The "Divine" Plant and Its Psychological Effects.* Chicago: University of Chicago Press, 1966.

Kripner, S. "Paranormal Effects Occurring during Chemically-Induced Psychedelic Experiences and Their Implications for Religion." *Journal of Altered States of Consciousness* 1, no. 2, (1974): 175–84.

Laing, R. D., and H. Esterson. *Sanity, Madness and the Family.* London: Tavistock, 1964.

Ludlow, F. *The Hasheesh Eater: Being Passages from the Life of a Pythagorean.* New York: Harper and Bros., 1858.

Masters, R. E. L., and J. Houston. *The Varieties of Psychedelic Experience.* New York: Delta Book, 1967.

McGlothlin, W. H. "Cannabis: A Reference." In *The Marijuana Papers,* edited by D. Solomon. 455–78. New York: Signet, 1868.

Michaux, H. *The Major Ordeals of the Mind: And the Countless Minor Ones.* New York: Harcourt, Brace, Jovanovich, 1974.

Naranjo, C. *The Healing Journey: New Approaches to Consciousness.* New York: Ballantine, 1973.

———. "Psychological Aspects of the Yage Experience in an Experimental Setting." In *Hallucinogens and Shamanism,* edited by M. S. Harner, 176–90. New York: Oxford University Press, 1973.

———. "Psychotherapeutic Applications of New Fantasy-Enhancers." *Clinical Toxicology,* 1968, 1.

———. "Psychotropic Properties of the Harmala Alkaloids." In *The Ethnopharmacologic Search for Psychoactive Drugs,* edited by D. Efron. Washington, D.C.: Public Health Service Publication no. 1645, 1967.

Newland, C. A. *Myself and I.* New York: Signet Books, 1963.

Pahnke, W. N. "Drugs and Mysticism." In *Psychedelics: The Uses and Implications of Hallucinogenic Drugs,* edited by B. Aaronson and H. Osmond, 145–64. New York: Anchor Books, 1970.

Reichel-Dolmatoff, G. *Amazonian Cosmos: The Sexual and Religious Symbolism of the Tukano Indians.* Chicago: University of Chicago Press, 1971.

Rosenthal, F. *The Herb: Hashish versus Medieval Muslim Society.* Leiden: Brill, 1971.

Shulgin, A. T., S. Bunnell, and T. Sargent. "The Psychotomimetic Properties of 3,4,5-trimethoxyamphetamine." *Nature* 189 (1961): 1011–12.

Taylor, N. *Narcotics: Nature's Dangerous Gifts to Man.* New York: Dell, 1966.

Turner, W. J. "Schizophrenia and Oneirophrenia." *Transactions of the New York Academy of Sciences* 26, no. 3 (1964): 361–68.

Watts, A. W. *The Joyous Cosmology: Adventures in the Chemistry of Consciousness.* New York: Vintage Books, 1962.

Woodroffe, J., trans. *Serpent Power (sat-chakra-nirupana & paduka-panchaka).* Madras, India: Ganesh, 1965, "Sakti and Sakta," 590–648.

Zaehner, R. C. *Mysticism Sacred and Profane: An Inquiry into Some Varieties of Praeternatural Experience.* New York: Oxford University Press, 1961.

3

Interpersonal Psychedelics

INTRODUCTION

In response to Julie Holland's invitation to contribute to her book *Ecstasy,* I proposed that she publish my talk on the feeling-enhancers at the 1993 Psychedelic Summit at the Unitarian Church in San Francisco, where I was honored to be the opening speaker. The following is a reproduction of the talk as it is printed in Holland's book.

As one who came to the United States in the mid-1960s from a country where there was neither a psychedelic movement nor psychedelic prohibitionism, I was particularly aware of how the American war between the government and the enthusiasts interfered with research and the utilization of psychedelics in psychotherapy.

It seemed to me that the refractoriness of the American establishment was not only a response to its unfamiliarity with the psychedelic experience but also an expression of this implicitly anti-Dionysian culture. And the intensity of psychedelic prohibitionism is not simply the

---

*Article originally published in the book *Ecstasy: The Complete Guide,* edited by Julie Holland (Rochester, Vt.: Park Street Press, 2001).

offspring of an ingrained, overly controlling tendency in the American character; there is also the issue that the psychedelic movement has vehemently insulted the institutions that traditionally control drugs and through which LSD might have found an official distribution channel. Take, for example, Tim Leary's romantic plea for total deregulation in the early 1960s plus his own disdain for the psychiatric world. One can sympathize with him in view of how slow mental health professionals were to realize the therapeutic potential of LSD and the fact that some of the early medical investigators of LSD were sponsored by the Central Intelligence Agency. Yet I have always thought that his all too heroic rebelliousness and his messianic eagerness to liberate the world have paradoxically resulted in an interference in the adoption of LSD by the establishment.

The American war for and against drugs was the background for my book *The Healing Journey,* published in the late sixties. I wanted to draw attention to psychotropic substances that had not been labeled dangerous or been criminalized and were not likely to be, for they constituted what were considered "tamer" psychedelics that did not elicit disturbances in thinking or psychotic-type reactions. Also, I focused on the specifically therapeutic use of these substances, which I classified into two groups: the *feeling-enhancers* and *fantasy-enhancers.*

Before I turn to the specific matter of feeling-enhancers I want to share my overall impression that the therapeutic aspects of psychedelic experiences are of more significant impact in personal evaluation than the wondrous spiritual ones. Whereas psychedelic-induced spiritual states are transient, therapeutic gains have considerably more stability. Moreover, the therapeutic process, which entails cleansing the psyche of dysfunctional imprints from childhood and recovering the ability to love, opens people up in a more stable manner and brings them closer to the depth of their spiritual potential. I think that the feeling-enhancers hold the greatest promise. I consider myself very fortunate that I had the opportunity to open the field of therapeutic application some two decades ago. Here I give an overview of what I have learned.

ON FEELING ENHANCEMENT AND
THE FACILITATION OF PSYCHOTHERAPY

In 1962 I met Sasha Shulgin, the most inventive of the psychedelic chemists, who introduced me to the potential that lay in investigating the substituted phenylisopropylamines. I was on my way to the Amazon, where I was to carry out my first psychedelic research project. I was interested then in the jungle brew known as *yagé,* or ayahuasca, the effects of which I came to interpret as an awakening of the reptilian brain and a sacralization of the "animal within."

If all psychedelics contribute to undoing the ego—the Little Mind that obstructs the Big Mind—it could be said that the effect of LSD-like psychedelics is most strikingly an undoing of the cognitive structure that constitutes the underpinning of the ego. The "ego death" they bring about is in the nature of a "blowing of the mind," and thus they may be appropriately called "head drugs." By contrast, harmala alkaloids such as ayahuasca seemed to be "gut" drugs—catalysts facilitating the flow of instinctual self-regulation, even at a physical level. It is against this background that I embarked on the exploration of MDA, a drug that turned out to be a psychotropic of a new species: a "heart" drug.

MDA: THE DRUG OF ANALYSIS

It was obvious from the very beginning that this substituted amphetamine had to do with the heart and not so much with the gut or the head. With the expression "feeling-enhancer" I wanted to convey that its primary effects were on the emotional sphere, and that these effects were not those of a simple stimulant. One facet of this enhancement seemed to be increased feeling awareness, and another was an enhanced inclination to express feelings, but this was not all. Today I would call it a "feeling optimizer" for the optimal feeling, which is love.

Our psychological heart's blood is love, but in academic life, love is an expression that is avoided as not being scientific. Since the subject cannot be avoided, however, it is regarded as more tasteful to talk about empathy or positive emotional reinforcement. "Feeling enhancement" seemed proper in terms of the academic speech ethos. It seemed appropriate to suggest not only the elicitation of warm feelings but also the happy feelings that frequently derive from the outflowing of the heart. This quality was later emphasized by the name *ecstasy* given to MDMA. Yet more deeply—as a precondition or foundation for love— I think that there lies another optimization, an optimization in our attitude toward pain. I believe that all our emotional problems have to do with a wrong attitude toward pain, a form of defensiveness to early experiences of pain that we were not ready to face that has become ingrained. Consequently, much of our learning to live right—the "gate to happiness," we might say—lies in finding another attitude toward pain, another way of being face to face with pain. This I consider to be the most significant aspect of the feeling-enhancers. Before sharing further thoughts on the characteristics of MDA, I turn to a story.

Sasha Shulgin had told me of some observations in Gordon Alles's laboratory notes. Alles, the discoverer of amphetamine, thought that MDA might be useful as a vasodilator (a medicine that lowers blood pressure), and he tried it on himself with a platismograph around one of his fingers to test this hypothesis. After some time he found himself becoming more talkative than usual. At a certain point he saw a yellowish smoke ring in the room, but nobody was smoking. That was suggestive of a hallucinogenic property, particularly in view of the fact that the structure of the MDA molecule is a sort of hybrid between amphetamine and mescaline.

I was at the right place at the right time, an eager seeker hoping to find more medicine for my soul, and so it fell upon me to explore the substance further. I was a psychiatrist working for the Center for Studies in Medical Anthropology at the University of Chile Medical School, which was ready to support me in such ventures. Since there was neither a drug scene nor a drug scandal in Chile, I found myself in a position very much like that of Dr. Stanislav Grof, who was able to investigate LSD during the same years in Czechoslovakia. Instead of concentrating on LSD, I went in other directions. One was the domain of the phenylisopropylamines, and another was the exploration of a South American shamanistic concoction (yagé, or ayahuasca) and the alkaloids of the African psychotropic plant iboga.

From early testing on myself and on a few acquaintances, it was clear that MDA was a drug, unlike LSD, that elicited an expansion of emotional awareness without interfering with thinking. Its effect did not take the subject away from the ordinary world of objects and persons, but rather seemed specific for the processing of unfinished businesses in the interpersonal world. In retrospect, I can say that I was exceedingly lucky to hit on MDA, for its effects are similar to the now more well-known drug MDMA, ecstasy. The discovery of this different kind of psychedelic was published in a succinct report, coauthored with Shulgin and Sargent (1967), evaluating MDA as an adjunct to psychotherapy. Afterward, I became involved in MDA-assisted psychotherapy, such as I have described in *The Healing Journey*.

I reported in that book what was found in working with people at the university clinic in Santiago. These patients given MDA would travel right back to early childhood and to early traumatic memories, particularly incestuous rape. Freud discovered this same realm of experience at the beginning of his career but then created a theory to explain it away. (I believe that he took the side of parents, not being ready to believe that they could do such things.) The undoing of childhood amnesia could involve other kinds of memory as well. In one MDA session, for example, a middle-aged woman remembered that as a child she had been locked in a room and had witnessed through a window the murder of her father by her mother's lover. I could not prove that this event was true, but I believed it. The understanding of herself and her life that resulted from this memory brought about a remarkable healing.

In *The Healing Journey* I referred to MDA as the "drug of analysis," because of the spontaneous age regression it induces and the interest it stimulates in reformulating—almost redigesting—the past.

Descriptively appropriate as that may be, a still more essential characteristic of MDA would be conveyed by calling it a truth drug, in view of the nondefensive openness it (as well as some other phenylisopropylamines) catalyzes. Unlike the truth serum of fiction, this is not a drug that leads to the disclosure of information against one's will. Instead, there is a concern for truth and a facilitation of authenticity.

Because authenticity is the chief vehicle of therapies geared to self-knowledge, MDA and the other feeling optimizers are impressive psychotherapy enhancers. Just as other psychedelics have specialized therapeutic applications, such as the induction of mystical experiences, work on dreams, or the experience of perinatal states, the feeling-enhancers open up what might be termed a *way of love*. This is a spontaneous willingness to keep the flame of love alive in the face of pain—rather than becoming defensive and manipulative and, in consequence, blind. The gift of the feeling optimizers is the ability to remain a healthy and loving child of Paradise in spite of the contamination of the past and pollution of the interpersonal world. This ability is supported by a radically different stance in the face of pain, a nondefensive attitude that allows for the transmutation of pain into bliss.

Suffering is inextricably bound to earthly existence, but it may be a narcotic or an awakener, according to our willingness to take it in and use it for our growth. Our pain can be a stimulus to defensiveness and selfishness or to compassion and love. The difference is like that between a contrary wind that obstructs our progress and one that, through skillful use of the sail, permits us to advance somewhat against it. Such willingness may be the fruit of an austerity developed along our psycho-spiritual journey, yet it is also the transient gift of the feeling optimizers. They may take users directly to the realm of Adam and Eve (as if in reward for openheartedness) or they may take them not to hell, as in the case of LSD-like psychedelics, but to a worldly place of pain, to the other side of earthly Paradise, which is purgatory. This is the realm of psychotherapy par excellence.

I think that the name Adam, with which Leo Zeff baptized

MDMA, was a very fortunate one. I was never happy with the overly academic and euphemistic term *entactogen* (which sounds like Latin and Greek and suggests the inner sense of contact more appropriately called "relationship"). I always liked Adam, because it indicates earthly paradise. And if psychedelic heavens can be related to the prenatal condition of life in the womb, earthly paradise echoes the postnatal condition of the newborn.

At the time of writing *The Healing Journey,* I thought it likely that since it is the more sick people who have the greater need to deal with the pain of the past, it would follow that the potentially addicted ones would tend to have "bad trips" and little enticement for the use of MDA as an escape into pleasure. When MDMA (with effects only subtly different from MDA) became available, I had occasion to see that I was wrong. There are people (with a hypomanic disposition) who manage to repress pain and experience instead euphoria and warmth in a way that seems to echo their customary denial of pain and anger. Instead of the therapeutic purgatory that they need, their hedonistic bias succeeds in directing them to a paradise, though their visits to paradise remain a sort of opium of the people, a spiritual exaltation that becomes a substitute rather than a remedy for their condition. In such cases, I think that preparatory psychotherapy and the therapeutic readiness of a person before the initial session—and therapeutic skill on the part of someone during the session—can make a great difference.

MMDA: THE ETERNAL NOW

Here I take up the thread of my story. I was ready to move into a new exploration, and this was to be MMDA. By the time Sasha Shulgin and I published its animal and human pharmacological characteristics in collaboration with Sargent (1973), I was using it in psychotherapy. The most important quality I found in MMDA—a sense of what I call "the eternal now"—was something that I was particularly ready to appreciate, in view of an unexpected source of frustration that I had just encountered in my attempts to conduct therapy under MDA.

I was a budding Gestalt therapist in those days, having come in recent contact with Fritz Perls, and I had attempted to bring Gestalt therapy to bear on the psychedelic experience. I was frustrated in this endeavor, because while I tried to have people focus on the here and now, they insisted upon the "there and then," keenly determined to dwell on their memories. I must confess that I was a little slow to catch on to the fact that just as the more remarkable potential of MDA is its ability to bring long-repressed memories to the surface, the potential of MMDA is an increased awareness of the present.

For this reason MMDA lent itself admirably to Gestalt work, better than MDA. It not only focused on the here and now but also enhanced work involving imagery—not archetypal imagery like LSD and the fantasy-enhancers but personal imagery, as in ordinary dreams. (I put iboga and harmala in the category of fantasy-enhancers.) Furthermore, I found that MMDA often triggered psychosomatic symptoms and lent itself to exploration of this domain. All in all, I think that through the use of MMDA in conjunction with Gestalt therapy I helped many people. Discovering the specific excellence of MDA and MMDA in the facilitation of psychotherapy was like having twins in more than an intellectual sense, but the winds of adventure inclined me to the new.

Sasha Shulgin's skill in the synthesis of new psychoactive molecules is now becoming widely known. In those days he already had produced a number of analogs that were waiting for human testing, and this prompted me to turn to comparative research with some of these substances. Shulgin, Sargent, and I (1969) also published a summary report on the testing of various isopropylamines and closely related compounds.

MDMA: A NONTOXIC ALTERNATIVE TO MDA

For me, the greatest news since the discovery of MDA and its healing potential has been MDMA—which differs chemically from MDA in the same way that amphetamine differs from nor-amphetamine. The effects are essentially the same as those of MDA, though it has a somewhat shorter duration of action and less of the toxicity.

While MDA is a therapy enhancer without the psychotomimetic potential of LSD, it has the serious drawback of toxicity. In my experience this was not a constant effect but one that became apparent every now and then in an unpredictable manner. In this sense it is like chloroform. In the old days, some patients would die from chloroform anesthesia, but this could not be anticipated. The reasons were unknown, and something similar seemed to be the case with MDA. I had observed at the time of writing *The Healing Journey* that once in a while MDA brought about skin rashes and that beyond a certain dosage (about 250 mg), some people became incoherent, which could be attributed to cerebrovascular effects. I had warned my readers, urging them to test a person's reaction to MDA cautiously, starting with a very low dose. I fortunately did not have any accidents during my work in Chile. Given the fact that about thirty people took the drug, I view this as a blessing. A Chilean colleague was less lucky (and certainly less careful), for he administered 500 mg to a friend who experienced aphasia. After that, several deaths were reported in the United States.

We know that with MDMA the case is strikingly different. It has been known and used widely for many years, and despite accidents attributed to high blood pressure or inappropriate use it is remarkable for its lack of danger to healthy people. I would say that it is the champagne of the feeling-enhancers. My approach to MDMA-assisted therapy (just as it was in the case of MDA) could be described as providing people with a special opportunity to talk about their past and present lives and problems, with a view to developing insight into their relationships and personalities. I emphasize this, because most people I know have used MDMA with a model borrowed from the use of LSD—that of listening to music through headphones while blindfolded. Much can be gained from that alone, but essentially the feeling-enhancers have to do with the world of relationship and with the enhancement of the sense of "I" and the sense of "You" (which are interdependent). They are remarkable for the greater openness that they elicit and the ability they engender to communicate better concerning relationship problems.

I also emphasize this aspect because at one of the Esalen ARUPA (Association for the Responsible Use of Psychedelic Agents) conferences devoted to an exchange between MDMA therapists, I found myself at odds with my colleagues in the psychedelic network. To my astonishment, everybody who spoke there professed to believe that the best way to take people on an MDMA trip is to urge them to withdraw into listening to music. I remember that Dr. Rick Ingrasci (past president of the Association of Humanistic Psychology) and I were the only oddballs in that meeting: we talked to people and listened to them.

I also use music, but frequently I prefer to begin a session without it. I see verbal interaction as an invaluable vehicle for guiding people and helping them go deeper into their difficult experiences. This became apparent when I would come back into the room after a brief absence, and a patient would say, "Oh, I thought the effect had gone away, but as we talk it is all coming back." It is not the case that talking needs to be a distraction; it depends on the kind of talking and the empathic understanding one can provide.

After some time working with MDMA in individual and group situations, my main interest became its use within groups of people who had ongoing relationships with one another, such as families and communities. In this situation MDMA lends itself to occasional sessions geared to "clearing away the garbage" so as to keep relationships healthy. I have worked in this way not only with associated psychotherapists but also with people concerned with the quality of their partnerships in business and with good friends who wanted to keep their relationship free from the deterioration that most are prone to undergo in the course of time. Typically, I would work with groups of fifteen to twenty people consisting of a number of subgroups, in each of which people are involved in ongoing relationships outside therapy, for example, a family of three, four partners in a business firm, or the staff of a spiritual community.

One case report might convey some sense of the nature of an experience of group therapy in the way I have conducted it. While I have used the expression "analytical psychotherapy" in connection with my approach to individual therapy with MDA and MDMA, the kind of group therapy I have developed is one in which I have intervened little, except in the preparation of the group and in the course of a session of retrospective sharing and group feedback. I not only coordinate and share my own perceptions but also assist toward further elaboration of the experience.

An important part of my role in preparing for the MDMA session has been to create an atmosphere of surrender and spontaneity within the boundaries of a simple structure that limits movement away from the group but allows for withdrawal, protecting everyone's experience from invasion. In the case of MDMA administered to a group of optimal size and composition, I have witnessed a remarkable coincidence between the need of some participants to regress and be mothered and the availability of others to give such mothering. Since the effect of MDMA can be a peak experience or a delving into pain (or both), it is easy to see how it is possible that some persons find themselves in the garden of earthly paradise while others undergo the fires of purification—and the experience of the former is a gift to the latter. Again and again I have had the impression that as the result of the catalytic effect of MDMA upon the participants, the group becomes a spontaneously organizing system, for the good of all.

I now turn to a personal letter in which one middle-aged woman tells me of her experience at a group session, as an illustration of the kinds of things that can happen. It is not an unusual report in its content, and it is particularly illustrative of how much can happen through appropriate group preparation, without one-to-one therapeutic interactions. I think that experienced therapists will know well that this non-interaction is not a matter of simple strategy but rather a sort of art of "not doing" developed through experience and supported by a faith in group and individual organic self-regulation. All in all, it is not something that can be explained easily, nor is it something that can be prescribed mechanically, for it seems to require an educated ability to be present in the right way with sensitivity to what is happening. I have to add that this particular group had prepared for the experience with several days of psychotherapeutic exercises and meditation. The woman identified as K was a member of the group who chose to participate without taking MDMA, and J, who did take MDMA, is a sex therapist.

After swallowing the capsule, I adopted an attitude of confidence— in myself, in life, before the unknown (which always scares me). Rachel's loving and strong presence made it easier for me. I felt strong palpitations that scared me, but I had confidence in you, who would assist me if it were necessary. I began to lose my skin sensations; I felt cold and as if I were lacking in air. This made me very afraid of death, afraid of dissolving or that my heart would explode. I lay on my side as if folded upon myself, closed in, and within me I began to feel more peaceful and secure. A moaning came from my body, soft and trembling, as if shivering from cold. Then I realized that I was a baby, or a fetus, still unborn and sent into being to realize "Being," emerging out of nothing, solitude and cold. I was very afraid of being born.

Then somebody covered me, and I felt that somebody was by my side and caressed me. I saw that it was K, and I told her, "I am being born into this world." This was certain to me like the light of day. I was then able to let go into pain and weeping, for I felt secure before another human being, who gave me much warmth and tenderness. I sucked my fingers and her fingers, and I felt my teeth with which I could bite. When I felt more at ease, I could uncurl my body a little and talk to her. I told her, "Don't leave yet." I very much needed to talk to her and to tell her what I was going through and what I had lived through with my parents. I felt no anger toward my mother, only pain; I said this with great conviction, as if coming to own it completely. "She was not able to do more; she didn't know how to be with me." I did feel angry toward my father. I gave him hard words for so much damage that he had inflicted on me in a subtle way throughout my life.

I told K that I had written a poem to my inner child, and she wanted to hear it. When she did, I saw her tears. I recited other poems to her, but then she left me alone a little. She asked me whether I could stay alone for a little while, and she went to somebody who was calling her, assuring me that she would return. For the first time I did not feel alone. I had her jacket over me, which I could touch and smell, and the fantasy of her remained with me. I felt happy, for I was sure of her return, and I could also be with myself. I understood that it was good that she left me alone a little, for after letting her come into me and fill me, I could now assimilate it, integrating it into myself. I had much need to touch and press against the ground with different parts of my body. J came by, and I received him too as a gift from God. I told him what I was living. I felt him and told him everything from the beginning of the experience and the deep abyss—how I felt lovingly interwoven with essence, as if all my cells were constituted of Him. I was sorry that in our "normal state of mind" we did not realize this Reality that we are. And we also talked about sexuality. He assisted me with his hands toward an integration of head, heart, and sex, opening paths. He helped release my father from my body, for I felt as if I had been possessed by him thus far.

It was in this moment when you came by, and I told you I was purging myself of my father. And so you smiled, in confirmation. I would have liked you to have stayed longer, but I didn't dare to ask you. Then J told me he needed to be alone a little, that afterward he would have to help somebody else and that he would come back. I thus learned from both of them that I could find my space of aloneness when I needed it and how that was all right; it was not bad. I continued to feel happy, neither alone nor empty. I continued to feel nourished while by myself. It all seemed a gift from God that filled me with gladness—I was receiving much without having to seek it. Yes, I felt that I no longer needed the compulsive seeking of another (mothers and fathers) but only to open up and receive what came to me at the moment.

K returned, and in her company I started to look around in the room, absorbing and opening up to the surroundings, listening to groups of people who conversed and laughed. For a moment I came in touch with an admonition that had been introjected earlier in my life: "You must go with the others." But I understood that it was more important at that moment to remain with my own experience. Afterward J told me of his experience, and I could listen to him and let him in, feeling clear and free from myself, with space for the other. Then I started to dance alone, feeling all my joy, my living cells. I found my body axis and felt that energy moved along it upward and downward. I felt that I danced like a serpent, undulating my body and feeling successively an Arab, a Hindu, a gypsy—full of strength and energy.

At several points J approached, as if seduced by me. I felt afraid, as if he were going to rape me. I told him, as if to discourage him, "Hey, wait. I have just been born." I was with him in a group in which also was V, to whose peaceful face I felt attracted. With him I could verbally express my aggression toward men. When masculine singing sounded, I said, "I would have liked to dance like a woman." But he said, "Precisely because it is a man singing. Why don't you dance now, and you'll finish with your father this way." I took it as a special challenge, and I danced. It was an experience of feminine strength—and self-affirmation before my father, of separation and autonomy. I felt as if in this destructive history, I had reached further closure.

Well, Claudio, I won't tell you more anecdotes, because this letter, I think, has reflected the most meaningful things in the experience. It was profoundly therapeutic for me. I feel as if some of my archaic, primordial lack has been covered and that it couldn't have been in any other way. I have returned to this experience many times to nourish myself, and I feel that I am coming to the end of a healing process with a more lucid, organized, and creative mind, more confident, daring to teach and share the riches I have been keeping to myself. I continue to write poetry, and I enjoy life more and more.

I hope that this session report will serve to convey a general understanding of how many issues that are distinct and separate in theory commingle in a single experience. The anonymous subject says that she has just been born, and the session as a whole may be seen as a step in a birthing process. Separation and union both have a part in this birthing. In asserting her individuality, she differentiates herself from her father; at the same time the event occurs in the context of a mothering situation—one in which she allows herself to regress through the support of others (the therapist, the group, and, most specifically, her companions). Yet regression is not all there is to birthing; just as separation and union are both part of the process, so there is here a regression to progress, the allowing of a fetal state that then becomes the stepping-stone, as it were, for self-expression.

I have said that the content of the session is not particularly special, yet it is rich enough to bring up many issues. Among these issues is the importance of the attitude with which the subject embarks on the experience—and more specifically, an attitude of confidence and even a measure of acceptance in the face of "death," or a sense of impending "explosion." It is the extent of this acceptance of ongoing experience that makes the deep surrender possible that is in the background of an organic unfolding. The classic elements of an MDMA experience are all here: awareness of psychological pain, insight into life and relationships, self-expression in verbal communication and movement, and a progression from defensive accusation toward an understanding of others. It is clear from the account just how important the relationship between group members can be, in the sense of both mothering and intuition sharing or, more generally, peer therapy.

Carl Rogers has claimed that therapeutic groups may be the most beneficial invention of the twentieth century, and I have not known a more effective form of group psychotherapy than the skillful use of MDMA. I hope that this glimpse into the nature of the experience may be a stimulus for future health authorities to give more positive attention to this neglected approach, for we cannot afford to squander resources in days when emotional health has become so vital to the human destiny. MDMA is an extremely valuable resource for processing past life experience and for healing relationships in the context of dialogue. Yet the great gift that heaven seems to be offering us through scientific know-how remains unused at a time when there is an urgent need for collective mental health. Given that the regulatory and medical establishment considers these statements unproven, I believe them to be research priorities.

REFERENCES

Shulgin, A. T., C. Naranjo, and T. Sargent. "Evaluation of 3,4-methylene-dioxyamphetamine (MDA) as an Adjunct to Psychotherapy." *Medicina et Pharmacologia experimentalis* 17, no. 4 (1967): 359–64.

Shulgin, A. T., T. Sargent, and C. Naranjo. "Structure-Activity Relationships of One-Ring Psychotomimetics." *Nature* 221 (1969): 537–41.

Shulgin, A. T., T. Sargent, and C. Naranjo. "Animal Pharmacology and Human Psychopharmacology of 3-methoxy-4,5-methylenedioxyphenyliso-propylamine (MMDA)." *Pharmacology* 10, no.1 (1973): 12–18.

3.2 A GROUP SESSION WITH MDMA

I will share next the retrospective testimonies of a group session with MDMA that was prepared with two days of meditation, "spontaneous movement," and work on the enneatypes.

I often respond to those who ask me about the therapeutic value of psychedelics by explaining how much it depends on some knowledge of the spiritual path and the nature of the therapeutic process or healing transformation, a certain familiarity with meditation, a previous introduction to becoming aware of one's own relationships and of one's personality, as well as an introduction to the practice of surrender through "spontaneous movement," which requires surrendering control over one's own acts.

The relevance of such things is obvious, since the nature of the psychedelic experience is similar to that induced by such exercises; in the case of MDMA it is clear that the experience is an invitation to non-doing (which is characteristic of meditation) and is directed toward feelings of peace and equanimity, which also spontaneously leads people to the search for understanding of themselves and to many liberating insights; and although the practice of "spontaneous movement" is barely known through the Indonesian Subud movement and the school of "authentic movement" originated by Mary Whitehouse (practiced by some dancers), it is easy to understand that the characteristic "letting go" of good psychedelic experiences can be developed through practice.

In summary: I am convinced that the best setting for a psychedelic group experience is that of a prior work that prepares people for surrender, "organismic trust," focusing on their inner being, understanding their problematic motivations, and for a spirit of mutual intimacy, and I will say no more than this is what was offered (for two and a half days) to those who participated in the group session with MDMA that was later shared retrospectively.

CLAUDIO: Today we will very succinctly share what was experienced yesterday, as only then will it be possible to have enough time to hear all of you. I am interested in knowing if the fruit of the experience corresponded to the wish you formulated, what you understood about yourselves, and whether during the session you received any indication, advice, or understanding of what you should do. I am especially interested in hearing the intentions that you have been inspired with during the altered state of consciousness, as if these are not explicitly formulated, they might easily be forgotten or invalidated later. Each of you will know what else you wish to share, but I am especially keen that you include these themes, and that you try to be succinct.

MAN 1: For me, the experience was very loving. I asked for the ability to receive, and what I received was my own love for myself; it made me feel enough, so I did not need to go out and seek affection. It was a pleasure to be with myself and to be able to indulge myself in a pleasant idleness, which is different from the laziness that leads me to escape. It was a very good experience and I thank the people who approached to bring me water or ask me if all was well. I came out feeling replenished. I have already learned to exchange hugs, but my difficulty was being with myself.

MAN 2: It was an unexpected experience for me. I went into it with the desire to love myself and to be more substantial within, and I felt an enormous energy, vibrations, intense tremors, and voices telling me to feel what was coming to me; and I felt that it was something to heal, and that it could also serve to heal others. I feel like a different person today.

CLAUDIO: Let us hope so.

MAN 2: It will be so!

MAN 3: When you told us to set an intention, I asked for a true love, for I find it hard to love, and to feel. A very hard heart. At the beginning, when people began to manifest joy I did not feel anything, and someone helped me. I let things unfold, and then I surrendered to feeling my emotions, and I encountered my nephew, whom I love. We had a loving exchange that moved me deeply, and then I went to meet others, to share love and to embrace them; quite a few people I did not know. I felt free, confident, comfortable, and very loved, and I saw that my difficulty in surrendering to love lies in not believing that I can be loved.

CLAUDIO: Is your nephew here?

MAN 3: Yes, and he is very much my friend. He was very lively, and I was half numb, so I hesitated to approach, but finally I went to hug him, and it turned out just fine.

MAN 4: My journey had many phases. It started with the desire to enjoy the experience, and soon led me to feel pain. I remembered a love relationship I had where I experienced great joy in sexuality, but not just with sex. I suffered a loss, and this pain, which I felt I should go through, is still very present in me, so I began to feel it, and it turned into another pain; it was beautiful to experience though, healing and sanctifying. It became an energy that expressed itself in movements and obeyed its own dynamics. My mission was to protect it. Considerable time passed, and the energy traveled up, then down and became a part of me. Then I realized that I felt alone, and I felt the need to share, so I began to lower my hand, which had been protecting me from an aggressive world. I was afraid, but I was able to get up, trusting that I would always be able to protect myself. I could see people very clearly, how they are and how they suffer, because I felt very present, and after a while I began to fall. Someone said to me, "Are you sad?" but it was not the same suffering as in the beginning, but a sense of very attentive desolation. I got up very alert, as if I had stopped thinking.

WOMAN 1: I asked [to experience] the three loves, and in the experience the Great Beloved, or the great heart of the world, welcomed me. Very gently, he approached me, and my spine. My neck was thrown back, in an uncomfortable position, and I spent a long time like this, in this position, it was a breathing exchange in which I felt that with each in-breath and out-breath he entered into me and I into him. It was an exchange of great subtlety, grandeur, and beauty. I touched love and it was extraordinary. An infinite movement in which, as in the Song of Songs, I felt the beloved beside the beloved, and he told me that I did not need to worry about anything, and he was saying to me: "Relax, relax," and my spine straightened again, and he said to me, "Those who come to you and touch you will be healed, and you do not need to do anything because I will always be with you"; so I did nothing. My only desire is to always be united with him.

WOMAN 2: Yesterday my intention was love, and the energy of the love of God came to me strongly; so strongly that several times I must have shifted my position because I felt I was going to explode. I had wanted to drink from the source and now I felt so much love that it did not fit inside me, and I did receive an instruction to move house, to start a family and to become a mother again. So, gratitude came to me very clearly.

WOMAN 3: I had an experience that was very sacred to me, in which I found my source of love and realized that it was inexhaustible for me; that the more I sink into it, the more love pours out of me and can reach others. I was very happy to encounter this love. I also had an experience of dematerialization in which I became ethereal and I met with the divine, and the divine and I were the same, and at the same time I was nothing, and I also felt that I can now assume a mission as priestess of Eros together with my beloved, to transmit to the people the sacredness of erotic love. Today I feel very joyful and I feel a tremor and slight heat in my body.

WOMAN 4: I found a heaven I did not know existed. When I was lying down you passed by me, Claudio, I saw your eyes and then I found a heaven full of arabesques, a colorful Indian heaven, full of music; I did not know that this existed and that I had been so limited here. I recognized the male and the female within me and I understood that I love him, and he loves me and that we are one, and this was something that gave me a lot of love. A love that loves like I had never loved before and that made me feel complete, that I do not need the love of anybody. At the end, when I thought the experience was over, I was very happy, and I encountered an angel. I had never seen an angel, but he seemed very familiar to me and I approached him and asked him things I had been anxious to know, and he embraced me and showed me where my death had taken place (I had asked him where the dead part of me was, and he accompanied me to the hell he threw me into, which I could not have done alone, and finally I saw that I am a planet that has an exchange with another planet and that a blue star lights up our family). This morning I woke up with a desire to dance and with the feeling that something possessed me.

MAN 5: At first, I went through a yellow doorway and there were guardians, and as I passed through it I entered into the experience I had asked for, but I also passed by a lizard made of geometric shapes, and the experience was of complete fulfillment, a total cure. Everything that had been missing in life was inside me, and also outside. The aim was to surrender to life and I felt that I surrendered, and that life surrendered to me. What a beautiful and complete experience, so beautiful, so sweet, so incredible. Then I began to see things that I needed to see. I realized that I do not know how to relate to a family. Here we are like a family, but I never had family ties, so I did not know how to relate. Violence was what dominated our relationships during my childhood, and I felt that I was violating others, but I think I put an end to it. Today I woke up feeling something different, softer and more connected, and I understand how I can begin to repair my crossed wires, and I feel that I must surrender to each moment. For coexistence, like a ceremony, is in every moment.

MAN 6: Recently, I have come to realize that I have always disregarded love for myself. In my search for discipline, rationality, doing things for others and serving God always, I neglected my own body, and myself. In yesterday's experience I felt it clearly and I asked for forgiveness from myself, and I also asked my body for forgiveness, realizing that I should take an interest in it; care for it, particularly realizing that without it one cannot truly love others.

CLAUDIO: You are giving us a very abstract version of the experience.

MAN 6: Yes, but yesterday's experience was abstract too, because it did not really affect me, except that in the end I was at ease dancing with my wife, with a tranquillity that I am not sure if it was the effect of what we took [laughter from the group]. I do not know, but I felt great and it was new, a very subtle thing.

CLAUDIO: But what subtle thing was it?

MAN 6: The feeling of liking myself and feeling freer, but without any image or tragedy or monster . . . nothing.

CLAUDIO: You say that at the beginning of the journey you understood the tragedy of being imprisoned, unconscious, and your own evolution impeded; I do not know whether to advise you to feel more self-love, or to become angry or moved at being so paralyzed that even this drug that has so deeply touched all those present here, cannot touch you. There is something you are doing to be so fossilized.

WOMAN 5: I asked from the experience to know unconditional love, and that is what came to me. First, my friend next to me went into labor, I accompanied her, and I helped her, and she gave birth to a baby named Love. We were happy receiving Love. Then I heard a music that fulfilled me in a different way, with great calm, and later I danced, and this was another way of receiving and giving love. I also received from a friend a message from my mother that did me a lot of good and that I needed to hear. Thank you very much.

WOMAN 6: Yesterday I asked for love and received many answers, even about why I have come, because I have never found meaning in my life and I do not feel attached to people, not even to my family. When I approached you and said I would be deserving, you said, "Yes, you deserve," and then, with a little help, I found something I was always looking for on the outside but that was in me, which is love for myself. Loving myself and trusting a little more rescued me. For I do not trust my work and I feel that I cannot help people; until now I have been guided by my intuition and I have to rely more on it. I also managed to connect with people who are always with me. I was very unhappy because I had lost touch with the inner work, and I feel that now I am coming back to the path that unfolds through the work for others. It is as if I have been wandering like a tormented soul, and now I have discovered a heart.

WOMAN 7: What I asked for was wisdom to be able to discern what I should do in my mature years, so that my next twenty years of life are beautiful and productive. It took a long time, but when I lay back I felt like a camphor bath, very cold but hot inside, tingling all over the surface of my skin, and then I sat up and felt waves of orgasms starting, waves of erotic pleasure, but also a lot of compassion. This seemed to me the great gift, for pure eroticism seems to me little and compassion also; I began to relate to people seeing their deep beauty; I also approached the women and touched their bellies; I felt the healing power of the earth in me, and did not want to be invasive, and when they welcomed me I felt that my hands had a healing capacity.

WOMAN 8: At first, I thought it was not having any effect on me, but then I felt a great heat in my body; and then I felt like I was fainting, as if I were dissolving with no control whatsoever. It felt good and I asked for confidence and I perceived so much beauty in people, and I understood that things are the way they are and there is beauty in them, and that control is false and that I must trust that everything is beautiful, and I can let myself flow.

WOMAN 9: I asked for a contact with my own love and a plenitude that I cannot quite feel, and the first thing I felt was physical rest. I was able to surrender, and I started to fill myself with myself, I nourished myself with myself and in this way, I was able to meet my parents and thank them for life, for the opportunity of being here and also to feel grateful for my four children, and I felt like their guardian and not like their owner as I imagined myself to be. This set me free and the love in me grew until I realized that I can love unreciprocally and that this is good for me. After filling myself with myself I was able to interact with others and come to you, with deep gratitude in my heart for being in your presence.

MAN 7: I did not ask for anything, I have everything, Claudio. With Catholicism, Spiritism, Claudio, G., S., R. and many others. . . . Only gratitude, only joy, and when I give love my being is illuminated inside. I work without effort, I act with joy and my work is only joy. I am complete, fulfilled, and satisfied, and I have nothing more to say.

WOMAN 10: For me it was the most complete and beautiful experience of my entire life. [At this point I ask the group if they feel the same way and most raise their hands.] Initially, I was not sure where

I was, and I am told that I was practically immobile for about two hours. I felt completely calm, with no thoughts, very connected with myself; sometimes I was aware of what was happening around me and it seemed to me I was in the stillness of the center of a hurricane. Then I felt myself falling, falling, and I felt physically unwell, I seemed to be dying, and I thought this could not happen, but I surrendered. Then I started to open my eyes and reconnect with the rest of the people, but what I discovered is that although I really like receiving, I feel happier giving.

WOMAN 11: I asked for what was best for me at this moment, and a lot of love came, a lot of sensuality, and so much light. Only this, and I stood motionless for some time, but after a while I could not stand still and began to share with those who were available. It was an experience of looking at people with unconditional love.

WOMAN 12: My initial question was why is there so much evil in the world and why is there evil in me. The beginning of the experience was of terror in relation to father, the creative father; I felt very unarmed and I called for mother, who came immediately: the divine mother, and I felt I was in mother's lap, and it was a very strong and prolonged experience during which I felt protected from everything that was happening. I felt a lot of understanding and a huge space opened up, so that I could forgive myself and reconcile with this love. Later, I also had the experience of approaching the father with much laughter, taking his hair into my hands and caressing him. It has been an experience of forgiveness and opening to love, which I am still vibrating with now.

WOMAN 13: I have experienced a personal process of perceiving that I am very different in my life and in my family, because I come from a family that chooses death and I choose life, and although in a good phase of my life I have been feeling many energy blocks and having many symptoms, yesterday I entered the experience with a prayer, asking our lady to allow us to find freedom. At one point I came into contact with my soul, which was a divine presence and was nothing external, not even God or the virgin. I called on my spiritual guides and mentors to protect my body and lead me to where I ought to go, and I was thinking about the illnesses that I have been attracting, and my body was taking me to my soul, to a place in my family of origin where forgiveness was needed, and I asked forgiveness of my mother, my sister, and my brother even in other lifetimes, and of my father, and I was receiving a healing through this forgiveness, and at some point I needed to come to a new understanding of the meaning of my birth, in contact with my inner father and my inner mother, and for this I sought out Claudio.

CLAUDIO: What do you think of this account? Is it the same experience as everyone else's, or is it something different? It seems to me that you all encounter love, but you build different theories around it. The central thing, however, is the meeting with the soul, from which love is born.

FINAL THOUGHTS

This transcript suggests that my observation is true that if Rogers is not mistaken in saying that therapeutic groups have been the most significant invention of the twentieth century, it is even truer in the case of group therapy with MDMA. The similarity in the experiences described here is remarkable, and I find it most interesting that not only do they speak of an awakening to love, but also of a discovery of one's own soul or essence, the nature of which is inherently loving. It is also remarkable that the journey to this encounter with the soul that is the source of love has been about letting oneself be in peace, and about trusting in the spontaneous development of one's own experience.

In addition, on this occasion many people felt guided from within, which I attribute to a certain group culture regarding surrender and appreciation as a partial explanation of the excellent results. I have also been struck by the little emphasis that these accounts reveal on the psychodynamic discoveries characteristic of other sessions. It would seem that they are people who, sufficiently aware of their main flaws, no longer get so distracted in wandering into the labyrinths of their neurosis, and prefer to enjoy the earthly paradise of love, freedom, and contact with their own profound wisdom.

Another important factor in the experiences described has been the simple opportunity to explore and develop healthy relationships with other participants that have been extensions of the encounter with themselves, which in turn has contributed to healing erroneous relational assumptions and established something like a healing contagion.

3.3 CONSIDERATIONS FOR FUTURE COMPANIONS OF EMPATHOGEN SESSIONS

Lao Tzu tells the emperor of China in his famous Tao Te Ching that the best way to lead his great empire is to do nothing, and although I doubt that a contemporary politician can go very far in the application of this advice, it seems to me that it is advice that would be appreciated by those who intend to guide others on their psychedelic journeys. In other words, those who are often considered "guides," contemplating what it means to guide, should understand the inappropriateness of the term in a situation where people should be helped to find a guiding principle within themselves through surrendering to a spontaneous and at the same time wiser psychic current than the rational mind itself or that of the therapist. I once met a group of people who considered themselves to be "psychedelic guides," to whom I asked the question what it meant to guide, and I was pleased that the first response I received was precisely that of "doing nothing":

Well, I definitely follow the school of thought of "simply sitting there," and with that "simply sitting there" I am referring to the Buddhist sense of the phrase "do nothing, just sit." Therefore, I wait [laughs]. Even so, of course, you have to be fully present for the person—I never know what to call them: the subject? No. The patient? Obviously not. So, you must attend to their needs, even in their changing breathing patterns, for example. However, I think the best way to do this is by using your expanded awareness from simple meditation, just sitting there and paying attention, dispassionately paying attention to all your sensitive perceptions. With a bit of luck, some of this awareness will rub off on the person who is having the experience, too. What I mean to say is that if you are able to relax your breathing and calm your heart rate, etc., through meditation, there can be a certain amount of resonant synchronization with what is happening to the subject. This is basically my modus operandi. And, of course, if anything comes up, if they want to talk about something, sure, of course, I will be there to talk to them about whatever they wish.

Is there nothing that can be said, then, in the way of advice for those who, whether they have therapy training or not, wish to accompany others in this inner journey so personal and yet so much better when undertaken in company?

To begin to answer this, I cite below a series of prescriptions that, although formulated impersonally, were written in response to the request of a talented disciple and colleague who was taking his first steps in this important capacity rarely permitted by law.

SOME PRESCRIPTIONS FOR THE PSYCHOTHERAPEUTIC USE OF MDMA

Individual use of MDMA is slightly different from its group application, because in the first case the possibility of turning one's attention to one person and staying in constant interaction with her through her process results in something very different from the group situation, where one can at most offer this kind of attention intermittently, and where, in my experience, other therapeutic factors become present.

Group interaction is so important that even brief interventions by an expert therapist are relatively less significant than group preparation and support given after the experiences. It is especially important, during the session itself, to have an artful way of being with the group, knowing how to understand what is happening and the ability to be present, even though the interventions are minimal.

Regarding the accompaniment of individual sessions, on the other hand, there is more advice to be given to a therapist on how to conduct a session, and on that I will concentrate now.

I shall begin by reiterating my belief that therapy is an art rather than a science, and more than an art even, it is the phenomenon of direct influence exerted by a person who has worked for his or her own evolution. Beyond one's own strategies or voluntary interventions, a relational phenomenon of contagion of humanity operates in the therapeutic relationship in the majority of cases—and especially under the effect of psychoactive drugs. It is in this context that certain basic elements of psychotherapy also become manifest, among which the main one is perhaps the healing power of understanding.

That is why the most important thing that a psychedelic therapist can do apart from doing nothing is to listen and to understand. One who understands what the other is saying and what is happening, does not even need to question what he is doing, because the one he is accompanying will understand the mere fact of understanding. Moreover, he will feel understood in a seemingly telepathic way, without even having to say: "I understand what you are saying to me," because the being that is understood, is understood in a very elementary way, like babies when they know if their mother is giving them their attention.

However, what is being understanding? It is, of course, something that goes beyond intellectualization, whereby a psychoanalyst believes she understands her patient because she identifies his "oedipal problem." It is, rather, an empathic experience, which involves a supportive connection and a suspension of critical judgment. Such is, it seems to me, the number one factor in healing.

It is important to allow the experience of others to unfold, to give it space; and this is intrinsic to deep and empathic understanding. Such tolerance for the other's truth is part of the person's real therapeutic ability, and is not learned in books, but is acquired, partly through the process of understanding oneself, and partly through not being frightened of life, of having befriended life and accepted life within oneself.

Rogers speaks of a factor of "congruence" of the therapist in reference to authenticity, mainly the nonmanifestation of false benevolence and more broadly with the capacity for encounter. Not all people have the capacity for encounter in the sense of sincere relating in the moment, in which one feels at liberty to tell the other what she thinks or feels about him in the therapeutic process. Not all therapy schools take this "encounter factor" into account, however, just as it is considered important in Gestalt therapy and in certain existential therapies, I find it relevant in psychedelic therapy—for falseness or compulsive good manners are perceived as something that does not correspond to the spirit of sincerity of the psychedelic state. This can easily surpass the capacity for truth of a therapist who has not gained an experiential learning in deep psychotherapy and who is only acting strategically from theoretical notions.

One who does not have an ability for sincere communication, is like before a child, who sometimes asks ingenuous questions that an artful adult does not know how to and cannot answer, so that the child ends up disappointed. Neither does a young boy have much patience with an adult who has fallen asleep and lost his way, like so many alienated people.

Psychedelic therapy cannot be practiced by people who are alienated or by people who have learned therapy from books in an academic context. This will require a healing training, or in any case a condition of health.

This is not to say that it is necessary to compulsively tell the patient such truths about himself or about his own feelings, but when one does not have the capacity to do so, the limitation of one's authenticity will surely become present, and the person in a psychedelic state might feel alone and will not establish such a profound contact.

If I think about how I have operated, about how I have conducted myself in individual therapy sessions, I would say that I have generally begun by recommending to the person to be with himself in silence or with the music, for I think it appropriate to make the most of the very beginning of the experience to move toward a state of deep consciousness. If you enter into the experience through conversation, waiting for the effect while talking, sometimes the exchange can deepen, and become increasingly open, rich, real, and authentic; however, there is also a certain risk that the person will be too absorbed in the world of ordinary consciousness, and although a certain superior inspiration may manifest itself, he will not experience the most singular gift that the drug can offer, which is a more loving state, or one more accessible to pain. However, it should be kept in mind that these are the possibilities that open up, similar to when one opens a game of chess: either one waits while talking or waits in silence, or one waits with music.

My impression is that, in general, it is better to start with music, for the musical experience is in itself intrinsically loving, and many words can be saved if the person connects with love before considering their problems. Let us say that the person spontaneously arrives at a state of plenitude and deep presence in which she not only feels good with herself but also with her surroundings; she will feel the sensations of her own skin as pleasant, she will feel at ease just by breathing, she will perceive the beauty of her surroundings. The time will come, then, in which she will want to talk about what motivated her to do this experience, but when she moves into the world of words and problems she will have the advantage of contemplating everything from a more loving and detached serenity than that of her usual consciousness, and this will bring her the advantage of being able to face life's pain with greater clarity.

However, it sometimes happens that when it has been hoped that music will suffice for the person to connect with the best of herself and her own health, this is not fulfilled. The person still feeling the impact of a trauma too great or whose level of health is not sufficient, can go into the experience with suffering, which sometimes appears as suffering in the present and sometimes points from the very beginning toward the past.

If the discomfort, physical symptom, or unease in the relationship with the therapist is perceived as part of the present, it is important to bear in mind that this may constitute a projection on the immediate situation of something that comes from the past, since one of the great potentialities of MDMA is the facilitation of regression, which in some way serves to correct the past, to be able to contemplate and understand it from the point of view of the adult, who has greater independence than the child who lived in a situation of defenselessness that, for this very reason, constituted a trauma. The way to get from present discomfort to the past is usually to simply sink into the symptoms: "Let us see, pay attention to that," "exaggerate." By going into the experiences of the moment and intensifying them, one naturally reaches the original painful scene that has been forgotten. Sometimes the face-to-face situation manifests a projection: the therapist becomes a person of the past, or his face is transformed into another face whose expression reveals by association what is sought in the past.

I would say that the work of helping the patient to unearth a traumatic childhood situation implies a detectivesque aspect. I remember, for example, a woman who felt cold: "Let us see, how does that cold feel?" I asked her, and then: "Does it remind you of anything?" "Yes, it seems to me that there is something very old, something from childhood." "So . . . you are in your childhood, how old do you think you are?" "I think I was about five." "You are five years old and it is cold; see if you can remember anything about where you are." "I have the impression that my mother is far away, that she is not there." "Try to remember, what are the walls like?"

The therapist's initiative sometimes seems necessary for the gradual retrieval of memories that become more painful, the more they become present. Certainly, the subject can feel the weight of this pain. It may be appropriate to take the subject by the hand, since that tactile accompaniment, with closed eyes, is more continuous than guiding with the voice.

Another word of advice that I would give to therapists is not to be afraid of the patient's pain, and not to fall into premature consolation. It is preferable to trust that the process of psychedelic healing is something like the bursting of a pustule, where above all, the rotten must be expelled. All that has been avoided must come to light, and this cathartic phase will take as long as it needs, but afterward it will leave the person clean, and with a well-being that could not have been brought about in any other way. It seems to me that it is important, in this reliving of the past, to allow the situation all the time it needs, to be open to everything the person needs to talk about and to what needs to remain, without precipitating its release.

These regressive episodes are one of the therapeutic results that appear, but there are also relatively recent or contemporary issues, things that are resolved under the effect of MDMA, for it is as if under its effects, the person's consciousness seems to reveal something like a compass that is very sensitive to what needs repair in her life. Therefore, it is better to avoid guiding the person prematurely to pay attention to this or that, and rather to have a lot of faith in the spontaneous movement of the mind in one direction or another, for it becomes more organismic in its function, and spontaneously comes to what needs to be brought to consciousness or reconsidered. The person can simply let herself be in a state of silence, enjoy the feeling of well-being for a time and then, after a while, say: "Something is missing, it seems that something hurts in relation to my family." Then she will discover: "It is as if my children are not well," and a bit later: "There is a problem with my eldest son." A process of focusing on one's own discomfort slowly unfolds, approaching its center like a camera zooming in. "Let us see, what is happening with our eldest son?"

In such a process, a question can be most helpful that helps to keep the person in touch with what is happening, and with her own expression of what is being perceived or understood, given the value of expression as an amplifier or as inspiration in the process of discovery. "The problem is that my eldest son never felt completely included, because the father . . ." Simply by giving enough attention to what begins to appear in the person's consciousness as a bubble of pain, and "tracking" the pain, she will come to an unresolved matter; and this matter will be concluded simply by paying attention to it and trusting in the person's ability to self-heal.

I have been following the alternative that arises if one begins in a state of pain when the pain appears spontaneously. However, what happens if the person goes into ecstasy and his well-being is prolonged? One knows that the person has problems, and perhaps he has been explicit in his desire to solve them through this therapy, but there are no signs that the problem is going to appear. It is as if the person was enamored of his pleasure, or at least of this special state, and has no desire to venture into the "descent into hell" that would be necessary to truly fix his marriage or to stop having the problems that he has with his children, or to find relief from his psychosomatic symptoms.

It seems to me that in such cases one must remind the patient of his problem, saying something like: "Look, you asked me for this session to look at . . . this or that matter"; or "What can you tell me about your problem with work?" We might hear in response: "That does not matter now; I feel very good," and it may be that this attitude of not worrying or becoming anxious about a usually problematic issue is a learning in itself; however, it could also happen that the self of this moment says one thing and tomorrow's self is completely unaware of the insouciance that has just been expressed. I therefore usually suggest to the patient that he speak to his future self. "Talk to the one who has that big problem and try to make him understand your point of view so different from his, so that your feeling of this moment is not something forgotten like a dream. If you want this understanding that you are having to be permanent, you should give it expression." Let us say that the "psychedelic self" should be in dialogue with the everyday self, and for this a gestalt technique can be used. However, the person may prefer to simply stay in the enjoyment of his peak experience, and when asked what he wants to say to his daily self, may answer: "Huh, I am not in the least interested," and insist that he does not want to trouble himself with considering the future. It may well be that it is not an option, and it may also be that the person needs above all to be nourished further by the experience of self-love and well-being, and he must be given that opportunity. Allow him to be permeated with this well-being for now, and time will tell whether in a next opportunity matters take a different course.

Let us suppose the person has started feeling the effects in the middle of a conversation. I have met with someone to have this session and she starts talking to me, and although I have advised her to remain in silence and breathe calmly, she has become very conversational and even I myself feel caught up by the interest of the matters that she raises, which elicit a response. The conversation takes that course. It can be interesting to follow how it is enriched, but at some point, it will be advisable to stop it, to disengage and to try another approach. One can then say: "Look, now I am going to ask you that we put a stop to this conversation, which is very interesting, but it would be better to try another approach to your problems. For this I want to ask you to focus on your breath (or on the music, or on both at the same time)."

Occasionally the person enters neither into loving well-being nor into her pain, so that her experience seems more superficial, limiting itself to a "here and now" that is neither problematic nor revealing. In such cases, I believe that it is justified to resort to a stimulating therapeutic intervention, since, although there is not a state of deep consciousness, surely a greater authenticity or ability to see the truth of feelings will be conducive to the examination of matters already selected before this day. Therefore, on the previous day I usually ask the patient what her questions are about herself or her life, and I even ask her what question she would take to an oracle—for it is likely that she will encounter something like an inner oracle.

I have already mentioned in *The Healing Journey* that I was disappointed by the results of gestalt techniques under the influence of MDA (unlike MMDA, which lends itself especially well to working with dreams and here and now situations). With MDA and MDMA I found dialogue, however, and work with memories, very important. The situation, therefore, resembles that of analytic therapy, where the patient's flow of thought becomes the starting point for interventions that can contribute to the understanding of what is happening, to guide the person to pay more attention to one thing or another, or to take something into account. At other times, however, it is advisable to stimulate the expression of rage, pain, or more broadly, of emotions.

The greatest potential, in any case, is loving, so that if one knows that therapy consists, in principle, in opening up the wounds and taking out all the putrid, including vengeful impulses, ending in understanding and forgiveness, both of oneself and of the other, that perspective can be useful to use it systematically as a technique: knowing that health entails healthy relationships, and that healthy relationships are a recovery of the bonds of love that have been interfered with by resentment and pain. So, it may be helpful to help forgive, sometimes as simply as: "Tell him that you forgive him; envision yourself embracing him and tell him, 'I forgive you and I forgive myself also . . .'"

To all that I have said so far, however, I would have to add that it does not seem to me all that important that a therapist operates through a systematic guidance such as I am providing, but rather that he acts spontaneously in accordance with his own mental health and empathic ability. Leo Zeff used to recommend to those who accompanied friends (particularly those whom they had met in their psychedelic group and who wished to experience a further psychedelic journey) the attitude of a babysitter: one who cares for small children or babies, and who is willing to do simple things like change the CD, open the window, run the curtains, accompany people to the bathroom, and mostly, respond to their wishes. Not everyone can be a good companion of babies or small children, for this requires availability, generosity, affection, and above all mental health; in coherence with this, one should not think that the training of those who are to guide others can be described as an intellectual learning, but inevitably it must consist in a human training. This seems to me to be particularly important in the case of group experiences to which I am not referring in this chapter—for in them the direct action of the therapist is less important as a situation of spontaneous mutual help is created in the group; this lesser significance of explicit therapeutic interventions, however, does not imply that the training and personal quality of the person supervising or supposedly guiding the session is not important—and this seems to me of great significance because of the possibility that healthy and robust people can provide great service by working with future self-help groups. However, I leave the subject here, as I shall return to it at the end of this book.

4

Oneirophrenics

4.1 INTRODUCTION

I borrowed the word *oneirophrenic* from Fisher, whom I located in upstate New York and visited in the midsixties after reading something about him in De Ropp's book, *Drugs and the Mind.* The justification for it lies partly in the prominence of dreamlike sequences under its effect and partly in the fact that such "hallucinations" or "visions" occur in the absence of the typical disruptions in thinking, identity distortions, and time alteration, characteristic of the effect of classical hallucinogens—LSD-25, mescaline, psilocybin, and DMT. Alternatively stated, the classical hallucinogens and ayahuasca seem to us quite distinct, and deserve a different name, just as in the case of the "empathogens."

When I conducted my first research on ibogaine, I found that, once again, it was appropriate to use the term *oneirophrenic,* and I am pleased that those who are using ibogaine as a treatment for substance abuse have retained the word. As I remarked in my discussion of drug-induced altered states of consciousness written for Wolman's *Handbook,** it seems to me that the three groups of compounds (the classical psychedelics, empathogens, and the oneirophrenics) seem to bring about a dissolution

---

*"Drug Induced States," in Wolman and Ulman, *Handbook of States of Consciousness* (New York: Van Nostrand Reinhold, 1986).

of the ego at different levels of the nervous system, associated with the head, chest, and belly (and corresponding chakras).

I am next reproducing two previously unpublished essays, without being concerned with some redundancy between them, since the attempt to correct it would destroy their integrity: the first, placed in this first section, 4.1, is a statement on my early work with both ayahuasca and ibogaine that was written in response to an invitation at the time of the LSD fifty-year anniversary (to contribute to a volume that never came to be published). The essay in section 4.3 has also never been published and is the transcription of a talk given as part of the University of Catalunya "U of Catalunya Online" program in the company of the prestigious Dr. Mia Fàbregas, a specialist in substance abuse who uses ayahuasca in his work in a way comparable to that in which others use ibogaine. Placed between these two essays, 4.2 is my contribution in a roundtable discussion at the 2014 World Ayahuasca Conferece.

FOLLOWING THE YAGÉ TRAIL

In the late fifties I read Lewis V. Cummings's *I Was a Head-Hunter,* and was struck by his description of an initiation ceremony, in which he had felt heroically impervious to the pain of whipping. I wished I could experiment with the brew that he had been given to drink, and even went so far as planning an expedition; but this did not materialize until 1962, when the photograph of a whipping ceremony among Colombian Indians in an exhibit at the Harvard Botanical Museum drew my attention to a paper ("On the Botanical Identity of the Malpighiaceus Narcotics of South America") through which I knew that the plants I sought had been determined and described. Its author was Dr. Richard Evans Shultes, who had clarified the issue after twelve years of intermittent fieldwork, and when I shared my intention of investigating the effects of the relevant alkaloids he supported my project. He had partaken of the drink but had found that for him it did no more than evoke the visualization of some abstract imagery—yet he deemed it was worthy of psychological investigation, of which he knew none.

Could he help me undertake it? Yes, he could introduce me to Dr. Idrobo, "the best ethnobotanist in South America" and also his name and picture might serve as a sort of passport to certain Kofan Indians upstream from San Agustin de Guamues.

Months later, during a visit to the Berkeley campus, I inquired from the secretary at the Department of Anthropology as to who had field experience in the South American tropics, for I wanted to know such things as the convenience or need to bring boots or firearms. She told me I might talk to Dr. Michael Harner, and after Michael and I met, we recognized each other as yagé brothers at the beginning of a new trail. Soon afterward, with some support of the Berkeley Research Institute (headed by Dr. Frank Barron) I stopped in Bogotá on my way back to Chile.

Now came the second phase of the adventure from which I was to return with plants, information, and rich impressions. At the National University in Bogotá, Dr. Idrobo instructed me in the collection of botanical specimens and suggested that on my way to the Kofan I might stop in Sibundoy, also by the Putomayo, but at a higher altitude—in the region adjoining the forested *tierra caliente*. He knew some Sibundoy Indians, and he also directed me to Dr. Mel Bristol, a Harvard botanist connected to Dr. Shultes.

I have told the detailed story of my early explorations of yagé in a book completed in 1970 that I only came to publish two years ago in Spain as *Ayahuasca, la enredadera del río celestial* ("Ayahuasca, the Heavenly River"), so I will only say now that, after a time in Sibundoy and a time with the Kofan Indians upstream from St. Agustin, I collected not only botanical samples and information, but enough of the yagé to analyze and test on human subjects. And then came the third stage of the adventure, when I returned to Chile and experimented, first with preparations from the plants I had collected, then with synthetic alkaloids.

Because a paper by Pennes and Hoch had reported that harmine was not a hallucinogen by mouth, I was more interested in tetrahydroharmine

and harmaline, which had been reported to be present in small proportions along with harmine in the South American Indian preparation.
Since J. A. Gunn (professor of pharmacology in the University of Oxford)
had shown that harmine, harmaline, and tetrahydroharmine (differing from each other by an increase in hydrogen atoms) are increasingly
active as antiseptics, I wondered whether they differed similarly in regard
to psychological effects. Indeed, this proved to be so, though harmaline
was scarcely more "hallucinogenic" than harmine had proven to be except
to people with a special sensitivity to it—and distinct enough from the
known hallucinogens to deserve a different name. I thought that the word
oneirophrenic (coined by W. Turner) to describe the characteristic elicitation of imagery with closed eyes was appropriate. Yet I then ascertained
that such imagery becomes even more pronounced when the subject is also
given DMT. In this regard I was able to verify the potentiation between
the activity of both substances that the Indians have known all along
when they add to the harmine stems of *Banisteriopsis caapi* the (DMT-
containing) leaves of *Psychotria viridis*. Unlike some who regard the harmala alkaloids as mere inhibitors of the destruction of DMT, I regard the
effect of the combination as something different from that of either substance alone, for DMT brings into awareness the feeling content of the
imagery. When later I came across a paper reporting on the transformation of serotonin into 10-methoxy-harmalan in pineal tissue through the
enzymatic action of HIOMT, I naturally became very interested in testing
this positional isomer of harmaline. Indeed, I found it to be psychoactive,
which suggests that it may be a normal hallucinogenic metabolite.[*]

At some point in the course of these explorations I decided to
focus on studying further the psychological effects of synthetic harmaline. Volunteers were recruited among acquaintances and the patients
of colleagues, and each would have two sessions—with two different

---

[*]Claudio Naranjo, "Psychotropic Properties of the Harmala Alkaloids," in *Ethno-
pharmacologic Search for Psychoactive Drugs: Proceedings of a Symposium held in
San Francisco, California, January 28–30, 1967,* ed. D. Efron et al. (Washington, D.C.:
U.S. Government Print Office, 1967), 385–91.

psychoactive substances. One of these, mescaline, was well known; the other, "a product from the Amazon country." Psychological testing (including the Rorschach and Cattell's 16 personality factor test) was conducted before and after.

My report on psychopharmacological findings is part of the volume that was published in 1967 by the Office of Health, Education and Welfare under the name of *Ethnopharmacologic Search for Psychoactive Drugs*, yet one is unlikely to imagine from that report the format or the spirit of the experiments: one that allowed for the observation of effects in an unstructured situation. This entailed giving up my original intention of remaining a mere observer for the sake of scientific objectivity. I forsaw that painful feelings or insights might arise and that, in such circumstances, an "asceptic doctor in a white coat," might not be the best company. Some needed therapy, and having a measure of therapeutic skill I felt it appropriate that I fulfill this need rather than sacrifice the potential benefits of the situation in the name of methodologic impeccability. On the whole, I proceded as an investigator of what happened as I enjoined my volunteers to let go and I set out to improvise as best as I could—that is to say, not only using my brain, but also my heart, and if possible, whatever "guts" the situation required.

Soon after returning to California (this time as a Guggenheim Fellow) about a year later, I wrote a paper on yagé-induced visionary themes, and when I showed it to Harner he was struck by the close correspondence to his knowledge of Indian descriptions of the yagé experience. He suggested that we present parallel papers at the forthcoming meeting of the Kroeber Anthropological Society. He reported on the snakes and tigers in the visions of South American Indians while I reported on the same phenomena in the experience of naive experimental subjects in Santiago de Chile. These findings have appeared (with Harner's companion piece) in Harner's *Hallucinogens and Shamanism*.*

---

*I took the "poetic license" of calling them "The Yagé Experience in an Urban Setting," though my report dealt with synthetic harmaline, in order to protect it from becoming illegal.

In *The Healing Journey* I have reported on my initial exploration of harmaline-assisted individual therapy that followed the above described volunteer study, yet I have never written about my experiments with groups. In regard to this, I will only say here that the inspiration and preparation for my therapeutic work with psychedelics in groups derived from my contact with Dr. Leo Zeff—pioneer psychedelic therapist who never wrote but influenced so many in Northern California.

A single LSD session with him in 1962 has been the occasion of a momentous healing, yet my season in "earthly paradise" had been followed after my return to Chile by one of turmoil, pain, and the felt need for psychotherapy. The wish for further contact with Dr. Zeff made me want to return to Berkeley after the time of a Fulbright scholarship was over, and Providence seemed to answer my wish through a mentor's suggestion that I apply for a Guggenheim Fellowship. Eventually I obtained it and had the opportunity to be part of Leo's first psychedelic psychotherapy group. This paralleled an exposure to Perls and Simkin, and through the combination of these I came to a plateau of emotional health. Yet an additional gain from it was such familiarity with "psychedelic group space" as permitted my own exploration of psychedelic group therapy. Also, as Dr. Zeff became acquainted with my observations of MDA and yagé, he had made these substances available to the members of his ongoing group as occasional alternatives to LSD, so when I began working with groups I also gave different substances to different persons. I had occasion to observe that this not only permitted individuals to use whatever pharmaceutical seemed of greater promise at the moment, but contributed a peculiar richness to the group process—as a consequence of mutual influences that seemed to make the archetypal and the interpersonal domains more present to all.

Since I returned to the United States in 1968 I dropped out of psychedelic therapy, for although a medical doctor I never applied for a U.S. license and I did not work under the sponsorship of a medical institution that might have provided me with the opportunity. I mostly conducted individual and group work with MDMA, when it was legal to do so at one place or another, and it took me a long time to reconnect with the world of the Malpighiacaea *phantastica* and related chemicals. This happened during the eighties in Brazil, where I attended several sessions at the Santo Daime Church and was empowered to lead sessions according to the traditional ritual. Acquaintance with its form of use (a Catholic-Rosacrucian hybrid) has given me greater understanding of ritual and group guidance in general and inspired me to explore the facilitation brought about by this South American alternative to *soma** in practices borrowed from the tantric legacy. Also, inspired by the ritual recitation of the creation story under the effects of ayahuasca by the Desana Indians,[†] I felt prompted to explore a possible facilitation in the understanding of mythical materials from our own tradition—and had occasion to observe that, indeed, ayahuasca could open an unsophisticated person's mind to an appreciation of subtle mythological texts such as the Homeric hymns.

In time I came to understand the snake, tiger, and eagle visions of ayahuasca as expressions of an activation of the reptilian brain of a similar nature to that obtained in kundalini yoga. Correspondingly, I regard the healing properties of the Indian brew a result of the extraordinary enhancement of organismic self-regulation that is inseparable from the "awakening of the kundalini *shakti*." Though eventually I came to formulate a broader "kundalini theory" of psychedelic action, it is the nature of the harmala experience that gave me the clue through the correspondence between the typical ayahuasca imagery and the traditional dragon.[‡] Indeed the somewhat felinelike and winged reptile traditionally associated with spiritual power is a composite of the three motifs that are so prominent in both harmala visions and shamanism in general.

---

*It now seems that most likely *Peganum harmala,* and not *Amanita muscaria,* constituted the origin of the Iranian and Vedic drink (See Naranjo, "A Posthumous 'Encounter' with R. Gordon Wasson," in *The Sacred Mushroom Seeker,* edited by Thomas Riedlinger, 1990).
[†]Now published by Gerardo Reichel-Dolmatoff in *Amazonian Cosmos: The Sexual and Religious Symbolism of the Tukano Indians* (Chicago: University of Chicago Press, 1971).
[‡]I develop this theme further in the article "Ayahuasca Imagery and the Therapeutic Property of the Harmala Alkaloids," in *Journal of Mental Imagery* 11, no. 2 (1987): 131–36.

A SORT OF AFRICAN AYAHUASCA

A new adventure began while I visited a friend in Santiago and met there a French missionary who had been stationed in Gabon. My recent yagé research came up in the conversation, and I mentioned how the prominence of big cats in the visions of my experimental subjects was congruent with the fact that shamans who use the *Banisteriopsis* drink identify with the jaguar. I mentioned that this identification is not just a subjective sense of kinship—and that their tribespeople believe that they objectively turn into jaguars. My fellow guest remarked that in Africa, witch doctors are believed to turn at will into lions, and he had heard about a lion that had escaped wounded after having been shot, later to find out that the local shaman had died at the same time.

Having been profoundly intrigued by a sort of "jaguar quality" in the yagé experience, it was natural to wonder whether a psychoactive plant might also be involved in African shamanism. Could this explain why the identification of humans with lions was so striking? There was reason to suspect that the plant involved might be iboga, for even though it had not been reported to be hallucinogenic, it was a polycyclic indole not very different in structure from the harmala alkaloids.

The use of the iboga plant by natives had led outside observers to think of it as a stimulant, and an electroencephalographic study had validated this interpretation. But this effect could be a matter of dosage, so that the ingestion of a small amount of the iboga bark turned the user a more energetic dancer, while a larger amount brought about visions. This was exactly the case with *Banisteriopsis,* chewed in small amounts to shapen a hunter's skill, and consumed in larger amounts for visionary and other magical purposes.

Since only a couple of papers on the effects of ibogaine had been published (on the vagina of the rat and on the intestine of the rabbit, as well as the cerebral cortex of the cat), it was not a taboo substance at the time and thus not difficult for me to obtain. I was my own experimental subject before offering the experience to anyone else, and when I reached an effective dosage—300 mg—I had a "bad trip." Not a complicated one, but quite unremarkable except that it told me I was not ready for such an "ally."

For the span of a very few moments I rejoiced in the sense of a cosmic dance, then became acutely aware that, while everything under the heavens orbited in the cosmic celebration, I did not—but remained isolated and still at the center of it all. Then there was a moment of choice: I could either say "Thy will be done" and go with it, or remain an outsider. It was like having my fingers on a switch. For a minute or two I procrastinated: what if it is God's will that I be dust? My self-importance was not ready to abdicate—and the occasion was gone. As in a play a scene leads to another, it all became a trivial cartoon show of which I could scarcely remember anything, for I felt very sleepy.

My next subject was a gifted dancer. I have quoted him in *The Healing Journey* already. Here are the first minutes of what he described, as it was happening:

"I see BLUE, blue, blue. I am on the floor, but with the body upright. I can rotate easily all the way round in a sitting position. All is blue . . . blue. . . . Everything is beautiful. I extend my arm and as I turn I draw a white circle around me and a smaller circle above . . . white, too. This atmosphere is dense. I try to look through my upper circle . . . a periscope? What is there? A ray of clear light is being formed in this dense blue atmosphere. It is becoming a shaft of light. I look, look through my white circle, look, and more light is coming into this tube, more white light, more and more, with blinding and filling force, and always more. And more, and more. I look through that ray of white light and I know that He is there, He, and . . . and that light, that tube, that immense white ray beyond is blue, blue, BLUE! (And this is a different blue from that of the first time.) This is a pure, clean blue, transparent, eternal, infinite, serene, that goes upward, that is the ALL! White-blue that is distance with no physics, enormity with no measure, Universe devoid of laws. It was God. It was God. God. God."

This is a report that fits in with what has been reported since concerning the use of iboga in religious initiations, and yet in marked contrast with the more recent findings of Dr. Bauman in Switzerland with ibogaine-assisted psychotherapy. In a report of his administration of somewhat higher dosages than mine to his patients (in the proceedings of a symposium held in Heidelberg, in 1985)* he concludes that it has the effect of a nonspecific psychophysical stimulant, and in the personal debate that we held during that symposium he emphasized the physical effects, and expressed disbelief at my own accounts of visual imagery. I think the difference is illustrative of the importance of setting, for by now I already expected ibogaine to resemble harmaline, and instructed my subjects to pay close attention to fantasy and imagery.

As in the case of harmine and its close relations, here was an alkaloid that elicited imagery and was a potential catalyst to spiritual experiences—though not a "mystical-mimetic" in the sense that the LSD-like psychedelics had been found to be.

In retrospect I would say that both the iboga and the harmala alkaloids are remarkable in the elicitation of what Dr. Grof has called "pranic phenomena," a point I failed to emphasize properly at the time of writing *The Healing Journey*. It is this kind of effect, I believe, that allowed Dr. Bauman to work well with ibogaine in combination with bioenergetics—though his report emphasizes the clearing of "energy blocks" over the observation of spontaneous "energy flow."

An additional similarity between ibogaine and harmaline was the fact that ibogaine could be either an opener to a fascinating realm or something very dull. It seemed to me that this was not a matter of personal preparation, situational dynamics or opportunity alone, as I had found out to be the case with harmaline. A personal affinity seemed to be involved, rather, much as it is with alcohol (in the case of which we know that extroverts tend to become euphoric while introverts tend to

---

*Hanscarl Leuner and Michael Schlichting in the symposium, "Uber den derzeitigen Stand der Forschung auf dem Gebiet der psychoaktiven Substanzen," 1985.

get depressed). As I continued to experiment with volunteers, I came to confirm the latter view, and soon concluded that for some people ibogaine works best in combination with a stimulant, a feeling-enhancer, or 50 micrograms of LSD.

When I reported my research to the French laboratory that was manufacturing an iboga extract (available at the time by prescription as a tonic), they proposed drawing up an international patent for a therapy-enhancing preparation. I agreed, and sent what case reports I had on the association of ibogaine and MDA—but my return to California put an end to my research. I am very happy to see that iboga is being used today at least in the cure of addictions. Howard Lotsof's claim to have effected cures in a single session matches my own experience in connection with various psychosomatic or psychological syndromes (as I reported at the 1967 LSD conference under the auspices of the University of California). My only published paper reporting in ibogaine-assisted therapy is one in which I speak of the "fantasy-enhancers" as oneirophrenics in general: "Psychotherapeutic Possibilities of New Fantasy-Enhancing Drugs," in *Clinical Toxicology* 2, no. 2 (1969): 209–24. (I will include it in this book as well.)

EPILOGUE

For a long time I thought that *The Healing Journey* had failed to stimulate the interest of either the medical establishment or the lay public in finding out how to put the new psychedelics I had described in it into use for the good of all. The book seemed to have been liked mostly by insiders—who needed it least.

Later, both the empathogens and ayahuasca have attracted widespread attention, yet I have been surprised to see scarcely a book about psychedelic *therapy*, and I think mine continues to fill, to some extent, a void, contributing to giving credibility to psychedelics as the precious therapeutic catalysts that they are. I hope that it serves to support my contention that we cannot afford the luxury of wasting their potential while we linger in a deadly police-minded mentality—for they constitute precisely the kind of remedy that we need as we approach a new collective "Red Sea" crossing.

I believe that it is the absence of a channel for the potential of psychedelics that is to be held responsible for our collective psychedelic disease, with its addiction and criminalization. I am convinced that abuse comes from bad use, and this has been the result of restricted opportunity for good use. Of course the repressive quality of government, vis-à-vis drug issues is an expression of a repressive bias in the very structure of civilization as we know it, as also of the prohibitionist leanings that we have inherited from our early Puritanical culture. We are living through times, however, where it has become critical to our very survival that we go beyond the overstability and fossilized spirit of the institutions that we have created.

I trust that our governments will come out of slumber before long and reconsider their disfunctional policy. What is needed now is not prohibition but true expertise: the training of specialists who can use psychotropic substances wisely and skillfully.

I am happy to see that we seem to be coming to a time when a reconsidering of psychedelics by the establishment is underway, and pray that enlightened government may perceive and put to use the potential of psychedelics for individual and collective healing.

4.2 REFLECTIONS ON AYAHUASCA IN HUMAN DEVELOPMENT*

Before speaking of ayahuasca in human development, I would like to say a little about what I understand as human development, and I would like to extend this with a parable: a story told by Idries Shah in his book *The Sufis,* where it is said that humanity was happy a long time ago, when each individual was a king and people had a level of satisfaction

---

*"Uses of Ayahuasca: Personal Growth," report presented at the roundtable of the World Ayahuasca Conference, Ibiza, Spain, September 25–27, 2014.

that is hardly conceivable today, until it emerged that they would have to brace themselves for a cataclysm, and a wise leader determined that everyone should be relocated to an island. On this island, people had to adapt to living conditions comparable to those of a sensitive person that has to take on the heavy work of a peasant and whose hands become so calloused, that he loses sensitivity in them. . . . Humans, then, lost many faculties that they had before, due to their urgency to survive.

The account goes on to explain that this is *our* story: we are living on an island and the only way to recover our human condition as such will be, firstly, to remember what we have lost, and then learn to swim or build boats: to take to sea to find the other shore.

I say this apropos human development, because when people speak of "development" they think of progressing from a satisfactory state to something much better, and I think that what we need to do is in the first place realize how *unsatisfactory* our state is, and then try to get out of the hole we are in by bringing our attention to our lacks.

Individuals do not realize they are in a hole, although the world is realizing that we humans are sufficiently deluded to not realize that we are already on the brink of the abyss.

Many of those who think of the world's problems are now speaking of a "crisis of civilization," and when María [Carvalho], our coordinator, asked me about the title of my presentation, I told her that "I would like to speak of the process that goes from the patriarchal mind to the total mind."

To refer to the civilized condition of humanity alluding to a "patriarchal mind" might seem slightly unusual or whimsical unless we realize that speaking of civilization is simply another way of speaking of patriarchal society—that is to say, of an authoritarian and repressive social order created by the males of our species.

I believe that civilization is a highly idealized barbarity, whose history has coincided not only with technological progress, but also with the establishment of slavery, exploitation, inequality, and as Freud observed, with universal neurosis. As we know, precivilized peoples tend to be considerably more humane, or less barbaric than we are: less ruthless, less driven by lack of solidarity.

For all that, what is the "patriarchal mind"? I wanted to begin with the parable of the islanders to highlight that it is something akin to living on an island within our own minds. Specifically, we live in our left brain, or more precisely, in our left neocortex; and although we have a "primitive brain" that has been characterized as the "reptilian" and instinctual brain, we have been domesticated by the spirit of civilization, whose despotic empire is affirmed above all in the idea that "we must step on the snake." This is what is said in the book of Genesis, and this is what has enabled the civilized (or patriarchal) mind to exploit nature and pride itself in its supremacy—not only of the outer nature but also of the inner nature—for millennia.

Nonetheless, what happens with a human being that is not only unaware of his animal wisdom, but also denies its recovery? This being loses his emotional health. For life is too complex to be lived from rational intelligence. Yet we are crazy enough to expect to.

One aspect of human development, then, seems to me to be the recovery of instinctual health; this has been the aim of psychotherapy, which has alleviated the suffering of many by helping them to reintegrate the world of desires. Freud was a great pioneer of this therapeutic task of helping people to recover the sexuality and healthy aggressiveness that constitute natural aspects of life; a task that has implied, above all, guiding them to become aware of their desires and then encouraging them to decriminalize pleasure, to break the taboo of allowing oneself to be more instinctual than a traditional millennial ethos has instilled.

This is precisely one of the ways in which ayahuasca has contributed to human development, and I suspect that it has done so even better than psychotherapy, as discovered by those who through surrendering to it have sometimes attained an awakening of the instinctual world that is reflected in the visions of their inner animal. Hence the frequent visions of animals and other images that suggest the world of the primitive, the world of the instinctual.

However, apart from the fact that our insular existence in the world of reason excludes our animal world, it also excludes our "inner maternal principle": our limbic or emotional brain—which in our collective life is both idealized and eclipsed by our patriarchal mind of astute hunters and predators. It was our ancestor mammals who developed empathic love, which manifests in the mother's bond with her offspring, and like them, we learned to live in the context of a loving mother-infant relationship—only being raised in a patriarchal culture has made us selfish, competitive, and violent. Snakes have not yet come to this, but horses are more loving than human beings. We humans are capable of a cruelty unknown to animals, and of a lack of solidarity that has now become problematic for our collective survival. Lévy-Bruhl, who wrote about the primitive mind at the beginning of last century, characterized it as a "mystical participation," but argued that the "primitives" have not yet developed the sense of self. However, during a recent meeting with Ivan Illich's intellectual heir in Mexico—Gustavo Esteva, founder of the University of the Earth—I was surprised that in the middle of our conversation he said to me: "The self does not exist." I thought, is this man reading Buddhist literature? Before I had the chance to ask him, he clarified for me: "We Zapotecas do not believe in the self." Zapotecas say "we," and not because we have not reached the required level of civilization, but because we consider individualism as something problematic. It is more noble to feel and say "we" than to say "I," but we have lost the ability to say "we." We have very little interest in the common good, very little empathic capacity for altruism, and it seems to me that with ayahuasca people become a bit saner. I am not saying that they become saints, but this exclusive concern for grasping and taking, this fierce individualism we are developing, this competitiveness without the balance of cooperation (that is part of the predominance of the masculine over the feminine in the barbarity that exalts itself as "civilized life"), this tendency to exploit rather than to cultivate . . . is leveled out. It is part of human development and health that people become a little more "human," as we tend to say. We have become dehumanized through our proud condition of *Homo sapiens,* and the very name *Homo sapiens sapiens* reveals the pride with which we have baptised ourselves. No wise man would say that we are "sapiens," for in our purported rationality we merit, rather, being called *Homo economicus.*

Then there is the matter of the two cerebral hemispheres. We have a hemisphere that processes things linearly; however, this discursive, rational, and linear thinking contrasts in us with an ability to see things in context: a gestalt ability to perceive what we see as a whole, as it has been described by Gestalt psychology. That is intuition, which sees things invisible to reason.

A Spanish economist is saying nowadays that scientific economics are very crazy because they regard everything as if commercial equations were a closed system, without considering that everything in nature is part of open systems, that everything is related to everything else. However, if we expect the calculations of the economy to have no relation to life or the environment, we are creating the fiction of an economy that is not even for human beings. It ends up being we humans subjected to an economic tyranny, and one finds oneself in the situation of the legendary golem: a human machine that we have created, that devours us and forces us to assimilate its ways of being.

Nowadays, we have become so scientific that anything that comes from the right hemisphere seems secondary to us, so much so that the humanities are disappearing from school curriculums. This seems to me a great symptom of our dogmatic blindness. For a good chemistry book becomes outdated in under ten years, whereas Shakespeare is timeless—as the writings of the Latin or Greek classics. Their wisdom is still relevant, and I believe the humanists were right in recognizing the importance of the subtle transmission of that wisdom of the mind of the sages through their works.

There is a famous book by a Scottish psychiatrist, Ian McGilchrist—not famous yet, but truly a great book—which is the best that has been written on the difference between the two cerebral hemispheres: *The Master and His Emissary: The Divided Brain and the Making of the*

Western World. I use the metaphor, borrowed from Nietzsche, that our right hemisphere, the intuitive hemisphere that sees things in context and that conceives values, as opposed to the rational hemisphere that does not have values, is the wise hemisphere: it is like the teacher in us that calls for a messenger, which is the astute brain, an emissary to deal with the matters of limits with other territories. The emissary started showing off. Better informed than the teacher, who is at the center of the kingdom and is unaware of all the details, the emissary within us, the barbaric hemisphere, the sinister hemisphere, believes it is the teacher and has already silenced the right hemisphere, does not hear the voice of intuition. I believe one of the most striking things about ayahuasca is that it numbs a little this emissary brain, this astute brain. The mind quiets. There is a feeling that one does not want to do, does not need to do, and just as the body goes into rest and the blood pressure can go down a little, this frenzied activity of searching for something and for someplace to go, goes into rest. This brings about the contemplative silence that was always sought through meditation to hear what is coming from the other side. Whether people interpret it as their intrinsic wisdom or as voices coming from elsewhere, or whether it is the spirit of a teacher plant, the fact is it can be heard when one is silent. In the most ancient of legends—the legend of the deluge in the Babylonian version, which is the most ancient of the versions—the secret of the gods is presented as something that was there with the Uptnapishtim, the original version of Noah, and the god of the wind whispered into his ear: "Forsake all and build a boat." Because he was silent, he was the only one who heard.

So, in a world of turmoil, ayahuasca helps us remain silent and therefore we can hear this deep wisdom. We are able to have a certain balance of the hemispheres, because just as we have two eyes to see deeply, we should perceive things with these two processors, not only with the reason of modern scientism, but also with our natural ability for in-depth understanding.

My time is up . . .

4.3 AYAHUASCA AND PSYCHOTHERAPY
(Interview with Mia Fàbregas at the Open University of Catalonia)*

MIA FÀBREGAS: I was reading a quote by Roland Barthes, a French philosopher of the last century, and there was a snip that seemed to me could be apt to introduce somebody like Claudio Naranjo. Barthes explains that there is a time in life when one learns, there is another time in life when one teaches what one has learned, and there is a time later on when one learns from what one knows not, which they call research, but then comes an age when one unlearns. Barthes says, concretely, that there is a moment for unlearning, for allowing the change of the unexpected to blossom, as only like this oblivion imposes itself on the limitation of wisdom. He says: "This experience has an illustrious name that is now outmoded, which is being wise: wisdom."

Being wise is equal to not having power: a little knowledge, a little wisdom, and maximum flavor; and I think today we are before a sage, somebody who has traveled this long path of learning, teaching, researching, and unlearning to now offer and share with us all this knowledge. It seemed to me a quote that really reminded me of Claudio, who I present to you with great pleasure.

The list from which he learned would need pages, for it is long, but the list of those who have learned from him is much longer. He studied medicine and psychiatry in Chile, and after some time in his country he moved to the United States, where he was a researcher and professor in several universities. At Ohio State University, he studied the work of Samuel Renshaw and Hoyt Sherman on the perception of totality. He worked in the Center for Personality Studies at Emerson Hall, under the guidance of David McClelland, where he took part in Gordon Allport's Social Psychology Seminar and studied with Tillich.

---

*Interview from the "Open University Online" series, November 20, 2014.

He then spent some time with Raymond Cattell from the University of Illinois, who invited him to become his associate in his private company (IPAT), the Institute for Personality Tests. Next, he worked with Frank Barron at the Center for Personality Research and Evaluation of the University of California and went to Berkeley.

There you were a student of Fritz Perls, the inventor of Gestalt therapy, after which you became its world's greatest exponent. It was the time of the revolution of consciousness and personal development in California, great numbers of wise men must have met there, who were your teachers: Idries Shah, Suleyman Dede, Swami Muktananda, Tarthang Tulku Rinpoché, the sixteenth Karmapa . . . you have always said that you were greatly influenced by the sculptor Tótila Albert, you always refer to it as a meeting in your life that was important, transcendental, that we would like you to tell us about some day: how a sculptor could have such a powerful influence in your life.

CLAUDIO NARANJO: When I read that Castaneda was making a distinction between teacher and benefactor, I understood that Tótila Albert was a benefactor to me, not one who leads me this way and that, one who fixes the workings of my mind, or psyche. He never assumed a position of authority, not even of a guide. He was a person who inspired many things in me. He did not like that I looked up to him, either. He treated me as a friend in spite of the fact that he could have been my grandfather because of the age difference.

However, I was looking for a teacher, so I left Chile in search of a teacher. I wanted somebody who would be stern with me if I needed it, and he was never once stern with me. I needed somebody to tell me what it was I should do, and when I insisted that I wanted him to tell me something, he would answer: "All that you need is to suffer. And that you do not need to look for." So, I went in search of a teacher, and there I met Fritz Perls, who greatly resembled Gurdjieff, who was my other strong influence; I had these two influences: Tótila Albert in Chile, and Gurdjieff who knows where, for he lived in Paris, but one I met personally, and the other not, and they spoke of more or less the same things in many senses: a Trinitarian vision of the cosmos and human beings, objective art. . . . There were a series of reinforcements. So, it was useful to me having these things in common from these two people who did not know each other and who were speaking about something quite ordinary; for me, they mutually reinforced their validity.

So Tótila was like a fertilizing influence in my life, and then I felt him like a spiritual father. The only thing he disapproved of in me is when I told him that I had an experience, my first experience with what today is usually called "pharmahuasca" (a mixed ayahuasca) and I sent him a poem that I wrote to him under its effects. For the first time he praised a poem that I had written, he liked it very much, but afterward, when I told him it had been written under the effect of something, he said: "What a pity!" And I said to him: "Well, we all have our limitations," I did not think it was very serious. However, it was like a violation of his faith that one should not push. The only piece of advice he could have given me, had I insisted: "Give me some advice," is "do not push." I believe he was right, that we rarely discover that all one needs to do is not push, because we push so much! We are like the mullah Nasrudin, who throws breadcrumbs around the house so that the tigers do not come close. And when a friend comes and says to him: "but there are no tigers in this region," he answers: "See! It is working!" We are doing so many things that we attribute to ourselves, that we make of them our achievements . . .

Once, I was in Las Palmas de Gran Canaria, at the airport, and I had two options: to get on a plane straight to San Francisco or to get on one with a stopover in London and make a detour to see Idries Shah, whom I had been in correspondence with for years, but whom I had never met personally. I had a very wise friend there who took me to the airport. So, I said to him: "What do you think, should I get on the waiting list for the flight to London or should I go straight to San Francisco on the flight that I already have a booking for?" And he said to me: "Do not push, do not push, one should never push." I followed his advice.

And the other plane crashed five minutes after having taken off.

It was such a clear confirmation, as if with the intention of showing me that my friend was right. I always had an inclination to that way of thinking: I have believed in spontaneity, in what arises of its own accord, in following one's own preferences, in the organic . . . and that was also Tótila Albert's belief. I am digressing, however.

MIA: I have only asked about Tótila Albert, and see already. . . . About research, you were a pioneer in the development of substances, in Leo Zeff's group work: ibogaine, harmaline . . .

CLAUDIO: They fell into my hands at a certain point in my life, and it seems to me I was in the right place at the right time, and meeting there the key people. I did not do anything. As for ayahuasca, before even knowing the name *ayahuasca,* or *yagé* (which was how I called it for the first years, because the beginning of my search had taken place in Colombia), it came to me through a book given to me by my father. He would very rarely do such a thing, for he hardly tried to influence my life, my father. I loved him dearly and I felt loved by him, but from afar.

One day he gave me a book: *I Was a Head-Hunter.* An adventurer, Cummings was his surname, he recounts in a sporting spirit, and a bit of defiance (like one who is proud of having done something tough and difficult), how he set off with an inflatable canoe and a machete on the Orinoco basin, which he had come into leaving from Colombia. After a long time, having to get in and out of the canoe to make his way through the rapids . . . he had to take the canoe out and put it in again farther along, inflate it, deflate it, I do not know how he did it, but the man was exhausted, hacking his way through the undergrowth with his machete . . . he arrived, completely spent, almost unconscious, with malaria fever, where some Indians named Yakalamures, cannibals, who seeing him so helpless, took care of him. No doubt they would have killed him if he had not been injured and unconscious in his canoe, but he lay at the bottom of his canoe adrift, and in his book, he narrates how the chief of a hamlet one day gave him his three daughters in marriage, and he was invited to participate in the initiation of the warriors. What did he have to do in that tribe where all the adults are warriors? They gave him something very bitter to drink, and he became excited during the ceremony in which he was flogged by a kind of demon. Of course, it was a native dressed as a demon, but under the effects of what he had drunk, he may have felt it as a real demon. However, he asked for more and more floggings, as if he wanted to withstand to the maximum and attain like this a certain distinction, even though it was frowned upon by the natives that he demanded to be beaten so much.

I would say that my first motivation in wanting to find ayahuasca was therapeutic, in thinking: "I would like to be a little heroic." I thought I was a very fearful person, too shy, and very little able to withstand pain. Would not a little of this substance be useful for people like myself, and for me? Although, when shortly afterward Chicho Maturana—a childhood friend who later became a very well-known man—and myself thought about traveling to the jungle, foregoing that we would manage to communicate in an unknown language with such "dangerous" people, as so many other "cannibals," we agreed that we were very attracted by the idea of enjoying the magic of the jungle, and I would assist him in capturing a certain insectivore that is in the human ancestral line and would help him in his research on vision. However, our project came to nothing, and in reality, it was an unattainable dream to find Cummings's plant without knowing its botanical name.

However, a long time afterward, when I was in Harvard in 1962, at the university botanical museum I saw a great banner across the street: "Economic Botanical Exhibition." I did not know what economic botany was all about; later I found out that it simply means plants that have economic consequences. There, at that exhibition, among all the little windows (each with its articles, its photographs, samples of plants . . .) I found a twisted vine with a museum publication entitled: "The botanical identity of South American narcotic *malpighiaceae*." I had not heard the term *malpighiaceae* before, but I was particularly interested in a photograph of natives flogging themselves. I said to myself: here is the plant that I am looking for, and somebody has already identified it, so it will be possible to find it. Since I was in the United States with a Fulbright scholarship, and would soon have to return to Chile, what trouble would it be to stop over in Bogotá? I had to take a bus to the Putumayo, I thought I could do it, and it would even be within my means to mount a small expedition.

Meanwhile, the secretary of the exhibition saw I was so interested in the matter that he allowed me to see the museum library, in which there were many things on ayahuasca, which I studied assiduously, reading articles by travelers, anthropologists, botanists . . . and then I was struck by the reiteration of certain themes in the descriptions of what I was reading, and also in the accounts of what the indigenous people say, as well as in the accounts of those who go to be healed by the shamans. Why so many tigers? Why so many jaguars? Why so many serpents? Why so many eagles? And the theme of flight. To feel oneself flying . . .

I had a more scientific than medical mind at the time; later I started to become interested in people, but at that time I was very aloof. I would say I was a bit autistic. Sometimes I wondered if I suffered from mild schizophrenia, one of the symptomless kinds that only loses the meaning of life.

As a scientist, I was interested in knowing if those images might be induced by culture (because a person belonging to an indigenous culture is told that these are the things that are seen, or perhaps they are instructed to see those things), or if indeed they were the effect of the drink. Later, when I was in the Putumayo, I understood, for example, that the serpent is seen as a guide, or as a representation of an encounter as the guiding inner principle. I wondered: Could it be that by giving this substance to somebody who is not of the indigenous culture, they will see the same things? This was one of the reasons I was interested in carrying out a study on yagé at the University of Chile. Another reason was the frequent allusion to the telepathic effects of the drink; as well as that it allowed to endure pain.

Fortunately, my boss at the Center for Medical Anthropology

Studies of the Medical School was very open-minded and believed more in the organic development of the initiatives of his subordinates than in organizing them. He did not have a master plan, except that he was interested that we help to bring some more humanity into medicine. He believed in people. He opened the doors for me. In truth, he was one of the great gifts of my life, Dr. Franz Hoffman.

I suggested to him doing a comparative study of harmaline and mescaline, and he allowed me to. I shall not explain here why I came to work with harmaline. Or, rather, I shall explain very briefly that I saw that the bacteriostatic effect was greater in harmaline than in harmine, and that a group of researchers had proved that harmine was not hallucinogenic even in quite high doses. I said to myself: perhaps harmaline, which is a better poison for certain cells, has a stronger effect on the nervous system. I found it at the Merck laboratory, which at that time used it because the aniline industry had not yet truly taken off (aniline had previously been used as a dye mordant). Merck was very happy to sell me some residual harmaline, and with it I started doing my comparative research. As I have been asked to speak of ayahuasca in therapy, I should explain that I had withdrawn considerably from psychotherapy. For in spite of having good teachers as an analytic therapy trainee (no less than Otto Kernberg, who was later president of the International Psychoanalytical Society), I felt I was not doing it right. Above all I felt bad when faced with people with great problems who came to see me at the polyclinic of the University of Chile; very poor people, toward whom I felt: "But what a fraud to be in a situation of being able to help people for whom I do not feel I can do anything truly useful." So, I had distanced myself from psychoanalysis and I had taken refuge in factorial analysis: mathematical analysis of the personality, studies of values, and such things.

However, accompanying people under the effects of ayahuasca made me feel useful in a relationship of assistance in spite of not feeling useful when I put on my psychoanalyst trainee costume. When I aimed to simply accompany people in an experiment, on the other hand, sometimes I was enthused by the things that enthused my experimental subjects in their experiences. One of harmaline's various effects was a great exaltation of intuition. Some people, who were thinkers, started to present arguments about the nature of the devil, of evil or of life itself . . .

In the course of these sessions I glimpsed that I could be useful without doing anything; but not "without doing anything" as I had imagined when I designed the experiment, for I had thought that I would be silent, a little like the psychoanalyst who more than anything, listens. Not so. For it seemed monstrous to me to do nothing in accompanying people who were so committed to their experience. I abandoned that role of scientific neutrality, and found the best approach was to do nothing; that is to say, not even to impose silence on myself. I discovered that I could be useful for psychotherapy when I did not set out to follow a model.

Subsequently, I did groups with harmaline and mixtures (forms of *pharmahuasca*, according to Jonathan Ott's term), and in these groups, I tried to offer therapy. Sometimes I moved about among people and found out what was happening; sometimes I carried out interventions, but I do not recall having been very useful in these. The overall impression that remains with me is that ayahuasca is therapeutic, but a therapist ceases to be therapeutic when he or she tries to compete with the ayahuasca. For when it is taken, one connects to the inner therapist, which is, I would say, the right cerebral hemisphere, the voice of intuition, which sometimes speaks to somebody as a voice: "Look, do you see this?" The inner guide is a wonderful thing when it can be contacted. Books have been written explaining that finding the angel that corresponds to one is quite a journey. In ayahuasca the inner guide sometimes presents itself as an angel, but sometimes as an animal friend, as in my book I describe the case of a woman that struck up a friendship with a Siberian tiger. For the rest of her life, that tiger kept appearing to her, even without ayahuasca.

I would say that ayahuasca therapy is very different from the therapy of therapists, and one way to begin to explain it is through the theme of the visions of animals. I was very interested in the visions of animals. All kinds of animals, and sometimes not the classic animals of the archaic and archaeological world, like the tiger, the eagle, and the serpent, which are so inherent to ancient Peruvian culture that even among the Incas they were still prominent; they are also Siberian symbols, but essentially, they are transpersonal and transcultural symbols.

In the beginning, it occurred to me that it could be a matter of telepathy; a mental contact of my volunteers with the indigenous people, but afterward the idea of archetypes seemed more plausible to me. It is as if there were in our minds impulses that present themselves symbolically, and as if there were in us a primitive strata subject to a certain taboo, and this would explain why a child is afraid of snakes, and also a monkey. There is a natural aversion to serpents in us, but the process of the cure with ayahuasca is a process of befriending terrible animals, or of identifying with them.

Now I have been asked to write a prologue to a book on Leo Zeff; perhaps somebody in the audience knows it: *The Secret Chief Revealed*. He was the person I received my first LSD from, and I accompanied him on his first harmaline journey (or harmaline-based pharmahuasca) and his experience turned out to be one of those "textbook examples," very similar to the one described by Mircea Eliade in his book on shamanism. He was telling me about a family matter, when he started to feel that the woman he was talking about started to turn diabolic, so his imaginary encounter with her transformed into a confrontation with the devil. He was smoking while he shared his vision with me, and at a certain point he became angry with himself and said: "How long am I going to keep smoking? I am going to give it up!" I said to him: "When are you going to give it up?" and he replied: "Right now." Indeed, at that moment he gave up smoking cigarettes for the rest of his life. He was so committed, so at one with himself that this act was like the trivial accompaniment to the fact that he was also separating from his wife. However, while he continued with this dialogue, and he was still presented with the feeling of something diabolical, the woman started turning into a great snake. So, having read Eliade, I dared to say to him: "Do not feel threatened by her devouring you, let yourself . . . see what happens." So, he allowed himself to be devoured. He let himself be swallowed, and now I can say that was one of the wisest therapeutic interventions of my life. However, what can happen after one has been swallowed by a large boa or python? To digest oneself, and to be digested. My friend let himself be digested, and through this he turned into the snake; but this coincided with a mystical experience, for the snake then revealed itself as divine.

It seems to me that is the process repeated in many variations in the deep ayahuasca sessions: that the animal feared becomes an animal friend. Today, I would say that is the translation into images of a process of integration of our own animal brain. We have a reptilian brain (that we even call the reptilian, primitive brain or archeo-cortex), but we have been very domesticated by the culture of our civilized world, which has educated us in the exploitation of the outer nature and also of our inner nature. We are not sympathetic to nature, but rather we have become its dominators, implicitly its enemies. The entire ecological problem stems from there, and today it is clear how limited ecology founded on reason is, so there has been a push for a "deep ecology," a loving ecology based on empathy with nature, of the kind Saint Francis embodied. However, the primitives are all "Franciscans" in that, far from sharing our alienating attitude toward nature, they feel part of it. They do not feel that they own the earth, but rather they feel that the earth is the owner of its settlers.

In view of everything that I have explained, today I would say that one aspect of why ayahuasca is therapeutic is because *it makes us befriend our alienated animal part*. Psychotherapy has done much good from that perspective, since it helps people to discover their desires, and becoming aware of their desires, to realize that they are not so illegitimate as felt during one's upbringing. One realizes, the more one knows oneself, to what extent the principle of pleasure was not only eclipsed by the principle of reality, but also forbidden by an implicit prohibitionism that is part of civilized culture.

It seems to me that instinctive freedom is one of the things that ayahuasca promotes, without it translating into explicit concepts that one labels as insight. One of the things that impressed me the most at that time is that people could get better without being able to explain why. I remember an obsessive man, for example, who told me: "I did not have a specific insight, but I feel much better." The same does not go for other drugs, which lead to the understanding of this or that. There is a healing that does not occur through the same circuit. We might say the drink acts as if it were a lubricant of spontaneity and desires. My thoughts are the same regarding the right brain, which is so prohibited in our current world because culture has become so scientific for us.

Two centuries ago it was not so much. When Freud formulated his ideas, he was very successful inasmuch as there was no scientific rigor as there is today. None of his ideas would be accepted nowadays. In reality, he looked for the contradiction in all of them. However, it helped that in that vision of things he was able to formulate it, to set in motion a revolution of consciousness. People started looking for the truth of their feelings, their thoughts, and their relationships. People were inspired to open up, to get to know themselves in a way that had not happened before Freud.

All because of some ideas, perhaps somewhat fanatical. Like the idea that sexual trauma was the root of the problem of hysterical women. Then Freud changed his mind, for he was a very open-minded man, who changed his mind frequently. He generated new ideas in each of his works.

Therefore, today, for example . . . I was in Russia not long ago. I was invited to be part of a Global Counsel for Change in Education. I had always dreamt of that. I have given many conferences about the need for a change in education, a change that will lead us from a patriarchal society to a society in which the feminine values and the child values are balanced within everyone's mind. A society that is not simply the perpetuation of the military order, of the old barbarian hunters turned predators.

So, I am very enthusiastically traveling the world preaching against the barbarity of civilization. I say it is such a highly idealized barbarity that it seems that people are not aware of how barbaric it is. It seemed like a dream realized when I received a letter to be part of the International Council for Change in Education. However, I came out feeling less enthusiastic. I came across very bureaucratic people. Yes, beside me was the president of Harvard and opposite me was the dean of the faculty of education at Stanford, there were people from all over the world: from Korea, China . . . but they were all very bureaucratic and lacking in vision. I even got angry and asked: "Where is the revolutionary spirit in Russia?" I was considered very rude and the Russians abandoned the meeting room. Just as they do at the United Nations.

Why do I say this? Ah, yes! Because, the day before yesterday I received a letter from the coordinator of that group, in which he writes to me: "But what scientific proof do you have when saying that patriarchy is the root evil? What you are saying is very serious, that behind all the social problems lies what you call the patriarchal mind." And I replied: "There are certain things that are difficult to prove yet are obvious."

The left hemisphere, the sinister hemisphere, is the one that has created today the religion of science, that is to say the dogma that only science can see things or is in possession of the truth. It is a hemisphere that does not see things in context, like the intuitive processor, that can be characterized as our humanistic mind; our poetic mind, that which the Romantic poet Coleridge called "imagination," and that we can also call "the gestalt mind," which seeing the whole, grasps the obvious. However, those who are only capable of thinking like a calculator, adding two plus two plus two, or rather of operating with bits of values zero and one, the discursive reason of science, can barely prove a hypothesis, and it is good when it comes to deductions, but not in the process of induction, which goes back from data to theories. When it comes to acting in life, pure reason is not much use to us, because while one hypothesis after another is proved, the patient dies.

I say all of this because it seems to me that one of the most important things about ayahuasca is that it gives individuals back their intuitive thinking: at times as a sort of philosophical stimulant, at others as an activator of stimulation; and the corresponding attitude of opening up to it, which is like an opening up of our rational being to the voice of our wise being, or of our left brain with respect to the right brain. I wonder if it is not this awakening of our wise brain that saves us from our habitual insular and one-dimensional lives, allowing us also to rescue our animal depth and to reach love.

I said it already at the conference in Ibiza during the roundtable on ayahuasca in human development, and I would say that the distinct therapeutic value of ayahuasca is secondary to its effect on human development, by dissolving the walls of the prison that development has left us within a patriarchal culture, implicitly repressive concerning the organismic instinct or function and intuition, which deprive us of the blossoming of love.

For this very reason, I have been saying lately that ayahuasca constitutes an antidote to the "patriarchal mind"—which I understand as equivalent to what Freud called universal neurosis, which he considered the tragic result of our civilized condition.

MIA: Can you can tell us about the comparison between children's stories regarding the matriarchy and patriarchy?

CLAUDIO: That was a researcher from California, Ravenna Helson. She was studying creativity in mathematicians. Her husband was a renowned mathematician. She suggested to him that some mathematicians had an intuitive vision of things before understanding their verification, and that others proceeded step by step, more rationally. She carried out a factorial analysis that showed the two types of creativity, and then she wished to repeat the study in literature. She used children's books as a field offering many books to be compared, a simpler field than that of the great literature.

In this study she carried out, she saw there was a type of creativity that she called matriarchal and another that she called patriarchal, leaning on Erich Neumann, who was a man much admired by Jung and who placed great emphasis on the evolution of consciousness, going through a matristic past (as it is called now) to the patriarchal, hierarchic civilized world based on violent authority. She had already chosen the terms *patriarchal* and *matriarchal,* and when she asked me to do a qualitative analysis of those books with these two contrasting characteristics, I ended up writing my book *The Divine Child and the Hero.*

Like in Saint-Exupéry's *The Little Prince,* the divine child is not going anywhere and is not seeking anything; he is only where he has to be, he is complete. On the other hand, the hero goes beyond the mountains and the mist, to a higher world, and battles with malignant forces. Ravenna Helson had qualified those two literary prototypes— the divine child and the hero—as expressions of a matriarchal attitude and another patriarchal. Matriarchal was, for example, a book that was also taken to the cinema, *Charlotte's Web,* which narrates the story of a spider that protects a pig. She wove her web on top of it and wrote something on it for that miracle to distract the exhibition agent and so prevent the pig being killed.

I think the reconstruction of history is not necessary for the concepts of "matristic" and "patristic" to be valid, nor to state that we live in a world in which men carry the political power, or that the world we have is despotic, police-like, insensitive, competitive, and shows little solidarity, that the common good is mostly ignored, in that each wants to grab for themselves. If we have a feminine side and a masculine side and one is associated with cooperation and the other with competition, we should recognize that the masculine side predominates in our society. By the same token, with respect to the polarity of exploitation and cultivation, exploitation clearly predominates over cultivation; and violence equally predominates over affection. Is it not highly obvious that the aspect we might call feminine is practically absent from the political and economic world? History has been marked by a masculine warrior ideal, with its wars and its rivers of blood.

Regarding this patriarchal mentality, ayahuasca seems to me a balancing medicine, not only that it brings out of the basement the animal we have alienated, but it also allows people to hear the voice of their inner guide, which to some presents itself in the form of angels, to others as voices or simply an understanding, and that can sometimes also be personified like the muse of poets. I believe what happens is that one cerebral hemisphere receives communications from the other, and this is perceived as if it came from another person.

MIA: This inner voice, do you think that it is a projection of knowledge, of culture, or is it really something that is there and becomes manifest? Sometimes people ask, is it wrong that I speak to a tree? No, it is not wrong to speak to a tree; what is wrong is that it answers you.

CLAUDIO: The big question is whether it is your right hemisphere speaking to you, or if it is something beyond yourself that is speaking to you, through this receptor that is the right brain. I am not sure, but I suspect that intuition perceives something that is beyond us, just as reason perceives qualities of the physical world. We have all the science created by reason, but it informs us about the external world. In the case of art, too, it is something created by intuition, but that is the vehicle of a truth. We have a right eye and a left eye that allow us to see things in depth because they are looking from different angles. I think that, similarly, it also occurs with our two brains: we would be complete people if we had (as should be normal) both instruments, reason and intuition; but nowadays the scientific mind says that intuition is only subjective and speaks of things not scientifically proven, like spirituality. Validity is refused to something that science has not verified.

I was very drawn to a book by an eminent psychologist, Steven Pinker, that appeared about fifteen years ago. I went straight to the index to see what he said about consciousness, and I was surprised that in that thick book there were only a few pages, three possibly, about consciousness. Therein it said that eagles had very sharp eyes that allow them to swoop down from great heights onto a mouse or other small animals, but that they have very bad hearing. It suggested that something similar occurred with the human mind, which has the equivalent of good eyesight that can reach a deep rational understanding, but has no use for studying consciousness. To that I would add that consciousness has to be studied by consciousness itself, through a diverse phenomenological scrutiny of the rational channel. Getting to know oneself is not like studying psychology.

MIA: Do you think that somebody who has been educated in a religion, or in a culture, can receive, under the influence of ayahuasca, presences or knowledge of elements from outside of our culture? Can Shiva or Buddha appear to a Catholic?

CLAUDIO: I think it is not necessary that Buddha appear to a Catholic. It is enough that Christ appear to him. Each has their own language. Each translates spirituality into their terms, their images. Although it might be that spirit wants to play a good joke on a Catholic, taking him out of his language, and once Christ appeared to me in the form of a horse—and that was without even drinking ayahuasca. I saw the head of a horse suspended in space and I felt it was Christ, but I could not prove it. I do not have scientific proof of it. Only that it transmitted great gentleness.

MIA: Visions are not only exclusive to ayahuasca.

CLAUDIO: Ibogaine was something that fell into my hands after I met a missionary in Chile, at the house of some friends, and I was telling him about shamans turning into panthers or jaguars. And he said to me: "It is similar to what we in Africa often hear that sorcerers turn into lions." There have been cases where a lion is shot, and the bullet is found in the shaman's body. It is incomprehensible that under the effects of whatever substance there are distortions such as these.

That made me search for what plants the Africans used, and so I came across a product under the commercial name of Lamabarène, which was available in pharmacies in France. I contacted the owner of the laboratory that produced the remedy and requested a quantity for experimentation. I was the first experimental subject with ibogaine, which was fairly harsh with me. I was alone in a house and I took 300 mg of alkaloid ibogaine. I felt like lying down, at some point it seemed to me that everything was spinning, that the stars were spinning. I was inside a house, but I felt like there was a cosmic movement, a dance of the cosmos: that everything was in its place, that everything moved in fixed orbits and everything was in motion except myself, here, at the center of it all. That I was not partaking in that universal dance. I started to feel I wanted to take part. But for that I had to say: God's will be done. There was one drawback: I wanted to be important. If I said: God's will be done . . . it might be that I am dust, that God has no other special plan for me. I was not prepared for that. I had a three-minute wait, feeling the switch was at hand, that I could change and be a part of the whole, as if I simply had to decide that now I would surrender my personal will, my control over my own life. But I was only given three minutes, and then the cartoons started, cartoons for the remainder of the hour. I felt that many people have no more than that. Well, ibogaine. How did I get to ibogaine? I do not remember.

MIA: Let us go into greater detail about ayahuasca. Ayahuasca has seen lately a process of international expansion and it is given a credibility that previously was totally out of place. It is accepted following the experiments with post-traumatic stress through the need that Americans have for treating war veterans suffering a difficult problem to solve because the psychiatry studied by you and I is more focused on treating the symptom and not really going into to the crux, the reason, or the depth of the matter. Do you think that ayahuasca can really be that window of opportunity to, instead of treating symptoms, start treating causes?

CLAUDIO: Yes, I would say that, beyond the symptoms, what aya-huasca mainly treats is universal neurosis; the universal neurosis that Freud postulated, and later Erich Fromm described as a shared defect, which therefore does not strike us as anguish. We find ourselves in the crazy situation of saying: How have we, normal people, created such a problematic world? Except we are not sane, healthy people, but we do share the same insensitivity, the same lack of empathy, the same exploiting tendency, the same authoritarianism, the same conquering spirit, that is characteristic of patriarchal society and culture. I believe that ayahuasca constitutes a cure for the patriarchal mind, and the rest are details. Part of the recovery consists in that in ayahuasca groups, a great spirit of fraternity arises, something like a recovery of the heart. Obviously, we have lost the spirit of fraternity of certain primitive cultures, while for the indigenous peoples the feeling of "we" or "us" is more important than the feeling of selfhood. I like to mention the "mystical participation" that Lévy-Brühl wrote about a century ago when describing the mentality of primitives. Only that he thought the primitives do not say "I" because they have not yet developed the self; however, I do not think they have not developed the self, but rather that the self seemed too little in contrast with the feeling of humanity, and therefore they prefer to say "we" or "us." I felt it very strongly during a conversation with somebody who I did not know was indigenous: Gustavo Esteva, the rector of the University of the Earth, in Oaxaca, Ivan Illich's intellectual heir. At one point in the conversation he said to me: "We, the Zapotecas, do not believe in the self. We say 'we.'" How could I say that this person before me did not have a sense of self? Rather, he was somebody that knew that the "we" or "us" is more, and it is greater to speak of us.

MIA: Do you think that ayahuasca is a solution in itself, or is it a tool that must be in the hands of facilitators, guides, psychotherapists, or therapists? Do you think the appeal lies in ayahuasca, or does its healing power lie in the use by those facilitators?

CLAUDIO: Nowadays, there are shamans and teachers, pseudo-shamans and bar owners, ayahuasca waiters. It is hard to choose among them, because we do not know if they are teachers or charlatans, and also with shamans it happens that there are many shamans for tourists, much business in satisfying the public's desire for drugs, so sometimes it can be healthier to attend one of Mia's groups, who will tell you: "I offer you a well-prepared drink and good music, and although I do not pretend to be a teacher, I will take care of you."

I do not doubt intuitively that under the effect of ayahuasca the mind perceives stimuli that come from a higher consciousness. If aya-huasca is taken in the presence of a true shaman, the shaman's presence has an influence. That is why music in ayahuasca can have a tremen-dous influence, because music makes present the mind of the composer, it conveys experiences.

Ayahuasca should be taken in the company of a mature person, with a certain wisdom and capacity for helping. However, where to draw the line between the professional and the amateur? It is very relative, like in psychotherapy itself, as Thomas Szasz says. It is a somewhat artificial line. Is a professional therapist always better equipped to help than a good friend or than a person with certain qualities who has gained a capacity for helping not through psychology studies but through life experience? I do not know, but it is my impression that psychology is to a large extent a sale of certificates, and it is not as important as thought in the process of personal development. Those who have learned psycho-therapy through a university are not necessarily good psychotherapists because psychotherapy, like music, is not learned in universities. One has to have a feeling for it; one has to learn from other parameters: the spirit of inquiry, the meeting of certain people that have something to transmit. Universities are not even conducive to learning experiences such as those required by therapeutic training.

No doubt those who take an interest in hallucinogens predomi-nantly wish for them to be freed of all control, and that people may do and eat as they please; however, I believe this anti-authoritarianism, although understandable in reaction to the repressive spirit of politics, is not all that wise, and it would be better that in the future we reached an order comparable to that of shamanic societies, where the particular capacity of specialists is recognized and the fact that healers and guides can contribute to the benefits of psychedelic trips by their mere presence. However, I do not believe that in order to achieve this, mere prohibition will be effective. It would be preferable to privilege the opportunity of a suitable training for the suitable people, and that the public ends up recognizing the appropriateness of turning to the most ideal guides.

I think it is important to recognize, moreover, that even when an ideal is good, the attempt to reach it through authoritarianism ends badly. It seems to me that nobody understood it better than Ivan Illich, who explained it very eloquently in an interview lasting five days that was done before his death and published later as *The Rivers North of the Future.** Essentially, in it he says that there exists in the modern world a form of evil that did not exist before, when it had not reached so much progress. As well as a theologian and an anthropologist, Ivan Illich was a historian of the medieval, and he came to the conviction that nothing contributed so much to the refined evil of today as much as the result of the church's attempt to institutionalize the Christian gospel. This is expressed by a theologian in the Latin phrase *corruptio optimi quae est pessima,* which means that "the corruption of the best is the worst of all." The same idea that Shakespeare formulates in a sonnet by saying "Lilies that fester, smell far worse than other weeds." Is it not true also that meat reeks more in its putrefaction than plant proteins?

However, in the case of the church's inquisitorial spirit, we must distinguish the imitation of Christ inspired by true devotion from the obligation of being a Christian and from the prohibition of sin, no matter how valid it be that "each carry their cross"—and smiling if possible;

---

*David Cayley, *The Rivers North of the Future: The Testament of Ivan Illich as Told to David Cayley* (Toronto: Anansi, 2005).

another, very different thing is the obligation of perfection stimulated through punishment. The effect is completely different, because where the superego is exalted at the expense of the freedom of the inner animal, mental health disappears.

MIA: You are an excellent musician. Is that a gift, or is it merit? Can it be compared to being a good guide, a good facilitator, or a good shaman? Is that a gift or merit? Is it something one works toward or is it something one receives?

CLAUDIO: I think one works toward it, but differently to how therapists are educated. Whoever wishes to train as a therapist by studying intervention modalities or strategies and not paying heed to the dialogic element, especially one's own training as a person, will not get very far. The training required is gained from self-knowledge, one's own liberation from obsolete conditionings, the development of love and other competences dismissed by university programs. That should be the main training of therapy, similarly to how in psychoanalysis it was always recognized that it was necessary to be psychoanalyzed to become an analyst. Only today, staying in psychoanalysis is a little retrograde, and there are faster ways, and I think it would be a waste of time to not use the three psychedelic shortcuts: the ayahuasca-type substances, drugs that open the heart, and those that dissolve rational thinking, like LSD.

MIA: Do you agree with the claim that ayahuasca is psychotherapy in syrup form? How would you define it? It is like psychotherapy in the form of syrup, a potion, in liquid form.

CLAUDIO: I think this is not the right way to think, because the experience one has drinking the medicine depends on many things. It depends greatly on motivation, it depends much on the ability to enter into relationship with the person accompanying you . . . even when an ayahuasca session is planned as a therapy session with your inner guide, the same obstacles as in ordinary therapy come into it, such as transference, and negative transference. Many people have negative transference with God and spirits and the intuitive. Some people are very closed to anything that is not their ordinary mind.

MIA: Fericgla coined a concept, he speaks of a dialogic consciousness in which the self is divided and one starts up a conversation with oneself, and that ability to recognize the other, not to see one's image in a mirror, but to see oneself as something estranged from oneself, which would be a psychotic state, a division of the identity of the self, not only does ayahuasca allow it, but one can draw from this situation, learn to see oneself, one being the one looking and one being the object looked at. Do you believe this is so?

CLAUDIO: I have not considered things in this way. Buber's idea of the dialogic is not that one can know the other, but that one must recognize the other as someone that one does not know. We respect the other more when we treat him or her as a stranger than when we win him or her over by thinking we understand him or her perfectly.

MIA: Is the inner voice myself?

CLAUDIO: The inner voice is a self that is not perceived as self. Phenomenologically, it is another. (Perhaps because what we call "self" is an identity too attached to the left brain.)

MIA: Is it a self with no identity?

CLAUDIO: Perhaps, with no identity. In the meditation traditions, the aim is to open the individual identity to find a universal identity, but that universal identity is a little like nothing. That is why what the quantum physicians argue is so exciting, who say that the quantum reality has properties of the mind and is not local. What happens in a particle is in resonance with what happens at greater distances than communication at the speed of light would allow. It is as if everything is united in the quantic world, and that constitutes scientific evidence that even in the material world there is a space underlying the observable that is like the mind. The mind has an ordinary dimension and a deep dimension, which some conceive as a deep self, but would perhaps more wisely be called "non-self," or not be called, or alluded to as mystery. So, what we call God in the West is conceived in yoga as depth of mind.

MIA: Education and ayahuasca. Do you, an expert in education, believe that ayahuasca can really be an element for education?

CLAUDIO: When educators uneducate themselves. They are so programmed by their academic training that education is the way it is, and that what is not part of usual practice is not considered education, that they tend to be the last to understand; especially, for what they have invested in dedicating so many years to getting that model into their heads . . .

Someone once asked me after a conference if I think it is appropriate to devote so much energy to changing the system, and if it would not be better to direct it in the creation of a new education, outside of the system. Perhaps so, as the bureaucracies are so unwieldy. The fossilized world is so difficult to change that perhaps the community should create alternative situations; unofficial educational centers, with different objectives and different people. With objectives of human development and not of individuals being meek little lambs that serve production.

MIA: You speak of uneducating and educating anew. Is that to reset and reprogram? Do you not believe in the possibility of the transformation of . . . ?

CLAUDIO: . . . of educators? They are so many, and they are steered by politicians that have been so unwise up until now . . . I sometimes wonder if it is the will of certain individuals that keep everything as it is or if it is a systemic will, something akin to what was called "the devil," which is not in any specific place, but that could be understood as a mind implicit in the inertia of the group, the government mind, and above all the mind of bureaucracy. Sometimes people with good intentions seem to get carried away by conformity to the spirit of a ministry, for example.

MIA: When you speak of education, you speak of the integration of the intellectual, of the emotional, and of the instinctual. Does ayahuasca influence the emotional, does it influence the instinctual, and does it also influence the intellectual?

CLAUDIO: It helps to become silent. What it most helps is that which yoga seeks: to let oneself fall, relax, not seek elsewhere; to let oneself fall inward. It is not a letting oneself fall so deeply into self, but enough for images or intuitions to emerge, or a sweet feeling of coming home. That is the peace sought in yoga. A good ayahuasca session is a great warm rest from which advice and visions arise; and from which a physical digestion begins to take place, which is something like rearranging things from the inside. I think it would be fantastic in education if educators opened up to such experiences, and it may happen, but up until now it has not been seen. So far, educators are slightly more conventional than other groups. Even commercial businesses innovate more, are more up to date, are more open. Education is the most obsolete of our institutions, modeled on the eighteenth century to create a workforce with people that do not think too much.

MIA: The majority of the audience are psychologists. What shall we tell them about ayahuasca regarding psychotherapy?

CLAUDIO: What shall we tell them? That it has to be discovered personally. There are so many opportunities today. A trip to Brazil, a trip to Colombia . . . it is worth having an ayahuasca experience sometime in life. Sometimes one wins the lottery and it turns out to be a life-changing experience. At other times not, and sometimes people have a rough time. Some people physically vomit a lot, and it is as if there was a defense against the visionary effect of ayahuasca. What on other occasions are psychic hells, here is manifested somatically. Some people are open to or prepared for ayahuasca, and others are not. Those that are not, at least realize that they are not on friendly terms with their inner animal.

MIA: Why does one speak of ayahuasca and psychotherapy and not so much of LSD and psychotherapy, or of ibogaine and psychotherapy? Why do you think that combination is better established than one with other substances that also have these capacities?

CLAUDIO: Well, the fact is, with ayahuasca the person does not lose their usual focus so much. He does not become disorientated, does not have alterations in time and space . . . he is saner. Essentially, what happens is that the person looks, sees, and so understands things. It is more within the acceptable and nothing worse than vomiting happens. There is no threat; the mind does not change so much; it is not as radical as lysergic acid, or even Mexican mushrooms.

MIA: Does ayahuasca depersonalize less? Do you think it depersonalizes less? Would that be one way to define it?

CLAUIO: It depersonalizes very little and is sufficiently unpleasant so as not be prohibited. If it were more pleasant, that would be in favor of it being prohibited.

MIA: Strawberry-flavored ayahuasca is not a good solution?

CLAUDIO: It would have to be an inner strawberry flavor.

MIA: I do not know if Nando allows people to ask questions, if there are interesting things. There really is an expansion. Our society is experiencing . . .

CLAUDIO: But it is not only ayahuasca. I have just had news that in Chile a law has been approved for the medical use of marijuana. In Chile, I would never have expected it, because it is very conventional. Something is changing.

MIA: Would you regulate, accept, are you in favor of the legalization of substances that are psychoactive enhancers of consciousness?

CLAUDIO: What I am certain of is that its therapeutic use should not be prohibited. This group of substances is too useful to close the door on. I believe a valid channel should be opened. However, opening a valid channel is different from proposing that it should all be available . . . I am not so sure of this second option, which could lead to complications. For me, the best metaphor is the one of fire, which placed in the middle of a living room, will burn your house down, but placed on a cooker or industrial oven is extremely useful. Psychedelics are like fire, in that they are a great force that would require certain measures, certain attention. The call for all laws to be abolished for once and for all seems to me very voracious.

MIA: Somebody is asking if in an ayahuasca session it is necessary to have an aim, an intention, something to achieve, or if the only prerequisite is just allowing.

CLAUDIO: I think it is good to ask oneself beforehand what one wants, and I have also heard it explained that the "Daime" is called this way because one asks "dame, dame, dame" ("give me, give me, give me . . .). Like prayer, it serves at least for one's own clarification. However, it is also true that when one is in the experience, surrender is advised and also a certain faith that there is something that knows better than we do what we really need. Sometimes one realizes afterward that it is as if one had received what one needed even though one had not known how to ask for it consciously.

MIA: Someone who was to go to Ecuador to do a session and to find a shaman, and go to the jungle and work with ayahuasca with him and feel absolutely nothing, what position should he adopt? Do you mean to get your money back? [laughter] Someone who had gone with that expectation, with that aim, and for nothing to happen to him . . .

CLAUDIO: I have seen that happen. I invited one of the most renowned shamans, a one-hundred-year-old man, and I had never seen so many people that felt nothing, that nothing happened to them.

Apparently, they were drinking the same as the others, but nothing happened to them. However, I cannot say if it was a good experience for them to be confronted with the fact that something was missing for something to happen to them.

MIA: The first three times that I took it I felt absolutely nothing. . . . Well, today is Claudio's birthday and instead of us gifting him, he has gifted us. We are grateful to him for this and we wish him a happy birthday.

[Applause]

4.4 RETROSPECTIVE OF A PERSONAL EXPERIENCE OF OVER ONE HUNDRED SESSIONS WITH THE UNIÃO DO VEGETAL

The document that I quote below is exceptional in that it pretends to summarize a person's experience of over one hundred ayahuasca sessions from the accounts accumulated over several years. It answers, then, the question about the effect of repeated ayahuasca sessions more satisfactorily than my interviews in my previous book with people who have been part of the ayahuasquera religions in Brazil, which were not based on an analysis of previous writings, but only on a long-term retrospective view. It is, moreover, written by a person with therapeutic training and experience, who was part of the União do Vegetal for many years.

It is of special interest, it seems to me, that in summary, Asunta de Hormaechea shows an evolution similar to people who encounter their "inner animal," their "spirit guide," and a "psychic death" in the course of one or two sessions, and I must confess that in the light of their account I feel less critical about the little visibility of the progress of the many that consume ayahuasca in Brazil's ayahuasquera culture. Perhaps they lack pride in their doctrines, a better understanding of the transformation process and its components, and of how to "work on themselves" between sessions, or a context more propitious to liberation than to authoritarianism. However, the following text suggests that, in spite of everything, ayahuasca is slowly leading some people to become aware of their aberrations, to trust in surrendering to a healing process, to awaken to the instinctual life of the healthy animal we all carry within us, to love, and even to devotion and to Spirit.

The Return to Innocence
By Asunta de Hormaechea, Madrid, January 31, 2015

Claudio has asked me to write a few lines about my experience with taking ayahuasca. Although many years have passed since those episodes, the memory is alive in me and they are still a source of inspiration and understanding of myself, of the human phenomenon, and of the unconscious psychic dynamic.

I wanted to call this article "The Return to Innocence" because, in hindsight, I can see a sequence, which I did not see so clearly then, from neurosis to reconnecting with my deepest self. What clearly marks the sequence is, if not dissolution, at least a softening of the character armor to be able to live my life from a different perspective.

At that time, I was fully immersed in my training as a psychotherapist and carrying out an analysis of my character. I was looking to understand what my difficulties were, how I generated difficulties in my life, how I repeated myself, and what my blind spots were.

A part of that personal work I was absorbed in was observing my structure using knowledge of the Enneagram. I had placed myself in enneatype nine, or Laziness.

For a period of several years I had the opportunity of having some experiences with ayahuasca. Between experiences, several months and even a year could go by, but still they had a clear unifying thread and a direct influence on the development of my personal work.

I can truly say that there was mutual feedback; as I made progress in my self-knowledge the experiences evolved and, at the same time, the insights through the experiences made my work progress.

Each of these was very intense and had a great number of images and symbols that I will not go into analyzing in detail here.

The first experiences revealed to me with great clarity and depth all that I had understood in my personal therapy work. Expressed in this way, it does not seem to be very significant, but it was highly transcendent, as what I already "knew" became a deep understanding that went far beyond the understanding I had until then. I could say that understanding was embodied, became alive, cellular, and organic. "The verb was made flesh" was a phrase that came to me at that time and that faithfully described what I was feeling.

I have to say now that I know that translating into words the experiences that take place on another deeper, and more symbolic plane of the mind is extremely hard, if not impossible. Verbal discourse belongs to the two-dimensional space-time sequence, past-present-future, whereas transcendental experiences of the inner world belong to a total, multidimensional present.

To describe in words a symphony of one of the great maestros of music is practically impossible. The number of instruments, notes, chords, silences that occur simultaneously are not verbally transmissible. To describe them individually would detract from its greatness and would not give us a reliable picture of what the work played was. We could have a mental idea but not the vivid experience of hearing it. This is also the case of experiences of the inner world: both if they occur spontaneously in the so-called states of grace or mystical states, through meditation, and as in this case, made possible by a wise and ancestral mixture of entheogenic plants, no verbal account can convey an adequate vision of what the experience is.

Following this digression, I will go back to the sequence of experiences.

To see how my character, and its multiple gestures, stood between reality and myself had a brutal impact on me.

I could see quite clearly how my ego, my neurotic structure, took charge on specific occasions in spite of myself, and this helped me gradually de-identify from the automatic behaviors conditioned since childhood that we habitually call "ego" or "self."

It allowed me to see with great clarity that I was different to what I had imagined up until then. I saw myself living, trapped, in a cage: character, structure.

We say: "I am like this" or "I am like that," when in truth what we really are remains silenced and hidden beneath a rigid and repetitive structure.

I call this structure "the cage" because that is how I saw it and experienced it and it seems to me quite a truthful image of what is really the matter with us. A metal cage we are imprisoned in. Depending on the different structures or degrees of health or neuroticism, we have more or less bars, thicker or thinner, uneven or straight, but bars all the same. I have to say also that without a minimum of structure, of cage, we would be in the field of psychosis. The cage, to some measure, is necessary; the problem is that it becomes too big, it becomes autonomous, automatic, unconscious, and takes control. We identify with it, convincing ourselves that "that is me."

We need, then, to become aware of what our cage is like, of what the automatic behaviors are, to recover the ability to make decisions in each situation of our life instead of responding mechanically. To shake off limitations, consciously put our strategies in service of our being. Ultimately, to gain awareness and freedom.

In one of the experiences I had with ayahuasca, I was able to clearly experience this division between what I really am and the structure that superimposes it. What is more, I was able to hear how in a moment of recognition of the essence and surrender to the unity of the whole, the structure said: "Well, if I cannot be in control, if it is not for my benefit, I will not give way."

So, the first discovery was seeing that I was colonized by a structure that was extraneous to my essence, to my true being, which had taken control, and within which I felt like a small and helpless child.

In later sessions, I was able to see concrete aspects of how my structure operated. One of the first aspects that showed up clearly was seeing how a great part of my daily energy was directed at seducing in general, and at seducing men in particular, while I rivaled with women. I could see myself alone in front of the men, and behind me were the women, where I could barely see them or pay attention to them. If the men saw me, they valued me, especially if they desired me, I had value, and, of course, I would get my way.

At the same time, rivalry with women was underlying and subtle—a secret conviction that I was worthier than all of them, whom I considered "silly."

In my daily life, I had friends, but now I was seeing that, even so, in the deepest part of me I considered myself superior, as if I was special and different from all of them.

Even seeing all of this I did not question my placement in the enneatype Laziness. The profound and vivid insights that ayahuasca gave me did not immediately translate into understandings of changes in my daily life. It was still some time before I was able to question my placement and move to the enneatype Pride.

I wish to pause here for a moment, for it seems to me that it is worth explaining how the process of change unfolds. The mere fact of having seen and understood something in a lucid state does not mean it becomes an immediate change in our habitual state of consciousness. We still have to do the work of bringing that understanding to our external life, make the commitment and effort to not forget what was experienced. We run the risk, back in the daily routines, of becoming trapped by mechanicity and forgetting what we experienced just like we forget dreams.

We need to become aware in our daily life of what has been revealed to us, for it is in daily life that we can really make the changes. That is to say, changing, evolving, growing, healing, involves a voluntary and conscious work, day-to-day. It requires remembering what we have understood and paying attention to how and when the mechanical shows up in our daily tasks. It really is Work, capitalized, as Gurdjieff called self-observation.

Although it is also true that some particularly deep experiences are transformative in themselves.

After returning to daily life and trying to see how seduction worked in me, I felt trapped in a spider's web. A web that I myself was weaving and in which I was the main prey. While I saw how this web was stifling me, I was able to see men as flesh and blood, and I learned to relate to them in a real way and not subject to my fantasies. At the same time, women also appeared before me in a real way, and I found with admiration that among them were very valuable women. I had never before seen a woman as valuable or "precious," in the sense the Tibetans give to this term.

Slowly, I began seeing other aspects of my structure, and how these were for me a living death. My tendency to please, to give in to the requests of others, to try to smooth out the differences, those factors that I had already pinpointed previously and that led me to place myself in enneatype nine, appeared now before me as part of my seduction strategies, and how this was detrimental to me also appeared clearly.

Gradually, I connected with my inner strength, which presented itself in the form of a panther with agile and gentle movements, clearly determined to reach its goal, and I also saw clearly the ego's tendency to use it for its own aggrandizement, to make me feel powerful. I also understood that it was about using strength with humility, without becoming proud, putting my strength in the service of something greater.

I wondered to myself what it would be like to feel more real and stronger, and at the same time, to use strength with humility; the clear answer was, "step aside for the energy to flow." At that, and other moments, my two realities appeared: my inner being and my ego, totally antagonistic and in competition. This understanding that it was about allowing the energy to flow immediately conflicted with the ego wanting to take over, as I have mentioned before. So, I felt trapped between surrendering and controlling. Being in the service of something greater or acting for a supposed self-benefit.

From this point on, two themes began to appear in parallel: feeling my heart was closed and feeling that the most instinctual was forbidden to me. So, from here two lines of work opened up and intertwined. I began to understand that to open my heart I had to "lose" my head. I had already seen this conflict almost a year before, but now it appeared with great clarity: either I let myself flow, and opened my heart, or my ego was in charge, which I was now able to clearly locate in my head, in all the preconceived ideas about myself and the world. That whole set of prejudices, beliefs, wrong conclusions that we are made up of and that largely remain out of reach of our awareness and our volition or, in other words, remain unconscious even though we act them out every day.

As the personal work continued between experiences, when I attended a new session it was with an idea that I wished to explore. It was not about directing or manipulating the experience from the head, but I discovered that if I approached a session with an intention, with a sincere question, one way or another, ayahuasca gave me the answer.

At this point I began to feel the need to connect with my inner "guide," that wiser part of us that we usually do not listen to. The session I came to with this intention began with a vision of the forces of evil unfolding with all their ferocity; at that moment I felt small, very small, and I understood that I am alone (we are alone), and that I alone have to confront this reality and find my way as best as I know how; all I have to do is to bring a little bit of light to wherever I pass. I also came to the understanding again that I have to blossom, that my heart is closed.

In contrast, the next experience led me to connect to the instinctual; I feel an irrepressible desire to suck my thumb like small children do, and I am immediately reminded of my father's forbidding us to use a dummy when we were babies; and I discover, to my astonishment, how sucking my thumb is directly related to the whole body's energetic circuit and especially with the lower part. As I am sucking my thumb, my lower abdomen, genitals and legs become integrated in the inner body image. I feel my entire body as a living unit, full of life. Suddenly, I need to touch the ground, roll around on it. I begin to understand *how the instinctual has remained outside of me: my father forbidding the dummy and sucking our thumb, my mother using euphemisms to name physiological processes (wee-wee and such like). The basic, the instinctual, the biological had remained outside of my interests in life. I felt it was shameful to have basic needs and give them a place. In my house, being hungry or showing one was very hungry was rude, and I was overeating also. One should eat little, with austerity . . . without giving it importance; everything was "ethereal."*

During the following months, I took care of my basic needs, food, contact, etc. The effect was that the next session consisted in feeling myself on earth, being a woman among women. It seems I have come down from the "ethereal" to be more real, more of flesh and blood.

I begin to question my belonging to the enneatype Laziness. I already have many understandings that are taking me in another direction, although I do not know what the key is, what my structure is. When I came to the next experience my intention is to connect with my little girl, my innocence. I immediately hear a powerful voice that says to me: "What you are is proud and all that you have done so far has been purely out of pride and wanting to get your own way." My whole life flashes before me and I see how I have been contaminated by pride. To get my own way, not accepting what life offers me, wanting to be lord and master of everything and above all else.

I feel deeply ashamed of myself. I feel like a little girl, tiny, vulnerable, and afraid. Another self appears before me, my character, furious, wanting to dominate me and take over again. I ask for help to whoever can protect me. I am terrified of what I am seeing: the little girl I am internally and the power that my "machine" has. It was a real struggle, an intense struggle in which I managed to avoid "the other"— my machine—taking control of me. I was exhausted at the end of the experience. In following sessions, I went deeper into this understanding of my whole life as a great farce. The feeling of shame is still very present. I ask forgiveness for so much arrogance.

I am beginning to understand, in my daily life (as I have already mentioned before, what is understood in a session takes time to become clear in real life), that the real work consists in laying aside the personal, interfering as little as possible with "what is"; becoming a channel somehow. The learning of non-doing that I am still immersed in so many years later.

Another strand of work, due to beginning to feel myself a woman among women, was the relationship with my mother and how I regarded her. How I had perceived her until then and how I could now see her with new eyes. When I was able to see her and accept her with all her greatness and her miseries, I was able to begin to reconcile myself with my own feminine essence and feel fully integrated in the great tide of women.

Slowly, I began coming down from my head and abandoning the warrior attitude. My scale of priorities began to change, becoming more focused on the inner than on the outer.

Over time, I am also reaching the understanding that I cannot do without my head. I need to learn to join my head and my heart, thought and intuition, knowledge and understanding.

In spite of all the experiences described, in 1993 I was still not able to piece together many of the understandings. As if it were a great puzzle, I had loose pieces and I could not see the complete picture yet.

My automatic behaviors still prevail; my lifelong characters still take over from time to time. With this battle, I come to a new session where I see my control, my control, my control. I cry bitterly for this reality and I wonder what is at the bottom of my heart, and all of a sudden, sweetness arises. Like a soft dance, shining, circular, sweet.

The struggle between my head and my heart was not over by far (and it still goes on today). I wondered then how it would be to be in the heart and not be so overprotective or condescending, how to be in the heart and establish limits, how to take care of myself.

I am coming to understand that opening the heart and inhabiting it means accepting all the immense pain inherent to life. Recognizing the pain of humanity made me cry deeply. We live surrounded by pain in our immediate environment, and of course, in everything that happens on the planet, but we learn to live as if none of all this had anything to do with us. We are desensitized, we isolate ourselves in our own little world, that is to say, we dehumanize ourselves.

At this point, already three or four years have passed since the first experience and familiar themes appear once again, but this time they have a new depth. The need to put myself in service and distance myself from anything that is not moving toward a concrete aim appears again. Men and seduction as the great temptation appear again. Either I give myself the chance to live life seriously, or I let myself get caught up in the mirage of conquest and seduction.

To open your heart and accept being in service of something bigger in itself requires renouncing the superficial in life. In one of the last experiences I had, I heard: "Have you not spent your whole life searching? Well, you have already found." The search for truth seems to end, at least in my case, in the acceptance of smallness and in putting myself in service of something that transcends me. I felt small, frightened, without knowing how to confront the return to reality from this new perspective. The only thing that reassured me was thinking that I simply had to let things be. Move softly, not wanting to do, attend to what is.

In one of the last sessions, I had the feeling that something wants to come out of my head, I need to loosen my neck even with massage. Finally, it comes out, I come out, it is myself leaving my body. Once again, I hear a voice asking me to show myself as I am, I feel naughty, shy, a child, even I do not know what I am like. I feel like a delicate butterfly of bright, delicate, almost transparent colors. I feel like a woman, now in this new way, and I want to be among women. I am reconciled with my mother, "I feel good, intimately satisfied, soft, feminine."

4.5 PSYCHOTHERAPEUTIC POSSIBILITIES OF THE NEW FANTASY-ENHANCING DRUGS*

I intend to speak here of two drugs, harmaline and ibogaine, which bear some resemblance to one another in chemical constitution and may be grouped together in terms of their effects.

Harmaline is the main alkaloid present in the seeds of the Middle Eastern plant *Peganum harmala,* and is also present in the bark of various species of South American climbers of the genus *Banisteriopsis.* This bark is the principal ingredient in the preparation of the drink used by the Indians of the headwaters of the Amazon, mainly in connection with ritual and divination, and we now know[†] that at least among some of the Indians it must have been the center of their culture since the Paleolithic times.

Aside from these two source plants of harmaline (and related alkaloids), this substance deserves special attention because of its close resemblance to another that is presumably a metabolite of the mammalian pineal gland. Both the pineal gland and the retina are unique in the presence of an enzyme, HIOMT, which permits the methylation of serotonin, a step to the synthesis of melatonin. And we know that melatonin, in the presence of pineal tissue can itself turn, by the loss of water, into 10-methoxy-harmalan,[‡] a positional isomer of harmaline.[§]

I have reported elsewhere[¶] that a study carried out at the University

---

*This essay was a paper presented by Claudio Naranjo (who was on a leave of absence from the University of Chile at the time) for the Institute of Personality Assessment and Research, University of California, Berkeley, at "Drugs, Psychedelic and Narcotic," Mendocino State Hospital, Talmadge, California, University of California, San Francisco Medical Center, Continuing Education in Health Sciences.

[†]G. Reichel-Dolmatoff, "Rock Paintings of the Vaupés: An Essay of Interpretation," *Folklore Americas* 27 (1967): 107–12.

[‡]W. McIsaac, *Biochemica et Biophysica Acta* 52 (1967): 607–9.

[§]Melatonin + C_2H_5OH + disulfiram ?? → in vivo human 10-methoxy-harmalan.

[¶]Claudio Naranjo, "Psychotropic Properties of the Harmala Alkaloids," in *Ethnopharmacologic Search for Psychoactive Drugs: Proceedings of a Symposium held in San Francisco, California, January 28–30, 1967,* ed. D. Efron et al. (Washington, D.C.: U.S. Government Print Office, 1967).

of Chile demonstrated that 10-methoxy-harmalan, when administered to humans, elicited subjective effects quite similar to those of harmaline. This naturally invites speculation as to the role of the pineal body in altered states of consciousness, desirable or undesirable. The similarity between harmaline and the pineal beta-carbolines suggests that the activity of the plant alkaloid may be understood in terms of its functional equivalence with a natural compound. If the latter is held under usual conditions in a state of chemical equilibrium, where it is responsible for the maintenance of the ordinary waking state, harmaline would disrupt such a state in a direction that already lies within the possibilities of the organism.

Ibogaine is probably the most important of the 12 alkaloids found in the root of the African plant *Tabernanthe iboga,* which grows mainly in the Congo and Gabon, and we know much less of the native uses of iboga than we know of the plants containing harmala alkaloids.

Dybrowsky and Landrin,[*] who were the first to extract the alkaloid, reported at the turn of the [last] century that it was used as a stimulant, as an aphrodisiac, and as an inebriant, which would produce an identical effect to alcohol without interfering with thought processes. While the last part of the statement may be said to be true, the comparison with alcohol does not fit with what we know of the drug. Ibogaine is not a CNS (central nervous system) depressant but is a stimulant[†] and the subjective effect induced by large doses has more resemblance to those of hallucinogens than those of hypnotics. Such a resemblance still is very fragmentary, for the effects of both harmaline and ibogaine are quite unique among the psychoactive drugs. No better term can be found to describe these effects than that proposed some years ago by Dr. William Turner, one of the pioneer investigators of the South American *Banisteriopsis* drink.

That author[‡] proposed reintroducing the term *oneirophrenia,* used

---

[*] J. Dybromky and E. Landrin, *Compt. Rend.* 133 (1901): 748.

[†] J. A. Schneider and E. B. Sigg, *Ann. N. Y. Acad. Sci.* 66 (1957): 765.

[‡] W. Turner, "Experiences with Primary Process Thinking," *Psychiat. Quart.* 37, no. 3 (July, 1963): 476–88

for the first time by Meduna, to designate drug-induced states that differ from the psychotomimetic by the absence of all symptoms of the psychotic range and yet share with the psychotic or psychotomimetic experience the prominence of primary process thinking. Harmaline* and ibogaine characteristically elicit such a state, for their psychological effect is one much like the bringing about of dream phenomena without loss of consciousness, changes in the perception of the environment, delusions, or formal alterations of thinking and depersonalization. In short, we may speak of an enhancement of fantasy that, remarkable as it may be, does not interfere with ego functions. Such an enhancement of fantasy, as we will see, is in the nature of both an increase in vividness of visual imagery (which takes on an eidetic quality) and an increased spontaneity of the content, which resembles that of true dreams more than that of ordinary daydreams.

In a way, neither harmaline nor iboga may be said to be new. Of course, each has been used for centuries by people in Asia, Africa, and South America, mostly as a part of rituals intended to bring the individual into contact with the realm of myth. But aside from such traditional uses, both alkaloids have been introduced into medical practice several decades ago. Iboga extract has been available in European drugstores for over thirty years as a tonic or stimulant, and we may well understand this empirically observed effect after the demonstration that the alkaloid is an inhibitor of monoamino oxidase (MAO). Harmaline, on the other hand, is a component of the alkaloid extract of *Banisteriopsis,* which, under the name *Banisterine,* was reported by Lewin[†] and others as an anti-Parkinsonian agent and, in general, as an inhibitor of extrapyramidal hypertonus.

It was probably the one-sided emphasis of the times on the somatic aspects of medicine that accounted for a lack of any systematic

---

*L. Lewin, *Banisteria Caapi. ein neues Rauschgift und Heilmittel* (Berlin: Georg Stiller, 1930).

[†]L. Lewin, *Banisteria Caapi. ein neues Rauschgift und Heilmittel* (Berlin: Georg Stiller, 1930).

investigation of the effects of these drugs which would be considered "toxic" from the standpoint of pure chemotherapy. By contrast, it is the harmaline and ibogaine intoxications that are of greatest interest from the point of view of psychological exploration or of psychotherapeutic endeavor. At the dosage level of 4–5 mg/kg* both harmaline and ibogaine elicit subjective reactions such as will be described in the following pages, which last for approximately six hours. In addition to this, about 50 percent of the subjects receiving either drug experience dizziness, incoordination, nausea, and vomiting at some point or other in the session. This vomiting is central in origin, for it is no less frequent when the alkaloids are administered intravenously, and it is greatly influenced by psychological factors. Some persons may feel nausea when dealing with specific topics, for instance, and in general there is an inverse relationship between the presence of physical symptoms and the richness of the psychological experience. This suggests that physical symptomology may be in the nature of conversion phenomena arising as a substitution and defense in the face of the psychological expression of certain experiences.

Harmaline is a mild parasympathomimetic, causing a slight decrease in heart rate and blood pressure, and an overdosage may also cause diarrhea. Both drugs most often elicit a state of drowsiness in which the patient does not want to move, open his eyes, or attend to the environment. Many are disturbed by lights and cover their closed eyes with their hands or ask for the lights to be turned off. Sounds or noises, too, can be disturbing, and this should be taken into account in choosing the appropriate place and time for a session. If the tendency to sleep is too pronounced, the patient's withdrawal may interfere with a meaningful communication, and this may be counteracted by other drugs. Many of my colleagues in Chile are now using associations of ibogaine or harmaline with methedrine or amphetamine derivatives with feeling-

---

*Or 25 percent of that dosage intravenously.

enhancing properties, like methylenedioxyamphetamine (MDA).* Such associations have interesting effects of their own with which I will not deal on this occasion.

In a study on the psychological effects of harmaline that we carried out in Chile during 1963–64, we noticed that one of the most remarkable aspects of the fantasy reported by the experimental subjects was its content-constancy. Even though the volunteers to whom we were administering the drug were not informed of each other's experiences or of the Indian medicine men's experiences under its effects, we soon realized that certain themes or images kept reappearing in the sessions of many individuals, suggesting a typical world of harmaline, shared by our sophisticated subjects and the Indians. Some of the more frequent and at the same time more intriguing themes to us, for instance, were those of tigers and Negroes, neither of which are seen in Chile, but which were reported by about 30 percent of the volunteers.†

By reflecting on images such as these with little apparent relevance to the subjects' personal lives but indicative of some shared domain of the psyche that harmaline was opening up to them, we soon realized that we were dealing with the same sort of psychological phenomena that Jung encountered in his study of dreams and active imagination, and for which he introduced the word *archetype* into psychological literature. Whatever our interpretation of these images and whatever our explanation of their repeated presentation among individuals of different interests and temperaments, they came to us as a fact. If a demonstration were required for the existence of archetypes, I believe that the content analysis of harmaline experiences is it. As far as I know, Jung did not speak of a "Negro" or "feline" archetype, but we need not be that

---

*C. Naranjo, A. Shulgin, and T. Sargent, "Evaluation of 3,4-methylenedioxyamphetamine (MDA) as an Adjunct to Psychotherapy," *Medicina et Pharmacologia experimentalis* 17, no. 4 (1967): 359–64.

†Claudio Naranjo, "Psychological Aspects of the Yagé Experience in an Experimental Setting," Institute of Personality Assessment and Research, University of California, Berkeley, 1965.

surprised at their presentation in a drug experience. Exotic as a tiger or lion may be as a physical reality, the Western mind has needed their image to signify psychological realities in literature, heraldic emblems, or plain advertising, such as "Put a tiger in your tank."* And we see the effect of the Negro together with the big cat as a psychological trigger in both the universal appeal of "Little Black Sambo"† and in the emotional involvement, much beyond politics and practicality, of the Black Panther movement today.

But the sphere of harmaline is archetypal beyond isolated images such as tigers or Negroes, prominent as they are. To give you a more precise idea of the quality of a harmaline experience, and as an introduction to the question of a therapeutic significance as well, I think that nothing may be better than quoting from one particular session. This is from one of our experimental subjects, a professional of average standing in terms of adjustment to life, according to interviews, and average neuroticism as judged by Cattell's 16 personality factors or estimated from the TAT (thematic apperception test). When questioned about his interest in volunteering, he expressed a feeling of incompleteness about his present life, which was too routine for him. This made him want to travel and also to know more about himself, about his real wants and possibilities.

Soon after the intravenous injection of 100 mg of harmaline, the subject reported a feeling of elation associated with the sensation of being suspended in empty space. Since nothing else developed spontaneously during thirty minutes, I decided to initiate a guided daydream in the standard fashion. Upon the suggestion of climbing a mountain he visualized and felt that he was doing so with a group of friends, and

---

*This is a reference to oil company Exxon's campaign "Put a tiger in your tank" (fuel) that uses the tiger as a mascot, a symbol of the fierceness of their fuels and their results in the engines of consumers. (*Note from the editor of the Spanish edition.*)
†*The Story of Little Black Sambo* is a children's book written by Scottish author Helen Bannerman, who lived in Madras, in southern India, for thirty-two years. It was first published in English in London in 1899. (*Note from the editor of the Spanish edition.*)

during the following half hour uninterruptedly described the events and experiences of the ascension. This was a very realistic sequence, which he related with a warmth and enthusiasm that I had never known in him before:

"We go as if wanting to prolong this joy of friendship . . . people made of a same fiber . . . we all enjoy this communication . . . "

My notes of the climbing occupy several pages and end with the image of the group upon the summit, thirsty and sweating, surrounded by a magnificent landscape, enjoying the feeling of having conquered oneself and that of being among friends, in contact.

Then there came, at my suggestion, the fantasy of flying, that of diving into the sea (at first postponed as deadly) and sinking to the ocean floor. There is much feeling at each stage, from dread to delight, and now a fairy tale began to unfold with the subject as principal character.

" . . . there could be a treasure here, as in the stories. I lie down. We'll see later . . . being measured by the sand. . . . Yes, it could be a story . . . I might invent some reason for having gotten here: shipwreck, attempted suicide, and so on. I might walk, and find a coffer behind a rock. One story could be that a princess has the key hidden in her bosom; or, alternatively, I may be able to open the padlock, and the Court of the Sea comes blaming me for the crime. Both are good. Let us start with the second alternative. I open it: pearls and stuff. There should be something else. What person that can fly wants pearls!

"But what is not in the coffer is next to it, with her father. She is what was missing.

"I am questioned. The old man speaks with a voice that conveys noble authority. Intrinsic nobility. A pausing, serene voice with authority, but sweetness too. He goes into things, into their essence. He does not get lost, he does not deceive himself. He shows cool passion. I believe he knows perfectly well why I am here. Not the others . . . "

The story goes on for about twenty more pages in my fragmentary notes:

Walking into the city, receiving absolution from the king, sitting next to the princess at the royal table, further acquaintance, until "the jigsaw puzzle of myself is complete. Such is love: being whole, finding the missing piece."

There is tragedy in the knowledge that he is going to leave sometime, and fleeting guilt in face of the princess's father. But his eyes approve, and his smile. Marriage follows, in "a church that teaches an aesthetic dimension of religion. . . . It is the Temple, purely so, without the surname of any religion. The place where 'communion' is effected with the Highest, with Whatever it may be. . . . Everything is as it must be . . . austere, yet regal." Then the altar, "like a pyramid; the priest, almost too human; and the music . . . just to hear this music, it would be worthwhile to marry a hundred times." There follows a party, with the villagers, peasants, and their songs. The newlyweds go to their cabin. They live, they work. "What I always longed to see in work: each does what he wants and when he wants it." He wants to know more of the people of this kingdom since he knows that he is leaving in a week, and he will not see them again. Where do they come from? They do not know. They have a vague reminiscence of having once been somewhere else.

"They know themselves to be different from ordinary men and don't envy them. They have carried civilization to the point to which it served them. Not further, like us, to the point of being left with nothing . . . with nothing inside, for all the advancement of technology. Science applied to nothing. . . . Not these people. They found their balance. They are there. They know that the energy that they did not spend in manufacturing they spend in something more essential: the perfecting of themselves. In a simple and clear manner, like a line. For love. In that they spend their energy, in loving quietly, in harmony, blissfully. And consciously happy, not happy like idiots."

The time for leaving comes, and he leaves without saying goodbye.

The name of the princess enables him to trespass the city walls. He returns to the starting point of his adventure, realizing now how far he had walked. After emerging at the surface of the ocean he understands that there is no signal that he can leave to show him the way back. He is about to let go of the only chance of returning. And he does. He flies away. He feels as if he had been flying all day. In face of the beauty of sunset he opens his mouth, since his eyes are not enough to absorb so much. He finally rests on a beach, feeling intensely alive, as if every pore of his skin were a complete being.

How can we understand that the conception of this story may have been a life-changing experience? For the subject reports, after three years, that this has affected his work, his relationships, and his feeling of himself up to this date. The words in which he explains it are close to those used by the subject of the session previously commented upon. He says that he had never before felt so much *himself* as during the telling of the story, and never before had he *expressed* himself so fully. Feelings and conceptions that went into the building of the tale proceeded fluently and obviously from himself as his real feelings and point of view, which always had been in him and did not have to be "invented." Thus, he experienced himself as *creative.* The consequence of the experience was self-assuredness, self-trust, and self-acceptance, related to the notion that he had heretofore unsuspected inner riches. He felt more a person, with a place and function in the world.

I think that we must not understand the self-assurance and feeling of personal worth stemming from the session as merely the result of being able to say, "See what a nice story I can make up," "See how imaginative I am." From the subject's comments it is clear that his self-confidence stems from an intense feeling of himself, a contacting of his inner reality, of which the story is but an outward manifestation.

In fact, several fragments of the narrative are clear expressions of this experience: the openness to friendship and landscape while climbing, the ecstasy and freedom of flying, the combination of wholehearted participation and the knowledge that all is transitory during the adventure under water; the feeling of aliveness in every pore, all convey the peak experience quality of the feeling of self.

In speaking of the "self" in connection with this session, I have been retaining the subject's use of the term, which was spontaneous and devoid of associations with psychological literature. Yet their experience might be adequately understood both in terms of Karen Horney's "true self" or what is called "Self" by Jung. Horney stressed the distinction between the "true self" and the "idealized self," pointing out that in a neurosis the person's true urges, feelings, and thoughts are substituted by others that he only believes are his. These are compulsive desires, emotions, and ideas stemming from the need to live up to the image, which in turn is the opposite of living from one's spontaneous motivations.

Jung, on the other hand, formulated the Self as the seat of consciousness in a state of psychic integration and completeness that entails contact with the archetypes of the collective unconscious. It is reasonable to expect that the more a person develops awareness of his own being, the more he will partake of a common core of human experience.

The long dreamlike sequence quoted above, with its forbidden treasure, kings, and good life is, of course, archetypal in every detail, and could illustrate many classical images, like the wise old man, the ideal woman, marriage, the cross, the pyramid, the guarded city, the ideal community, etc.

The mythical style of harmaline sessions is only one side of them, though, and by attending to another side I think that we may gain some insight into the nature of archetypes. This other side is as extremely instinctual as I have seen in fantasy, both in the domains of aggression (mostly predatory aggression) and sex. Just as some sessions appear to be the reenacting of myths or fairy tales, others consist of a series of bloody scenes of all sorts, scenes of incest or other forms of sexual activity, or combinations thereof. These dreamlike sequences are in their spontaneity more extreme than anything normally reported by the subjects or patients in their free associations or dreams, and unlike the visions that some of them have reported under mescaline or LSD. In fact, the effects of both types of drug seem to stand in polar opposition, those of the common hallucinogens being a lofty and "angelic" domain of aesthetic feelings, empathy, and a sense of oneness with all things, whereas the domain of the oneirophrenics is that Freudian underworld of animal impulse and regression.

In general, the more destructive the content of fantasy, the less archetypal or mythical it appears, so that one is tempted to believe that the archetypal expression proper (particularly when it involves images such as tigers, snakes, or dragons) corresponds to some kind of harmonious integration of instinctual forces, where they are still recognizable but not fragmenting the individual in their conflict. In some instances one can witness the transition between these two styles of expression, the instinctual and the mythical, and understand how myth is to passion as form is to content or like the skeleton to the flesh, and instinct may either animate myth by becoming its blood, so to say, or be complete chaos.

The session here reported is of a patient with a compulsive character neurosis and various symptoms of anxiety and depression for which he had been in treatment for over five years. The fragment reported here constitutes about 75 percent of the total session after the intake of 300 mg of harmaline by mouth and consists of my notes of his continuous monologue from a time shortly after the onset of the drug's effect. Naturally, the succession of the images took place in a tempo much slower than that of the reading of this transcript.

"This is a dark cloister. There are white and red tiles. The sun filters through purple curtains. A nun appears. She has Christ's stigmata in her feet and hands. The mermaid appears and laughs. She says, 'I have never seen such a stupid woman.' The nun says, 'Only the spirit is of value.' The mermaid says, 'Only the body is of value.' Suddenly, the nun begins to be illuminated from above. It is celestial light. She begins to rise in a cloud. Several little angels are with her. She drifts on

the cloud over the sea. The mermaid appears behind a rock. With her is the nurse, who kills babies to make sausage. 'See, my friend, how this nun travels on a cloud,' says the mermaid to her assistant. The nurse produces a broom, puts on her hat, and flies after the nun. She scratches the cloud with a pin, and it deflates. The nun is drowned, but she is in ecstasy so that she doesn't notice it. She reaches the bottom of the ocean. Her clothes are gone. She is naked. She doesn't look like a nun anymore. The stigmata are gone. The fishes bring her a crown made of algae, and she becomes a mermaid with a fish's tail. She forgets what she has been, and sets out to travel along the ocean floor. A triton is now kissing her. They make love on a rock." (Subject feels nausea. Music in the room conveys "repressed feeling" to him.)

He continues: "They had sex. This was the first time the nun had had intercourse. She became settled on a rock where she had a house made of jade. There was a large mahogany bed with a cherry-colored spread. She is nothing of what she used to be. She is stark naked and is wearing a coral necklace. Her hair is loose. She has a beautiful body with large breasts and wide hips. She is not a mermaid anymore but has two legs. She is insatiable. Proserpina is her name. Silvery fish wait on her. The mermaid is desirous of sexual intercourse. She calls tritons to make love to her. In the evenings she wanders about with the attendant nurse, who is also naked. They look for dead sailors and bring them back to life. Proserpina makes love to them and kills them again. Now she goes to the beach and sleeps on the sand. Some fishermen come. She calls them. After making love with all of them, she is bored and she goes to the city. She dries her hair and wears stockings. She is a whore. She earns good money and buys herself a pretty house. She likes beautiful objects—silverware, ebony, jewelry, antiques. She goes about in nightgowns, even in the street. But one day she passes in front of a poor church at the time of a funeral mass. Upon seeing the burning candles and smelling the incense she remembers what she had been. She sells all that she has and gives the money to the poor. She gives her house as an asylum. She goes about in poverty, barefoot. She walks for three days and three nights until she reaches a distant monastery. She becomes a nun once more. But she does not live long. She becomes ill and dies within a week. She rises to heaven with the angels. The mermaid tries to destroy her again, but it is impossible now, so she commits suicide. She leaves her jewelry to a friend and drowns herself."

I have quoted at length because this was one of the most remarkable sessions in terms of its beneficial effect. The patient had been in psychiatric treatment for five years—psychoanalysis, analytic group therapy, Schultz's autogenic training, and all of it—with poor results. At the time of the session he felt ineffectual and overly submissive, burdened by anxiety, depression, and interminable brooding, fearful of other people's opinions and of his own homosexual inclinations. The session with harmaline, as can be seen, was practically a monologue uninterrupted by interpretations, questions, or attempts to direct the development of the experience, and was, like the previous sessions reported here, like a fairy tale, quite unrelated (in its superficial appearance) to his life and problems.

The immediate effect of the session was a state of irritability with some impulsivity and assertiveness, which the patient described as a tyrannical streak and took him by surprise more than it worried him. Still, within two months he felt stronger and more independent, capable of taking the authority needed in his work, but concerned with his excessive violence. His depression, anxiety, and fear of others had disappeared. His violence, too, diminished gradually within three more months, without further psychotherapeutic aid.

In considering this session I feel tempted to speak of an "archetypal catharsis," a mythical outlet for the instinctual, in contrast with the more personal types of abreaction that we come across more frequently in psychotherapy. The orgiastic fantasy described above was as opposite as it could be to this patient's life—unfree and compulsive in the literal sense of the term—and apparently served as a bridge between his ordinary lack of spontaneity and a type of behavior closer to the style of his fantasy. Just as the training of a behavior pattern through imaginary display serves as a bridge toward its enacting in real life in the practice of Behavior Therapy, it seems from sessions like those quoted above that the process of self-expression in the domain of imagery, made possible by this drug, can serve as a link toward further self-expression in life, in the case of persons that are constricted in their spontaneity by peculiar personality patterns.

Compared to the effects of harmaline, those of ibogaine seem less exotic. Though archetypal contents are common, animals are prominent in the visions and, in general, man-the-animal is reflected therein, the quality of fantasy is in general more personal, involving the subject himself and his parents or significant others. At the same time the fantasy evoked by ibogaine is easier to manipulate by the subjects on their own initiative or that of the psychotherapist, so that more often than with any other drug that I know he can stop to contemplate a scene, go back to a previous one, explore an alternative to a given sequence, reenact a previous dream, and so on. This ease with which the events in an ibogaine session can be handled and the experience channeled through a desired domain is probably part of the reason for the success observed by many psychotherapists using the drug as an adjunct. In my own experience, I have been more impressed by the enduring effects resulting from ibogaine sessions than by those from sessions conducted with any other drug. Time limitations will not permit much clinical illustration of the effects of ibogaine, indispensable as this material seems to me if the aim is to communicate more than a very abstract notion of the reactions to the drug. I will therefore not attempt to give you a detailed view of any complete session but rather focus on a few images and upon their significance in a psychotherapeutic context.

The following sequence was described by a young psychiatrist as soon as he decided to lie down and close his eyes, about forty-five minutes after the onset of the drug's effects:

At first he saw as in a closeup, the face of his father. He was making faces at the patient as if in a game, with a contented smile. He commented at this point that this is how his father must actually have appeared to him as a small boy. It was an "unfamiliar yet very familiar" sight, as something forgotten by him for many years. But suddenly, the expression on his father's face changed into a contortion of rage. As he was attending to this, the scene changed, and now he saw a naked woman hiding her face behind her arms in obvious fear. Next to this, he saw his father also naked, falling upon the woman in a sexual attack. He could sense controlled rage in the woman, whom he now identified as his mother.

At this point I asked the subject to have his father and mother talk to each other, as a means of bringing out the latent content of the images. "What does she say?" "Go away." "What does he feel?" He could not imagine that. "Maybe perplexity," he suggested. This was an appropriate moment to take another step in the direction of making the feelings involved in the scene conscious and explicit. "Be your father now." I said to him. "Become him to the best of your dramatic ability and hear what she has said to you." Now, impersonating his father, he felt, not perplexity, but great sorrow, suffering, and anger at being rejected.

Short as this episode was, it brought about a drastic change in this subject's view of his parents, and therefore in his feelings toward them. In the following days he commented that only now he saw how much he had been identifying with his mother and looking at things through her eyes. Part of such a view was the blaming of his father, and more than that, of man, which had interfered with his own assertiveness and masculinity. In contrast to his habitual idealization of his mother as fully loving and his perception of his father as a selfish brute, he now had a feeling of "knowing them as they really are." He wrote: "I see my mother as hard, with no affection and afraid, and I no longer regard my father as that insensitive being who has hurt her with his love affairs, but as somebody who wants to open the gates of her love, without succeeding. Yet I feel compassion toward my mother."

Compared to the dramatic quality of the psychedelic experiences, the episode under discussion might appear to be insignificant or trivial, and yet it was the key to a radical shift in attitudes. I think that this may be said of ibogaine experiences in general when compared to the effect of LSD-like drugs. The type of contact that is affected with unconscious material is here symbolic, rather than in the form of free-floating emotions, and therefore is articulate and possible to assimilate in the form of enduring insights. Such insights generally arise when a fantasy or assumption that was hitherto unconscious or implicit becomes consciously revealed with such clarity that the person's mature self cannot but see its deep-rooted fallacy.

One more instance may clarify this further.

I was showing a patient a photograph of his mother. At first he saw what he had always seen and what he wanted to see: his idealized mother, the mother that he needed to see to avoid an anxiety too great for him to cope with. She was shown there knitting and looking down fixedly at her yarn. For some time he saw her as he usually did—as a loving mother devoted to the things of the house—but by looking further there came a moment when he could see through his image. Once the habitual pattern was obvious and discussed, he was naturally free to go beyond it; to inquire whether the reality caught by the camera truly fitted the form of his automatic perception. Then he noticed hatred and hardness in his mother's glance. He writes: "I then realized that she had hated me, that in her hatred for my father she had included my sister and myself. I realized that she had utilized us, desecrating our feelings.

"I hated her and stimulated by the doctor I confronted her with her attitude, her lack of concern for our feelings and her battle with my father. I insulted her aloud with violence in all the frustration and withholding of a lifetime, calling her a witch, a hysteric, a monster."

Since his voice still didn't convey the violence that he said that he was feeling I had him repeat his utterances again and again until he could translate his emotion into the nonverbal aspect of his expression. Finally I asked him to beat his parents in fantasy. He pounded the pillow that stood for them until he felt physically tired. The patient's anger was something so alien to his everyday awareness that I was afraid that if he did not experience it now as fully as possible, he might repress it once more. Much of the session was devoted to experiences such as this one confronting and impersonating different persons in his family and expressing much criticism in the process. The end result in terms of insight was a lasting one and can be illustrated by contrasting an autobiographical account written in the week prior to this session with what he wrote in the week following. Before the session he had written:

"The first eight years of my life I lived in the countryside. This was a magical time! In these years I knew the taste of dust in summer, of grass in spring, the river where I would go out bathing with Peter, my idol of that period, a young dark-skinned peasant with a mole near his mouth. My parents seem like cardboard figures in my memory. Peter eclipses all the rest. I don't remember feelings of guilt or frustration. I lived in a primitive way. Like a sponge I absorbed local superstitions, I searched for hidden treasures, and believed in God and the Devil with the same force as my peasant companions.

"I was a loved boy, and my mother was not the frustrated woman that she became later. She gave me the love that I needed and beat me when I deserved it. Nothing more."

And he ended the first chapter of this autobiography with the following overall view:

"I was an ordinary boy who was lucky enough to be liked by everybody. Neither masturbation nor my love for Peter nor my amorous attempts with some girls had blurred that innocence that children have when they know no frustrations or traumas and who live in an atmosphere where things are given, not explained. There was something in me of that myth of the 'innocent savage uncorrupted by civilization.'

And yet my mother was a civilized woman—or should I say balanced?— who provided me with reading and a wonderful, unforgettable Christmas.

"Yes, all that time was truly magic!"

Notice the contrast between this version and the following paragraphs written after the session:

"As a boy I was always hiding behind Mother's skirts. I went from one woman to another. My father seems so nonexistent. Maybe he was not there already . . . I was a rather timid boy, very prone to crying, very fearful. I had many fears, of a thousand things, supernatural and natural.

"Many times I wished that my mother would die. I once attempted suicide to punish them. So that they would learn! In their reciprocal hatred, my mother forgot what she always displayed with pride: her capability of being a mother. And my father was hypocritical. I used to suffer very much in the beginning. According to my mother we had to hate my father. Neither of us wanted that at first, in spite of seeing that she was right in some of her complaints. But not in her yelling or her dramatic scenes. This lasted for about eight years. I thought I would go nuts, at first. When they had their fights we were helpless, used as weapons. 'This is your son,' they would say, to point out the negative qualities of the other. One was fighting against two sides without fighting. I used to cry, but later I took refuge in books. And I started to hate without saying it. I withdrew. They could not know what I thought or felt. The thing was to be invulnerable.

"After doing that for so long I cannot open up anymore. Perhaps the fear of that time is the same as today. If I felt hatred they would point at it as a defect and use it as a weapon."

The two cases presented thus far are similar in that they constitute a liberation from a mother identification and a breaking through to an independent view of the world. However, fantasy that can be exposed and reexamined with the help of ibogaine may be simpler than a parental image and still very important. I want to present you with one last example in order to give a broader perspective of the possibilities of the alkaloid and the exploration of unconscious fantasy.

This was the case of a woman in her late thirties who recalled very vividly at some point in her session an episode from her childhood. Her father had returned from a journey and was distributing gifts among the children. Before leaving, he had asked each one of them what he wanted. To that question our patient had answered that she did not want her father to spend more money, and would be quite content with anything inexpensive. In recalling this, it was obvious to the patient that she had wanted to be her father's favorite daughter in playing . . . a sweet considerate and understanding role, in contrast to that of her achieving sister. In this she had succeeded.

As she attended to this memory, she became aware of how frustrated she had felt when her father actually carried out her suggestion, bringing her a gift that could not be compared to her sister's. This was a little brooch in the form of a dog, which she recalled putting inside a matchbox. But now she remembered something that felt like a discovery. She now saw very clearly that in her disappointment and anger she had imagined the little dog biting off her father's genitals. In recalling this, she felt that it was herself, greedily and revengefully castrating her father, using the image of the dog, and it seemed to her that not even at the time of this event had she allowed herself to become aware of this fantasy.

After remembering the scene, she also remembered feeling guilty for her imaginary action, and then she realized that she had been feeling guilty toward her father throughout her whole life. The transient mental event, or what appeared to be that, had radically altered her relationship with her father, to whom she was not close anymore. After realizing, now, that up to this very moment in her life she had been feeling guilty for her childish fantasy, she could not fail to evaluate the situation with more mature eyes. Upon the suggestion of looking at the situation from her father's point of view, it was clear to her that he could forgive her, and she could forgive herself too. Her relationship to her father was actually reestablished with joy to both of them during the last months of his life.

I think that the therapeutic event just described may be understood in at least two ways. One is that of taking the patient's words literally, in which case we must accept that an imaginary action and even an unacknowledged one may weigh as much as an overt action, and be treated as such by the unconscious mind. The other alternative is thinking that the patient did not actually have the fantasy of castration at the moment evoked, but this is in the nature of a screen memory and the projection in symbolic terms of feelings of chronic grief and anger that were triggered by such an incident. That is to say, the translation of such feeling into a visual display would be only part of the ibogaine experience. If this were so, it is evident that this may be of crucial importance for the process of becoming aware of such feelings, for merely feeling them throughout a lifetime, in this case, had not been sufficient to understand them.

I would not like to leave the impression that I am regarding ibogaine like a psychiatric panacea bringing about changes by itself. I believe that many drugs may be utilized for the purpose of psychological exploration, but that drugs can be no more than an instrument. Just as the hypnotic state may be used either for theatrical demonstrations and entertainment or for therapy, and in the latter case the ways of utilizing it can range from overt suggestion to hypnoanalysis or hypnosynthesis, also drug-induced states may be used or not, and if used, there may be room for many approaches.

I doubt that there is anything that can be achieved with a drug that is not possible without it. Still, drugs may be psychological catalysts or facilitators that can compress a long psychotherapeutic process into a shorter time and may alter the prognostic picture in a given case. If ibogaine does not open a door by itself, it might be likened to the oil on the hinges.

4.6 IBOGAINE IN SMALL DOSES IN A PREPARED GROUP CONTEXT*

I think it was in 1963 when I found myself at the home of some friends in Santiago de Chile with Irineo Rosier, a Catholic missionary who had just published a book about the presence of God in the minds of coal miners in France. I was at that time absorbed in my studies on the effects of harmaline in experimental subjects, who, as research required, knew nothing of what they were ingesting, and therefore I had been struck by the fact that very often jaguars, tigers, and panthers appeared in their visions.

Regarding this, I explained to Rosier that the jaguar is an animal that the shamans of Colombia not only identify with, but whose appearance they seem to take on, at least in the eyes of others who have drunk yagé. Only then did Rosier tell me that he had lived in Gabon for a time, and that there he had encountered a similar fact; which is, that sorcerers identify with lions, and that on one occasion when a lion was shot, the bullet was found in the sorcerer's body.

This led me, naturally, to the idea that in Africa there might be a plant the effects of which were similar to those of yagé, and so I started to search for it in the literature on alkaloids that I was able to find in the library at the medical school, and it was not long before it seemed to me that ibogaine, an alkaloid somewhat similar to beta-carbolines in its chemical structure could, for its African origin, correspond to the substance in question.

Searching for more information about the effects of ibogaine, however, I found nothing about its psychological effects on human beings. I could only find two experimental studies—one on the effects of the alkaloid in the vagina of rats and the other on its action on the intestine

---

*Written in response to the invitation to close the first international conference on ibogaine in Tepotzlán, Mexico, March 2016.

of rabbits. Fortunately, however, I had no trouble obtaining ibogaine from a laboratory to carry out an experiment on myself, and although I have referred to it a couple of times (once in an interview filmed by Jonathan Dickinson), I will repeat here the essentials, for it was a teaching for me that will surely be useful to know for those who take this remarkable medicine.

Shortly after following the impulse to lie down, I felt the effect of the drug come on, and it seemed to me as if all the celestial bodies moved around me in circular orbits; even though it was not a hallucination as such, and not even a precise image, I had the clear feeling that everything in the universe was subject to a precise law of divine nature, while I, in the middle of it all, remained removed from that magnificent dance like a mean-spirited witness that implicitly refused to join in a celebratory and sacred movement of the whole. Such an ascertainment inspired me, naturally, to want to join that sort of universal dance I was contemplating, and I felt that I was willing enough to embrace that act of surrender. Only, I hesitated in taking the necessary step toward it; it was about taking a step that, translated into words, would be something like saying to God: "Thy will be done," but I hesitated because I understood that such a surrender to divine or cosmic will implied that I was nobody special. This came into conflict with an omnipresent wish to be important, which had always been a part of my life, and that is why I procrastinated, as one who had his hand on a switch, so that with a simple movement I could take that step so desired and so resisted. However, I rejected the possibility that in relinquishing control over my own life I would end up being just "dust," that is to say, not in the least remarkable; and so, in this way, seconds, or perhaps minutes passed, until I knew that a time that was given to me had come to an end, not as part of the pharmacological effect of ibogaine, but rather as an expression of a higher intelligence that considered me unworthy of greater attention. From then on, I experienced a simple cartoon: an animated film of which all I remember is the comic strip started with a rabbit going into a tree trunk, the triviality of which, as the hours of the effect wore on, was nevertheless a subtle torture—the torture of simple banality.

I was impressed by the experiment, for I felt that I had come across something bigger than I expected in the fleeting encounter with an intelligence that had rejected me. With this conviction, I began my experimentation with volunteers, to whom I offered individual sessions during the course of the following months.

The first of my subjects was Hernán, a talented dancer I had met shortly before, and in my book *The Healing Journey* I described his ecstasy over the beauty of a ray of blue light that dominated a great part of his experience. My friend's encounter with the light was something akin to an encounter with the divine, and the first session that I offered and witnessed turned out to be the most important one of all.

The thirty individual sessions that I accompanied confirmed my anticipation that iboga was, like harmine and harmaline, an oneirophrenic: a drug that does not produce the distortions of time and space characteristic of the better-known hallucinogens, nor the emotional effects of phenethylamines, which I had researched previously (and that today are mainly referred to as empathogens). People saw many images, including images similar to the ones described under the effects of yagé or ayahuasca, as characteristically, those of animals.

Ibogaine also helped people to understand themselves, or more specifically, to understand their pathologies; and this was sometimes combined with the appearance of an "inner voice" or guide, or with occasional regressions.

Like in the case of harmaline, however, it seemed to me that only some individuals especially predisposed to it had profoundly transformative experiences, and that led me to think that perhaps the best use of the drug consisted in associating it with another substance, similarly to how harmine is associated in ayahuasca with DMT.

I was just finishing my experiments with volunteers when I received a call from Richard Baker (subsequently successor of Suzuki Roshi in the Tasajara Zen monastery, who at that time was organizing the university extension courses and specifically, this conference), inviting me to take part in the now famous conference on LSD that was organized by the University of California. I asked if him I could, instead of speaking of LSD, talk about my recent studies of ibogaine; he accepted my proposal and this was the stimulus for writing the report that I then sent him and read on the day of the conference—which unfortunately has disappeared from my files and that Dick Baker himself was unable to find when years later I asked him for it following his move to Colorado, at a time when many of his papers were still in cardboard boxes.

Only after presenting at the LSD conference this report on ibogaine (the title of which included the expression "There and Then," alluding to understanding the past in contrast to the "here and now" so in vogue in the therapeutic culture of that time), did I meet Howard Lotsof, who had been in the audience and who briefly explained to me that he had experimented with ibogaine on himself, curing himself with it of an addiction to opium. I believe it was also him who told me about the existence of the D'Ivry-la-Bataille laboratory, who at that time had the monopoly over ibogaine, which was sold under the name of Lambarène and could be acquired in pharmacies in France as a *tonic*—a medication that had a stimulating effect and was recommended for convalescents. The owner of the laboratory, Dominique Bocher, showed an interest in my findings, and mentioned that one of his workers had once taken an entire tube of Lamabarène and seemed to have got drunk; sometime later, having shared with Bocher my observations about the value of the combination of ibogaine and MDA (to facilitate pharmacologically assisted therapy), he proposed registering a patent and carried out the relevant procedures. However, although that patent still exists, the combination of ibogaine with MDA never came into use, for MDA was prohibited shortly after, as it is toxic for some people and yet it was neither able to be predicted or even explained afterward how these are distinguished from those who tolerate it well.

Later on, I did a test with MDMA and this seemed to me a useful combination without the dangers of the previous one, and others also, among which the one that most struck me was the combination of ibogaine with MMDA-3A; but it was soon time for me to return to California (this time as a resident), and so my psychedelic research was put on hold. Only, in some way, my research was continued when I shared with my friend and colleague Leo Zeff the results of my work in Chile (as well as information on how he could obtain iboga extract from the French laboratory). Then I was intrigued to find that the first people who used this new drug in their group (in which I myself had trained in the previous years, and consequently the participants had heard me say that an inner guide may appear under its effects) began talking among themselves of "Mr. Iboga." I specifically remember a lady named Helen who suffered from irritable colon that had brought her lifelong affliction, and that healed in a single session thanks to a conversation with this character.

I have not followed closely the research that has been done since then through the work of Lotsoff, who inspired so many to become interested especially in the use of iboga as a therapy for fighting addictions; therefore, when I received the invitation to this conference, my reply was that I have nothing new to contribute, nor am I somebody who is particularly well informed on the subject, although I would happily carry out another study on ibogaine if I was provided with the medicine. Thanks to the positive reception of my proposal, I have conducted a new experiment almost fifty years after the one carried out under the auspices of the University of Chile in 1967.

This was done in Colombia under the auspices of the Center for Human Transformation, only this time it was not a study on iboga's effects on isolated subjects, as the case was in the sixties,* but in a group context, and similarly to how I have administered ayahuasca

---

*Another difference has been that on this occasion I have used the synthetic ibogaine that is being produced in Canada under the name *Remogen*—in view of the near extinction of *Tabernanthe iboga* in Gabon resulting from considerable medical consumption in ibogaine-assisted drug rehabilitation clinics that have appeared in many parts of the world.

during my recent works in Brazil. As I did then, I have once again used small doses of ibogaine (from 270–300 mg, in general) and not the large doses used in the context of African ritual and in rehabilitation clinics.

Many of the participants in this group were colleagues and disciples of Jorge Llano, the renowned therapist and shaman, author of *Las tres llamadas del alma* (the three callings of the soul), and the experiences that I shall examine in this report took place in the course of a single session that began at around five in the afternoon and went on until two or three in the morning. This group experience was preceded by certain preparatory activities, just as I have described previously concerning my transcriptions of retrospectives of group sessions with MDMA and ayahuasca.

Firstly, the group participants came to the ibogaine experience with a certain notion of how to meditate, and of an introduction to the psychology of the enneatypes; and also following a series of psychological exercises that had not only brought them awareness of themselves, but also had led them to establish bonds of intimacy and trust with their fellow participants. In addition, this preparation included an invitation to surrender—whether to the flow of verbal communication or to *spontaneous movement:* an invitation to a kind of spontaneity that goes beyond artistic improvisation, for it fosters what arises "of its own accord" when people do not voluntarily seek to move, and thus it favors the emergence of phenomena that are usually termed as *possession.* Lastly, participants of the group also took part in a series of sessions inspired by my "theory of the three loves"—with its concept that mental health not only depends on the recovery of erotic freedom, but also on the development of compassion and appreciative love.

When the group was gathered again the day following the experience, I carried out a short inquiry that confirmed my impressions of the sixties: a great deal of people had felt the impulse to remain lying down, particularly because trying to move or walk made them lose their balance; a few vomited, they had practically all seen images, many felt guided, they almost all said they had learned something about themselves, many relived childhood scenarios, and several mentioned experiences of regression to forgotten scenes. More frequently even than with ayahuasca, there were those who felt they went through a death, or they felt in contact with the spirit of deceased people.

As for the visions, I was intrigued not only by the descriptions of beautiful geometric, kaleidoscopic, or fractal shapes, which seemed to suggest a creative superabundance of the cosmos and the workings of a universal mind, but also by the appearance of animals and black people (which during my study on ayahuasca in the sixties I had interpreted as manifestations of awakening or a reintegration of the instinctual mind). In this case the images seemed even more archaic, suggesting that psychedelics can be classified according to proximity to the well-known domain of the chakras, with LSD in the crown, *Psilocybe* in the forehead, interpersonal drugs in the chest, and ayahuasca in the abdomen, while ibogaine seems to affect a region of the lower abdomen—even more earthly and bodily than the customary under the effect of ayahuasca—and accompanied by more aquatic images, as suggested by the visions of fish and turtles.

It is true that I cannot now say, as with my experiments with harmaline with Chilean volunteers during the sixties, that they were taking something unknown to them; on the contrary, this time they were all aware that they were ingesting the alkaloid of an African plant; however, I have no doubt that the images of snakes, felines, or fish were a translation of forms of consciousness rather than the result of a mere association of ideas.

When afterward I asked who in the group had had "a highly significant experience," almost all the people present raised their hands, and likewise they almost all reported having had a deeply healing experience. I then asked, with the aim of eliciting the most extraordinary statements, who had had "the most important experience of their lives," and now only nine people of the forty that had participated raised their hands. It seemed a significant proportion to me, although many of them had already experimented with yagé and mushrooms, and I shall begin this report citing their words (phrasing in roman type added for emphasis):

L.A.: *I started very fast and it was really nice for me as my body was guiding me. And it was guiding me to the pending issue in my life: to cry. I remember that I cried and cried. It was not a heartrending weeping, but a sweet weeping. I cried until there were no tears left. When I stopped crying, I felt I could breathe. That was one of the gifts: to breathe.*

I felt that my heart opened; and when my heart opened a very beautiful journey began. God told me there was still something I had to say. I started checking, and I realized that I still had to say yes to God.

Then my ego started: "What if the thing is very big?" And I thought: if it is big or small, it is equally valuable. Here began the great journey of my life, the one I needed. I said to myself: "Total surrender." I heard Luis say to me: "A great act of love." Then I approached him, and said to him: "Teacher, you are the expert; I would like you to explain it to me: what is a great act of love?" to which he replied: "You tell me." I thought for a while and said: "Total surrender, of course." Ultimately, in reality that was my whole journey. I understood that surrender must be total and in everything. Even when making love!

J.: *I was afraid and started to feel things in my body: that I was losing control and my head was shaking. I surrendered to God, somebody opened the door, and a feeling, and also an image of Jorge came in. I said: "Well, God and Jorge, may this medicine show me the way," and I surrendered. I closed my eyes and went on a deep, very deep journey: I started to cry and did not know why I was crying. My son appeared on my father's shoulders. I understood that I been fighting with my father for many years. He had done the best he was able to do for me all that time, and my son had understood it, before me. This was one of the great insights I received: to honor my father I am going to be the best father for my son, and the best husband for Laura, and really make it worthwhile that my father died for something. To give me life. And to pass life on, which is my son.*

Then I left the room (I asked David to accompany me) and I had a strong urge to vomit. As soon as I went out a silence sounded within me, everything was dark. My whole family started arriving, and from this lake huge black birds emerged, lifting me up. They put me down at one point, and that is when I felt even dizzier and vomited. Some spirits came, some black shadows, and they pulled me into the bathroom. I went into the bathroom and when I looked, the bathroom was a coffin. I looked back, and all my family was there. Was the coffin mine? I opened the coffin and there was nobody inside. I was being pushed, and I thought it was David that was pushing me, but I turned around and David was already far away. I began to feel that I was going crazy. Then I started to pray and ask the medicine again, and I went in. The bathroom was getting smaller and smaller and smaller: it was the coffin. I closed my eyes because everything went dark, I could only see if my eyes were closed; if I surrendered to the darkness and did not fight it. I closed my eyes and saw my son, Laura, my parents, they were all there. If this is my death, I shall die with dignity. I closed my eyes and died. From one moment to the next everything started vibrating and the bathroom exploded. Everything exploded except me. I looked at myself and I was complete. Everything exploded, and I felt a new spirit. All that darkness that had surrounded me now had color; I could now see the green of the grass. I could see my family that was saying to me: "Stand up then, do not lie there any longer." That is where I speak of a being born anew. There I was born to love. One of the greatest insights was experiencing things simply. Living from simplicity is so fulfilling. All this wanting to have so much, be so much and do so much is so egoistic, to fill up an emptiness I had. It is, as Jorge says, like having a cake here and to be thinking of another that does not exist; when I want to eat cake, there is none left, it has been eaten.

Then Igor approached and told us: "The medicine is shown to us like in dreams." It is like connecting with the Great Spirit and asking him. Letting the Great Spirit reveal images. Within all the chaos that I felt in my head, there was a lot of clarity, very precise things. Regarding one of them, I said: "What do I do to be a part of my partner and to be in a relationship?" Two little balls came from the sea, like when one skips stones, but very fast. Then they jumped to the clouds and then like into a funnel and they fell onto a casino roulette. They fell on a number and a door opened. The feeling was: "Roll the dice." "Bet on something and give it your all." That little ball was the heart, which was leading the way.

I also understood that concerning the relationship with my mother, what I have now is the best there is, and it is not going to change. That I must make the best of what there is. To live from what there is, to appreciate the small things. Another thing I saw is that there are so many things: animals, bushes, people, things that I had never seen before. And I said: "Ah, more things exist. And those things are simple." I felt content with those things, at ease. There was a moment when an image of God came, of Jesus perhaps. But it was a super modern Jesus. He sat down. I told him about my neglect, that I felt a lot of abandonment. He said to me: "Yes, but you have neglected yourself. Close your eyes and see what is wrong. Why it is that you cannot be with yourself?" I began to imagine things and I began to hear my body. Speaking nicely about me. I felt like touching myself. I looked at someone and said: "This is another person, another human being who is beside me." I understood respect. Relating to the other from respect. We are worlds apart, yet ultimately, he is a human being like myself. It would be wonderful if everybody felt how I felt.

S.: I have to say that I started in heaven, because I felt confident and I surrendered. It is the first time that I say: "I am going to trust, I surrender." I closed my eyes and started to see white. I felt calm, confident, and began to see many images. Cities passed, people passed, images of me passed. I saw myself as a girl. I saw myself as a baby, my father was carrying me and kissing me. I was wearing a little pink hat. I went into landscapes. I saw an eagle that went into a tunnel and flew through me. I saw the sea, a whale, a rabbit, a dove. When my journey began, I thanked the medicine, for coming to heal me from so far. And it said to me: "We are a single planet; a single universe and the goodness is for all." The voice of my other self appeared, so my ego appeared. What I most understood about myself is "the ideal of the self-realized ego." I saw scenes of my self-realized ego: I saw myself as a queen in England. With a chauffeur and a huge house. The voice said to me: "Look at yourself there, like a queen!" My self-realized ego in the ideal that I had created. All those images started to fade. They moved on and they faded. "Let us do something, let us not fight. Let us come to an agreement. Do not keep treating me like this," I said to it. I connected deeply to the meditation of spaces, and to you saying: "Breathe, and realize where you are." I remembered Luly, a friend from the school here, who died. She could turn things around in a way that amazed me. I said to her: "How do you do it to see things from there?" She said: "It is easy, it is the spaces, things can be seen in many ways." I started to see how my mask was falling away. I saw myself dead, buried. I saw a little heart, all romantic with a small petal. It was my tomb. I experienced all this with such peace, with acceptance of all this that was unfolding before me. The gift I received was compassion. I realized today, when I was writing, because at one point many things happened. I said: "If the key is to love myself, how to know if I love myself?" I did not receive an answer. Today I understand what compassion is. It is not to be so hard on myself, to stop mistreating myself. There are other ways to be and other ways to live. As everything was going on, suddenly I found myself in cyberspace. It started to be like in films, everything fleeing past and everything fading away. The word impermanence came to me. I started to feel it, to experience it. Of course, the here and now, all that I have learned. Depression is to live in the past, anguish is to live in the future. I have spent my life not living the present. Then everything took on a meaning for me. I felt everything in my skin and experienced it. This undoubtedly changes my perception of myself, of the world, and of everything. I feel that this is a very deep transformation and understanding.

CLAUDIO: *Tell me in a sentence what that deep compassion that changes your perspective of everything is like.*

S.: *That we are simply divine sparks and we are in this existence and that everything that occurs is. It is neither good nor bad. They are things that happen and there can be other ways; there is not a single way. Because there is definitely a lot of space. Because I understood there is much created, and that there is space to create more, because everything fades. I feel moved by it (weeping) and I feel gratitude to everyone and for everything. It has been a journey of plenitude and bliss. I feel very at peace. Thank you.*

D.: *I have been working on enneatype six. What happened is that I finally understood where it started. I was abused when very young. I only remembered the scene in which my parents discovered that a worker had been abusing me. It was not violent, I never felt it like that, so I never remembered it like that. On the entire journey what happened was a great cleansing. I come to this scene in which he was telling me it was a game and I was saying to him: "Is it ok, am I not going to be told off?" That was the end of the scene and what the medicine said to me was: "You asked." I felt the deceit and I felt the lies, and I felt the rage, and I felt my parents' pain. I understood why I did not know, why I could not be trusted. Why if I asked and made a decision and it was wrong, how was I to decide anything from there on. Because I did not believe anything of what my body was telling me. If I did feel, I never knew: Was it right or was it wrong? I was always asking and had the feeling that somebody was going to tell me off. Whenever I arrived somewhere, if somebody did not greet me, I had the feeling that I had done something or that I was going to be told off. I did not understand where that great feeling of blame I felt came from, because I had not done anything wrong. The medicine was telling me that I was good, no matter what I did. This is the paradise I had lost. I understood that my father had loved me with a great deal of guilt. And that my mother did not want to see me because she felt pained by* *what had happened and could not see me without getting angry. And that my father could not love me because he felt he was to blame and he gave me more things. I understood that I did not owe my brother anything because I always thought that I owed him because my daddy loved me more and had given me more and had been more patient with me. I realized it is not like that. That I had my own pain. That his love sustained me until I was able to reach this point. I understood that I do not owe anything, that I am not to blame.*

CLAUDIO: *And what was your father guilty of?*

D.: *Not having avoided it. Not having protected me.*

Among the gifts, was the weight of the word yes and no. I enjoyed that the whole night. The medicine was saying to me: "Allow, for the body is finding out." It was lovely because I saw it as a blue color in all the ramifications of my body making me understand what a "yes" is and what a "no" is. What a "yes" feels like and what a "no" feels like. Without so much noise, without so much craziness. Without the ambiguity. I felt that the medicine was saying to me: "Nothing is right, and nothing is wrong." "It is the decisions that are important. In the decision, you will do." And that ends in a great yes. And I felt it in my whole body. For me this is very new.

I asked how many times it had happened. It was painful because a calendar started flashing by, with many numbers. And I was saying: "It cannot be that many times." And the medicine said to me: "Yes, it was every time that you allowed yourself to be penetrated without love. It was every time you gave satisfaction to another. There you violated yourself."

I had the image of a serpent going into my crown and coming out of my vagina. Going in and coming out, cleansing. Then it raised itself straight up to my eye level and with its tongue started hitting my third eye.

V.: *For me, in the beginning the experience was quite hard, I was very afraid. It started with there being a lot of blood. Rivers and rivers of* *blood.* All the dead in my family. The dead of my grandfather, my father, of my uncles, and then my own dead. *I thought I was going to be reprimanded, what I always expect: punishment. I did not for a moment, however, feel afraid or anxious. After this, seeing so many images of death, seeing* how my lineage had killed so many people, how we do whatever we feel like doing, I saw myself as a child; I understood that I am a child having a tantrum. A boy who when he was very little discovered that everything was unfair, and who believed that his task was to bring justice. I understood that for this I did not feel guilty, that I am only claiming what is mine. *It does not matter to me what I have to do for something to be mine; I simply consider it is fair and that is it. I have never felt guilty and I am beginning to see it. I understood how I fled from Colombia saying that I am fleeing from my lineage, from my uncle, from the mafia, from everything that it has been my lot to live. At that point,* my dead more or less said to me: "We are not demanding anything from you, but if you do not stop, that is, if you stay on the same path, what then?"

CLAUDIO: *Let me see, explain it better.*

V.: *"We do not judge you, we do not punish you, but stop, you coward!" I saw myself as a boy, when my childhood was erased, I prefer not to remember. I have never been able to visualize my inner child, but now I saw myself as an angry child, filled with rage. Until I made my mind up and embraced him. I saw him ride a bicycle, I saw him play football. I saw my son also, and I understood that if I continued along the same path, he would experience the same thing. Finally, I was able to embrace myself. Finally, that boy received love. I told him he was grown up now, that he no longer had to be afraid. That he no longer had to escape from anyone and that fleeing from predators, he was the greater predator. I also saw myself with half the face of a good child and the other half of my face so demonic and so ugly. . . . As for the gifts, I have always felt that my gift is to corrupt people. I have enjoyed this very much. I have always felt that, if I feel bad, why should someone else feel good.*

Throughout my life, I have corrupted in several ways. However, I also understood that I do not have the gift of corrupting, but I have the gift of transforming, and I have used it in the wrong way.

L.: *I was afraid, I have always been afraid. When we took the medicine, I asked the Holy Spirit to accompany me. When the journey started I asked to reconnect with joy, happiness, enthusiasm, and willpower. Images started moving past and the main image I saw was my own face. A sad, aged, and shrivelled face. That face was turning into many faces, into many people.* I saw all of my dead. They were turning into my mother's face. She was calm and young. My mother is already dead. I saw the faces of my dead on a beige stage, like an old black and white photograph. Then I saw my father in a lovely image. *I could not see his face very well, but his arms were open, and he was wearing a white tunic. He greeted me with a nod. I saw all my children, I saw my husband, but who I saw most was Laura. I saw how my sad, aged, and listless face turned into hers. However, in the middle of the dream, I saw all this but without suffering. This is what stays with me as an understanding.* All that I experienced, I did not experience with suffering but through seeing things just as they are. *Then came all those* lovely images of rhinoceros, of lions in the desert, of orange colors. The animal I saw most was the rhinoceros. I find the rhinoceros ugly, but it looked lovely to me. *It came up to me and touched me. All those images made me understand that I saw things differently, not as they really were. When I wanted to reconnect with joy and with happiness and all this,* the clarity came to me in a moment that I was the one who did not see it. I understood that I was the one who could not feel it. *Then came all these angelic images, I saw heaven. Then, here I had what you mentioned: "The most important experience of my life." The thing is I do not trust, and I do not believe if I do not see. I find it hard to firmly keep faith and that is why I have no willpower.* In those moments I am in the cloud, and from a higher cloud, a dove takes flight. And I said:

"Oh, the Holy Spirit! I saw him, I am not happy, I am not joyful, but I saw him!" *Then I understood that the most important thing you must trust in is the most sacred, the Holy Spirit. From this moment on I am going to be in communion with him to reexperience myself. I also had a very deep understanding with regard to joy and happiness.* I said: "Oh, yes. I saw him: I have to serve, because I can see him." Serve more and not ask for so much. Do not ask for joy, but to serve. *To understand then that perhaps I, who have spent my life longing for this, may find it when I begin to serve. Surely, when I give to others, I will see myself differently. I saw my grandparents, whom I did not know, when they were young. I saw Laura getting married, in a beautiful white dress walking up the aisle. Seeing her in that white dress, radiant, beautiful, also on a journey of transformation. If I take this journey, she will too.*

C.: *I come from two families. One Jewish and another Catholic. I grew up in a very intellectual family, they were atheists, and there was no religion. So, I think my first experience in heaven is this one. What I contacted was a space (that arose from my body and was expanding all over) of happiness and joy.* In this space, I was rising until I saw the heavens and I felt the beauty, the joy of the magnificence of space. I was crying with happiness. It was ecstatic. I felt free of this feeling of nostalgia for a place, for a home that I have not had in this life. *It was an old nostalgia that has been chasing me from who knows. . . . Through generations and generations. I felt: it is over! It was a liberation.*

CLAUDIO: *First time that you feel complete.*

C.: *I am so happy, and I say: "Where is T.?" I am in complete bliss, I look to my left and I see him lying down at a distance and I say to him "T., come. It is so beautiful here!" And him, lying down. I was told four years ago that I was surrounded by angels, that I was protected. I do not see, I do not feel those things, and for the first time, I saw them. They were wonderful, these angels, these protections, numinous spaces that were close to me. Then, from this heaven, angels came down that freed T. from nets of rusty chains. I said to him: "Come, come, let us go!"*

Then I found myself in the dynamic of expectancy, I saw the eagerness in me. I said: "I am leaving," because I did not want to get into that dynamic. And then, in the sky, it was a very comical journey; a beautiful, light journey. An advertisement appeared that said: "Compassion," it was huge. I felt it in the middle of my heart, which was opening. Then I saw Claudio and felt immense love. I saw the people that work here, the cooks. The word service was something that opened my heart wide. I saw vampires. My neurotic impulse was to sever their heads, but the happiness and the compassion were so great that I did not let it bother me.

I would like now to add to these reports one more that I found remarkable, among several no less significant of people that did not raise their hands in response to my question:

The visions that I had shortly after taking the medicine, which I did not want to see, made me refuse to delve deeply into them. I have interpreted it as a self-protection, like not feeling ready to confront the pain they could bring with them, especially one. The childhood memory of being abused by my father. I did not see details, I just had the certainty that came, rather than from a vision, from an auditory experience, or simply of a certainty without images of what had happened. My rational voice, however, appeared, questioning this certainty, telling me that it might all be my imagination. I still wonder today whether this was real or not. The only moment I contacted a lot of pain was when Claudio asked me to share my experience. About the rest, I have been ignoring it or thinking that I really could have imagined it all. . . . . I suppose it is a chapter that I will have to open at some point. I still have not done the SAT II, so I think it would be the right time to do it. The other vision or certainty I had was that my relationship with Gonzalo, my husband, was spent. There was a question that kept arising: Why are you still there? When are you going to make the decision? I saw Gonzalo's face clearly, and I saw the choice I was faced with: to stay or to leave. It depends on you the voice was telling me. You know. You already know. I did not want to go deeper into that image and even my heart was saying to me: you are making this up . . . I do feel this vision as absolutely real, so much so that on my return I made the decision to speak to Gonzalo about it and suggest a separation.

Both visions remained firmly engraved in me in spite of not wanting to see them.

At the same time, I had two very strong experiences: one in which I connected with my breath and followed it all over my body, becoming aware of all that was happening without doing anything. I felt very serene thinking that my purpose in life was simply to breathe, to be able to step back from the whirlwind of doing, of seeming, of pushing in life. Simply to breathe! The other was about discovering my little ego number three hidden behind every thought and every urge to act. But it is so devilishly astute that it is difficult to see it, to discover it. I had an idea to do something and a chain of motivations immediately appeared that I ended up tracing the primary motivation, wanting to be seen. I saw it, I saw it throughout the entire experience and it was healing. It was like discovering myself, in a light and joyful tone, with an element of surprise and fun.

The following day was marvelous. I think that this workshop has been the catalyst of a process that I began a few years ago. The work with Lluís, taking the medicine and my visions, and meeting Eduardo, make this one of the most transformative experiences of my life. I am opening up a new space that I feel is much more real and serene. It is as if finally, I feel like an adult and I am owning myself, and my decisions. The infinite confidence that Claudio radiates in human beings has been for me a model that before, I still sought to emulate, and today I embody it and I live it.

I shall not reproduce the accounts of each of the participants of the group, but instead I will continue this report illustrating the themes or experiences that seemed to me the most striking due to their frequent recurrence.

1. Dissolution of the Self, Trusting Surrender

The experiences often begin with a description of an attitude of surrender, and it seems to me that in general, not only does the ability to surrender (as also the effect of psychotherapy or the influence of a spiritual teacher) depend on the effect of psychedelics, but surrender is in itself a valuable therapeutic act (and implicitly, a loving state, as sometimes implied by expressions such as "I surrendered with trust, with love").

2. Help, Guidance, Feeling Cared For, Gifted, Assisted

The same person quoted above continues: "The medicine was loving my whole spirit." One might say that the state of love is personified in this statement, just as in mysticism the love of God is personified; only that love of ibogaine itself is being personified, like in shamanic cultures, where the spirit of the plant is conceived as a teacher or guide, and what is probably a valid way of speaking about *an inner reality, for there is something in us that loves us, call it our own soul, or life itself, our inner child or our maternal spirit. The fact is, that love is not a mere abstraction, and where there is love there is a relationship, and where there is a relationship there is another.*

The following experience seems to want to make the person understand the nature of his relationship to his guides. He says: "At a certain point in the journey I felt as if somebody was making me sit. He said to me: 'Let us play at you repeating what we do,' and the hands of two beings were showing me how to move objects without touching them. They showed me, and I repeated it, my physical body was doing all those movements seeing the objects in my hands."

In the following fragment, God himself is the guide: "There was, during my entire experience, a constant dialogue with God. I would ask, and images appeared that gave me answers."

A theme so related to the theme of guiding entities that cannot easily be separated from it is that of dialogue: a dialogue with wisdom, with God, with the guide, the encounter with another entity who knows more.

Somebody reports: "It was loving, it was sublime, and at the same time great fun. There was equanimity, more space, with so many images and a permanent realizing. However, I stayed on the middle path receiving the messages, but with a focus on the deep . . ."

In another case, the "inner teacher" was the Virgin of Guadeloupe, who said to someone: "Surrender. Be free." "Her chest opened like a portal and out of it came colorful fractal images. When she said goodbye to me she gave me a bunch of violet flowers, with a yellow center. When she gave them to me, she said: 'Honor yourself, you are beautiful.' Then she disappeared."

3. The "Letting Oneself Fall" of Surrender and Renouncing the Superfluous

"My body was paralyzed like a corpse." This is common: that the body is instructed to not move, that it is hard to move it, and also: "My inner world started flying and feeling, my head was spinning, and I was turning into many things that were leaping into the void, into emptiness, and I was falling and falling with such pleasure and trust."

This falling with pleasure involves detachment, surrender, that we often conceive as an aesthetic effort, but that here is experienced as a satisfying resting in life itself, beyond our control. Is not this letting everything go something like dying? The same person says: "At times I came back to my body, because at times people moved past above me and stepped on me, and suddenly I started to feel like a dead person: nobody saw me, and I was not interested in them, it ceased to bother me; and *I began to feel the emptiness, I was nothingness, emptiness, my body started to melt like a candle, until I went beyond the earth and merged with the whole, with a beautiful shower of stars that was opening my heart, and my heart was also relaxing and was falling, everything in me was falling.*"

I find this description of surrender wonderful, somewhat similar to iboga and ayahuasca, something like a principle of exaltation of gravity, of letting go, in keeping with the spirit of Zen, a thinking downward, as is characteristic of surrendering to the earth. In contrast to the "classic hallucinogens" that take one to heaven, oneirophrenics are earthy drugs, of letting oneself fall to earth, to the animal and primitive or archaic.

4. Understanding of One's Own Childhood, Personality, and Illness, and Going into the "Dark Side"

"The plant decided to guide me and show me my mistrust, my madness," says a participant, and then explains that he saw his madness in a wounded child that does not trust others. He felt that everything in his life was reduced to relationships of power and money, and that the spiritual path was a farce. His whole life was a farce, and this workshop was also madness, and the world was full of people wanting to impose their vision of things on others. However, when he understood that his state was that of a frightened child, he decided to embrace it, and in taking this loving maternal approach, he felt amused by and compassionate about the child's tantrums.

Another patient reports having perceived that "with all that strength and loving support, the journey into darkness, the ego, addictions, traps began."

Beyond the scientific understanding of some dynamics, however, I was surprised by the following allusion to a broader-reaching insight:

"From a therapeutic perspective of my whole personal process, it was the way to integrate all that I have done so far. It was lovely to see how in a single experience I was able to see the process I am going through, the work of many years, finding things and events that I was very clear about in my head and that I had not been able to bring down into the body, and almost everything materialized in a single structure."

5. The Prescriptive Aspect: The Vision of an Alternative Life Stance

A person given to complaining writes that she understood she had to approach life gently, sweetly, accepting what comes to her: "The struggle wears me down, in fact, I am learning that fighting for what I want is not to fight: I can earn the right, I can belong, I can disagree without the need to fight." She explains that she must not *"let my life be wasted in worrying about it, simply live it, without trying to be prepared for everything. Likewise, if I find myself thinking or acting repetitively, to realize it, and above all, not judge myself."*

"Life is a process, I am alive, I am in the process, everything is part of it, humility to accept things as they are. Opening up space for my partner, even my inner partner needs space."

Another participant says: "I realized at several moments that I am so uptight, or rather, I am so restricted by my own mental attitude, it limits me to that narrowmindedness. Thoughts like: 'You will not succeed,' 'you are not capable,' 'not you'; and in those moments of course, envy of others also. I think that one of the greatest insights is becoming aware of this subtle notion of greed . . . and the medicine showed it to me clearly and as it is. I resisted, saying that was not true, that is not the way I am . . . but in the end, reluctantly and yet with a smile, I agreed."

Another person in the group reported having had the necessary clarity to make the decision to end a relationship that led her to a conflict with her preference for a stable long-term partner, and this clarity when faced with decisions could also be cited; in this case, it can be said that not only was she able to perceive the right step, but also find the strength (or detachment) to take it.

6. Death and the Deceased

I was surprised by how frequently people experienced something like going through death, to then be reborn to life, *and even more frequently coming across the spirits of dead people, known or unknown.* I have already highlighted this element in the first experiences reported in our retrospective session, and I quote another next:

Following the description (already quoted) of a "letting oneself fall" that leads one to the feeling of being nothing, one of the subjects goes on: "I began to feel nothing, I was nothingness, emptiness, my body started melting like a candle, until I moved past the Earth and became one with the whole, with a beautiful shower of stars that was opening my heart, and my heart was also relaxing and falling, everything in me was falling.

"I saw many people, some were going up, and others down: They looked at me, some made a gesture, many were only shadows, others grimaced, I do not know if this was the presence of dead people, I felt it was. It was curious because it was clear that some necessarily went up, and others down. Some tried to enter into me, one managed to, and I had to ask him to go out of me, and he did.

"Also, at one point I was remembering one of my family members, my grandparents, great-grandparents, their presence came to me.

"In other moments, the medicine led me to many episodes of death, and I was able to see them calmly, as an observer. I saw several of my own deaths and also felt them; likewise, seeing how I returned to existence. This experiencing death has not been a mental or emotional understanding, but a spiritual and bodily understanding."

Another says: "I felt myself die, but not externally, this time internally: it was a death of the ego, the condition was that I had to previously make all my pending apologies, without forgiving or asking for forgiveness I could not die in peace. Initially, I thought I had nothing to lose, but gradually people appeared, and in free association, past scenes that still needed to be healed. Once I had finished, I felt myself empty from the inside, like deflating inside a skeleton; then, a final sigh came from my mouth in which the ego was diluted.

"I saw death elegantly; I felt it, recognized and honored it. I finally reached the end of my life project: to serve and to start a family. It became clear to me for the first time that I love my partner, with whom I have shared a long path, full of challenges and beautiful experiences."

Another participant says she saw all her dead, including her parents when they were young. The images appeared as old photographs. The father in sweet, angelic images. Herself on a balcony, very beautiful and sweet.

In the following passage, I have not wanted to separate the relative to the death of the experience of rebirth that followed it, leading to love and the "Great Spirit," which in this case carried out the role of guide or inner teacher.

He started to feel unusual sensations that inspired him to pray to be able to get closer to God and his deceased. *"I experienced my death; I was swept away by a black shadow and tormented by voices reproaching me. They were all at a funeral and gave me sympathetic looks. I felt a very strong energy and the box exploded: it was a rebirth. When I opened my eyes L. and M. were in front of me receiving me into love. I connected with the great spirit and it showed me my father and the pure love I feel for him."*

7. The Mystical or Spiritual Dimension, and Its Happiness; The Cosmic Order, Universal Evolution, The Revelation of the Unity of Everything and the Intuition of Nothingness—or Space

Beautiful places never visited before often appear in the visions, and the wonder of the aesthetics of imaginary places; the paradisiacal, we might say. This is a theme related to the beauty of everything when it is intuited as part of a universal order, with the perception of how everything is interwoven with everything else. This is about the vision of the entire universe or of life, which is different from the beauty of imaginary figures or aesthetic stories or constructions.

For example, one of the accounts says: "There were lovely images of me floating, flying, rising suddenly into infinity, and I saw myself from below disappearing into that cosmos. There were stars, then a deep darkness. I was not afraid. I felt I belonged to that dynamic, to that vast world where everything fits.

"The medicine was showing me images all the time, galaxies, cylinders, tunnels through which I moved rapidly and that I could put a stop to at will.

"In space, there is a force that brings everything together and always knows what it is doing, even though I do not understand it.

"I was then carried by infinite space where everything fits (my imperfections too). Feeling that I belong to this universe as another particle, with no greater or lesser importance than all else that wondrously exists in the universe."

Someone begins wanting to connect with the spirit of the plant, and from there goes out into the universe. He feels how everything is related, how each thing is influencing everything else. Traveling into the universe, he is first guided to visit the spirit world. He is asked: *"Do you want to know who you pray to?"* He could see many light beings, a lot of light, a lot of peace. He understood how each movement with light generates the divine material we breathe in.

Then came the invitation to go to the dark side. He was accompanied by a protective eagle that showed him how the dark side is part of a great web, together with the light. It showed him the importance of staying in the light and amplifying it, and how this generates grace, happiness, and tranquillity.

"I also saw a little star on the floor, and then this little star . . . I was widening my vision and it was as if somebody had left a footprint, and the footprints were stars. Then I saw the steps and said: God has come. They were God's steps, I felt very afraid in the beginning because of this perception of how bad I am. Then God was coming, and it was time for the judgment. God was coming. I never saw him, I only saw him in the fish I described earlier. I had not seen God, I saw his steps. I said to myself, well, there is nothing to be done now, so I will receive my punishment. Instead of that, I stepped into those footprints, and I was taken to see the entire structure of the universe. We traveled supremely far, until we found, reaching some columns, the pillars of the universe, columns made of diamonds, with many extremely strong structures. On one of those columns, one of those diamonds was me, supporting, not as something exclusive, not like the great support of the universe . . . I was one of the millions of diamonds that were there in the universe. From there, from that column, other columns appeared, and I witnessed all the vastness of the universe and again fell to Earth."

8. Clarity, Lucidness, and Acceptance

This experience might be described as something characteristic of ibo-gaine in that it is repeated several times through the accounts. It is a meditative state, again, very close to what is sometimes described as space.

"Above all, equanimity, I feel that the ogre I carry inside is not that bad. The last words of the voice stay with me, telling me to *trust, trust.* I managed to sleep, to rest, to let go, loosening my left arm and left leg, which I felt were disappearing and were no longer vibrating, but were going into a deep calm."

9. Animals and the Sanctification of the Body

One of the subjects says, succinctly, among other things: "Animals: felines, jaguars, looked me straight in the eyes."

One woman feels accompanied by an animal she recognizes as her "power animal": "Then several landscapes changed, and I moved many times with my protection animal (black panther) that I already know is with me. It was beautiful company because I felt strengthened, the panther was showing me its left paw, in which it held a little deer made of white beads, and I said to myself: this is yours, take it. I took it and immediately appeared in another landscape, it was greener at times, and at times it was desert. Then a big deer appeared, white, with large shiny horns. I stretched my hands pulling strongly on my fingers and these turned into the body of the stag, and its head lay on my chest and that brought me great calm and tranquillity, decisiveness, safety, openness, space."

Two of the forty subjects encountered an immense fish with divine qualities, and as their experiences are remarkable, I quote their corre-sponding accounts, with some of the context corresponding to these images.

"It was not like a regression of this lifetime, but like the history of humanity. At one point, I felt that I had two eyes, and my physical eyes, my eyelids, were closed, but behind there were some other eyelids that were opening, like eyelids opening to the subconscious and to another dimension of reality. With these eyes, I could see my eye, my physical eye, my left eye. This part of the eye positioned itself in front of me, and this eye started moving backward. And it got older, older and older, until was very old people, and then went back to being, passing through different genders, like the eye of a man, like the eye of a woman, then of a man again, and of many women. My eye was in the body of many women and of many men in a kind of regression. I could see all of time going backward, backward, backward, until I went into water; I did not feel the damp, but I could physically see the water. Suddenly, a fish appeared in the water, the most beautiful fish I had ever seen. I assume it is not a fish from this era because it was a fish with very bright colors, yellows and reds and blues, with whiskers and a majestic size, with a majestic structure, which I saw in my eyes, and then I saw God in that fish. A spectacular fish, it is the most alive and beautiful image I saw throughout the vision, and then there was a pause, I did not want the vision to vanish, but then the vision began to fade and drops of water emerged from it, as if the water was also going backward. Then the water began to fall, and it started to rain, rain, rain and I saw the evolution of life, I saw the first fish being formed, as if on one of those school posters where we see a small fish and then all the other fish going by, all the fish, and then again, a fish dancing on the water. I came out of the water. I saw packs of animals, some known, others unknown, many flocks of birds and birds and birds, until coming to the first aborigines, I saw the face of Jorge Llano, but not as Jorge Llano, for clearly my teacher, with all his wisdom, was there, but all I could physically recognize of him were his eyes. I knew it was him, but he was a black man, one of the first settlers, a spectacular black man. I could only see him from the neck up, with his white beard and his white hair, gray and chestnut hair."

"At one point, I saw myself, and I was standing in front of myself. I started seeing a series of animals, very big, huge, huge animals. It was as if I was in front of them. I saw some dinosaurs, and the idea came to me that dinosaurs existed. I saw different species of enormous dinosaurs looking at me intently, saying: 'Here I am. I exist. I existed.' Then I saw myself surrounded by water as if I was in the ocean, and in truth, nothing but the ocean existed, only ocean, there was no land. In that ocean, I started to see some enormous fish that were also looking at me intently, making themselves present in front of me, saying: 'Here I am.' I felt the history of the world, I felt the passing of the history of the world, how we have been so many species, and how we have been so many beings, we are so full of that history, and I surprised myself by telling myself: it is evolution, evolution. At one point, I saw up close a fish so much bigger than me, that I was the size of its eye. It was a gigantic fish, I do not know, it gave me the feeling of a huge whale, a whale-fish. It was looking at me with its eye, and I was the size of the eye, and it smiled at me with its eye, or with its presence. It saw me, and I saw it, and it was something like recognizing each other among the species, and recognizing history and the joy of knowing we both exist."

No less significant, perhaps, than the visions in which a symbolic projection of the instinctual world can be recognized, are experiences of the sacred nature of one's own body and sexuality. I quote one next:

"I met some women who received me in a very loving, shining pink space. Suddenly, I was naked among them. I was moved. They said to me in a single voice: 'The vagina is a gateway into the universe.' They showed me that when a soul decided to go back to Earth to have a human experience, it came from the universe and into our vagina, and that is why our vagina is a sacred place at the service of all souls returning for their evolution and the evolution of the universe itself. I asked, unsettled: 'Is it only to bring souls into the world?' With loving smiles, they answered no. They explained to me that it is through the vagina and its powerful energy that it is possible to connect with everything and with love. They showed me that, at the moment of having sexual contact with somebody, this energy spreads all over the body, even to the universe. I saw how that energy that I had received from the earth through my vagina in the conscious sexual act could be physically pleasurable, but that it also transformed into more subtle energies. When it reached my heart, I sensed it fill me with a feeling of deep, immense, total love. Not only for my partner whom I was making love with, but for the whole world. As the energy kept going up to my head and beyond it, I felt like I was making love with God, with the whole. I could see that my partner was God, and myself at the same time. I understood spiritual ecstasy. Then I started to see a large, beautiful, pink vagina, from which emanated a warm energy that enveloped me. I began to see the vagina turn into a virgin. The clitoris was the virgin's face, and the inner lips were the veil and the dress. At the entrance to the vagina, a bright sparkling light. I understood that the instinctual energy of the flesh is merely the trigger to meet God. Man's task goes beyond the body."

10. Pranic Phenomena

Someone describes "snaking sensations in my body and a lot of vibration," and several mentioned tremors and vibrations of the type that Grof suggests calling "pranic phenomena"—sometimes associated with images like the snake, such as in the classic kundalini descriptions in the tantric traditions, and it seems to me that such a phenomenon is related to the liberation of the instinctual world and the resacralization of sexuality. The vibratory phenomenon may barely be mentioned, or it may appear associated with an ecstatic plenitude, like in one of the accounts transcribed earlier—just as also occurs sometimes under the effects of ayahuasca or other psychedelics.

"The plant was entering through my head, I could see my entire nervous system, moving, cra! cra! cra! filling all the nerves like blue passages. I could see something like those school diagrams depicting the entire nervous system, only that it was lighting up, bit by bit. I felt afraid."

I will also include in this category the experience of somebody who observed acutely how he becomes disconnected from certain areas of his body, specifically from the three lower chakras. This led him to do an original work of integration through which he proposed to bring his soul to his penis and then to his digestive system. "To really integrate it, I need to be present."

11. Love and Service

Many people experienced something akin to an awakening to love, and they also frequently discovered that they should serve. Here is one:

"Snakes of bright dots of light were going into my body and were cleansing it with a high frequency of love, what I understood as love, joy, and plenitude."

"When I saw what love was, I thought: right, that is it. I can go out into the world. After other stages in the journey I perceived that this, with all its strength and loving support, was the beginning of the journey into the darkness, the ego, the addictions, and the pitfalls."

"Finally, I came to my life project: to serve and to start a family. It became clear to me for the first time that I love my partner, with whom I have shared a long journey, full of challenges and beautiful experiences."

Another narrates a profoundly transformative experience:

"The first thing I started to see on my mental screen was the Virgin of Guadeloupe approaching me. I am a strong believer in her, and it was very beautiful to see her again. Then I felt her hands touch my heart. I was deeply moved and felt an emotion that I have trouble putting into words, similar to the plenitude of a very deep understanding, and I cried profusely for this understanding, and for feeling love and for feeling loved. I stayed with that sensation of feeling love and of putting a stop to the belief that there is no love for me. It was restorative for me in that sense."

12. Discovery of Shamanic Abilities

"My body was filling with air, my legs felt huge, and my hands tickled. I could hear voices saying to me: 'use your hands, they are powerful,' I looked at my hands and sparks were flying off them, which were connected to electrical waves, which were all over the room.

"I communicated by telepathy with the people in my group, and it was magical, I was very happy. I was a very powerful little girl. I heard Jorge tell me to work with my hands. I heard a voice telling me not to eat any more meat; I asked if I could eat chicken or fish, and the voice said to me: 'I am telling you to stop eating meat, not to be vegetarian.'

"I was told: 'You are clairvoyant.' I saw a car accident in which I was in the front passenger seat and we were crashing into a red truck, I think this is how I am going to die. Also, at another moment, they were showing me about telepathy, they were showing me how it worked, and I had the feeling that it is possible and easier than we are all used to thinking it is."

Is this pure imagination, or a case in which ibogaine has served to activate a latent disposition? I imagine so, and only time will tell.

13. Sequences with the Nature of a "Mythical Journey" That We Can Perceive in the Description of Certain Experiences, and the Language of Which Resembles That of Fairy Tales

"Afterward I saw the image of a small skull with a very angry face that was falling down a dark river, it was very unpleasant, and it was falling, and the voice was saying: it is your childhood resentment, let it go, and it fell away. Then others came, like a little devil, and the voice said: that is your rebellious adolescence, let it go, and in this way other images came of different times in my life."

"Many catastrophic images started appearing and a slight anguish, and I said to myself: What is the need to create those imaginings? To support what? To sustain the fiction that you can neither trust nor be hopeful? There the voice again said to me: that is not you, that is what you learned, and everything was dissolving."

"Buddha appeared radiant, golden, with a great golden light that welled up before him. Then Jesus came, who had a wheel in the colors of the rainbow spinning clockwise in his heart, slowly until it came to a stop, and then it started spinning the other way and the colors started expanding all over space, very gracefully."

"At one point, the silent voice said: there is a mystery of the universe that has not yet been revealed, soon you will discover it. Thank you, thank you, thank you."

14. Transformation

Naturally, the experience of healing cannot be separated from the experience of transformation, which in turn, is inseparable from the encounter with the spiritual, from the understanding of illness, from surrender and from detachment of the known, death and the encounter with love.

The theme of transformation is predominant, for example, in the account of one woman who describes going into the underworld, where *the goddess with a skirt of snakes told her to let herself fall to her death. There, many of her traits started to disappear, like her excessive criticism or demandingness, through everyday scenes that appeared parallel to an intellectual certainty. "I understood that these were my addictions and they started falling away. I came to a river of mud where I was able to dissolve after feeling myself mud for some time. A baby's face then started taking shape, and I understood that is what I was like in my essence: sweet, beautiful, a being of love. There I started to grow, and I became a girl of three running freely through the forest of the south." The goddess with a skirt of snakes was saying to her: "You already know how to do it. Help others." "I understood that everything that had been, had been a response to external stimuli. I was not the one my mother and my brother had forever told me I was: cold, arrogant, selfish, troublesome, intense, unbearable, and more. I told myself: 'She no longer holds any power over me.'"* She then felt like telling her new family that she was beautiful, sweet, wild, free, loving, joyful, and she pictured herself kissing each of them in turn.

Sometimes the healing process is not explicit, however, and it is not translated into thoughts or words. Somebody says, for example, "I had the feeling that this medicine works very subtly, that feeling like when one knows there is a work being done, and there is no need to understand it rationally."

Just as in Arthur C. Clarke's *2001: A Space Odyssey,* brought to the screen by Kubrik, the influence of a mysterious monolith triggers the evolution of the human species and the final transformation of the astronaut who falls on Jupiter, the experience of contacting guides or teachers can converge with the experience of transformation, like in the following episode:

"Alien images appeared; beings from another dimension, who were leading me through a kind of neon green tube or vacuum that was absorbing me, and I felt they were making changes or adjustments to my body, first in my brain, and others that I did not even understand. I felt myself lying on a simple stretcher, made of shiny glass and very high-tech. They were telling me it was to recharge my body with things that I needed. Then, polyhedron-shaped pendulums came down from the sky, and in the end, when they were almost touching me, they turned into a gigantic diamond that went into my heart."

In the following lines, written by another subject, *calmness and gratitude stand out as the main characteristics of the healing experience, and it seems to me that this can be fairly general: I would say that the calm that many perceive is an expression of the detachment induced by ibogaine, which in turn is nothing but the state symbolized by a journey toward the world of the dead:*

"The experience has left me in a strange state of calm that I would like to be able to bring into my life," he says. He then adds that during the session he saw beautiful images that made him feel how fortunate he was, in spite of his apparent wish to die, and that he understood the importance of valuing what he had, instead of attaching so much significance to what he once had. He ends by saying that in spite of his fears, he was able to give himself another injection of hope. "It has been a very good experience, positive, healing, and hopefully permanent," he concludes.

15. "Great Truths"

I shall include in this section quotes of people whose understanding has broadened from personal matters to encompass universal thoughts—which are still relevant to their personal experiences. For example, several witnessed a vision of the evolution of life, and the understanding of this fact of universal history seemed to significantly influence their sense of life itself—just as Terrence Malick's film *The Tree of Life* aimed to depict. I have already quoted one of them as a precedent to the visions of giant fish, and here I add another quote, which reveals an understanding of the human condition:

"Then I understood original sin as living in service to the ego and adoring it above God, that is egocentricity: it is like adoring a false god, like forgetting the first commandment. It also seemed like the work of the devil to make us adore ourselves, that we are ego-fed personalities, and in that way, we forget about God. Therefore, it is important to pray several times a day, to remain aware of what truly matters; that is also the explanation of the biblical idea that first I have to die to the ego for the essential and divine to be born in me."

16. Resisted Experiences

One woman says that her entire body was shaking intensely, she felt very dizzy and off-balance to walk by herself. She also had diarrhea and vomited after eating a chocolate someone gave her. "I did not want to go back to the room. I felt like staying somewhere more peaceful and quiet. I grew desperate thinking about going back, because the noises were very loud. I felt everything I heard was very close, and my racing thoughts were driving me mad in the room. Alone in bed, after vomiting, I managed to better surrender to the journey. I felt as though I spent the whole night in a very deep state of meditation."

Another woman reports a "horrible experience, not for having conflicting thoughts in my mind, but for the external noise and for not knowing if I was doing it right."

A third, writing the following day, says: "I got up feeling

disorientated, confused, a failure, feeling not only physically nauseous, but also nauseated by what I had experienced." However, we cannot help but feel that the experience implied for her the destruction of her pretty mask, the revelation of her murderous impulses and the beginning of the disintegration of her ordinary personality.

A fourth also felt unwell, withdrew to her room "for a moment" and there she stayed. The next day, her fellow participants helped her come out of her depression and she was able to cry, and her exchanges with them led her to the conviction that she should get help and understand who can provide it best for her. She also reached the conclusion that she must express her anger, because otherwise it turns against her.

It can be said, in synthesis, that even the experiences that were hard to swallow and were resisted had their therapeutic effect, as well as no doubt the understanding of such a resistance to surrender, as in the psychoanalytical process, will be a favorable factor in a greater surrender if the opportunity of a similar experience arose in the future. I also find relevant somebody's observation that it was helpful to understand that she was present here, and at the same time, it was as if she was in an unknown place in another dimension.

The Nature of the Therapeutic Effect of the Experience with Ibogaine

I have mentioned, regarding ayahuasca, that the integration of the instinctual mind with our ordinary mind—habitually repressively domesticated both with respect to the pleasure principle and the rage principle—is precisely the foundation for the traditionally therapeutic effect known and sought. I believe it can also be said of ibogaine that it is at least one of the components of the benefits it offers. However, this opening of the instinctual world does not necessarily manifest in the form of visual images. An alternative expression is, simply, opening to the movement of the body's energy, or prana, which the tantric culture has always recognized as an aspect of the awakening of the "inner serpent." We can also consider the following experience as an alternative expression to images:

"I felt that through the perineum, a warm energy began to emanate that went up my vagina, passed through my womb, and my entire body up to the crown, and it began to envelop my whole body. I felt a lot of heat, but it was very pleasant. It was an energy that moved in waves, that had a very fast, but very soft vibration."

This pranic experience preceded the one I have already described as a recovery of sexual innocence, and culminated in a sequence of images that I have already described and that seems to me very illustrative of a phenomenon, also universal, in the process of self-realization—the transformation of sexual energy into maternal love:

"Then I started to see a large vagina. It appeared beautiful to me, it was pink, a warm energy emanated that enveloped me. Then I began to see the vagina was turning into a virgin. The clitoris was the virgin's face, and the inner lips, the veil and the dress. At the entrance to the vagina, there was sparkling radiant light. This was one of the most valuable things for me. I understood from a different place that my body is sacred and that my vagina is sacred too. Instinctual energy of the flesh is only the trigger to meeting God. It is man's task to see beyond the body."

The account of another of the participants in this group session confirms it:

"I learned that only by taking the energy that emanates from sex, and separating it a little from the flesh, can it be channeled and open the heart. I want to be able to make love from this space and find somebody who—like myself from now on—understands sex in the same way."

After reviewing these common elements of the experiences, which could be multiplied, I now wish to add a broader point, suggested by something that I have been saying of ayahuasca and that seems to me to be equally true of ibogaine: *that having the effect of reintegrating our three alienated brains—the primitive and instinctual, the limbic or empathic, and the intuitive or wise neocortex—it could be said that it is an antidote to the "patriarchal mind."*

In other words: the "civilized world" or "patriarchal society" shares a mentality that has systematically criminalized the instinctual world (like in the myth of the demonized serpent of Paradise), in its violence eclipsed love (which corresponds to our mid-brain, inherited from mammals), and in its predatory technological astuteness, disregarded our intuition (function of the nondominant cerebral hemisphere), as well as its potential to enlighten and guide us.

Of ibogaine, as of ayahuasca, it can be said that it leads to a greater awareness of the instinctual (manifest in a greater awareness of the body and its "energies," as well as in images of animals) that, besides contributing to the mental health of people through a reintegration of their vilified and forbidden instinctual world, contributes also to a great extent to their opening up to intuitive thinking, which entails not only a reconnection with the spiritual, in itself healing, but also a learning guided from a level ordinarily inaccessible to consciousness.

Lastly, the ibogaine experience leads many to the recovery of their capacity for love, for appreciation and for service; and this not only through a transitory stimulation of such motivations, like in the case of empathogens, but seemingly through the peace arising from detachment, from which love, the spirit of service, devotion, and gratitude seem to emerge naturally.

So, it can be said that, *in bringing innocence back to people's instinctual world, reconnecting them to an intrinsic wisdom that is like their own inner spiritual guide and giving them back their loving capacity, ibogaine has the effect of healing three anguishes shared by modern man that constitute the three fundamental aspects of what Freud called "universal neurosis."*

To conclude, I should explain that the experimental design was that if some people felt that the dose of ibogaine was insufficient to have a satisfactory or productive experience, they would be given a supplement. To my surprise (in view of the impression of 1967), only two people asked for such a supplement, although I wonder if it might not have been better to administer it to them, since some of the written accounts are not so indicative of a therapeutic change as would be expected from so many people raising their hands in response to my question regarding this. One possible explanation could be that with iboga, the therapeutic aspect operates slightly beyond intellectual awareness of what is happening, so in the course of the following days, they had better knowledge of it than what we can infer by reading their accounts.

Still pending, of course, is a retrospective study to inform us of the persistence of the short-term benefits perceived, and also being able to compare the effect of ibogaine on its own with ibogaine in association with a complementary substance, such as MMDA-3a, which seemed so promising to me earlier on but that I never got to evaluate through an experiment specifically designed for such a comparative study.

4.7 ANALYSIS OF THE THERAPEUTIC PROCESS IN AN IBOGAINE SESSION

PROLOGUE

I transcribe next one of the ibogaine sessions that so far has seemed to me to be one of the most powerful in its transformative impact, and I believe that it might be useful to shift the font of certain passages to emphasize their significance. I have also added a few words in square brackets in reference to aspects already mentioned about the typical ibogaine experience.

ACCOUNT

"The experience began with a female voice asking me to let her come into my mind [guide]. I did not know who it was, and I questioned it. I began to question my mind: What does it mean to go into the mind, what is the mind? I touched the center of my cranium (my crown) as if wanting to check that it was 'open' to receive that which wanted to enter. I felt air coming in through that opening and I visualized a circular

layer dissolving, literally opening the cement barrier that was preventing the substance from entering and the beginning of the experience.

"*When she entered, I felt a large ring being formed that pressed into my brain; it was the second door of resistance: control. I felt it tightening around my mind and I asked what I could do with it. That ring, which before was made of metal, turned into a ring of rapidly circling birds that, after I saw them clearly, left. As they flew away, I waved, saying goodbye to them: at the same time, I said goodbye to the control that they represented. [Becoming aware and relaxation of egoic resistance.]*

"*While everything started moving, my heart was beating faster and faster; I felt something like fear, but I could not rely on the definition of fear that I already knew because something was telling me that 'the known' had nothing to do with what I was feeling, as it represented a cognitive limit. So, the new sensation of nothingness and of speed, on the one hand made my heart race like mad (as if I was traveling in a spacecraft being hurtled into infinity), and on the other, it was exciting, it was pure adrenaline, if it can be defined in any way. [Opening up to the unknown.]*

"*My body was still, immobile; I could not move even a cell; I perceived it in all its stillness while I journeyed inside and above me the air, the wind, the light, the clouds, were flashing by and were giving me the feeling of something similar to the universe, to life, to time, to eras swiftly slipping by. [Intuition of the universe.]*

"My eyelids were immobile, but I could perceive that they opened and closed in a gesture that was neither physical nor concrete; I could see it clearly and perceived it opening and closing; however, I still saw the light when my eyelids closed. I wondered if it was really me executing that movement that could not be physical, but an inner movement, as if I could see with my eyes closed or open in the stillness.

"The light did not become shadow when my eyelids closed; everything was very strange and natural at the same time.

"*I tried to see beyond the limits of everything that slipped past above and disappeared behind my head. I tried to see beyond my field of vision, pushing my eyes upward and into my cranium to see beyond the horizon limited by its own movement.*

"I felt that the luminous clouds drifting rapidly above me were taking me back in time at an ever-increasing speed. Suddenly I had the vision of a forest where a vibrant green bush stood out; I could hear the birdsong and silence in the background: it was the virgin forest. In front of the green plant was a huge black gorilla that could have been a male or a female; I heard it breathing heavily, deeply. [The primordial, archaic, nature.] In that place there were only plants and animals. The vision only lasted briefly, but I felt that I had seen the origin of the planet, when man did not exist yet and it was only populated by flora and fauna, before anything else. We came later. [The origin, primeval.]

"The 'spacecraft' set off once again and took me to another place. [Craft, vehicle.]

"It came to an abrupt standstill because I felt a jolt. This time I was surprised by the sensation of not knowing where I was; I did not have time to ask before the answer arrived: in my mother's womb. [Regression.] I immediately rejected that information because I felt that something was not right and that I could not be there, where everything should have worked perfectly. Something was happening that made me not want to be there. I perceived shouting from afar and the echo reached me, as if there was something outside that was speaking and made me alert, but I could not decipher what it was about. Then I was able to come out of the perspective of the womb, as if a camera had displaced the vision from inside to outside, and from the lens of the 'camera,' I saw my mother sitting in the armchair of her house (that she still owns); she was nine months pregnant and punching her belly while she screamed: 'Don't move! Don't move!' She kept punching herself with closed fists, overcome by hysteria; she was unable to sleep due to mine and my twin sister's movements in her belly. [Traumatic situation.]

"That feeling of paralysis, of not being able to, or allowed to move, lodged deep into my body and I carried it with me all my life. [Insight.]

"At that moment I felt that something was splitting in me; it was

the first fragmentation between what I was feeling and what I was understanding concerning what was happening: it was myself and the self that were splitting apart to never meet again. I felt a separation in my brain of the rational part that thinks and acts, and the intuitive, creative, sensitive part; the split between the two parts was filled by the fantasy. [Retrospective insight.]

"Relinquishing control (by letting the metal ring fly) had given free rein to fantasy, which often was confused with reality, allowing me to integrate it. The experience made me see situations of the past that I could have interpreted in a realistic way but that I then transformed into something creative and imaginative. It showed a scene that happened when I was five years old (I asked the age and the reply was: 'Five'). I was walking down the corridor of my aunt's (my father's sister) house; at the end of the corridor I could see my cousin, who was a few years older than me, holding on to the edge of the bed while my uncle, her father, penetrated her from behind. I was shocked and rooted to the spot by this scene; I began to ask myself why I knew this, why I received this information. I felt guilt, disbelief, disgust, pain; I knew what all that was about, but there was nothing I could do; I did not have time to stop at this image and analyze the sensations, the feelings, or the consequences because the upset and dislike would immediately disappear and be replaced by another vision. [Traumatic memory.]

"There was no place for emotion. I automatically tried to be empathetic to what I was seeing, but I was not able to get to the bottom of what I was feeling, and if I struggled to feel, I felt nothing. So, I had to give up the warm filter of emotion, which is the resource or instrument I usually use to confront what comes up and that my identity is linked to. What am I without emotion? Do I exist and does the world exist without emotion?

"If I tried to stop and reason about or interpret something that I was seeing to get in touch with my feelings about it, new information or a new image would sweep away that intention; it was impossible to stop the flow. I saw images that seemed like cartoons in succession and

there was no way of stopping to look at any of them; I had no power of decision, I was not able to control it. [Neutral contemplation of the flow of consciousness.]

"Furthermore, when I felt that I had understood something about my life or about my past, if I tried to include it in a definitive understanding of a fact or of an event, something took the memory away from that scene, so I was always back to square one. On more than one occasion I wondered what I could have narrated about the experience if everything that I saw disappeared in the void without leaving a trace, and while I struggled to remember by 'rewinding the tape,' a voice would stop me, asking me why I wanted to go backward to listen to the song before it was finished. This tells me a lot about my life: sometimes I put everything on 'pause' and I get lost in memories without paying attention to the present; in this way I 'lost' part of my life: in thinking, in ideas, in false memories, in imaginary constructs.

"Ultimately, if I wanted to hold on to a fact, the voice appeared and said to me: 'The mind lies.'

"Everything was losing meaning and significance. [Learning of noninterference.]

"At some moments I felt squashed by the weight of what I was seeing and perceiving. Then a completely different scene opened up, of sheer beauty: unexpectedly I saw the light, heard the music louder, and the scene included a feeling of space and freedom. It was as if the substance wanted to tell me: 'Do not forget that paradise exists, that happiness exists. [Do not become attached.] In one of those moments I was seeing a blue sky and black spots that were becoming swallows crossing the sky. I felt in awe of all that beauty and exclaimed: 'Look, the sky!'—voicing the marvels I was seeing. A harsh voice would answer my exclamation, saying: 'Do not be superficial!' in a disdainful tone. I do not know to whom I uttered the sentence about the sky, but judging by the tone of the reply, it seemed to come from my father. [Insight about her father's arbitrary and authoritarian invalidation.]

"I did not understand what being superficial meant; I did not

*understand the meaning of that word in relation to what I had stated;
I wondered what superficiality was for him; perhaps it was beauty,
the wonder of nature, being able to attest to the world being a place
overflowing with wonderful things. Then I realized that for him, and
what I know about him, things that could be considered not superficial
were profits, appearances, ostentation, well-being ensured by possession
and luxury, effort, great effort, and all that is obtained through money,
what is done with money to obtain a substitute for what nature already
offers: freedom of experience and of existence. I heard my father's
voice inside of me and then I understood that that voice belonged to
an inner figure that talked and constantly tried to devalue the things
that I understood, as if it were a call to remain immobile, to not grow,
to not see, to remain within the limits of a small world, a labyrinthine,
complex, difficult, sterile, dry, dead world. Feeling that voice inside of
me, I understood how in life I had taken on the same empty way of being
in the world and how I had taken on the same role in relationships. That
presence was so strong that I had identified with it, with its discrediting
and critical way of acting, seeing, and feeling. [Insight.]*

"My hands were tense, as if all the rage that I did not express had
concentrated in my muscles and tissues. My fists were closed, and I felt
a lot of aggressiveness that I turned against myself, as if I was unable
to contain the evil that came from inside and I turned it against myself.
That is how I saw the ego, the mind within the mind in which the
father's figure and voice held a dominant position. [Insight.]

"Understanding was moving parallel to a personal level where I
became aware of the idealization of the father figure, at a level where
I recognized his image had been fixed as a dominant introjected figure.

"At a certain point, I was looking up and I felt that I was rapidly
climbing up a mountain; while I climbed it, I understood I had put him
up there, and before I reached the summit (which was very high), I
wondered what figure I would find; it had to be immense and powerful
if I had placed it so high up. At the top I found the figure of my father
when he was about thirty years old, and that represented the moment

in which his idealized image had crystallized in me as a child. I knew he had to come down this way, and suddenly I was behind him, whereas he was on the edge of the cliff. I did not know whether to push him or ask him to jump, or if I could suggest he did, or if I should push him and then tell him what I wanted him to do. While I reasoned, I touched him, and I saw him fall. [Metaphorical thinking relative to the deconstruction of the idealization that is taking place.]

"The scene does not end, and my mother appears. It was as if I had been inside and outside of her. She appeared sad to me and I felt her voice in my body because suddenly I felt spasms that accompanied the words: 'My God, how I suffer!' It was as if that feeling belonged to me. In reality, that was my mother's voice that I had made my own and the image of the woman embodied in her that I had introjected. My mother was almost always sad and unhappy, and her suffering tended to manifest through physical discomfort, and I carried this inside in the form of physical contractions that represented an existential pain. I had never so clearly felt her presence and her 'affection,' understood as emotive presence as I experienced it. This was the woman who was a point of reference for me, and something of her had become my own way of being in the world as an incapable, suffering, and needy victim. While I recognized my ego structure, I worked on the figures and reasons that had given rise to the formation of character. I felt the enormous unbearable weight of myself. The more I saw the facts of my life, the more I realized the great need to cover up all that pain. I felt how much pride I had put into the compensatory answer to the problems and situations I had come up against. [Insight.]

"I also had the chance to work on the figure of my mother to free myself of the identification with her introjected image. Under the effects of the substance I see her as a caricature: her hair was standing on end and her arms were open; the features of her face were deformed; she looked like a madwoman. This was how I had never seen her and how I had refused to see her. Inwardly, I perceived her this way, but I had a great feeling of guilt and I justified her actions because she

suffered. Seeing her caricature allowed me to separate the emotion from objectivity, and in this way access awareness of the mother I had and that in reality had not been a beneficial presence for me. [Insight and individuation, and implicitly, inspiration.]

"*I felt what she truly was, and* I sensed profoundly the absence and abandonment; *she was there to feed me, but otherwise, I did not feel that she was present, and emotionally she was nonexistent. I realized with the sufficient clarity and distance to remember that information that I have not forgotten. I finally saw how she was not there for me. I believe this is the only path to forgiveness.* After having accepted the undeniable fact of her absence and her madness that distanced her from me and from herself, I can look for a way of repairing the relationship with the parts of her that I carry inside me.

"*Then I went back to my father, whom I had left while he fell down the mountain I had placed him on as an unreachable person, figure, entity that I could not see for who he was, because it was so far removed from reality that I did not even remember what he was like. It was a fantasy.*

"*I knew that the process of deconstructing the idealization that I had to experience was similar to the one I had gone through with my mother. I saw him fall off the cliff while his clothes disappeared, and* the voice was urging me to have the courage necessary to see him as he really was in his essence, how I had to see him to free myself. *Not only did his clothes disappear, but also layers of skin; it was like opening something to see what is underneath; only at the end did I see him naked, with something covering his genitals. I wanted to undress him completely but was unable to; a great resistance warned me that I could not go beyond that point because there was something that could not be spoken, something deep and hidden, that had to be protected. It was the taboo of the denouncement of sex, of abuse, of aggression, of power, of conquest, and of man's possessive domination, as well as* the complicity with man that is part of this world and that belongs to me as a woman and to women in general. *I could go no further, and then I asked myself, beyond what might be behind the cardboard that covered part of his body,* what was the worst of all the wrongs that my father had done to me? The answer was that he had killed my dreams. He had exterminated them as if they were enemies of war. I grew up without having a dream in life, or a direction, because everything that stirred from within was short-lived; I had ceased to trust in what I felt.

"*I was telling my father that* I no longer needed him, *and I was deeply convinced. It was not a material need, but the dependence on the idea that had kept alive in me the wish for him to be a part of my life, albeit as a purely ideal and idealized presence. I shattered the illusion that was hurting me because it annihilated the possibility, though ethereal, of realizing everything that was concrete and that could have overruled his dominating authority, crushing and annihilating beyond all limits.*

"*It was a declaration I did not expect to make, born from the deepest part of me. I realized the truth of those words as if I had said (but before, saying it to myself) that the time had come to turn the page and pursue the creativity that had been suppressed for so long, beginning with the possibility of putting into words what I feel, as I am doing now.* . . .

"*The substance made my body adopt twisted positions, and while I felt pain and sadness, I was hoping to receive new information or a useful memory.* But the voice was explaining to me that the twisted and suffering position represented my real inner mood when on the outside, I showed myself to be happy. [*The "holy voice," and the insight inspired in a situation of intra-psychic teaching.*] *I adopted different positions in which I was shown how I was inwardly regarding what I was convinced I felt.* My mind denied in its origin any painful feeling or mood or reaction, suggesting to my consciousness that they were positive states.

"*I felt disconcerted. The distance between what I felt inside and what I told myself and what showed outwardly was dichotomous and abysmal. I reviewed my whole life again and recognized how ancient and stable in me was the split between 'inside' and 'outside.' [Her insight in this moment is none other than recognizing her histrionics, or dramatization of false emotions to hide her true feelings.]*

"In some moments, the difficulties found spaces of well-being in which, sometimes, through the music and light and pleasant images, Claudio appeared, as if coming to remind me of where I was and to bring me back to the present. I saw him more than once shirtless, gliding over turquoise waters, with his eyes half-closed; he was smiling. When I saw him, even if for a moment, I breathed again, and my peace of mind was restored, he was like an angel that allowed me to go on.

"In my mind there was a chaos of overlapping murmurs and voices; I did not know who was talking; it was as if several people lived inside me, each separate from each other; they each spoke as if in a monologue, as if they were alone. I felt afraid and at the same time I realized that all that noise had always existed, but that I had not been able to hear it because it showed up daily as a silent chaos that produces the same feeling of fragmentation that I perceive as confusion and dispersion.

"Then the voice led me to formulate a question *that represented the beginning of a phase of the experience* that culminated in the meeting with a girl inside of me that had always been waiting to be seen and heard. *The question was: 'The inner child, what is the inner child?' I spelled out the words as if hearing them for the first time, all together, while they took on the connotation of experience and lost the dimension of simple concept. While the question was repeated, I began to visualize inside of me, at the level of my vagina, the head of a young girl crowned in a golden halo. She was sitting in a small wooden chair and she felt bored. I knew that she had always been there and that she was waiting for me.* When I properly focused my attention on her, I said to her: 'So, you exist?' She stood up and started jumping up and down with joy, celebrating the fact that finally I was seeing her. *She was in a sort of cardboard skeleton and I could just see her head, but without a doubt it was she, that is to say, me as a young girl. I was amazed that she was still alive after all that I knew she had endured; I marveled at her strength and her resistance and the fact that she was intact, happy just because I could see her, the rest was not important.* Her voice had always been present, but I had not heard it or recognized it in the midst of the chaos, the murmur of thoughts and abstract ideas; she existed, and she was concrete. *That encounter marked one of the most important moments of my life. Overcome by incredulity, we hugged while the music accompanied that moment like in a love story film scene where the characters meet and good prevails following many challenges and obstacles. It was THE meeting and THE moment of my life up until now. I was aware that I was experiencing something absolutely unexpected and extraordinary. [Intra-psychic encounter.]*

"*I started up a dialogue with her and there was no room for anything or anyone else. I have never felt so complete and at home in my entire life. I understood that the emptiness I felt inside and part of the murmur that I heard was her call; she had always tried to catch my attention, to no avail. I spoke to her and asked her whether all the murmuring was her doing and she answered me yes. I imagined her with pots and pans to make noise like a child wanting her mother's attention. Then, when the experience led me to another situation and I felt lost, I went back to her, saw her, I was afraid of forgetting her existence again, and when I focused on her the calm returned. [Encounter, reintegration.]*

"The fact of seeing so much life in her made me feel that I was burying my old wish to die and to leave this world. *[A surprising statement, for one who knows her as a person so full of life, the depressive background of her experience is not so easily perceived.]*

"*The substance made me see my mother and the fact that it had been her choice to give up on life before life gave up on her. 'She chose to die while alive,' the voice said, 'so it is better that she dies now.' I could see my mother's body and face transform into that of an old woman. Before her appeared a riverbank and a boat that looked like a gondola; she got in it and left. She died. As she sailed away, something was telling me that I could say goodbye to her and I did: I said goodbye to her. [Liberation of introject.] Then the doubt arose in me that I might need her, and I wondered what I had done. But no answer came; the scene changed once again. It was the representation of movement, of the current, of the flow of the mind and of experiences that appeared to me for the necessary time before disappearing. The substance kept circulating through me; I felt that it was cleansing the inside of my body and at a particular moment I also had the impulse to heal. I ran my hands all over my body, as if in a ritual of healing myself; healing my body and my wounds inside and out. [Purification.]*

"*Sometimes I felt the masculine voice that came to devalue me, ridicule me and make me feel weak and valueless; it was horrible. In the beginning I identified with the voice completely, but at a certain point I felt that it came from a part of my mind, as if there was a man hiding, talking behind my head. It was the masculine figures I had encountered in my childhood. Older, it is as if I had lost the ability to recognize that that part did not represent my essence but was a toxic pressure that repressed the freedom, movement, and expression of other parts belonging to me. [Insight. Detachment.]*

"*The dominating voice was the one that Claudio defines as 'patriarchal ego.' Taking it to a higher level, the experience led me to discover that there was a different plane of the mind that was the 'realm' of emotion.* I had the feeling of not having a heart and of not being able to feel emotions coming from it. Unexpectedly, I saw my heart explode and beat fast in the center of my chest, as if it was bursting, strong and visible. *[Reintegration.]*

"*In that region of the mind there was no space for a self-regulating voice. When I tried to ask my heart what I felt, the voice that answered was the voice of reason and of the father that I had learned to recognize and that silenced the true feeling.* Compassion and empathy, so hard for me to feel, were, therefore, under the control of reason and responded to that which, following the moment, I ought to have felt and not to what I genuinely felt. *[Insight.]*

"*While I was discovering that level of consciousness, I moved to another center (also separate from the center of reason and of emotion).*

It was the lesser known because it was the furthest: the center of instinct. [Reintegration and change of 'convergence point.'] They were three isolated worlds; there was no connection in terms of information; it was as if they had been different planes of consciousness, separate and with no knowledge of each other. Each would seem complete, but in reality, the distance I perceive between emotion, instinct, and reason is equal to a real intra-psychic split that separates, fragments, and distances from the center. [Insight.]

"*It was impossible to reduce to silence the mind that talked incessantly, as if it had been the control center of the whole system. I was a spectator of everything that happened, like consciousness looking at itself. It was like* a meditative state in which the silence of emotions allowed the incessant rapid flow of information and that, not becoming attached to anything, flowed with the current. *[Spontaneous flow, neutrality.]*

"*Today I feel that this experience has been revealing for me.*

"I constantly looked for peace in silence and in listening to what moves inside with an attention that does not intervene. *When the mind gets stuck, I am able to relax by recognizing the thought as something impermanent and I wait for it to pass.*

"*A greater awareness has arisen of my moods and a greater coherence between what I think and the action corresponding to what the image or the thought suggest. Nevertheless, I feel more aware of what is united within me; I also feel more centered regarding 'what is' when I observe without too many veils or superstructures.*

"After the experience, I felt the imperative need to speak a few truths about my past with reference to forgotten events and emotions that resurfaced *seeking an outlet and acceptance on my part.* [Memories, acceptance.] *I think it is all connected to the fact that after having seen in me the presence of the 'child' and having felt what it was that called for justice and truth, I have begun to answer that call with greater attention. Somehow, the gag that oppressed that voice has fallen away and it has allowed me to look inside instead of seeking or demanding outside. Part of the blindness regarding the child was linked to the fact that there was not a woman to attend to what she needed because she had not grown up;* now I feel that an adult presence within me has the sufficient courage and strength to sustain that call for caring for myself that before I ignored. *[Self-love.]*

"*I also feel that it is calming down, aided by the detachment that the substance allowed me to experience, the self-perpetuating thirst for love that finds no satisfaction on the outside. In spite of being distanced from emotion,* I felt the completeness and the richness of the experience that I did not wish to interrupt even to go to the bathroom because it seemed like a waste of time to me. *It has been an opportunity to experience intensely and in first person a part of what Claudio teaches during meditation, and to internalize his message about the need to liberate the patriarchal mind that desensitizes consciousness, limiting it to the point of reaching the extinction of the force of instinct and of love.*

"After the experience I felt bad due to the weight of the charge of the denouncement and of the enormity of the crime toward the feminine aspect, which proceeds like a destructive machine perfectly engrained in the system and that refuses to reveal itself as the evil that is annihilating us.

"*The pain I felt was not only mine, but also deeply connected to the evil that I perceived as belonging to humanity that is blindly moving toward its own destruction. [Compassion.]*

"*I am infinitely grateful for the opportunity that has been given to me and I hope to use everything that I have felt, seen, and integrated in the best possible way.*"

EPILOGUE

The session starts with her feeling guided and led to not knowing and the search for understanding: "I did not know who I was, and I questioned it . . . I began to ask myself questions about my mind," and it seems to me a wonderful start. I would say that it was the inspiration of her inner guide that led her to look inward, to discover that she does not know who she is and to question it. And what higher practice do we know in the journey of consciousness than that which takes an interest in the nature of the mind?

What she describes next when she touches "the center of her skull" seems to me an indication that the question she is asking herself about the mind is far beyond intellectual, and since in virtue of a deep parallel between consciousness and the body, the crown is related to the encounter with one's own mind, I would say that she seems to be intuiting that to open her mind she needs to open something akin to the "crown etheric sphincter" that is known as the seventh chakra; what she says conveys to us that indeed, she does achieve this, as she suggests when she writes: "As if the cement barrier literally opened."

However, the spiritual experience not only depends on the body but also on the psychological experience, and this is what immediately becomes manifest: "It was the second door of resistance: control"; and again, perceiving things clearly transforms them, as her metaphorical thinking reveals: "That ring that was made of metal turned into a ring of birds."

Understandably, a relaxing of the ego's resistance gives way to a greater flow of experience, and this is confirmed by the account: "While everything began to move." It is understandable that fear arises when leaping into a greater space of freedom, although our psychonaut seems to have gained enough courage to be able to overcome it. (When I spoke about it with her, she explained to me that I also helped her and that her trust in me was fundamental.)

From the experiences of the universe and the primordial she moves to the personal with a memory of unease during intrauterine life, and after describing this she makes an unusual comment: the absence of emotion in her memories, which is in contrast with the emotional nature of her usual experiences. I would say that here becomes apparent the characteristic neutrality of the "typical ibogaine state," and also an insight about her usual "emotionalization" of life—a typical trait of histrionic people, as rationalization is of intellectual and fearful characters.

Then begins a series of comprehensions relative to her inner world throughout her entire life; first concerning her invalidating father and then regarding her mother; understandings that give rise to changes— at least in her inner world. The sequence with her father is one of progressing from the perception of the critical voice of the father within, to the understanding that his disdainful attitude has been the consequence of an excessive value attached to "earnings, appearances, ostentation, the well-being guaranteed by possession and luxury, effort, much effort, and all that is obtained through money, what is done with money to procure a substitute for what nature already offers," and to a liberating criticism of the paternal values that until now fear had not allowed her to express, which in turn inspires rage in her. Then she understands, more broadly, that she has idealized her father by accepting his dominion, and immediately she experiences in her mind the equivalent of a de-idealization, first in finding on the top of a mountain, not a gigantic being but simply the father of her youth whom she had idealized, and then in seeing him fall to an abyss after barely touching him (a perfectly appropriate representation of the fact that she did not need to show violence to rid herself of her paternal introjection after having understood it so completely).

Following a healing process with her relationship to her mother, she comes back to considering her father, and I find it surprising that after seeing the image of her father naked hiding his genitals, she asks herself about the harm he has done her and comes to an answer that has nothing to do with sex, but with the blockage of her creative activity. I imagine here a leap in consciousness, for in the autobiography she writes following this report she says she realized her father's secret homosexuality, and yet it seems true to me that his cynicism had been more destructive, scorning all kind of ideals, which is, moreover, typical of people with his character, which seems to me (due to information that is not in these pages) to be a preservation seven enneatype.

I find striking the perfect order of this process of reelaboration of the childhood experience that arises from surrendering to a seemingly chaotic and uncontrollable experiential flow of experience. First the de-idealization and liberation from the father's and mother's introjections, and now finding again her past identity as "inner child." So, I ask myself, might it be the case that the emphasis on the "three intra-psychic persons" in my explanation of neurosis has constituted something like a shortcut that facilitated the process for her?

With the logic of a systematic renewal of her inner world that presents itself perfectly spontaneously, with no apparent deliberation, the mother becomes again the central focus; the suffering and complaining mother with whom she had also identified and had introjected, without ever understanding it so clearly as now, and she understands how the existential suffering of carrying that suffering mother in her had manifested through a physical pain caused by contractions.

Immediately there is, as in the case with the father, a freeing herself from her introjection, which presents itself this time as a caricature-like vision. "Her hair was standing on end and her arms were open, the features of her face were deformed, she looked like a madwoman. This was how I had never seen her, and I had refused to see her." She also understands then how her mother's suffering had become her own attitude of "helpless victim, suffering and needy." However, not only does she understand her experience of victimization and devaluation, but also the effort with which she had wanted to always hide that aspect of herself through a mask of arrogance.

I wish to end this retrospective commentary by noting that many aspects of this experience will be recognizable for those who have read my report about the group experience in the previous chapter, but certain elements toward the end of this account impress me as a new category that I have classified as episodes of "intra-psychic integration": first with the inner child, then with the habitual "patriarchal Self," which is now perceived with a distance that allows it to be explicitly discerned, then with the heart and finally with the instinctual Self. In view of this woman's previous familiarity with my thoughts (about the patriarchal mind and the tri-unitary ideal of health), I could not help but feel that my theoretical formulation of those matters might have acted on her mind like a fertile teaching that has offered her a shortcut on a usually very long journey. I also take the opportunity to comment on the singularity of the description that she offers us of how in looking at me she was able to free her perception of the usual projections (from father and grandfather). In wanting to classify that experience in the terms already analyzed from the group experience mentioned, the most pertinent category has seemed to me "reality," although, obviously, it is not an ordinary reality, but a deep or mysterious reality—coherent with her previous implicit experience of spiritual contact when seeing me as somebody similar to Buddha and finally feeling herself to be on the right path.

I conclude by pointing out a curiosity that I find enigmatic: the likeness of the image of the "eye behind the eye" that I have emphasized by shifting the font and that I gathered at another time and even in another country. I would say that it is one of those cases of metaphorical or symbolical thinking, which suggests a different type of perception, more inner than that of usual self-knowledge, but without attempting to interpret it better, I shall limit myself to reproducing the strikingly similar experience of one of the subjects in the group mentioned in the preceding chapter.

"At one point I felt like I had two sets of eyes, and my physical eyes, my eyelids, were closed, but behind there were other eyelids that were opening, like eyelids that opened to the unconscious and to another dimension of reality. With those eyes I was able to see my eye, my physical eye, my left eye. This part of the eye came to stand before me and this eye started to go backward. And it got older and older, until it became people who were too old, and then again, it went through

different genders, the eye of a man, the eye of a woman, then of a man
again, of many women. My eye was in the body of many women and of
many men in a kind of regression."

This account suggests to me that it is a metaphorical representation of
the way of seeing induced by the alkaloid, as if a higher intelligence were
announcing that it is both a very special and different seeing and one that
occurs in a different sphere, different both from the external world and the
usual internal world.

5

Psilocybin

5.1 SURRENDER AND PEACE, INSPIRATION AND SELF-KNOWLEDGE IN THE SELF-REPAIR PROCESS INDUCED BY HALLUCINOGENIC MUSHROOMS

I have often said that whatever the mechanism of action of psychedelics in the nervous system, it would seem that the nature of its effect was something akin to an anesthesia of the ego or neurotic personality that ordinarily limits us, and that the simplest consequence of this liberation was the simple recuperation of a state of happy tranquillity; a simple letting oneself be without imposing obligations or obstacles; a state of acceptance of the experience of the moment where "everything is ok."

This is how one of the participants of a therapy group with psilocybin mushrooms describes it: "As soon as it began it was very easy to go to a place where everything is possible, where anything can happen, where whatever my problems may be are unimportant, everything is ok there."

The feeling of all being well and inner peace, however, can be complemented by an element of numinosity or sacredness, at times also transmitted by music and at times by light: "A lot of golden light and a lot of being at peace with myself, with myself and with life; everything is fine as it is. All I have to do is to do what comes up for me each day . . ."

Also, just as how in the quote above the state of peace is compatible with doing what needs to be done in the moment, more broadly, it can be said that it is like a still place that the ever-changing flow of experience passes through: "I was completely still; while, within, was a rapidly flowing current."

Since the current of life that flows through the mind in stillness is an evolutionary process or a healing personal development, it is understandable that it is represented as a process of blossoming: "A visualization came to me that I was a bud, that was opening very lovingly with the notes, the musical notes were caressing me and opening my petals and I repeated over and over again: 'Thank you for trusting in me, thank you for trusting in me.'"

Those familiar with meditation will recognize this deeply satisfying place of inner tranquillity as something that, far from being the artificial result of the suspension of thought, is like a natural backdrop of the mind, with which we have lost contact in our agitation or neurotic paralysis. A condition of freedom, also, in that not only "anything can happen," but also in that one feels a plenitude that seems to derive from one's own essence or being, and therefore one does not seek extrinsic satisfaction. It is like an open space, where one can allow oneself to be penetrated by life, but this open space can also reveal itself as a great treasure with no describable qualities at the core of all the phenomena of consciousness.

"The experience has been, ultimately, one of going beyond thought. Something happened that I would not know how to translate into words that belong to thinking. I have made contact with my vital core, which I did not think I had, and that allowed me to be for a long time in a state of total serenity. I know this will allow me to penetrate the world without the need to step away from it, and that difficulties will only help me grow, and they will not be something menacing that I need to worry about."

It is as if the open space of this serene and receptive consciousness was the precondition of the richness of what shows up in the "inner journeys," and an aspect of this richness is something like an inspiration that manifests through these inner journeys as a guiding principle that can sometimes present itself as a voice or as a person, and at other times as simple creativity in search of the next step in a process of healing.

Thus, one woman explains in her retrospective account:

> "A soft voice was telling me: 'do not judge, simply see what is coming'; ok, I was only here to observe . . . not to put words to each thing I saw. . . . It was as if a mother, a sister, or friend were talking to me, and then the cathedrals opened to me."

The guiding principle does not need to operate through words, however; it also operates without them when the person feels "accompanied" or "carried," as in this case:

> "At this point, I started journeying but very lightly; I was carried by angels . . . I am not used to that . . . and I began to travel through so many places, which seemed to be made of petals; very soon floating images appeared, and I was saying: 'I want to know the important things.'"

It is very interesting that it is precisely this "I want to know" that makes us feel that she feels accompanied, that is to say, in dialogue. Or, even more subtly, the experience of a wise influence can become manifest: "I felt the presence of a guide constantly, but it did not have dialogue, and that for me is wonderful because I always have an inner dialogue or monologue, and that did not appear."

However, it is perhaps an oversimplification to speak of a "guiding principle," as if its sole function was to signpost a path. Sometimes the "inner guide" gives explanations, like the ones a person who is aware of what the "journeyer" needs to know would give, or other information that seems to come from a clairvoyant or omniscient faculty. "I started to hear voices that were saying: 'Now we are going on a journey, and you will be cared for." Or, further on: "The voice comes to me that says:

well, the day that you are going to die is the same day that you were born, and now the journey continues . . ."

Could it be that it is the intuitive cerebral hemisphere that behaves like a person and manifests to the mind that, after having silenced thinking, opens to something "magical" beyond its ordinary limits?

The following account is revealing:

"The first part was like a kind of anchoring; all I could hear was the voice of a woman that I felt was my mother, and she spoke to me when I was a child: 'Rest assured, my pretty girl, rest assured, trust, trust.' Then, I allowed myself to sink into my body and I surrendered to follow this motherly voice, and from there I began to feel secure; I began to play with her, something that was fun, and she said to me: 'Come, I want to introduce you to Claudio.' And I was saying: 'No, no, no, not Claudio,' and like that, in a low voice, she said to me: 'It's ok, come, I want to introduce you to Claudio.' And I said, but how am I going to reach him, across the long room, and the voice said, well, let us build a bridge together, it was all like a game, like Pan's labyrinth, something like that; then I said: 'Oh, ok, the bridge thing is cool, but people will see us, how scary,' and so on. 'No, no, because we are going to use some magic powders so that nobody sees us, but let us go to Claudio, come.' And I say, ok, but do not let go of me; 'No, no, I am going with you, come, come'; then I open my eyes and I see Claudio standing here, and I say, sorry? [laughs], and there was no bridge to speak of, and I did not know what to do, I mean, I saw you standing there and it was like feeling: this is magic. You crouched down and said to me: 'Tell me something,' and I was wondering, should I tell him about the bridge? [laughs]. Then I said: 'I am enveloped in love, I am with mother, I am calm . . .' And I spoke with mother again: 'Mother, this is so strong, can you believe it?' and so on. I was amazed, it was a fairy tale, a complete fairy tale, then I stood up and after a while I said: 'But I want to go also, I want to walk, I do not want Claudio to come, I want to walk toward him'; so I stood up in the room, and I

had mother behind me, and I said to her: do not leave, and she said: 'No, no, you walk, walk, go toward him, go toward him.' Then it was as if for the first time I started to walk, I started to crawl, then I stood up, feeling that I was beginning to grow, and I started to walk toward Claudio, and as I was reaching him, I felt like surrendering; surrendering to love, surrendering to trust; and what I dared to ask was: 'Are you here, are you here for me also?' And you said to me: 'Of course!' And it was marvelous, it was amazing, I have never felt that before in my life, you are here for me . . . [She is moved.]"

These two aspects of the psychedelic experience—the self-sufficient neutrality of detachment that allows surrender to the organic flow of the experience, and intuition or the "guiding principle"—can be sufficient explanation of the self-healing process that takes place throughout a good session, regardless of occasional therapeutic interventions that can (in the best of cases) facilitate the process. However, sometimes one barely intuits the open and receptive state (that allows the magic of a healthy organismic function), and the person has to be willing to surrender to be able to give up their usual excessive control.

"I could not allow myself, I could not let go, I had the feeling of being grabbed, I was looking to see what was grabbing me, I had concrete experiences such as, for example, with my mother, with . . . But I was restless, restless, restless; I approached you, Claudio, mmm . . . I felt oral, then I liked to do it this way, as if, give me, give me, I need, and that is when you said to me: 'Take what you need, I am giving it to you,' I was like, well, yes . . . but it helped me afterward to realize that what I need is contact, and at the same time it is like I want to do it by myself."

"You are conditioned to saying to yourself that you can manage on your own," I fill in here in this retrospective, and she continues:

"When I was able to accept: 'yes . . . I need,' it was very good for me. Like something simple. Thank you very much for this space; I came

searching for that although I did not know it, I mean, I knew it and I did not know it. . . . Anyhow, that is what you generate, what you have generated and what we can enjoy. That we know how to maintain it and continue to do it is another matter."

It may be that I have a certain capacity to evoke that open space of detachment through a lengthy experience in meditation, but I also suppose that a great contribution to creating this space (that constitutes an important aspect of what I teach) is the theoretical background that I have added to it through previous contact with those who have experiences of this kind. This understanding of the spirituality of detachment or of the neutrality of deep consciousness, which is so present in the spiritual traditions but is lacking in the theories of psychotherapy, may be relatively exceptional in regard to the professional culture of therapists. It can be said that those who have participated in psychedelic experiences are fully aware that the "work" consists, paradoxically, in surrendering, in letting oneself be guided by a will different to one's own, in allowing oneself to be penetrated by the experience of the moment—perhaps even to "disappear."

However, those who have already entered into the place of serene contemplation of the present can be guided toward a greater depth.

"I have just realized that I entered into the experience without voracity, without wishing for anything, I was very, very relaxed, I did not expect anything, I was very, very present there, and at the very beginning of it all, when the colors, the wonderful shapes, the bliss began, it came to me very clearly: 'Step aside, step aside, Raúl, step aside.' Also, curiosity to see who appeared if I stepped aside, right? . . . And a creature began to emerge very much in the present, it was feeding off the present, contact with the music, with what it was seeing, and I began to feel very strong trembling up and down my spine, and then also here, at the nape of the neck."

Naturally, for the one contemplating, contemplation is already a path of transformation, for it allows the healing influences of music, of nature, or of healthy human contact—and much could be said about each of these spheres of psycho-spiritual nourishment.

Thus, for example, one pondered the question:

"If this space exists, if this place exists, what is the meaning of life? If we can be here, why are we alive, why are we incarnated in a body? Then that led me to see the others, to see myself from the perspective of humility, of simplicity, of a child. That perspective, when I was together with C., was telling me: 'I can hear your heart'; or people approached and asked me things, and everything was like seeing the other from a deep space, of being embodied; it is like giving sense to that spiritual part. In that spiritual space that is pure joy, is pure love, I think that space needs the color of human beings."

The following is an experience where the most striking is not the interpersonal relationship, but ordinary perception—which in some way becomes extraordinary:

"Well, I feel very, very grateful because the experience had to do with the annihilation of the mind . . . it was like waves after waves; I realized that I am beginning to learn to navigate this thing of 'surrendering.' It is the only thing there is, right? And I saw how the ego resisted, like 'aaagggh'; and I could say 'no' to it. 'Allow yourself, annihilate yourself, there is nothing you can do here,' I said to the 'aaagggh,' and the mind was like . . . destroying itself, and when I thought that I had reached something, I would say 'this is it,' there I realized and would say 'no, do not get attached because it is not,' and something else would appear. There were strong moments of feeling nature. I saw my feet and the sky. My feet were like the feet of an old lady, and I felt (as had never happened to me) devotion toward myself; toward the steps I have taken in life with these feet. It was very restorative."

Lastly, I quote an experience where music is in the foreground, both as a vehicle of love and as devotional incentive:

"Then my right hand facing firmly upward, connecting me with the true reality, and my left hand completely fused with the music, I felt sexual love to the maximum, emotional love to the maximum, I felt the subtlest delicateness, precise like violins, each sound was absolutely beautiful, devotional, utterly beautiful, feeling that also meeting God was not from below to above, but from above to below."

However, such experiences do not suffice to account for the extraordinary therapeutic effect of hallucinogenic mushrooms. For although detached consciousness and intuition are always the factors that support the therapeutic process, the work sometimes requires digging deeper into the mind and the past in view of the need to reelaborate traumatic childhood experiences—and especially, the need to remember the pain and rage underlying current relational problems. I illustrate this, above all, with an experience that presented itself to somebody who had already lost their bodily perception and ordinary identity.

"I encountered a distant part of myself, a part of deep anger and great resentment and a lot of repression and a lot of humiliation, it was like . . . I was . . . something came to me that was like 'I have no head, I only have a bad temper, I have nothing else,' I felt there was no head, I was unable to answer anything, I had a lot of common sense, but something that was from a bad temper, it seemed to me that everything was wrong, that something had to be done, that there was no solution for this, that. . . . And that is when you were approaching Rebecca, and when you were about to stand up (well, before that), I began to connect with all the resentment I felt toward my father. Why did he become ill; why the hell did he leave us; why was he sick; why did I have to place myself above him?

"And then I was overcome by resentment, and it was circle, and

there was no escaping the fucking circle, from resentment to omnipotence,
from omnipotence to resentment, not forgiving him, not forgiving myself.
When, at a given moment, you were about to stand up, Graciela and
Juan went to help you, and you said: 'I can manage, I can manage'; there
was the pain of feeling that my father was not capable; he could not
manage alone; and I felt such pain, pain, a tremendous pain!—and at
least I entered into the pain.

"*I felt my husband deeply; it was marvelous; I felt him so strongly*
that I forgot about him, so that was wonderful, that he was so deeply in
me, but he was there for me, for the first time I was letting him be there
for me, and at one point it was asphyxiating, and I felt: 'He is here for
me, and I have to leave this place, but then the burden of projecting the
father will remain, right?'

"*And from there, I have no idea, I am really lost, I am left with the*
feeling: 'Well, and now?' As if I had lost the sense of doing something.
My life no longer has meaning, as if I had lost. . . . It might have
something to do with having to save my father from something; now it
makes no sense. . . . So, well, as God wishes; put myself in service to
something else . . . I will take it as it comes."

No doubt the text transcribed here is not enough to fully understand
what it means for her to have lost "the sense of doing something," and
therefore, I must explain that she is a person with the type of personality that in the psychology of the enneatypes is known as an enneatype
preservation three: the conservative variant of vanity, not recognized by
the DSM-5 and that is so widespread in the United States that it can be
said it is a typically North American type of character and that it is not
considered pathological, for it does not lead so much to suffering, but
to a compulsion to efficiency and loss of contact with the inner self. A
person of this type is constantly doing because he or she expects to be
loved for what he or she produces, and it is understandable that when
the person manages to let go of the compulsive need for doing, he or she
feels at least some perplexity, or experiences something like a mourning

for the part of himself or herself that has been left behind. However, as much as from excessive humility she says that by being free of always having to do something "she is lost"; I do not doubt that she has taken a great step toward her liberation, which will have positive effects on her life.

Here is another illustration of a process of healing regression with the implication of an incipient change of character:

"During the first part, highly important, there were feelings of fear and rage; as one dissipated, another arrived; it was really being in that pole continuously, and there I realized how anger was my response. The only thing I did not know was to what question, to what situation. . . . And a scene appeared that I already knew but had never visited in this way, a scene of when I was eight years old, where my father, in a fit of anger, was really strangling me, and I felt rage, fear, and tremendous pain. . . . Moreover, he was strangling me, telling me to: 'Speak up, for fuck's sake.' At this point it was liberating for me to shout out . . . that's enough of that! The only thing is that once again I came across anger, fear, anger, and fear, and did not know how to get out of there. . . . And I had, I do not know, the inspiration or the courage, or the lack of strength to stay there, and something began to happen that I did not understand, that my mind was rebelling against the possibility of that happening . . . and my father's spirit came. . . . His spirit came, my father's, about twenty years before he died; his spirit came and . . . [cries] asked me for forgiveness . . . and that undid me. I no longer had to be angry, or afraid; it threw me off center, and it has thrown me, because next he accompanied me to heaven, and heaven was here, it was this; and I felt how the barriers fell away, the barriers between the spiritual and the human, the psychic, I do not know, and I still feel that I am there, like I understood there is no barrier. I felt like a child, I could only be there as a child, and he even said to me: 'Well, now you have to go and meet God,' and I was searching for him, but he is not there, I mean, he is not placed there, but rather he is . . . he was like

*air . . . I felt very good, until, until something showed up that prevented
me from being here, which was when I came to say to you: 'I am in the
presence of God and I feel dissatisfaction and, how to deal with this?'
You replied something like, I do not remember exactly: 'Of course, after
a lifetime of trying to achieve everything on your own'; I understood it,
and I have been pondering this ever since, it is like I do not know how
to be satisfied: it is something strange to me; I am focused on achieving
satisfaction . . ."*

In this episode of remarkable change of perspective regarding a
childhood experience that allowed the person, through forgiving his
father, not only to free himself of a chronic hatred but also to remain at
peace, a characterological change has also occurred, only very different
from the previous one. In this case it is a personality type that in the
psychology of the enneatypes is identified as a social two—a proud and
ambitious type, which we can evoke through the well-known images of
Napoleon or the powerful Louis XIV, the Sun King. In both cases they
can be described as people of great "stature": powerful people who have
reached positions of power through a remarkable will to conquer. The
ambitious person always wants more, and seeks out greater triumphs, so
much that in the case of Napoleon, his ambition leads him to the exaggerated enterprise of wanting to triumph over Russia and through this,
his downfall.

However, what happens if an ambitious person, in view of a practically miraculous transformation, finds himself or herself devoid of his
or her desire to achieve more and reach higher, and no longer feels dis-
satisfied? Will he or she know how to accept the placid acceptance that
life now has in store for him or her?

The apparition of the father in the experience of this man at the
peak of his desperation may seem enigmatic, and one may wonder if it
is his own fantasy, induced by a deep desire to free himself of the weight
of guilt about an aggression that until now he had not allowed himself
to express, even though he had carried it his whole life in the form of

chronic resentment. Or was it, rather, as no doubt it seemed to him, an unexpected real visit from the father's spirit; that is to say, a moment of mediumship in which his mind, turned more receptive by the effect of the hallucinogenic, was able to perceive the influence of his real father?

Few in our secular world today believe in the survival of spirits, and even Buddhists would say that our parents have already reincarnated, following a brief sojourn in the Bardos, or worlds of transition. Yet, how much do we know in our certainties? And perhaps those who wonder about what they do not know, know more than those who pretend to know . . .

Many investigations and testimonials demonstrate that interventions by shamans and healers are effective—even though there are also charlatans—and that both clairvoyance and mediumship are real phenomena; if this is so, might it not be that the mind, under the effect of a hallucinogenic, can transiently manifest such abilities?

Here is another illustration of something that I would personally interpret as a paranormal phenomenon and not merely a paranoid fantasy:

> "Something appeared that unsettled me, which was something like as if there was a curse stuck to my soul, as if somebody had cursed me with black magic, and something was stuck to me that has not had its full development partly thanks to my form, my light, or to I do not know what, but there was something stuck there; and that is when I thought: 'What a paranoia with black magic,' because it is something that I know is there, but that is not for me. Then it came to me that this (and I say it just as it is) was the result of an ex-partner, whom I married here; some of you were at the wedding, and had such a bad time with the separation that she decided to take revenge; so, she cursed me with that black magic; I am not sure if it is a paranoia or what, but it felt the same, the way I experienced it. Then it came to me that the black magic has turned against her, for she has been ill, she is ill, she is still very much alone, and for me, it was on the one hand feeling the pain

and wanting to get rid of that, but I had to do that not in kind, but with love; then came a long time of undoing this operation, like a surgery, like one of removing from my soul all of that black magic, all of that stuff I had stuck there, deep down, gradually remove it, remove it, remove it, and I even thought: 'You have to speak with Vilas to see whether this is the case or whether it is all my imagination'; so I was removing it, removing it, removing it, and with love, and wishing the best for her, with love, that she heals, that she finds a man that makes her happy, and it was very long. I do not know how long it lasted, it happened once, it happened again; it was like unraveling something that was very deeply threaded there."

The theme of the re-elaboration of the experience has led me to the subject of the transformative insight of one's own personality; however, regression to traumatic experiences is not necessary for understanding to be revealed about the dysfunctionality or irrationality of the attitude that has constituted the implicit fundamental problem of one's own life.

A woman of type E8, characterized by a fighting spirit and by lust or a thirst for intensity, for example, wrote the following:

"I felt the weight of this old skin, of this fighting character of mine, of a warrioress that is already fifty-two years old . . . that I must do it differently because I am not going to get anywhere like this, forcing, forcing myself, but for what? Because there I felt overwhelmed, a fatigue of my excessive efforts, of not being able to simply say 'I do not feel like it, no, no, I do not feel like it' I also see how I have a great tendency to please others; well, I forget about myself."

And further on:

"But I feel that something has gone out of me, I want to live in peace, I seek peace, I see that I am always overexcited, I am tired, I want to be calm. And I felt that I need to let this old Muriel go a little, that I

am transitioning to another passage in my life, simply, and to be calmer, and I feel that something has gone out of me, I feel much happier, very tired, but happy to have released this thing, and I want to start over in another way."

Another example, this time taken from the account of a social E7, which is the personality of a "goodie-goodie," who sacrifices himself in excess for others, and who for a desire to be appreciated, behaves too idealistically.

"I started to get more real, not loading myself up with anything, but stripping down to the true essentials; and as I became more real, the day was finer, and I felt more present and more complete with people, and there was no division between the holy and the unholy, between the divine and the human, there was. . . . It was I, was it not? I inhabited myself from within, I was complete, and I was working. . . . And slowly I started to realize that if I resolve my issues I feel very good, and if I do not pay attention to my stuff, I feel like a good person. There is a great temptation, 'I am good, I am very nice, I go down really well with people,' and when I attend to my stuff I am much more serious, more boring, more problematic; but I think that my patients, my friends, my family, and myself, we deserve that Carlos be here, not that Carlos no longer be here."

The following passage is of a sexual E2, a seductive person who has confused the false love that is expressed to attract external love, with true love, and who in her account refers to the discovery of a "dry love" that she had not perceived, and now discovers as more real than the "damp love" of seduction.

"There it was as if I left my body and it was a journey, I do not know, in another dimension, where every time I felt afraid, Claudio's smile appeared; then I started seeing Claudio's smile everywhere, and it

accompanied me. And then I connected with a lot of dry love. It was dry and there was a part of my ego that was saying: this is not love, you are getting confused, this has no validity. . . . And I would look at him and go to that love, which was a love that flooded me, which was immense, but it was like feeling love in the middle of the desert, and at the same time, it was a calm love, quiet, without affectation, it did not need to be expressed much; love for my father also came to me, I could see him, and I went out to keep him company, to be with him, but it was a very calm love. Above all I felt great love for Claudio; I felt at one point that . . . that it was much greater than the love for my father, the love that in that moment I felt for Claudio, and that gave me a more compassionate perspective of him and of myself, of my father, of myself. . . . I do not know, of my son, of my husband, but everything was very calm and very solitary also."

5.2 THE AWARENESS OF ILLNESS, THE AWAKENING OF LOVE, AND THE GLIMPSE OF KNOWLEDGE IN EXPERIENCES WITH PSILOCYBIN

I wish to address next three themes, each of which can be considered a healing aspect of the experience with "magic mushrooms": becoming aware of one's own illness, the awakening to love, and the glimpse of wisdom.

I. THE AWARENESS OF ILLNESS

The Christian tradition says that we must purify ourselves from sin through recognizing and confessing it, which leads to the desire for amends, and similarly, in the spiritual traditions much importance is given to recognizing certain destructive emotions such as attachment or aversion as a starting point of the possibility of being able to free oneself of their slavery. All of this is no different from what in the language of psychotherapy is designated as the "awareness of illness," which the psychology of the enneatypes describes as the comprehension of the "passions" underlying one's own personality. The starting point in this recognition is the simple feeling that one is not truly living, or that real life is being disregarded in an excessive dedication to worldly purposes, which sometimes happens spontaneously or due to the influence of certain people or religious ideas. However, it is particularly common for this to occur under the effects of psilocybin, during which a sort of "descent to hell" takes place that leads people to adopt attitudes of amends, through which they can recover well-being. Here are some examples taken from a retrospective account of a group session:

> "I have realized that I have been shutting myself off; I have shut myself off so much recently for fear of what I carry inside, or perhaps for fear of having nothing inside. I even resist meeting up with a friend to chat. I came to ask you during the session what I should do, and you told me that I should let what I carry inside come out, and that affected me deeply. I think that is what I will do, rather than keep taking refuge in work—which is a space where I can be strong, recognized, and where I express my power. However, it is a space that is killing who I am, as who I am is not expressed anywhere else. Even, when the telephone rings, I hope it is a work issue, and not a friend. But now I have decided that I will give up my job, and right now."

On occasions such as this one, the encounter with one's own inner self constitutes a great spiritual incentive, for we are all seekers rather distracted from our guidance and inner work by mundane distractions.

In the following statement, someone feels that, through the effect of the mushroom, she has discovered her spiritual vocation, and now wishes to place that quest at the center of her life. We could say that it is an impulse of the same nature as in the case mentioned previously, which she had apparently invalidated as presumptuous due to her compulsive modesty, only that here it appears alongside a rare understanding and acceptance of one's own imperfection.

> "My experience of yesterday was one that I can describe as being about my vocation, or about being called. I have something to confess: that all I am interested in is spiritual growth. This is my life's priority. I was not able to declare this because it seemed too presumptuous. But neither can I deny it. At one point, I visualized a sort of scale, on one side of which was all the luminous, spiritual, divine, and on the other all the negativity, my presumption, arrogance; and this scale was in perfect balance. I have wondered: Could this be equanimity? They were in perfect balance, and both were fundamental. And I saw that I must change my attitude regarding my character, and that I need my tenacity to achieve what I have to achieve. I feel honest in saying what I am saying. We all have a vocation, and life makes us go toward where our vocation calls us. God calls us and we all go to him."

The following illustration is also about somebody who has learned to overcome a dysfunctional attitude (of demanding explanations or asking unnecessary questions); the trigger of her change of direction is an approach to death, which presents itself to her through a "visit" from her father, recently passed away:

> "I felt a great fear of dying; I was almost certain I was dying, and my heart was beating very fast in my throat, and my left arm was hurting. I thought of A. and told myself that I would call him to me, and with him by my side, I would calm down, and it was as if he took me by the hand and accompanied me. That strong pain in my heart lasted for about half an hour, and A. left me in my father's hands. And I begin a journey. We are facing a door, and my father says to me: 'Do not worry, let us go through.' I enter with him and my heart automatically calms down. He looks at me and says: 'This is death,' and I feel a deep peace in my body. A lifetime's tension dissolves and from one moment

to the next there is nothing left. I am impressed, and I say: 'It cannot be like this.' He says to me: 'No: it is like this. Do you not trust?' And for about two minutes an intense pain returned to my heart. 'And now, do you trust?' 'Yes, yes, yes.' 'Do not worry, you will be in peace. The sense of everything is precisely peace,' he tells me. 'You must not worry anymore,' and then he guides me to go deeper into the experience.

"Words mean nothing compared to what I was fortunate to find. It has been a deep experience, complete, as if I had released a reasonable doubt. I was speaking out loud because I did not want to have any doubts. Every time I doubted again the pain presented itself to me anew, and it said to me: 'You have not learned yet.' My whole body was hurting, and I felt a great tension in my belly. I was saying: 'Now I have understood,' but I kept asking questions. I wondered: 'But what do I do with this now?' 'Tell me what I should do with this other matter?' and it made me feel pain, until I stopped asking questions it made me feel pain. When I stopped asking them, new doors opened. My heart seemed to give me access to a new space, and step-by-step I was finding it, only when I was stripped of pretensions (this is the word that seems most intrinsic to my character: a continuous pretention). Every time I wanted something, the pain came to me, and that led me to understand very clearly that my suffering comes from my demandingness. The teaching I have to learn is not to ask: 'Just be present and wait for what comes to you in peace.'"

Just as how in the preceding illustration the subject must give up an excessively demanding attitude, in the following testimonial the main thing is the recognition of the falsification of oneself; the concealment of one's own "shadow":

"I said that I had seen an inner light and I did not need recognition from others. When I started speaking I felt that was true, but while I was saying it I realized it was not like that, and that I sought recognition, and this caused me a lot of frustration; for I felt my character had

again taken possession of me; I had discovered self-deceit; but instead of stopping and saying: 'No, I do not feel like this,' I have kept saying that everything was fine, in spite of it not being true. That is how the experience started. And I wondered: How can character be so strong? And the experience led me to see my dark side, my hell. I visualized a cave at the center of my heart, I turned into a black dragon; as I was going through the cave I saw the dark side: vanity and all the passions, arrogance, competitiveness, and as I moved forward I realized that these things did not belong to me, they could not hurt me, and I could reveal them; it was not necessary that I hide them. I made so much progress that from a dragon I turned into a butterfly, still seeing these dark parts; and then I became a human being, with all these dark parts and now without fear, confronting them and integrating them. I thought the dragon was the instinctual part; the butterfly, the emotional part; man, the rational part . . . and I turned and saw all my dark side to my left and to my right all my luminous part, and it seemed clear to me that life is simply a combination of that light side and that dark side. This gives life momentum. . . . My dark part was hidden, and the luminous part was not even mine, but was what others wanted. It became evident to me that I had made myself ill by covering this part of myself that I did not want others to see."

Confessing a fault does not always take the form of a confession of a fault, however, and the following illustration is about somebody who discovers that what she must leave behind is an apparent moral duty to help others. For those who suffer a compulsive need to help, naturally, this constitutes a pathology they need to be freed from—just as in the case of the sins more widely recognized as such. The day after her experience, this subject said:

"I want to take care of myself. I want to take care of others, but I want to be able to choose. When I am tired, I sleep. Sleep, rest, regenerates me. I cannot spend my whole life always feeling obliged to

do something, to save humanity; I am not saving myself; I have already become physically ill. I have understood it, and I have also understood at a very deep level that I did not perceive, I did not really trust in God. I have always felt that I have had to make great efforts to help God, and this implies a delusion of omnipotence. And not only have I understood that although we are alone, there is God. Also, sometimes God does not do anything, and lets the universe follow its course. I have often wondered about evil, and I have said to myself: 'How is it that God exists, and children are violated, and people kill,' and I told myself that there is nothing I can do about it [CLAUDIO: He has to sleep occasionally; every seven days he rests]. It is like knowing that one can trust; that God exists, and the universe has its balances, and I must trust, and not always feel obliged to do something. I was very tired, and I said to myself: I choose now to be in this home and remain with this person, because I do not have the strength now to go anywhere else."

Perhaps subtler than the pathology of those who have the compulsion to help, is the compulsion of those who overidentify with those who suffer, and in that way, suffer the suffering of others:

"I have seen that it is difficult to understand the suffering of others. I have understood the other's pain, but it was as if I had to become the one suffering, unifying myself with the other. I do not say 'merging,' because it is not a psychological concept."

What another woman says is similar:

"I was worried about the pain of others and I started thinking about people in the group who might not be feeling good, and at the same time I said to myself: 'That is enough; this is not what you need.' I respect the pain of others and I go into it, but it is an old mechanism that I developed with my mother, a mechanism derived from guilt. I understood yesterday

that I had to put a filter, and that it was not genuine, that it was not about that. I stayed still then, and I enjoyed a carefree connection with the people I was with. I was very peaceful, and that brought me great fulfillment. But it is difficult, given my life story: I have always been a mother to my mother, who suffered intensely; and if I do not act as a mother to her, I feel that I am not loved."

I will add the declaration of another person who, after discovering this seemingly virtuous way of deceiving herself, was able to overcome it:

"I have been able to see the character's deception . . . that has consisted in using the pain of the world as a sounding board, becoming hypersensitive. This has led me to distance myself from myself; for as soon as somebody felt bad, I felt something like a fatal attraction for her. I become that pain and shed her tears, and enter into a futile madness, because it does not serve anyone. Her, because I cannot help her by suffering with her, and let alone myself, because I distance myself further and further from who I truly am, and I miss out on the opportunity to see myself, to know myself, to know who I truly am."

In the following statement, however, the "sin" or pathology is not relating: a woman now recognizes that self-sufficiency, which had always seemed to her a virtue, has been a problem, and consequently, begins to open up to relating to others:

"In synthesis, the first thing I understood is that I do not believe in others, and I do everything alone. I believe I know whether they love me or not, whether I am worthy or not . . . I have never been in the relationship where it is the other who tells me, who sees me, who tells what he sees. I have acted as if I knew more about myself than the other, and it is not like that. It has been very beautiful, because I have understood deeply this relationship thing."

II. THE AWAKENING OF LOVE

Just as in certain experiences what is most striking is how a person frees himself or herself from some important aspect of neurosis, in other cases the most striking aspect is the awakening of love. Only, noncompulsive love is not necessarily contrary to indifference, but principally an expression of inner freedom. The subject I cite next, precisely, is one in whom the new capacity to love is founded on a new freedom to respond to certain situations with "to hell with it!"

> *"I can say: 'I love you' to the person that I love, and I felt love, an extremely beautiful love, without my mind interfering; the three loves: admiration, heart love, erotic love, and it was very beautiful. Knowing how to recognize love and be in love; but also knowing how to say: 'Go to hell.'"*

Here is another case of loving release, this time predominantly erotic:

> *"I have felt for the first time something truly authentic, which was love without thought. It was pure love, and I also gave birth: I crouched in the birthing position, but I did not give birth to children, but to something like balls of love that were flying through space."*

In this third case, the opportunity to establish a new relational learning process—an exploratory element of restorative contact—that presents itself in groups, has contributed to the recovery of erotic health:

> *"I allowed myself to take without feeling guilty; for I understood that my giving and giving came from not knowing how to take, and that I had a feeling of guilt that came from the relationship with my father; an unconventional relationship in which I felt as a child that something was not right and I was ashamed, and confused, I ended up believing that I was not right, I was not beautiful. The fact of being chosen seemed*

something dirty to me; and if I assume an attitude of grandiosity in life, it comes from that old feeling of low self-esteem. But yesterday I experienced taking without guilt, and it was wonderful. I have always feared men without recognizing it for fear of my father, and I have kept men at a distance through seduction . . . and all this disappeared yesterday, and I wanted a loving contact, and I am very happy with the experience."

Another specific aspect of the awakening to love can be compassion, as in the following account:

"I have journeyed through the sensations, first on a physical level, and then I was carried away by a sort of inner vortex that took me beyond myself, to a kind of cosmic connection. It was beautiful, tears were rolling down my cheeks and at the same time I was very present, aware of the room and of the people. The experience, then, became one of great compassion for those who suffer, for the wars, as if there ought to be more compassion in this world, not only for people close to us, but also toward situations that we feel overwhelmed by."

Devotion is also a part of our loving potential, which is inhibited in certain forms of the neurotic character, like in the experience of one in whom an implicit superiority had made it difficult until now to cherish feelings of appreciation or admiration:

"A subtle eroticism permeated my entire body. It was a state of bliss and not of sexuality. I spent quite a while thinking that it was also a way to meditate. Then I went into a kind of hell. I wanted to understand my story, my relationships, my mother, the usual stories, my children, etc., always discovering new things, but with a deep anguish, and I said to myself: 'This no longer serves me.' At the same time, I felt the whole group here, all the people, and a love enveloped it all. I was with the others without judgment, and this was important. Then I said to myself: but this does not mean that I should always say yes; for I had asked for

acceptance, but I told myself that did not mean I always had to accept,
and I remembered what Fritz Perls said: I am me and you are you, and
if we meet it is beautiful, but if we do not, there is nothing to be done.
Then, listening to the music, the miracle of admiring, devotional love
occurred, for behind the music, was you, Claudio, who was offering it
to me, and I felt that with the music you conveyed to us your teaching."

I also include the statement of a woman until now unaware of devotional love, for whom the recovery of the capacity for appreciation ends up allowing her to repair the relationship with her father.

"I realize that I have come back to life, because in the last two
experiences that I have had I was always on the frontier between life and
death, and it seemed to me I was always on the verge of extinguishing
myself. Now, however, I felt that my energy is not yet completely full,
but I am alive, and I have finally been able to experiment admiring
love. The music has been a guide for me, it always has been, and it is
so more and more; in truth, also when I am not under the effects of a
substance: if I listen to the music, I enter into the same states again.
But when my state is altered by something, I can clearly feel all the
emotions that the music stirs in me, and this time I was also able to
decide whether to follow it, or at least to explore it, and find out if
it is something owing to my choice, or my state, whether to be in it.
Well, you, Claudio, presented yourself in the form of an eagle, and you
showed me your flight, your swooping, your nobility, your confidence
in flying, and when I could admire you, admire your flight, learn from
your flight, in those moments I sobbed at such beauty, and it was not
necessary for me to do anything to try to reach you; it was enough to
admire you. Your teaching, your guidance, taught me with this example
that I can fly according to my abilities, my level, that I can develop what
is there, for you are above me, and you have already reached those
heights, and so it has been beautiful to be able to admire something
higher; I think I had never done this before, and I had the courage

to explore the information I received about my father, to explore the deep bond with this man and that I had never recognized before. I took some time to thank him for all that he gave me, to express to him the anger I felt about the way he left and about the way he always showed me indirectly, and because he has left me an onerous legacy: that of having to fly in his place, to reach those heights that he never managed to reach. But I do not have to outdo my father, I thanked him for everything he has given me, and I put Antonio, Vilas, and you above myself. I do not want to fly alone, I do not have to fly alone, I need a guide or several, I have to be contained and I must allow myself to be contained, so I thanked my father but I said to him: 'That is enough, I take everything that you have given me, thank you, and I honor you for so much, but now I am going to follow my path.'"

CLAUDIO: *An important day.*

TESTIMONIAL: *Afterward, I danced.*

III. GLIMPSES OF WISDOM

Of wisdom it can be said, as of real love, that everything can heal. This is what is proposed by Buddhism, for example, by assuring us that all that is problematic in our lives could disappear if only we understood that our conviction of existing as separate individuals is something like a great illusion.

Someone (a lawyer) who had never had a psychedelic experience before reported the following the day after a group experience:

"When I realized that I was talking with the spirit of the plant, I wondered: Who is speaking, who is the one that says 'I'? And then something marvelous happened: I saw that several entities, for want of a better term, lived in my body, as well as my consciousness, which at this point clearly answered that 'I' that I was wondering about: there was the spirit of the plant, the spirit of the music, the spirit of Querube,

who in that moment was at my side, and my ego; then came the pain, like another independent element.

"That understanding, which fortunately for me was not intellectual, but loving, from the heart, brought me the incredible experience of seeing how all those elements that made up the self within my body, and my body itself, diluted in space, everything: heart, lungs, blood vessels, all disintegrated as if in a dance, first in the room and then in the entire universe . . . and just then I understood (because I had heard Deepak Chopra say this) that in reality we do not exist; that we only exist if there is an observer who is watching us. And I had the feeling that that body and those entities, which no longer existed as a single body, but were part of the air, of space, regrouped to make up this being that from the ego answers to the name of Francisco. In this sense, I felt one with all the beings present, and one with the universe. I did not exist independently, I was nothing, yet I was part of the whole."

Also, in the following statement, the central thing is not something that is part of the content of the experience as such, but rather, a notion that the subject has regarding her own identity:

"When I entered this higher level of consciousness that is called emptiness, pure consciousness, the word that seemed most appropriate to me was pure source, flowing. It was like a river that has always existed, and will always exist, that dispenses with man. Yet, at the same time it is the deepest part of each of us. I felt that this was the essence. On the riverbank I could see Jesus with his disciples, Buddha with his monks, Mohammed. . . . Oscillating between the two levels, I took questions that I did not understand at an ordinary level to a higher level. For example, I have a friend that I have not seen for some time who suddenly felt a strong pain in her eyes and lost her sight. I was not given an answer, but I felt as if in the waiting the pain dissolved, and it was as if I was being told it was not important to understand it. The same occurred with each question I asked myself, and I understood that the

answer was to fully trust in what shows up, for there is a higher wisdom operating. . . . The experience teaches me that there is nothing that is needed to be done, and thanks to your teaching I have had the chance to reach that source, and the only thing I have to do is be here in my body, aware of its limits, and trust in the permeation."

Also, in the following statement, we can appreciate that the healing element has been a new understanding:

"I always felt there was no place for me.

"What I want, I must take for myself, so what I expected always seemed like stealing. What yesterday's experience told me was: 'You do not need to take anything, you just need to go inward.' To be able to love, to love myself and to love others, all that comes from being inside myself. This is difficult. There is a great force pushing me, and there are two conflicting forces. When I am able to relax in being in myself and to feel love, then I can look at the world with peaceful eyes. *But the force that pushes me to come out to take is much stronger. I have discovered the fear that moves me to fill that emptiness. Possessiveness is a reaction to an undeclared and unfelt fear."*

As an epilogue, I wish to reaffirm my overall impression that psilocybin mushrooms have been the most transformative of the experiences apart from the ones induced by ibogaine. I have already mentioned how, very frequently, people under their effect not only encounter their pathology, but they also suffer it intensely, and the examples I have given will have conveyed an idea of how they are not able to overcome their discomfort until they correct an attitude or do something akin to an act of surrender, like entrusting oneself to God.

I will leave for a separate chapter what is relative to the inner fire and the "serpentine power of healers" that I have also witnessed, especially under the effects of "magic mushrooms," but that can also be activated by other drugs.

6

Spiritual Aspects of the Psychedelic Experience

6.1 INTRODUCTION TO THE PSYCHO-SPIRITUAL NATURE OF THE HEALING TRANSFORMATION PROCESS

Are the experiences induced by psychedelics therapeutic or spiritual? Palpably, both simultaneously, and they are so interwoven that nothing in human experience reveals to us so clearly how the therapeutic and the spiritual are two sides of the same coin.

Naturally, this complementarity between the spiritual and the therapeutic is made present to us not only in light of the psychedelic experience, though there are plenty of nonspiritual therapists and those who only take an interest in the spiritual and disdain the therapeutic; some of us who help people through their transformation process like to speak of "psycho-spiritual development."

Only, this inseparability of the spiritual and the therapeutic is disguised if instead of taking an interest in the spiritual as such, we attend to the religious, and also when instead of taking an interest in the profound transformation of people, we focus on their apparent "mental health," possible to assess through a relief of the symptoms or an improvement in social adaptation. Thus, inquiry can easily reveal that religious people are not necessarily healthier people, or that healthier people are perhaps not so interested in spiritual matters. However, practically all psychedelic experiences reveal to us how we must understand that the therapeutic and the spiritual are simultaneous facets of a same process of evolution of consciousness, by showing us a process through which the sick aspect of our personality—call it neurosis, ego, or character, which has developed as a defensive response to the painful impact of our family circumstances and relationships during childhood—seems to dissolve temporarily in the presence of certain higher emotions such as detachment, trust, surrender, love, or devotion.

Although the dominating image of the Christian culture is that of a spiritual path that undergoes a "purification of the sins," the medieval church criminalized the sins as offenses to the will of a punishing and authoritarian God to such a degree that we have lost awareness of these as illness; Buddhism, however, often presents the Buddha as a doctor who brings to man the cure for universal suffering. More broadly, we can say that to conceive the path of salvation as a healing process or as a path of development of our intrinsic spiritual potential are essentially one and the same.

I will begin this chapter dedicated to the spiritual aspects of the psychedelic experience with a chapter in which I illustrate the frequent appearance of what I will call "the kundalini phenomenon" in the psychedelic world, and although I shall not presume a precise definition of such a phenomenon or a systematic treatment of its relationships to the different drugs, I expect that the section that I have titled "The Relationship between Psychedelics and the Inner Fire, the 'Serpent Power' of Healers, and 'Pranic Phenomena'" will serve not only to outline an idea of what I wish to say with the expression "the kundalini phenomena," but also demythologize somewhat the traditional teachings, which entail such a schematization of the corresponding experiences that they do not even serve as a clear reference point when it comes to undergoing them.

Secondly, in this chapter I present an analysis of psychedelic consciousness based on an analysis that I once did about the facets and dimensions of the meditative experience. It was written many years ago, in response to an invitation to participate in the *Festschrift* for Dr. Albert Hofmann, and it constitutes a detailed analysis of the process I have described as a reciprocal interaction between the dissolution of the ego and the emergence of people's essence, spirit, deepest self, or Being.

Thirdly, I include an autobiographical report written by a person who has not only healed through a succession of sessions with MDMA and ayahuasca, but who, due to her philosophical training and Sufi culture has been capable of explaining very eloquently the process of encountering herself, that is to say, in the experience of the encounter with a "deepest self" or "being" beyond thinking, feeling, and wanting.

Moreover, I will add to this set of reflections a synthesis of my overall vision of the processes of disintegration and darkening of consciousness and the reciprocal aspects of the healing and enlightening process.

6.2 THE RELATIONSHIP BETWEEN PSYCHEDELICS AND THE INNER FIRE, THE "SERPENT POWER" OF HEALERS, AND "PRANIC PHENOMENA"

Different spiritual traditions know the experiential realm that today is most often universally alluded to as *the kundalini,* adopting the term from Hindu tantrism, which alludes to a power that is represented as a serpent coiled like a spiral at the base of the spine and that spiritual aspiration and certain practices have the effect of awakening. Aided by breathing exercises, this "serpent power" ascends—until it reaches the crown, and then induces a state of mystical ecstasy. However, the awakening and ascent of the kundalini is but the initial phase of a process that is followed by a slower and more complicated descent, which unlike its ascent, leads the person through unhappier and less lucid states that have given rise to some reservations regarding the benefit of reserving knowledge of this process for people most fit and able to overcome the potential dangers of the process that will spontaneously follow this awakening.

Although the ascent of the kundalini is explained in many popular books on Hindu tantrism, its descent is far less known, and evidence of this has been the autobiographical account written by Gopi Krishna in collaboration with James Hillman,* where the main author explains that despite having lived in India, where spiritual instructors abound, nobody recognized what was happening to him during his long "night of the soul" that followed his state of cosmic ecstasy and accompanied the descent of prana through his body. In contrast, the process of such a descent has been explained very well by Joseph Campbell in reference to *The Tibetan Book of the Dead*—a work that not only constitutes a manual for the living to be able to accompany the deceased beyond death, but also a map of the subtle path of the consciousness of those who die in life and whose consciousness then goes through the Bardos or "intermediate states" until, having achieved a certain integration of the spiritual experience in the body, they return to the world transformed.

I have made an implicit reference in what I have said so far to Hindu tantrism and also, implicitly, to tantric Buddhism, but it is clear that esoteric Taoism has been very aware of the movement of the "subtle energies" in the body during an advanced stage of development that precedes the birth of a cosmic individuality, and in view of archaeological remains, I have no doubt that the phenomenon was also well known by prehistoric American cultures such as the Chavín people, in Peru, of some four thousand years ago—for in these cultures we find representations of serpents inside the human body that no doubt allude to the basic phenomenon of the "development of the kundalini": a sensation of inner flow that Wilhelm Reich rediscovered as a result of a natural relaxation of the "body armor" and that neo-Reichians call "bioenergy." Naturally, this movement of a "subtle energy" in the body that has been described, alternatively, as a flow of air (prana) or "nectar," and that is

---

*Gopi Krishna, *Kundalini: The Evolutionary Energy in Man* (Boulder, Colo.: Shambhala, 1974).

known by different names in different cultures (ki, chi, lung), is not part of ordinary experience. Theosophy speaks of an "etheric" body in which such phenomena occur, and in the tantric tradition it is thought that the mysterious prana flows through subtle channels of the body; however, such channels have not been observed, and personally I have argued that the vibrational phenomenon in question has its basis in the stimulation of isolated muscle fibers.

I shall not propose here a detailed commentary on the "kundalini phenomenon," but I will say that the explanations found in the literature (that describes the channels and energy centers or chakras, as well as their associations with certain shapes, colors, and animals) are so far removed from the individual's experienced reality that Gopi Krishna, as I have said, narrates that despite living in India he did not find anyone who was able to recognize what was happening to him or help him.

It can be said, however, that the liberation of the "inner serpent" occurs as an advanced stage of ego transcendence, which begins in the realm of behavior and attitudes but reaches a level that can be called a "body ego" (as Reich described when speaking of an armor of muscular tension associated to neurosis and its excessive control). Thus, liberation of the "instinctual brain" and the vibrational phenomenon that can be conceived as the subtle physiology of advanced meditation are parallel phenomena. Only, in the case of the psychedelic experience, this phenomenon of bodily flow (resulting in the opening up to spontaneous thought, emotion, or movement) can occasionally occur already in one of the first sessions.

I have known of someone in whom the classic "awakening of the kundalini" occurred without any other stimulus than a usual dose of MDMA, and I have mentioned in my book on ayahuasca its close relevance to the kundalini (that we can consider the fundamental matter according to what is said in shamanism about the medical profession). In what follows of this chapter I shall illustrate the frequent appearance of such phenomena in experiences with psilocybin mushrooms and with ibogaine.

I begin with an experience (under psilocybin) in which the pranic phenomena do not appear, but what does appear is an episode of recovery of sexual health and innocence—which seems to me the starting point for them:

"The title of my experience would be 'Total Ecstasy,' absolute pleasure, ability to enjoy, delicacy in every movement, recognition of my body, the wonderful experience of finally feeling that I inhabit my body, my sensuality, and my sexuality. Acceptance and love for myself like never before, to feel that I can love myself just as I am, leading to the bliss of feeling that I am happy to be who I am. To be focused on myself without becoming distracted or inhibited by the gaze of others. Only at one moment did I need C.'s gaze, and I had a deep impulse to approach to make contact with him, to convey to him my infinite gratitude for making me connect with so much pleasure and help me to dilute my ego and connect with my essence.

"I have learned that I can connect with pleasure and hold the gaze of others without losing myself in it.

"The spiritual gift was the exquisite sensation that God lives within me and that he is also unrepressed and guiltless 'pleasure.' As I said before, the sanctification of my body and of my sexuality.

"I realize that in spite of my fears, each time it is easier for me to open myself up to experiences where I lose control with the marvelous result of touching heaven with my hands."

I will also reiterate here a few lines of a report already cited in a previous chapter, in which the serpent appears to someone who had already recovered her sexual innocence:

"There was a moment in which I had the image of a serpent entering through my crown and coming out of my vagina. Going in and coming out, cleansing. Then she raised herself up and began banging my third eye with her tongue. At that moment, there is a blue light coming down,

and she says to me, calmly, that my body is realizing what yes is and what no is. That my body is becoming aware, and that this needs a process. Then the blue light travels all over my body. I visualize new connections being made throughout my body, and I begin to feel the sensation that I am healing, that I am recovering, and that truly I am becoming aware. For me, this is becoming aware with my whole body. Perhaps in therapy I have realized, but this is a total realization. I had never felt what a yes and a no was in my body before, there had always been that mental ambivalence. Now I do feel a clarity in my body regarding that."

I now turn to an experience of body heat (or internal fire) that reminds me of those that present themselves in the tantric path. In this experience, the heat leads the subject to an *insight* about an ego mechanism, and finally, to love:

"I surrendered and felt an incredible heat in my body, like a fire; and then I felt my heart beating, which spread over my entire body. After this stage, which was rather physical, I visualized a cloth puppet, which represented my fears, and it was not terrifying at all, but quite expressionless, gray, rather sad. I realized that the hand moving this puppet was mine. Following which I felt an incredible love that penetrated me, and I loved everyone with a total love. Later I remained in that loving state, meeting with other people, hugging them, kissing them, very simply, without thinking and feeling this was enough. Wonderful!"

Here is another very rich experience that also begins with the sensation of a body that is on fire, and leads to the rare comprehension of a harmony between what is healthy and what is sick—which in turn implies recognition of the divine undertone of what appears as evil:

"It started all of a sudden, first with an itching sensation in my body and after this internal fire images appeared continuously of ineffable and wonderful geometries. It was like a continuous production, creation, and

destruction of geometries that were constantly changing, like fractals, and I felt that was the truth of what has been called divine design. God was the artist of all this wonder, which was not only good, but also evil; I saw it and also took part in it. The color of evil was black with red dots, while all the others were the colors of good. I saw aspects of my character, and now I particularly remember the arrogant pride of my 'self-sufficiency.' Only it is not at all real, I am not self-sufficient, but I have nurtured that pride."

Later on, the subject says:

"In this divine design, moreover, everything made sense, good, evil, ego, no-ego, everything had a purpose; there is a meaning to it. I felt that when one speaks of divine plan, of sacred geometry, one is speaking about something real. Then, God for me was the artist, the divine child that produced and produces this cosmic and infinite game in which everything has a meaning. If this has a meaning, evil does too, only that we are all on a different stage of the path, but the path is the same for all. I understand what compassion is, because we are all on the path toward the same source, and in reality, there is no truly evil human being. I felt gratitude, and a deep commotion."

Here is another report that begins with "a great inner fire":

"I started with a state of great internal fire, like a kind of physical excitement, and everything started from there. At one point, I wondered: 'But if I feel exactly as I feel in life, there is no difference.' I began to observe within and did not find anything, and I thought: there is nothing to think, there is nothing to see, and in the moment that I felt this, I understood that what I had to see was vacuity. When I felt this was the key and looked at vacuity, it was as if a door opened leading to a state that I can define as one of total perfection, in which everything was perfect, it was an unimaginable perfection for me,

where the perfection was such that even the imperfect was perfect in its imperfection. Then I felt perfect, as absurd as it may seem to say, and I felt that my character is perfect, I felt grateful for my character, it is neither beautiful nor ugly, it is what has served me and it has been fine like this, I felt there was a very profound intelligence, a true wisdom that inspires everything, for which each person does what he or she must do, and each person also has a profound wisdom. It was like an orchestra, a symphony, and I was saying that everything is fine, anything goes, there is not a word spoken that is not fair. I feel that the problem for me is that I want to give this vacuity a shape, but I do not know what the shape is, and in the face of such perfection it was clear to me that life will show me what I must do in life, for it has taken care of me so far, and therefore there is nothing else I need to do."

The greatest interest of the experience described here is not in what has been set out so far, however, but in the strong anticlimax of the day after and the difficult time that followed, which confirm that the awakening of the kundalini can entail serious complications:

"I stayed for a long time in this wave of love and beatitude: it ebbed and flowed, like jolts of energy coming from the belly. Like a breath, it rose and fell. Often it reached my head, and then the impression that it was coming out from there was very strong, like when I was drawing energy from the air with my hands and making it go in and then out of my chest. On this occasion, it was the energy coming out that was coming from my lower belly and going out through my spine. These two movements alternated: coming in and going out of my chest, and the energy going out toward the top from the bottom, which sometimes went out of my chest and other times from my head. In both cases it was wonderful, infinitely blissful. I felt I should have the experience with my eyes closed to avoid going compulsively toward others, in a need to be within, and it has done me good. I felt that my character makes me

lose touch when I automatically reach out to others, and it was very helpful to keep my eyes closed.

"Also, when I approached different people, I allowed myself to say no, to not be friendly always, as both good kids and social E7s are; and I felt good. I went toward others guided simply out of pleasure, and I was happy because of it. In the end, with the music, I surrendered to dance, to a very beautiful and pleasurable movement.

"When this immense wave of love diminished, toward the end, I suddenly felt an icy mantle of lead reaching me, very heavy. My gaze became subdued, the gloomiest and darkest thoughts came to me: 'Now how do I get home?' The improvised understanding of my family's drama hit me like a speeding train. I was crushed, devastated, I felt an intense cold all over my body. I felt very tired when it was time for dinner, too tired to eat anything. I felt like a zombie."

I reproduce another similar testimonial:

"It has been a long and tiring process, as well as difficult, because it was as if I had to keep repeating that I choose the light, and finally the light came, the warmth came, like an opening, like the other side of life. It was beautiful and I was able to see the delusion of my character, the deepest delusion of my character, which has do with pain, and this is how I had used the pain of the world as a sounding box, becoming hypersensitive, and this made me distance myself from myself, for no sooner did somebody feel bad, I would immediately feel a fatal attraction and become that person, that pain, and shed that person's tears and go into a madness, a futile madness, because it is not useful to anyone: I cannot help the other person by suffering with her, let alone help myself because every time, I distance myself further from who I really am, and I deprive myself of the opportunity of seeing myself, knowing myself, knowing who I really am. There is no possibility on this journey, I did not have the strength to think of anyone but myself. I did not have the energy to help anybody, I felt that I could only think of myself and *nothing else, there was no space; there was only space for truth, for the path toward the light, to who I really am, and it was a difficult, painful path. I drew strength from Katriona, but it was an individual path, it was clear that nobody could walk in another's shoes, and nobody could walk in mine. At one point, I came to a space where I found my soul, which initially was hesitant, it came and did not come, as if it was afraid, as if it was not sure that I would welcome it. However, I was truly convinced and made space for it, and in that union, I found paradise, something wonderful in which nothing was lacking, where there was a great love, warmth, erotic love, it was very pleasurable, I heard the voices outside and I could see how my character leads me outside of myself because I have the feeling that I am missing out on things. But this is another self-deception, because everything is already within, what is already inside is not outside, and I stayed like this, so the miracle that I had asked for finally occurred: how to integrate in life the solitary woman that I am, in an intimate relationship. The integration is to take the other into my garden, into me, into my world, and in doing so, go into it, and if I am welcome, going to visit his world, loving and being loved freely because it is clear to me that there is no love if there is no freedom, if there is no trust and space to be able to follow my path without having to feel cautious or fearful of losing the other. I have also understood that there is no more possibility, there is no manipulation, there is no deceit, there is no time. Time is alone, in truth, also around me."*

I cite yet another experience, in which sex and death coincide:

"The experience began, I suppose, already wanting to die, although wanting is not the word. There was not a wanting, but a music that was very tuku, tuku, tuku . . . and my body wanted to fall and become undone. I started to feel a great heat in all of this area (belly) and felt a serpent begin to coil around me. It entered through my vagina and went up to my head and came out of the top, and it would not let me stop; it seemed to be moving to the beat of the drums. Every now and

then my body would fall, and it was like 'that's enough now,' but the serpent went tuku, tuku, tuku, again and again . . . and all this time I was lying down. Then the music changed and there were no more drums and my body finally relaxed . . . and then I started to expel water, I think (I don't know). At last I could move, I went to remove my knickers, I have thrown them in the bin, and my trousers were soaking wet. I thought: has my period come? It is not due, I looked at myself and it was not blood, it was water. I don't know what it was; I was completely soaked."

CLAUDIO: *"Did it feel like having an orgasm?"*

TESTIMONIAL: *"There were palpitations, and I totally felt what must be the whole inside of the vagina, I could even feel the folds, and from there, when my body relaxed, I entered into what I experienced as my death, and in that death space, the only thing that connected me to life was that my body needed to breathe; it is as if suddenly my body started going down toward the earth, and my mind started going out like this . . . and I began to see myself from the outside, but it also smelled, and it smelled bad, but who is smelling if I am outside of myself, and where am I? I could see myself from the outside the whole time, and the moment came when I was able to leave, and then I felt I was in that wonderful place where there was nothing; and I felt my mother's fear of death. I think she is very close to that moment; I knew it and connected to that fear, and then my body (because it was not me so much) felt moved, and I cried; it was as if I could explain to my mother that there is nothing to fear, that this is wonderful. It is the same, but with peace. When everything had ended, and I left here, at night, to call Bruno, I had seventeen missed calls from my mother. From the experience until we left she called me seventeen times, and when I managed to speak to her she said (and she could barely speak, for she was high on painkillers) she had had a horrible afternoon, that she could not take it any longer, and it was like phew! . . . which convinces me that I really was there [she is moved]. Well: I* *was in heaven, and I call it heaven from my human form. I could also see you all, and distinguish you by your clothes, which I had noticed, because you were all like entities and I said: Who is that? I could see Rosa, I had noticed a bracelet she was wearing, which I like, and then I said: 'Ah, Rosa . . .' For that thing she is wearing, it is Rosa. I could not distinguish human beings physically, and then G. came and said to me: 'I know you are in heaven (perhaps that is where the word comes to me from), but please, come down and bear your fruits, bring them down to earth, your fruits'; and I said to him: 'Yes, but a little bit longer, let me stay a little bit longer.'"*

CLAUDIO: *"You have won the lottery, in experiencing death so profoundly. It is not the case for everyone."*

These citations taken from experiences with psilocybin confirm something that has become well known in the ayahuasquero community—and although it has been speculated that the frequent and meaningful visions of serpents under the effects of ayahuasca may echo the structure of DNA, it seems to me that in the experiences I have witnessed and been through, the serpent experienced physically reveals itself both as bodily energy flow and as a personification of something that we can consider the symbolic reflection of an aspect of our own archaic mind, most likely the psychic or experiential counterpart of our own "reptilian brain."

Assimilation of the experience just cited, however, tells us that the awakening of the inner serpent—with its innocent instinctual freedom—can be an entry point to an even deeper awareness of a vacuity that is both death and spiritual reality.

I will conclude with the reflection that beyond the visions of serpents and pranic phenomena, the fundamental aspect of the "kundalini phenomenon" is the deep surrender to the healing "current" of a restorative organismic process that lies dormant within us, and this constitutes the *sine qua non* of the visionary psychedelic "trip."

6.3 THE DIMENSIONS OF THE FIELD OF PSYCHEDELICS IN LIGHT OF THE PSYCHOLOGY OF MEDITATION

In what follows I propose that the categories of analysis derived from my earlier reflection on traditional spiritual exercises are also applicable to pharmacologically induced states of consciousness, so that what I once presented as a dimensional theory of meditation may be extended into a theory of psychedelic states.

NOT DOING AND LETTING GO

What does all meditation have in common? The usually shared answer in academic circles, since Benson's work (1975), is the "relaxation response." In the view that I am suggesting here, however, the answer to this question is sixfold rather than single.

Yet let me begin by reiterating Benson's notion and assert that at least one component of meditation (most striking in some forms, such as Buddhist Samatha) is inner stillness.

It is the attitude of effortlessness (wu wei), and the action the stilling of the mind (Patanjali's *citti vritti nirodha,* in the extinction of the agitation of the mind) that are here essential, though outer stillness and muscular relaxation may be considered as appropriate supports.

Yet, just as stillness is most prominent in certain kinds of meditation, the opposite is characteristic of others that I have characterized as "Dionysian" (cf. Naranjo and Ornstein 1971, and Naranjo 1990); and this aspect of meditation may be also recognized as a generalized quality of meditation beyond its particular forms: letting go, noninterference, surrender of control, so as to allow the spontaneity of the mind and its natural flow.

In the dimensional model of meditation I contrast not doing and letting go—as opposite ends of a single bipolar dimension of experience. We may refer to it as the "stop-go" dimension. Yet stillness and flowing are not the contradictory states that they might seem to be when we only regard their conceptual contrast. If we attend to experience rather than discursive thought, we observe that they are, somewhat paradoxically, complementary. For in giving the mind free rein, what takes place is neither chaotic freedom nor dead stillness, but a dynamic experiential flow; and while the two poles (not doing and letting go) may be found in comparative isolation at the beginning steps of meditative practice, deeper meditative attainment may be best characterized by the convergence of peace and inner freedom, and as a stability without fixity, as in the Zen metaphor in which the mind is compared to an empty space that, like the sky, allows birds to fly unimpeded.

Turning now to the consideration of psychedelic experience, we may say that letting go is most relevant to pharmacologically induced states of heightened consciousness. The evidently Dionysian aspect of psychedelic states—from the twitching of muscles to the arising of feelings, memories, and visions—seems to be the expression of a noninterference on the part of the everyday mind, so that the "flowing" aspect of the experience, the experiential unfolding popularly likened to a "trip," may be understood as the other side of a suspension of a habitual inhibition. And just as the suspension of ordinary perceptual schemata and habitual behavioral dispositions is well known to observers of the phenomenon, sometimes the stilling of the conceptual mind may be directly observable as well. As Henri Michaux (1974) describes in his essay on "What Is 'Coming to Oneself'?" when the effect of a psychedelic wears off, the individual is then "restored to thought."

While both "ego-suspension" (which may be experienced as impending or actual "ego death") and release of spontaneity from customary inhibitions are part of the general psychedelic experience, there are also differences in the states brought about by different classes of psychoactive drugs. While it is the Dionysian aspect that occupies the foreground in the case of the (sympathomimetic) LSD-like psychedelics or hallucinogens, psycho-motor relaxation is relatively more prominent in the case of the (parasympathomimetic) harmala alkaloids of ibogaine and ketamine. The feeling-enhancing drugs, such as MDA and MDMA, stand between these two groups. In their case a peaceful state of mind typically serves as a background (particularly in the presence of skillful guidance) for a spontaneously unfolding process of self-discovery, as the suspension of habitual defensiveness opens the way to suppressed emotions, unacknowledged perceptions, and repressed memories.

MINDFULNESS AND GOD-MINDFULNESS

I have characterized a second bipolar dimension in the realm of meditative experience in terms of the polarity of "mindfulness" and "God-mindfulness." While in certain practices (such as Vipassana) the meditator's task is concentration on the givens of perception and emotion, in others attention is focused on symbolic content (mostly conceptual, visual, or auditory) as a means of evocation of the sense of Sacredness that transcends the field of mental contents proper. In these cases the meditator is enjoined to become so totally absorbed in the meditation object (a divine attribute or a mantra, for example) that nothing else remains in the field of awareness. There then arises a sense of subject-object fusion—an identification with the contents of creative imagination.

From the point of view of the second dichotomy, both kinds of experience are included among psychedelic states. They include "visionary" states in which, just as in traditional contemplation, there takes place an identification with imaginative or symbolic content; and states of enhanced awareness of the "here and now." As Huxley (1954) stated using William Blake's expression, the "doors of perception," usually clouded by stereotypes and habituation, become open to greater clarity and complexity. It is common for both states to be superimposed, so that things realistically perceived take on symbolic and numinous overtones with the subject-object fusion characteristics of visionary experience.

In traditional spiritual methodology, the two complementary

techniques of meditation—object focus and attention to presence itself—merge upon the cultivation of samadhi. So too in a psychedelic situation it seems that a single quality of consciousness may be manifested in alternate ways, according to the form of attention. There are differences among psychedelics in terms of this dimension. The feeling-enhancers rarely elicit symbolic representations (spontaneous "meditation objects"), but characteristically facilitate the perception of physical and emotional states, whereas the harmala alkaloids and ibogaine are mostly "visionary" drugs.

NONATTACHMENT AND LOVE

The third dimension of the nature of meditation and its variation is an affective one (in contrast to the active and cognitive dimensions just explained). It involves the complementariness of nonattachment and love. While the cultivation of nonattachment is predominant in yoga and in most forms of Buddhist meditation, and that of love is the main characteristic of devotional religions, it may be said that both love and nonattachment are interdependent—even when one or the other is in the foreground of experience. Examined from the point of view of this polarity, we may say that it is the experience of love that is emphasized in LSD-like peak experiences, though a nonattached attitude may be said to underlie it and sustain it.

Applying this dimension of meditative experience to psychedelic experiences, it may be said that the expanded states of consciousness induced by LSD-like hallucinogens are different from those typical of the harmala alkaloids and ibogaine. In the latter, it is frequently cosmic indifference rather than universal love that is the foreground of the peak experience. Similarly with ketamine the nonattached quality predominates, while in the feeling-enhancers, the dominant characteristic is warmth.

I have spoken of not doing and letting go, mindfulness and God-mindfulness, nonattachment and love as six "inner gestures" that are balanced in the maturity of meditative experiences (see Naranjo 1990, *How to Be*), and have described higher consciousness or meditative depth as a multifaceted experience in which there is a convergence of peace and surrender, awareness of the here and now, numinosity, equanimity, and compassion (see Naranjo 1992). Psychedelic peak experiences are similar, so that these different aspects of consciousness are present in them, sometimes in isolation, but most commonly in combination, and it would be superfluous to illustrate psychedelic cases of the experiences of love, detachment, intensification of attention to the here and now, contemplative experience with symbolic content, the stilling of thought or the facilitation of letting go, for all these are so characteristic and well known to all acquainted with the field. It is my contention that through the suspension of the conditioned personality and the liberation of the deeper organismic process of self-regulation, both meditation and psychedelics have therapeutic results, as is clear from numerous papers in the medical and psychological journals in the first instance and from both shamanistic and modern psychotherapeutic use in the latter. The underlying commonality between therapeutic and spiritual practices is a view now generally accepted in transpersonal psychology. (For a general discussion of the issue, see Naranjo, *The One Quest*, 1972.) A summarization of these thoughts on meditation that I am proposing to apply to the psychedelic domain, is illustrated in the diagram in figure 2 on page 294, taken from "Bringing Eastern Meditation into Western Psychotherapy" (included in Grof's *Ancient Wisdom and Modern Science.*)

PSYCHEDELICS AND THE DIONYSIAN POLE OF MEDITATION

In addressing the relationship between meditative consciousness and psychedelic experiences, I further think that it is useful to propose a "kundalini view of psychedelic experience," and to show how it is relevant to the three bipolar dimensions of consciousness. For this, it is still

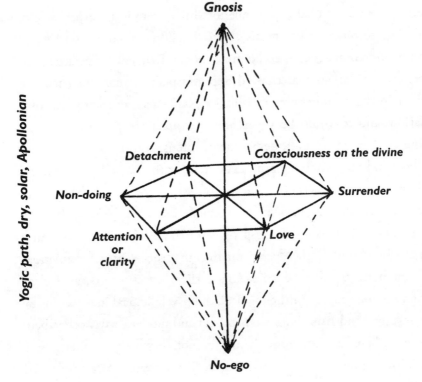

Figure 2. The two predominant orientations in spiritual practice—the Apollonian and the Dionysiac, sometimes called the "dry" and "wet" pathways, or the solar and lunar pathways—are not incompatible, and thus they have historically been described as complementary by the archaic Western Mysteries, by the tradition of the teachers of wisdom in Hindu Tantrism, and by the tradition of teachers of wisdom in Tibetan Buddhism. Figure 2 shows the interdependence of non-ego and spiritual knowledge or awakening, and how each of the six basic exercises cited contributes to both. In this figure, I have highlighted in solid black lines (in contrast to the dotted lines) how the process of suspending the ego is emphasized on the yogic path, while the awakening of the higher self is emphasized on the religious path.

necessary to introduce another concept from my earlier formulation of meditation: that of a polarity between the Apollonian (or solar) and the Dionysian (or lunar) aspects of experience—which underlies each of the three dimensions of meditation.

While the practices of tranquillity, nonattachment, and bare attention (more prominent in East Asia) tend to go together and may be said to constitute a "yogic complex," the practices of surrender, love, and God-mindedness also tend to go together, constituting a "religious complex" of attitudes.

Since the Indian tantric tradition, which orients itself to the activation of the kundalini phenomenon, may be regarded as Dionysian in that it emphasizes devotion and surrender, it is more accurate to say that it constitutes an integrative approach, in that it presupposes a background in classical yoga (and thus should be conceived as a sequence of classical yoga and its tantric extension, with its respective yogic and religious or devotional aspects). The Apollonian and the Dionysian aspects of tantric experience (embodied in Shiva and Shakti, respectively, in the Hindu tradition), are parallel and contrasting disciplines and also (ideally), successive schools. And since the tantric way of surrender is an advanced discipline that presupposes experience and success in classical yoga, we may say that the path of austerity and restraint are preparatory to the success of the path of surrender. Also the path of classical yoga, beginning with behavioral, postural, and breathing restraints and aiming at the attainment of one-pointedness, permits the individual to "get out of his or her own way," and this permits pranic phenomena to be unleashed.

While in traditional spiritual practice it is the Apollonian cultivation of *ekagrata* (development of mental control) that constitutes the ground out of which kundalini manifestations arise, in the psychedelic experience surrender has not been arrived at through the voluntary control of the mind, but through alternative, psychopharmacological means, and it would seem that the Dionysian realm of free-flow has been allowed through a sort of ego anesthesia rather than through a deliberate stilling of the mind.

PSYCHEDELICS, NOTHINGNESS, AND BEING

My intention here is to portray the six elementary *gestures* or ways of meditation as means of suspending (and eventually transcending) the *ego* (in a traditional and transpersonal rather than psychoanalytic sense of the term). Because psychedelics—through such ego suspension—remove the veil of obscuration, they constitute gateways to the experience of Being. Psychedelic peak experiences may also be said to have aspects of something more basic and encompassing: different degrees of *ego death* (i.e., dissolution of conditional personality) and a breakthrough to spiritual perception. They are states rather than stages of consciousness, and yet states that can powerfully influence the individual's growth process.

The apprehension of being, through which everything seems more real and in which the individual feels that "it is enough to be," is the core of spiritual experience. I believe it is also behind what may be described in merely aesthetic or sensuous terms, and in common psychedelic properties such as a more intense light or color or sharper contours. These may be symbolic translations of a spiritual event that the person is not familiar enough with to describe otherwise. Also, there are states of reaching after being, apparent being-scarcity, and struggling toward intuited spiritual reality that may be assimilated to the traditional concept of purgatory. Psychedelic births may be associated with memories, but I think that it would be a mistake to regard them as only that. Images of biological birth, whether memories or fantasies, can also be understood as the symbolic visionary expression of a nonbiological, spiritual birth taking place at the moment when the veil of egoic obscuration is "torn" away.

Similarly, mystical experiences are found in "nothingness," and experiences of moving toward nothingness (i.e., dying). In the case of an "annihilating illumination" (Andrews 1963), it may generally be said (as in Western mysticism) that the birth and Being aspects lie in the foreground. In the harmaline and ibogaine experiences, as in the case of ketamine, it is more likely that dying, nothingness, and cosmic space will predominate. This is surely related to the fact that the word *ayahuasca,* given to the *Banisteriopsis* drink in Quechua, translates as "vine of death." It may not be a coincidence that the subjects who have been administered ketamine frequently interpret their experiences as a glimpse of death or a journey into after-death states.

Teachings of the more sophisticated meditation schools, particularly those of Tibetan Buddhism, emphasize that techniques of meditation are only means for attaining an understanding of the nature of our mind. This involves a consciousness beyond its objects, similar to the awareness that an empty mirror might have of itself beyond the images it reflects. This self-apprehension of the ground of consciousness is understood to be the source of the intuitions of both being and of nothingness.

I think that while being and nothingness are closer to psychedelic than everyday awareness, they are still mostly veiled in religious, archetypal, biological, and aesthetic symbolism. Consequently, they are not always clearly apprehended as that "transcendent knowledge" of which spiritual traditions speak. If this is true, then an orientation toward being and emptiness—such as that provided by Buddhist or Sufi discourse—may constitute a valuable context and preparatory "set" for psychedelic experiences. For just as birth and death experiences are central to psychedelic phenomenology, Being and Nothingness may be regarded as the core of its spiritual philosophy or "theology."

CONCLUSIONS

To summarize the practical implication of this view of psychedelic experience suggested by my dimensional model of meditation, I want to first point out that understanding psychedelic experience as a transient activation of the kundalini (or as the elicitation of states comparable to those brought about through traditional tantric meditative disciplines) does not mean that meditation and psychedelic experiences are identical in nature. For inasmuch as chemically induced states are artificial rather than intentional, their repetition does not necessarily entail the development of an ability to bring them about willfully. While it is clear that the pedagogy of the spiritual traditions makes it possible for serious practitioners to undergo a transformation of consciousness, the transformation of consciousness achieved through psychedelics alone may be less stable, and the example of shamans does not serve to document the transformation of consciousness through psychedelics, since the education of shamans involves much more than the ingestion of psychedelic substances.

It is my personal view that psychedelics should remain initiatory experiences, agents of mobilization at an impasse, or means of facilitation at choice moments in a person's life, but never a diet. Consequently, those with an inclination to spiritual advancement are well advised to engage in spiritual learning and practice, so that their meditation is not circumscribed to occasions of psychedelic use. Further, just as in tantrism, a good grounding in *tapas* (austerity) and in the practice of concentration are regarded both a preparation and a safeguard; I think that an individual's ability to use psychedelics well may be optimized through a similar preparation.

It has been part of the wisdom of shamanism that the use of psychedelics occurs in the context of an austere way, in which sacrifices and "the path of the warrior" are central characteristics. Through emphasis on discipline, courage, and the development of the will, it would seem that the wisdom of the past has sought to counteract the dangers of mere passivity and quietism, and I think such old spiritual pedagogy provides good recommendations for the new shamanism in our new therapeutic culture.

To finish, I would like to remark that though I believe meditation methods are highly suitable to a mind "lubricated" by psychedelics, I do not consider the "spiritual" states elicited by psychedelics as necessarily those of greatest spiritual significance in a person's life. Despite the intrinsic value of psychedelic states and the lesson they provide in opening the mind to wider domains than those of everyday consciousness, and despite the great inspiration that has come to many from psychedelic mystical experiences (and even despite those instances in which a single visit to "psychedelic paradise" has changed a person's life profoundly for the better) it may well be that it is the visit to "hells" and "purgatories" that are more transformative in the end, for through the healing that takes place in the course of these painful journeys, the person's receptivity to spiritual experiences increases in a stable and reliable manner. I have wanted to say this so as not to give the impression (through the choice of my subject matter) that I think of the mystic-mimetic domain as the most important psychedelic domain, nor that I am personally more interested in it. Just as spiritual greed is not conducive to the best spiritual results, I think that there has risen a sort of "hedonistic spirituality" among psychedelic users that is conducive to incomplete assimilation of psychedelic experiences, and indirectly to abuse. Correspondingly, among those who find themselves in the position of assisting others in their psychedelic experiences, it would be best not to be biased by the search of peak experiences, but to have the ability to guide others through the psychodynamic and interpersonal mazes as well as in heavenly flights. In this, too, I think we may do well to stay close to the inspiration of the shamans.

I am convinced that drug problems are mostly the consequence of misuse. This, in turn, has been a function of the tension between the psychedelic potential and the lack of a cultural channel for its implementation. I want to end by offering my opinion on how to achieve the mobilization of the positive potential of psychedelics throughout the world. This would be greatly assisted through the creation of a national or international training center for specialists that would bring together the wisdom of present-day therapists, spiritual teachers, shamans, and psychedelic guides, and further the transmission of their knowledge and experience to the coming generation.

REFERENCES

Alexander, Gerda. *Eutonie.* Munchen, Germany: Kosel Verlag, 1977.

Andrews, G. "Annihilating Illumination." *Psychedelic Review* 1 (1963): 66–68.

Bauman, Peter. "Uber den derzeitigen Stand der Forschung auf dem Gebiet der Psychoaktiven Substanzen." Symposium. Berlin, Germany: Express Edition, 1986.

Benson, Herbert. *The Relaxation Response*. New York: William Morrow, 1975.

Campbell, Joseph. *The Mythic Image*. Princeton, N.J.: Princeton University Press, 1974.

Feldenkrais, Moshe. *The Master Moves*. Capitola, Calif.: Meta Publications, 1984.

———. *The Potent Self*. San Francisco: Harper and Row, 1985.

Fremantle, Francesca, and Chogyam Trungpa, trans. *The Tibetan Book of the Dead*. Boston: Shambala, 1992.

Grof, Christina, and Stanislav Grof. *The Stormy Search for the Self*. Los Angeles: Jeremy Tarcher, 1990.

Grof, Stanislav. *The Adventure of Self-Discovery*. Albany: State University of New York Press, 1988.

———. *Beyond the Brain*. Albany: State University of New York Press, 1985.

———. *LSD Psychotheraphy*. Pomona, Calif.: Hunter House, 1980.

Hartmann, H. *Essays on Ego Psychology*. New York: International Universities Press, 1964.

Huxley, Aldous. *The Doors of Perception*. New York: Harper Brothers, 1954.

John of the Cross. *Ascent of Mount Carmel*. Translated and edited by E. Allison Peers. New York: Image Books, 1958.

Kluver, H. Mescal. *The "Divine" Plant and Its Psychological Effects*. Chicago: University of Chicago Press, 1966.

Krishna, Gopi. *Kundalini: The Evolutionary Energy in Man*. Berkeley, Calif.: Shambala, 1971. (Republished with additional material in 2017 as *Living with Kundalini*.)

Laing, Ronald D. *The Politics of Experience*. New York: Ballantine Books, 1969.

Lowen, Alexander. *Bioenergetics*. New York: Penguin Books, 1978.

Maurer, Maja. "Uber den derzeitigen Stand der Forschung auf dem Gebiet der Psychoaktiven Substanzen." Symposium. Berlin, Germany: Express Edition, 1986.

Michaux, Henri. *The Major Ordeals of the Mind*. New York: Harcourt Brace Jovanich, 1974.

Naranjo, Claudio. "Ayahuasca Imagery and the Therapeutic Property of the Harmala Alkaloids." *Journal of Mental Imagery* 11, no. 2 (1987): 131–36.

———. "Drug Induced States." In *Handbook of States of Consciousness*, edited by Benjamin B. Wolman and Montague Ullman, 365–94. New York: Van Nostrand Reinhold, 1986.

———. *How to Be*. Los Angeles: Jeremy Tarcher, 1990.

———. *The One Quest.* New York: Viking Press, 1972.

———. "Psychedelic Experiences in the Light of Meditation." In *Gateway to Inner Space: A Festschrift in Honor of Albert Hofmann,* edited by Christian Ratsch. Bridport, Dorset: Prism Unity, 1989.

———. "Wesen und Erscheinungsformen der Meditation." *Dialog der Religionen* 2, no. 1 (1992): 2–58.

Naranjo, Claudio, and Robert Ornstein. *On the Psychology of Meditation.* New York: Viking Press, 1972.

Reich, Whilhelm. *Die Funktion des Orgasmus.* Vienna: Internationale Psychoanalytische Verlag, 1927.

Swami Muktananda. *Chitshakti Vilas.* Ganeshpuri, India: Shree Gurudev Ashram, 1972.

Wilhelm, Richard, trans. *The Secret of the Golden Flower.* London: Routledge & Kegan Paul, 1969.

6.4 REACHING AWARENESS OF BEING
An Autobiographical Account by Mónica Udler

My experience with psychotropics was radically transformative. The first of these was when I was eight or nine years old, and certainly it was neither in a therapeutic or spiritual setting, but in a hospital one. It was terrible. My father was an anesthetist and had introduced Ketalar in Brazil, that is, ketamine for anesthetic use. He would give me ketamine so that I would not feel pain during dental treatments. I would take it frequently and each time that I found myself under its effect was equally dreadful and traumatic. Invariably, they were bad trips, and it could not be otherwise, because I was afraid of both the dentist and my father. My mother never went with me. Besides, my mother was never with me. For some reason, I never told my parents or anybody else how horrible those experiences were. I suffered in silence. On dental appointment days, I would start shaking inside, and break out into a cold sweat, filled with fear. But I did not say anything. I felt enormously impotent before my father, I knew—or that is what I firmly believed— that my weaknesses and "cowardice" would not elicit any tenderness or compassion from him. I was totally subjected to them. Those episodes would deeply mark my life. First, they made me feel that my father had complete power over my psychic life—he could "go into" my mind, as the ketamine did, and create nightmares—and also my physical life, as in the times he gave me general anesthetic, I could no longer access the sensation of my own body. The afternoons on the sofa, when the effects of the anesthetic were wearing off and I tried to move my body and it did not obey, were like horror films. Yet I told nobody about any of this and I suffered in silence. That neglect was to accompany me my entire life and would erupt years later.

Those episodes with ketamine must have opened a portal of increased perception in me that never closed. When I was sixteen, I withdrew from everything and the only thing I wanted to do in life and that made sense was to read, to read and read all the works of Carlos Castaneda. Only that was my world. There I could consider my reality, A Separate Reality, as Castaneda's second book was called. A reality that encompassed the strangeness that I had experienced with ketamine. I wanted Reality. And an ordinary consciousness only brought me unreality. But I did not want drugs either. Marijuana and hashish provoked in me the same bad trips as ketamine and I ended up feeling a deep horror of any drug. However, I was enormously fascinated by Toltec shamanism. And so, I plunged into spirituality.

When, years later, I suffered a situation of sentimental abandonment, I was overwhelmed by a sudden crisis and my illness began to emerge and escalate with every situation of abandonment or loss that I experienced. Abandonment emerged as a strange and recalcitrant psychiatric illness accompanied by crises of great anxiety and despair. After years and years of different therapies and spiritual practices, I sought out the SAT program to heal myself, as nothing before had really had positive or decisive effects on the pathology, apart from controlled drugs.

Claudio Naranjo told me he suspected that if psychotropic drugs had triggered that state of terror and abandonment, then they were the best remedy to cure myself of them. They could teach me how to deal with abandonment and to transform it into something else. And that is exactly what happened . . .

The First Experience: MDMA

I was in Bogotá. I had been left by a lover, and I succumbed to an anxiety crisis and started losing control. I wrote to Claudio, who invited me to come to Bogotá to get treated. He told me he had the intuition that my participation in a certain group could get me out of the crisis and help me reconnect with the courage to keep on living. His welcome, and that of his colleagues would be the basis of a critical structure that would lay the foundation for my experience with the substance. I am aware that without that full week of preparatory psychological work and without the genuine love and friendship present there, the substance would not have had such a deep and decisive effect on my process of healing and individuation.

I was part of a group in which together we took the "dove." It was a starry night, in a cozy room. In a corner of the room, Claudio, who was in charge of the music, was carefully selecting the classical music that would be playing. From the first moments, as the substance started taking effect, I was overwhelmed by an indescribable ecstasy. Each piano note of the music that Claudio chose vibrated inside me announcing paradise. My body did not bear such beauty well. Sometimes I closed my eyes to let myself be transported by the music and sometimes I opened them, in a state of contemplation, to look at our "spiritual DJ," as we called him later. Claudio had a lovely smile, half-sitting on that swivel chair. The elation increased, as did the peace. My eyes would close to allow the sublime to penetrate each cell. Until something strange happened: In the middle of the blissful feeling, I opened my eyes, and this time . . . I did not see Claudio there. I only saw the swivel chair. It was immobile, wine colored, still a swivel chair, but . . . totally empty. With no Claudio! Claudio had gone to the bathroom. I heard myself let out a piercing scream. The vision of the chair without Claudio would have been unbearable if I had not been under the effects of the emotional anesthetic of MDMA, an effect that allowed me to access emotions that, initially, were unbearable. In some region of my being, which I now had access to due to the strange analgesia, it was unbearable, but my consciousness was barely aware of my reactions. I would not stop screaming. The empty chair was a vision of horror, Claudio's absence was a terrible experience. An empty chair was Claudio's abandonment. Like 2 + 2 = 4, the equation was: empty chair = you have been abandoned. A tragedy. But not for me. Only for somebody inside me. Somebody I was witnessing and that surprised me (and that still surprises me today). It was as if I was clearly split. There were two selves, one that suffered, or seemed to suffer, and another that contemplated everything and was in ecstasy, in spite of any tragedy. In that scream, all my abandonment was present. The childhood of neglect that I carry in me was so palpable. . . . All the traumas were there, present, I . . . was in ecstasy, in spite of everything. The word ecstasy does not do it justice, for it was a kind of bliss that is unchanging in the face of joy or pain. A bliss that accompanied every event, whether it was witnessed, internal or external, joyful or sad. A bliss that stayed with me for several days after that night.

My dependency on Claudio surprised me. Such an obvious and literally . . . raucous (aaaah!) transference, that it was embarrassing. I turned my attention to a gradual emancipation, to a degree of dependency. From then on, I felt tempted to transfer the axis that Claudio represented to the music, so that it became the axis, the support, that Claudio represented for me. At that point, he had already returned from the bathroom, but I did not dare to look at him again. It was dangerous . . . I stuck to the music; it was now my safe ground. Claudio could now leave the room without me shouting. But then there was another strange occurrence.

What happened was that, between compasses 16 and 17 of the intermezzo that was playing, someone came to talk to me and asked me something inane. The interruption was so fatal, so disastrous for me, that it seemed like the vibrator had been pulled out of my hand an *instant before pleasure. I was left disorientated, out of orbit, spaced out. Then, in contrast to an orgasm, a fit of devastating rage exploded in me, I remember walking around in circles like mad and finding some old newspapers, which I began to tear apart crazily, sitting on the cold floor.*

Afterward I returned to my place and tried to find some sort of balance, on the floor. I searched for it all night and it was easier to find alone than with other people. I withdrew. Completely. Nobody could give me anything in that state. I felt alone, very alone. But the ecstasy had not left me for a moment. Not even during the fit of rage. Everything that I did or felt was delicious.

Solitude and bliss were mutually exclusive yet were together. I did not understand how it was possible. When Claudio announced that he was going to retire and that we should continue the work without him, I told him he could go at ease, for I would stay with my "loving ferociousness." I have no idea where that came from. In fact, and from that day on, I learned a kind of unique ferociousness, a way of being evasive and not available to what distracted me from myself. I think that is where I started to say no, to respect myself, to close my doors and antennas, and to come back to myself.

I needed to protect myself from what made me lose sight of myself. Up until then I did not know how to do that.

It was absolutely delicious to be alive and with myself. Throughout the night I felt like that, and also the following day. It was a completely new state for me, but paradoxically, I experienced it as a memory, as if I was revisiting a state that I already knew and had forgotten. And more than that. It was as if I was being myself for the first time, but I also remembered what it was like to be myself. I was alive for the first time, truly alive. And being alive was to remember what it is like to be alive. Perhaps that is how I felt as a child. Perhaps being a child was like that and that is the paradise lost, the paradise that we lose as we grow up.

There was a sentence that stayed with me during the entire work that night and in the days that followed and that still resonates with me today: "Oh! What longing I felt for myself!" I went to tell Claudio about it the following morning, wanting to kneel before him in gratitude for the experience. "What a longing I felt for myself!"

After this experience, nothing was like it was before. Everything transformed! All my values changed. What I had longed for and chased after was revealed as futile and opaque, with no interest or use. What seemed wonderful and unattainable was revealed as having no sense and being undesirable. From then on, only one thing mattered. To find myself again in that level of presence, in that intensity of being, to be in that state of indifferent completeness, a state of being awake and alive. To dive into the real Reality again, for only that deserved the name real.

It was certainly the most important night of my life. I know that my life is divided in two great periods. One before that night, and another after it.

The First Experience with Ayahuasca

The wound of neglect and the wound of solitude are the same in my case. They are two names for the same wound.

Less than a month after having taken MDMA and having been through an experience that would change my life so profoundly, I had a second experience with psychotropics in a therapeutic context. For some reason that I am unaware of, I decided to do a SAT 3 in Brasilia, in the course of which was to be included a visit to the Santo Daime Church, the sacrament of which was ayahuasca. A little while after my first ingestion, I started to feel a clear sensation of having a child against my breast, on my lap. It was not a vision; it was not visual at all. It was sensorial. But I had a baby on my breast. And I was holding the baby close. It felt very good. It was totally unusual. How did I know that I had a baby on my lap if I did not see anything? The feeling was one of complete ecstasy. An ecstasy perhaps similar to the one I felt in the experience, I do not know. What I do know is that I suddenly stood up and put the baby on the ritual table and said: "Stay here. Mummy is going to go to hell and then I will come back." I left the baby with complete confidence and went to drink the brew a second time. There was no voraciousness in my action.

It was an order from above. The ecstasy that I felt was not serving me and would not be of any use to me. Something had to be done. I had to dive in. I felt this with all of my being. The wound had to be visited to be healed. It would be of no use to me to stay there enjoying the ecstasy. I gathered up all my courage and valor. I put on the hero's cloak.

I drank the brew a second time and sat down next to the shamans, Luciana and Eduardo, close to the head of the table. There I began to sing along with them. I felt accompanied, in community, singing with them. Suddenly, I started crying. Crying without feeling any pain. It was as if the pain in me was being released, as if the door to its cage was being opened. Tears welled up because it was pain that was leaving. It was an utterly physical and metabolic weeping. It was the pain coming out. Seeing me crying, Luciana took me by the hand and led me to a mattress to sleep. I hated that she did that. I did not want to leave there, I wanted to stay beside her and the community. But she took me so I would be by myself. I headed to the mattress as one going to be sacrificed. That is when I did feel pain. A grief of solitude. A sharp pain, but with analgesia: the same analgesia of that night in Bogotá when I wept my helplessness and abandonment and felt bliss at the same time.

The same as that night, I started shouting. And talking nonstop. With no control. An assistance group gathered around me. A whole lot of people wanting to help, unknowing that I suffered without suffering. What I felt was that if I stopped talking or screaming, I would find my loneliness so extreme that I would disappear, and nothing would survive the real pain that would follow without warning. As if I had to feign pain to escape pain. As if pain feigned by myself was the only known survival technique. They were all there with me trying to get me out of a tunnel, a hole, that only they saw. I did not see any tunnel. I did not have any control. I just screamed, moaned, and talked incessantly. My inner dialogue turned into external monologue. I could not understand what those people were doing all around me. Neither was I aware that I was shouting. Later on, I was told that I had been shouting. For me, they were cries that had been trapped inside me for a very long time. And the door to the cage was now open. And the cries were flying out. Finally.

I remember that what I most repeated was: "Oh, oh! I am so alone! Oh, oh. I am so alone here. Oh! Now you know the loneliness I feel inside! Oh, oh!" It was what I said and in fact how I felt, although with analgesia and with the joy that came with everything that unfolded. Nevertheless, at some point, they had the brilliant idea of leaving me literally alone. I think they perceived their presence, even their warmth, in no way alleviated my loneliness and did not help in any way. It was completely intrinsic. A fundamental loneliness, an a priori solitude.

They moved away. Each returned to their own story, their own work. I experienced a literalization of my trauma. I was abandoned. Only then was I able to really begin the work. Only then did the process start. All that followed—that here would be inexpressible—led me to that space of solitude, to that dusty cellar of my own soul. I discovered that abandoned cellar that was in me, and that was my most ancestral, most primordial self. My access to it had been interrupted for a long time. I perceived how wonderful it was to be there again. And I perceived the reason I had stopped visiting it: for fear of loneliness. For fear of the solitude that is the guardian of the threshold.

A distinct truth emerged, which even now I can barely formulate with such simplicity: the abandonment I feel, a syndrome of helplessness that I was diagnosed with and that makes me dependent on both people and psychiatric treatment, is due to a self-abandonment. I am the one that neglects myself. I abandon myself systematically and immediately I feel defenseless in an impersonal world. I disconnect from the feeling of myself and from my presence for one reason only: being with myself makes me feel alone, terribly alone, light-years' distance from any other living being. Then I alienate myself from the world, pretending to be with everyone, in symbiosis with my environment, ceasing to feel myself and forgetting about myself. Being with myself is too close to the intense wound of loneliness. But the tea showed me that the wound is the cure. And I was not sabotaging myself when I left paradise with my baby in my lap (I do not know if it was my child or myself) and went to hell, to the core of my wound. The price of reconnecting with myself is to cross a narrow gateway of solitude. But once crossed, I can reconnect with all that there is, with all that is. It is a threshold of death, which must be crossed to reach real life.

Rejection has followed me my whole life simply because I always approached others in a way that was not genuine. My coming close was nothing but a fleeing, an escape from myself. People warmly welcome free and whole people, not fugitives. Those who saw me did not welcome me and moreover did not find me. And nobody can find someone who flees from finding herself.

It was as if I had resolved a puzzle. I spent almost the entire night awake. And I had not slept the previous night. I spent the whole day in an altered state and in the evening, I danced in the middle of the room when all were sitting watching the video of Mozart's Requiem. My ecstasy on hearing it was so great that I could not remain seated like the others and I started dancing. I danced the entire Requiem. Little did I care what they thought. Afterward I managed to sleep, in the early hours of the morning, but at eight they woke me up to be at the next work session. When I finally managed to wake up, I realized that I was as unnerved as the previous nights. The effect had not subsided in the least. What is certain is that I seemed to be stronger, extremely lucid, present, and full of power. However, for the others, what I was, was even crazier.

The work that had to be done with the group was a regression, where we would go back down the timeline, visiting all our hardest moments from the moment of birth, even before: from the moment before being born! After an immersion in the moment before birth, we had to be reborn and go over the difficult times from the perspective and the strength of that wider context, the context of prenatal indeterminacy.

The exercise seemed to be fascinating. When I carried it out with my therapeutic partner, I did it so deeply and seriously that after working for two hours I still had not gone into the momentless moment, into the spaceless space, of the prenatal. The regression was carried out with my *partner being the therapist, and there I relived all the difficult moments of my life, going backward in time, from the recent abandonment of my German lover, to my mother's terrible accident, and all the previous abandonments and losses, all the traumatic moments, even the postnatal traumas, when I was left in my cot to cry for hours on end without my father allowing anybody to hold me in their arms, and perinatal traumas, like the incubator I was put in at the hospital where I was given birth to, or the hospital bed where I was conceived (my father took my mother to the opening of a hospital in Porto Alegre and there, in one of the rooms, where they stayed, I was conceived). When I went into the prenatal state something very intense happened. Something that took me back again to the same peak state of the experience with ayahuasca two nights before.*

Backtracking and heading to where I was before entering my mother's womb, I found myself, to my surprise, in something that was neither a place nor a space. It was a Presence: that of an Eagle.*

I was in the Eagle; I was an eagle; I contemplated the eagle. In that level of reality, those three perspectives were true and did not exclude or negate each other. The logic of the prenatal world worked in a completely different way from how the postnatal world works.

The eagle occupied the whole horizon, so that there was no horizon, or space, only presence. Nothing was outside of that presence. And that presence was the Self. The Self was Eagle. With definite article: definitive article. The Eagle.

Before her, in her, being her. And I was not moving. And there was no outside. Or inside. Only her. Surprised inside her. And though my partner insisted that I be born, that I leave the Eagle and be born, I could not come out of her presence. I could not be born. I did not want to be born.

My partner insisted. Firmly, I asked him to leave. He did not. I shouted. My partner desisted. And he left. I stayed there motionless. In

---

*Capitalization of the term *eagle* follows capitalization in the Spanish version of this piece. (*Note from the editor of the English edition.*)

the state of Eagle. For hours. Sitting on the felt top of a billiard table in a room adjoining the large meeting room.

At that point, a committee of real therapists had been informed by my partner who was acting also as therapist that I was not in my ordinary state; that I had not come recovered from my ayahuasca experience, which after thirty-six hours should have passed. They considered I must be suffering from a crisis. But I did not feel that it was. I simply felt I was still immersed in the journey. Every detail of that adventure was something delicious to remember, because that "fit" was what transformed me forever, what individuated me, what taught me to have a true self.

It was a holy madness, and it lasted three weeks. Two people who I trusted considerably were the only ones who confirmed that I was not suffering from a fit. One of them was my psychiatrist, the renowned Dr. Ángela Lobato, who examined me two weeks after the experience. They both said they perceived that I simply decided not to return from the journey and that I did not come back. I think they are right, but that it was possible because the effect of the ayahuasca was enhanced and prolonged by the Paroxetine, an antidepressant that I have been taking for fifteen years.

My intention was to then put down on paper my whole life from the state of eagle, going over all the difficult moments that I reexperienced in the first phase of the regression. That is why I stopped writing the moment I came out of the bubble, in which I was born again.

What happened next, on the last day of the SAT, was that they took me back to the room with the mattresses. I stayed there for a few hours, on a pile of mattresses, trying to sleep. What happened was something ineffable that, although impossible put into words, is something that I shall never forget and that was decisive for a new stage to develop in my life. Only now do I realize that what happened there was the next step of the eaglet experience, after leaving the incubator, coming out of the maternity ward, and being put in the cot, alone, with nobody's lap to cuddle up into. It was as if the mattresses were my cot, being alone with *myself and that Presence, luminous and protective, was indescribable and definitive. There I was taught a new mode of presence, which I could access whenever I felt unprotected.*

I spent three weeks in an altered state of consciousness. Many considered it a breakdown, as they said. They offered me antipsychotics, but, thank God, I did not accept them. Taking them would have aborted a "madness that heals." They were three very intense weeks in which I continued to learn ferociousness and to individuate myself decisively. I felt a love for myself, as I had never felt before. I felt as if I was passionate about myself. And I felt power, a lot of power. I felt powerful and beautiful. And when I saw myself as ugly, it was a delightful ugliness, for it was MY ugliness. And I felt a lot of love.

No. Power and love were one and the same. Power was loving, and love was coming with a lot of power and a feeling of power.

Although I had caused some confusion in my family with so much spontaneity—snapping at people, stealing chips off clients' plates in restaurants that I went into, calling my sisters to tell them I had murdered our father and things like that—they were three weeks that made me absorb into my daily life a new mode of presence that the two experiences had introduced me to. I realized that in truth, I had never really been in myself. The "breakdown" was a healing madness. It made someone who lived dissolved in an external world for fear of loneliness become psychotic. I experienced the psychosis as if all that there was in the world were in my own psyche, as if people were characters in my dream. The mandate of the sun in my experience with ayahuasca, about: "Not to live in the world, but to make the world live in me," had to be experienced literally so that I could then experience in an integrated way. Sobriety and ordinary consciousness came with time. But I had already discovered a way of being in the world that was unknown to me and that saved me from complete helplessness and dissolution.

I assimilated that new way of being in the world over time, until the present, through ordinary experience, through further uses of psychotropics in a therapeutic or spiritual context, and above all through a method of remembering that I use often: writing. I committed to two literary works that consolidated me in what I narrate here. One was a literary work, a story called "A Butterfly That Became a Caterpillar," and another was a philosophical work, my doctoral thesis, which will be published shortly and is precisely about spiritual individuation and the visionary experience. It is called "From Exile in Space to the Space of the Soul," and is four hundred pages long. Many people are wary of using these substances (as a cure) for fear that they distance them from reality. However, little do they suspect that precisely they can lead us back to reality, pierce the veil that separates us from it. Contrary to giving up the world in a psychedelic journey, hallucinogens brought me back to the world. Contrary to taking us out of ourselves, what they do is bring us back. I was brought back to myself and I finally discovered what it means to "be in oneself." The most remarkable thing about that experience was that I immediately became a mother. Although my daughter was already six, then I truly began mothering. I started to love being a mother and to be a good mother. Only from then on did I truly feel I was a mother. Perhaps because, after all, I took back into my arms the baby that appeared at my breast at the beginning of the experience with ayahuasca and that I had lovingly put on the table and asked to wait for me until I returned from hell. And I came back. And here I am. I took myself into my arms. And my daughter too. Finally.

The Second Time with MDMA

Two years after the "fit" of (healing) madness, when I was forbidden the use of psychotropics, I was allowed to take ayahuasca again. However, no experience was as transformative as the ones I had in the presence of Claudio Naranjo.

The second time I took a "dove" was a few months ago, four years after the first time. It was an experience that is also worth being narrated, for it completes the process that began in 2011. The years from 2011 to 2015 were years of going within. I myself had announced after Bogotá that I was sorry but that I would withdraw, retreat, back into myself—whom I had abandoned for so long—and that I hoped in the near future I could come back to live with others, a living together that I hoped would be genuine and loving. In the end, I was to discover I was incapable if this. The last experience, which was with a dove, finally taught me the path of coexistence, the mode of presence, rather than the possibility.

The day after the experience with MDMA, I wrote: "The most beautiful night of my life returned. It happened four years earlier, in Bogotá. That night, in which I took MDMA for the first time, came back to me yesterday. It is not that it had disappeared, or that it was not present during those four years, like a starry night that cannot be seen in the light of day. Yesterday I saw that that night was with me and has been with me since I was born. Since I was born, this starry presence has been here, even though I abandoned it systematically to surrender to the clarity of day."

I will attempt now to recount it more clinically. Once again, I had clear access to myself. Four years ago, I encountered for the first time a mode of presence until then unknown to me. As if for the first time I was truly present, truly alive. Like four years ago, I was overcome by paradoxical sensations all at once; ecstasy came hand in hand with solitude and an atrocious feeling of abandonment. Again, I took refuge in Claudio, who reminded me of what I had already discovered, that to be alone is to be the sun. The hours that followed were experienced in terms of that solitude, experienced as a threshold. It was the great teaching received that night. I will try to describe the threshold:

1. The feeling of solitude approaches gradually, like a colic of the soul, like a cramp in the psyche.
2. I make an effort to bear it, like one who bears a birth contraction.
3. Receiving the energy of my attention, the muscle begins to relax a little and what was unbearable begins to become bearable and borne.
4. As I bear it, the pain begins to give way to a growing feeling of pleasure in being and of being present.

5. *That transition from pain to pleasure and to plenitude is most mysterious. I do not know how it happens. What I know is that if I had fled from the pain and had alienated myself in the external and in thought, I would not have reached the pleasure of Being. And I would have avoided life. Now I know that I must not do so. I know that after the pain of solitude comes the pleasure of individuation.*

The moment in which the pain of solitude is approaching, the great Barzaj,* I experience as a death. And death pulls me away from everything and everyone to take me with her. But it is to take me away to myself. And after reaching myself, I feel an immense relief. It is as if I finally had a true self—like Pinocchio, who turned into a real child. It is going from being a tormented soul to having a true self. When one has a self, no pain is unbearable; nothing that can happen to you is bad. Indeed, what happens to you is irrelevant, if you have a real self. In reality, everybody pretends to have a self. MDMA awakens the heart, opens the heart. To awaken the heart is to bring back the self, it is to awaken the self, numbed or silenced by the ego, which is a false self, a ghost.

At the beginning of the evening, when an emotional or mental cramp was coming on, I would shriek, then I cried, but as the night went on, every time I surrendered to the pain and had to cross the threshold, I looked for a corner where I could die in peace, without disturbing anyone, without making a show. After being reborn, I stayed there enjoying the feeling, or I approached the group. When I approached the group, I did not "socialize." I did not chat with anybody or smile at anybody. I did not interact. I was not able to come out of myself to be with others. I wrote:

How good it feels not to have to express anything with one's face. How good it feels to be able to not smile when somebody smiles at you,

---

*Barzaj: According to the Koran, it is the intermediate state in which the deceased soul remains in a dreamlike state between the day of its death and the day of Final Judgment. (*Note from the editor of the Spanish edition.*)

and you do not feel like smiling. How good it feels to not have to talk when you do not feel like talking. How good it feels to be able to write "how good" without having to finish a sentence with an exclamation mark. How good it is to not be afraid of people thinking that I am crazy. How good it feels to not be afraid of people thinking that I am sad. How good it feels to not be afraid of people thinking that I am ugly. How good it feels to not have an ego. How good it feels to not have anything.

I did not come out of myself to be with others, even though I was better with them. I did not share. I did not interact. But very soon I was able to make small gestures that were truly genuine and not pretended (under the effects of MDMA it seems it is impossible to pretend. I was incapable of pretending anything. That is why I did not smile back at anyone who smiled at me and I did not feel obliged to do so, although, inside, I was in ecstasy). After a long time, I began to be able to interact without interrupting being with myself. It was like balancing two bottles on both sides of a cane. I had to pay great attention without losing myself. Like in that story of the disciple who had to contemplate the palace without spilling a single drop of oil from his teaspoon. After some time, it was easier to be with others and still be with myself: as long as I did not forget my solitude, as long as I did not stop dying in every instant. When I say "die," I mean "return to myself." The condition to be able to be with myself and with others at the same time—that was the great learning of that night and of life—is not to neglect my solitude, not to put it on hold to be able to be with others! That is what I understood and experienced. It was a mode of presence that the Dove taught me that night.

If in that sharing I forgot about myself, alienated myself, I had to go and die again, in a corner. After being able to die in stillness in a corner, I moved on to being able to die while being with others. To die dancing, to die talking, to die caressing friends. I died outwardly and was born inwardly. I did not flee from the solitude that separated me from others, but also, paradoxically, I genuinely joined with them. I lived as if for the first time I understood what it is to relate without symbiosis, without dissolution.

I crossed that threshold so, so many times in one night, so many that in the end I found myself constantly on the threshold, as if my place was exactly that one, on the threshold, in the aperture of that cosmic vagina that swallows everything up. It was a continuous autophagia. That happiness is something I intend to keep. To seek that happiness is the only thing that really matters.

The day of the experience and the days that followed, I felt that I was going into a deeper mode of presence, in which I was the center of the world. I was only able to reach that state of being the center of the world because I surrendered to the solitude that I had been fleeing from. That, however, was nothing new, for I had already learned it through the first two experiences in 2011, which had left me in a state of healthy psychosis. Now, the big novelty was that others could also, each one of them, be center of the world, without that threatening my centrality. The other no longer needed to be abstracted, be impeded, be avoided, for me to be in myself. The other's gravitational center no longer pulled me out of my orbit, or of my axis.

I understood what had made me flee from the SAT workshop last year, in 2014. I understood why it had been unbearable for me. There, the others prevented me from having myself. I felt that I was dissolving, becoming invisible. It was unbearable to be "just another," "one among others." I lost contact with my centrality, with my axis. I immediately went to Paris for three months and there I came out of myself in the wrong way, I dissolved in the crowd, I had a panic attack and had to return to Brazil. However, in this recent SAT, in 2015, I accessed the key, I accessed the threshold. I discovered the secret of being a satellite (peripheral) outwardly and the sun (central) inwardly. I discovered that I was living in an unhealthy reversal: I wanted to be the sun outwardly because I felt like a satellite inwardly. Not assuming my centrality, my true self, my state of sun, I became a mere satellite around the gods of appearance, and thus pretended to be the sun outwardly and the center of attention. I stopped longing to be sun outwardly as now I feel sun inwardly. That makes it possible that outwardly I can be a satellite: feel part of the whole, feel involved, participant, planet as the others, and sun also, as the others.

6.5 A COMPREHENSIVE VISION OF THE PROCESS OF DARKENING AND ENLIGHTENMENT OF CONSCIOUSNESS

When the Buddhist vision is presented in the great synthesis that has been called "the four noble truths," it begins with the explanation of the reason for suffering, continues with the elucidation of its causes, moves on to the affirmation that there is an alternative, and finally, to the description of the path. It seems a valid framework to me, and now that I intend to share an integrative vision about the nature of the healing process that psychedelics can contribute to as an important catalyzer, I shall also start with the question of why we suffer. To answer this question, I shall begin with the first of the explanations that I believe has been given for the problem of the "fall of man" or degradation of consciousness: ignorance.

Yoga, which it seems has its origins in prehistoric times, says as much, as testified by certain clay bas-reliefs that show somebody in the upright sitting position of a yogi, beside a tree and a serpent. The yoga aphorisms collected by Patañjali in a period of time close to that of the Buddha no doubt constitute a timeless knowledge, and in them we can find the interpretation that in order to return to ourselves we need to recover the vision that we have lost. The very word *ignorance,* in Sanskrit *Avidya,* etymologically means "nonseeing, nonvision," and differs radically therefore in its meaning from what today we call ignorance, which is, rather, an absence of knowing. For those who use the word in a spiritual sense as yogis, Buddhists, or Christian theologians (like Saint Augustine), ignorance (*ignorantia*) is essentially the opposite of wisdom, and intrinsically, blindness. From the point of view of the spiritual traditions almost all of us humans are blind, having forgotten our fundamental nature and believing in things in a world of things through this nonvision that has despiritualized us, alienated us, confusing our essential nature with what awareness of the moment presents to us: sensations, emotions, thoughts, fantasies.

Buddhism also states that the fundamental root of suffering is ignorance, but suffering is often presented as part of a triad: ignorance-desire-aversion, which are usually represented in turn as three animals: ignorance as a hog, desire as a serpent, and aversion as a cock, chasing each other, though they constitute three aspects of a single phenomenon. Because we do not find ourselves, we desire this and that, wanting to fill ourselves up with what we perceive, and to the extent that we desire this and that, we reject that which stands in the way of our desires. The idea in this triad of what is usually called the three poisons and that we can recognize in our omnipresent experience is that ignorance has its psychological offshoots, and the list of offshoots varies depending on how yogic, Hindu, or other reviews are considered. In Christianity, seven capital sins are often mentioned, yet in the most recent historic expression of what is called esoteric Christianity, long predating Christ, the list of sins or passions includes nine, as represented in a geometric design called enneagram. In this Christian concept, which essentially does not differ from oriental concepts about the *Kleshas,* or obstacles to spirit, we suffer because we are susceptible to certain "sins" or deviations of our psychological energy, and these sins are like mental parasites, energies that distract us from ourselves and from our evolutionary direction, or as traditionally it is said, from God.

Such are the main theories of suffering before the emergence of modern psychology. However, it introduced something radically new to the world of Freud's culture with its particular theory of neurosis, by attributing human suffering to the fact that, in developing a civilization, we had to endow it with a police-like character, as a mutual protection guarantee against our aggressive and destructive impulses. This is what he suggested in his last book, *Civilization and its Discontents,* by proposing that universal neurosis is the price we have had to pay for our civilized condition in view that we are not intrinsically altruistic beings. Only, over the years Freud's pessimism has been questioned, and not only have the existence and the relative success of psychotherapy demonstrated that human suffering can be alleviated through the assistance of specially trained people, but they also further the arguments in favor of the human brain being basically designed for collaboration, so that the destructiveness that we have shown throughout history constitutes, rather, an expression of our collective illness.

In any case, I believe that Freud was right in suggesting the we suffer because we are animals that, through a process of domestication since prehistoric times, have ended up criminalizing our own impulses and our healthy orientation toward pleasure. We suffer like chained animals, it could be said, and part of the therapeutic process will be not only to reawaken our instinctual nature, but also to lovingly embrace it instead of feeling guilty for our biological legacy.

An alternative vision of suffering promptly emerged in the psychoanalytical world that emphasized the thirst for love that manifests in us from childhood as mammals born in a situation of dependency regarding our mother, and also as people living in a world in which motherhood is often interrupted by other values that imply the devaluation of the mother, life's excessive orientation toward the aggressive satisfaction of one's own needs, and that has led, over time, to the need for mothers to increasingly focus on the struggle for subsistence in a world of growing shortages where, paradoxically, wealth is growing on a par with poverty. If we wish to get to the bottom of this suffering for love, which we can all easily recognize in our life experiences, it is not so much about crying over a love that was lacking in our childhood, as they say (when it is said that we suffer from bad memories), but that we suffer mainly because of a chronic self-frustrating thirst for love, for the more we fall into the temptation to chase the love that is lacking for us, the more we betray our nature. Whether we try to be smarter or more attractive or sweeter, or we want to attract the maternal love that we lacked through the dramatic magnification of our needs, or express our wishes with aggressive feelings of guilt, we develop ways of being that make it harder for us to find love. Ultimately, those who succeed in resolving the problem of love in life—which are not many—reach the surprising conclusion that it is not so much the love that can be received from others that can bring happiness, but love for ourselves, which we were desperately trying to replace with appreciation from others, with being cared for, or with the erotic attraction of others.

The answer to the problem of why we suffer, then, from the perspective of love, is that we suffer for the loss of our loving capacity, and that, by extension, in the healing process, it is the recovery of our capacity for love that will make us not only whole, but happy.

Taking a step forward in time and in the history of psychological thought, we find another theory of neurosis according to which we do not suffer so much because of an animal or instinctual frustration, or because of a romantic frustration, but because of an existential problem: we have lost the meaning of life because we have lost ourselves, we look for ourselves without finding ourselves like one who has lost one's own soul. Here we find modern psychology, in this existential vision of neurosis, with Buddhism and ancient yoga, which spoke of ignorance. Because "to have lost ourselves" is to have lost the subtle basis of consciousness from which stems the awareness of the Being that we so seek in "being this" or in "being that," in achieving such or such a thing. We live with a hunger for what presents itself to our consciousness because we have lost the *awareness of our consciousness,* or awareness of ourselves as subjects.

Such are the theories of neurosis that have been presented historically, each of them as a valid explanation in itself, but to me it seems important to understand that all these visions are equally true and that they all partially describe a single phenomenon: it is just as true that we have lost our instinctual inner animal, as it is that we have lost our maternal mammalian brain, and that we have lost our wise right brain by becoming so exaggeratedly interested in the world of astute reason and its instrumental technological advantages.

Let us say then that we suffer because a part of us—the rational mind that we usually associate to the function of our left cerebral cortex—has become for us an island on which we have shut ourselves away, losing touch with the wealth of our whole being. Correspondingly, then, healing must consist both in the recovery of our mammalian limbic brain, and also in the recovery of our intuitive, caring, mammalian brain, deactivated by a chronic deafness.

However, this is not all: How did such a tragic condition arise, of becoming practically ghostly beings that know only how to think and that feel voraciously compelled to exploit all that they come across to fill their painful emptiness?

In very simple terms: we are born healthy, carrying the seed of a prodigious developmental potential, but as Rousseau observed, we are born into a sick world that precipitately conditions us, limiting us, and somehow infecting us with its millenary affliction. We might call it simply the "civilized" world. However, more useful or objective than the word *civilization,* which has been so idealized, seems to me the more neutral and scientific or anthropological designation "patriarchal society."

Yet, how can this notion that we suffer for being contaminated with a collective hurt help us to heal? I will only very briefly say here what I have explained more broadly in my books on education and politics: that although it does not seem plausible that we can change patriarchal society, which is too immense, varied, and resistant to change, in principle, a healing education could be possible, wisely designed so that children and youth can transcend the dominating patriarchal mind of the settings that we have witnessed through millennia.

In light of this point of view, then, to heal is to heal the patriarchal mind, and patriarchal mind seems to me the best name that we can give to what Freud called universal neurosis and Pierre Weil has called normosis, and that the apocalyptical Christians called the Great Beast— whose spirit characterized the great power centers in the civilized world.

Yet, how does all this apply to the world of psychedelics?

Fundamentally, it seems to me like a divine gift that psychedelics are in the world as agents of dissolution of the fictitious and small mind that has established itself at the pinnacle of our inner world, exerting a repressive and destructive force on the rest of our nature. Some psychedelics, like ibogaine and ayahuasca, are very notably characterized by the liberation of the instinctual world, which explains the frequent visions of animals that characterize its effect. Other psychedelics, the interpersonal ones, are associated more with the recovery of the loving world, the caring, empathic maternal brain; but they all seem to me activators of that realm of thought that rationality does not allow and from which both religious consciousness and psychological understanding arise. It seems to me that we ought to understand our intuitive world as similar to a navigator in our brain structure—a navigator that we have disconnected in our implicit scientism, which denies the nonrational. If, through our culture of civilized man, we have come to disregard our animal instincts as subhuman, we will understand, through this comprehensive vision of the process of darkening and enlightenment of consciousness, that the spiritual is not a territory separate from the animal one, but, rather, is an inclusive space that allows the synthesis of all that we are—an intrinsically neutral space, as the sapiential traditions that insist on detachment have so well described. In the light of the traditional dichotomy between the Apollonian and the Dionysian, so expressively integrated in the Hindu symbolism of the erotic hermit, plenitude has two sides: on the one hand the neutral space that allows and embraces everything, and on the other hand the perfect flow of life.

Psychedelics are characterized both by the activation of the current of life, as for enabling the transparency of the mind through which this current can flow and carry out its healing work.

7

Matters Related
to Method and Training

Although the understanding of psychotherapy and the spiritual path I transmit has probably been a factor in my influence on the people who have had psychedelic experiences with me, I shall limit myself in the following pages to explaining a little about the preparation of people with respect to such experiences through the workshops prior to the session in itself, as well as a little about the way I intervene during the sessions, and then, during the elaboration and shared feedback of the experiences. Additionally, I shall include some explanations of my use of music, which seems to me to be an important spiritual influence that people in an altered state of consciousness are more receptive to than in their ordinary consciousness, and surely contributes to the therapeutic effect of the experiences.

EXPERIENTIAL PREPARATION

What experiences are relevant as a means to prepare for a psychedelic experience? Firstly, an introduction to the practice of non-doing—or the stillness of meditation; for such a practice implies voluntary control of neurotic needs, or unmet needs, and is aimed at the detachment characteristic of the serenity of higher states of consciousness.

Secondly, the practice that I have called "spontaneous movement"— which I have adopted from Indonesian latihan, in which the interest lies in letting go, rather than movement, letting go of control and learning to surrender to what occurs of its own accord beyond our deliberate intentions—seems to be a most relevant preparation for surrendering to the psychedelic "healing journey."

A third practice relevant to the psychedelic healing process seems to me the understanding of one's own personality through the psychology of the enneatypes—which is an invitation to recognize the destructive motivations that sustain the neurosis itself.

Also, I have often included a series of psychological exercises of insight and communication about one's own problems that serve not only as preparation to the "journey," but also to create a group atmosphere of intimacy.

Finally, an introduction to music as a vehicle of sacredness, compassion, and enjoyment seems highly relevant to me—that serves to make better use of the effect that music has on us in itself in the best of cases.

THE ACTUAL SESSIONS

Always as a way to prepare a group for their experience together, I usually ask participants to write something about what it is they are mainly seeking or hoping for from the session, and also a statement of what might make them uncomfortable in relation to any of the other participants. I say "statement" because it is not about solving anything at this point, but simply making it present so that it can be addressed in the course of the group experience.

I then explain, before the session begins, what the "rules of the game" will be: surrendering to one's own spontaneity within the limits of noninvasiveness of others, a commitment to sexual abstinence (though with erotic freedom) and physical nonviolence.

Once the substance has been ingested, people wait for the effects in stillness, either in horizontal position, or seated on chairs (in the case of yagé), in an attitude of self-observation. Later on, music will alternate with silence, and when in silence, I recommend participants to be mindful of the meditation instructions—which comprise silence of thought, attention to breathing, and "remembrance of self"—that is to say, attention focused on the center of one's own consciousness or "deep self," rather than on thoughts and emotions.

It is common that if people do not become prematurely distracted from their process of solitary learning, carried away by the temptation to make contact with others, a period of self-encounter occurs before they feel prepared to take what they learned to the sphere of the encounter with others—and I cite next the description of the experience by one in whom these two phases were made particularly present:

> "The experience was divided in two parts, the first very brief, in which it was as if I had received a series of clarifications, of teachings about so many things, about energy, what is the energy that serves me, the integration of love that I am lacking, about my partner, death, practically everything, as if receiving a teaching from a teacher who is telling you, reading it to you very quickly.
>
> "This phase did not last long, so to speak, it must have lasted approximately an hour and a half, but the problem is that at that point, the experience had come to an end, but the substance had not, obviously, for it lasted until nine in the evening. So there was a second phase, in which I understood how I start doubting, because when I have a certainty, when I am clear on what I must do, it is not enough that I am clear about it, but I have to control it, I want to stop it, I want to have it, and this, I believe, has been the experience for many yesterday, stop nothing, which means, you only know it, you have to trust what you know and give up controlling it.
>
> "My starting point is how I am now, the fruit of yesterday's experience. Using an image, it is a little like knowing how to drive a

machine; you guide it and you do not know all the gestures you have to do while you guide it, you simply guide it and that is enough. The feeling I have now is like being able to trust that I can guide a machine without thinking about how to do it, as if I had understood something further, in this experience, about obsessive thinking, what obsessive thinking is for me."

In view of the desirability that each have the encounter with his or her own inner world and the opportunity to correct his or her attitude following the "oracular power" typical of the psychedelic experience, I recommend people not to move from their place for about the first hour, so that contact established with others does not constitute a premature evasion of the encounter with oneself; however, some people begin to move around the room, some also approach me—either to communicate something to me or ask me a question. Only in response to such initiatives do I usually intervene explicitly, although on more than one occasion, I approach each one in silence, or I exchange a few words with them, and my presence is strongly felt by many in spite of me not moving from my seat (at the front of the room, by the music equipment).

THE RETROSPECTIVE

The next day is dedicated to what I usually call the "integration session" (as Salvador Roquet used to do), for in it, the interest is to integrate the recent experience into the present moment and also into their lives, and the perceptions of those narrating their experiences are also compared with the experiences of others.

However, as a way to prepare for this group meeting, I recommend that each put their experience in writing, as I am convinced of the importance of a circumspect recollection, as the time they will have for sharing will not allow for detailed accounts. Likewise, as a way to prepare for the session (in which only the essential points of the experience are shared), I asked those present to meet in pairs or in groups of three to analyze certain aspects, such as:

1. What has been more deeply understood about oneself or about one's own life;
2. What was extraordinary, marvelous, or spiritual in the experience, beyond the ordinary mind; and
3. What inspiration or understanding one has had regarding what needs to be done in concrete life.

My interventions in such sessions usually take the form of very brief comments of appreciation or irony in the course of the accounts, or at the end of them, or a guidance toward a better understanding of what has been said, as illustrated by the transcripts in previous chapters.

7.2 REFLECTIONS ON THE USE OF MUSIC

When I experienced for the first time a psychedelic-therapeutic journey in the company of a great expert, Doctor Leo Zeff asked me, after I arrived that morning, to select among his music what I would most like to listen to over the following hours, and I chose Bloch's *Shelomo,* which I continued to listen to inwardly for days, or perhaps even years. However, my entrance into the beyond was accompanied by Handel's *Water Music,* which I had not thought about choosing. Since then, I have also invited my patients to bring a selection of their own music, which is used as well as what I select for them from a certain repertoire.

When it comes to advising a repertoire for others, it seems to me that to induce spiritual states, nothing is more appropriate than sacred music of all cultures, but also classical music from diverse cultures can have a sacred content. Thus, when I attended Leo Zeff's group, I was deeply moved on several occasions by the music of Ravi Shankar that was popular in those days, and I think it ought to be part of a psychedelic guide's music collection.

Coming back to Western music, of which I have mentioned just a little with Handel, it is of interest to pay great attention to Bach, the great genius of sacred Baroque music whose work constituted something like the foundation of later European music, until the beginning of modern times. When I was working with groups in Chile, I particularly used the *Musical Offering* and the *Passion According to Saint Matthew;* however, just as in a concert, usually, a classic piece is included in the first part, followed by a Romantic piece, and then something from the modern repertoire, it seems to me that in a good psychedelic session, it is advisable that all these influences reach the participant in his or her inner journey. If one had to choose one of Beethoven's works above all others, none would be more appropriate than the Ninth Symphony, whose first movement sounds like the voice of the Transcendent Father, the second movement like the voice of the Son in all of us, and the third—a lake of compassion—like the Mother, whereas the fourth choral movement represents an expression of humanity in harmony.

Perhaps there is no Romantic work that I have included more often in my sessions than Schubert's final string quintet, which, reflecting the composer's encounter with his very premature death, speaks to all of us mortals when, with the aid of psychedelics, we are able to open our ears to the experiential world underlying the musical world of sound and in this way receive nonverbal teachings from the composers.

Over the years, I have spoken at length about Brahms's very particular therapeutic power, who it seems attained a more balanced spiritual maturity than Beethoven, the titanic fighter in whom heroism prevailed both over tenderness and the spirit of play. Likewise of Mozart, whose works so much communicate both this element of tenderness and the spirit of play and the disposition to the pleasure of childhood. However, if we wish to find, in one single person, the full spectrum of the forms of love, it seems to me that Brahms sings with a fuller palette than the others, for the strong presence in his music of the empathic and maternal, almost oceanic component. I have made frequent use of Brahms's first two quartets, and also of the first sextet, as well as of Symphony no. 1.

Parts of my repertoire have also been the quartets of Debussy and of Ravel, and Ravel's Piano Concerto in G major and his Bolero, as well Stravinsky's "The Rite of Spring" and "The Firebird." On occasion I consider, as part of the preparation of a session, giving people the opportunity to become familiar with the music so as to better be able to understand it—as occurs spontaneously after a repetition, with the view that understanding music requires understanding its form.

However, what to say of the opportuneness with which these musical works are offered to the group? Or of the sequence in which they are presented? I would say that in this I have known how to practice a certain art that I never attempted to put into words, and that I do not know if I will be able to put into words, when I can barely remember the finer details of what I have done. On occasions my musical preference of the moment has been induced by the experience of a particular person or, sometimes, by a wish of his or hers, or by a simple wish to say "hello" to him or her, but in general I allow myself to be guided by what I intuit as appropriate to the "group atmosphere," and many times people in the group have told me that the music reached them in the most opportune way for their inner process that could be imagined, as if programmed from an omniscient mind.

I confess myself innocent of such omniscience, but open to the idea that spontaneity can be very wise, and the situation reminds me of a time during which, upon receiving teachings in a small group surrounding Tarthang Tulku in the seventies, nothing seemed more mysterious to me than the way in which he answered all my questions before I even had a chance to formulate them. I learned by talking to other people in the group that they also shared the same idea. But then, how could it be conceived that Tarthang Tulku satisfy all of us? Might one think that he did it consciously? Rather, it seems to me that a person that teaches from a certain level of inspiration is secretly in touch with what happens without realizing it, like how we are not aware of the activities of our superficial and deliberate conceptual mind.

Is that not really art, which encompasses more levels than our ordinary mind can encompass; this element of art in people who have used popular music in their group works, as Memo Borja did, and Jorge Llano does, resorting to songs in vogue that fit perfectly to people who are working on issues of grief, or pain, or unrequited love, or complaints, or cruel reproaches. I would not be able to do the same because I have not paid sufficient attention to popular music, and therefore my repertoire is limited to a few songs from my youth, up to the time of the Beatles, more or less.

However, I believe that classical music encloses a greater power than popular music, in spite of the immediacy of the latter; because classical musicians are people that have come far, not only in music, but also in the great journey toward the source from which all great inspirations arise. For this, it seems to me that future guides of psychedelic journeys would do well to get to know the vast repertoire of classical music and to have some idea also of how this repertoire adapts to the expression of the different qualities of love, each of them as important for our life and desirable to be cultivated, as well as each of them evoked with more happiness by music than by the words of poets or even mystics.

I have written a book that I have called *The Inner Music: Towards a Hermeneutics of Sound Expression,* in which I develop the idea that music, rather than a pure architecture of sound, constitutes a vehicle for experiences, and that music would not interest us if it was only about ordinary experiences or states of mind. Not only have I argued in that book that music is something akin to a crypto-religion that functions as spiritual nourishment and as language of the depths of the mind, but I have also attempted to convey in it something of the attitude through which we can learn to attend to that inner aspect of music, which is none other than the experiential flow of the one who sings it. Not only the repertoire matters then, but it matters also that we be invited to listen in a different way from how one listens in concert halls: to listen to music not as a simple aesthetic phenomenon and to please the ear, but as a heart-to-heart communication from the composer who wrote it, so that contact with the great musicians of the past may reach us as a great spiritual communion. Above all, for this, we must learn to become the music, laying aside our personal thoughts and day-to-day emotions, identifying ourselves through this with the will of the music, moment to moment, which is but the reflection of the will of the creator of that texture of sounds.

I am convinced that the great composers of the West have been teachers of humanity whose spiritual influence is ignored; and whether this statement is true or not for the majority of people today, I believe it is still true for those who listen to great classical music in their psychedelic journeys.

In the same way that psychedelic experience makes us more permeable to the direct spiritual influence of shamans or people more advanced than ourselves in our spiritual development, it also makes us more permeable to the spiritual wealth of music, be it religious music, the Western classics, or classical Hindu, Arabic, Turkish, or Chinese music—and no doubt the psychedelic experience of many in the sixties explains why such a great deal of ethnic music from all over the world has come into our culture. Certainly, a factor in this has also been that our own classics, for being well known to us, have seemed less attractive to us than the music that reaches us with the prestige of the remote and mysterious. However, I reiterate: more important than the emphasis on the repertoire seems to me the notion that the great musicians, both from the East and the West, have been transmitters of experiences that belong to that higher stratum of the mind to which also belong compassion, true joy and ecstasy, kindness, and detached serenity. For this notion to penetrate us more than intellectually, it is appropriate, before the psychedelic sessions themselves, to listen to music as a way to stimulate the experience of these facets of spirit.

7.3 RECOMMENDATIONS FOR THE TRAINING OF FUTURE PSYCHEDELIC HEALERS

Many people resort to the word *guide* in reference to their role in the work with psychedelic groups. In response to the question, what do they do when they guide, they usually say "nothing," and when I have insisted on wanting to know something about their "therapeutic interventions," they have given me scarce answers, which I have considered confirmation that their experience has led them to feel it is appropriate that—apart from adopting a certain structure or, at times, a certain ritual order—they have let their patients surrender to their own spontaneous inner journey.

For my part, it took me many years of experience before deciding that my novice expectation that in psychedelic therapy I would make greater use of the techniques of my profession than Leo Zeff did, in whose group my learning took place, had been no more than that: the expectation of a novice.

Unlike Leo Zeff's work, however, mine has been characterized by an elaborate *preparation of people before the session*—whether it is for a day or a few days, or for a longer period—and also by the retrospective session (usually the day after the take), during which I tend to intervene in a meaningful way, at least in the case of some people, depending on their reports.

Moreover, it could be said that in spite of my scarce verbal interventions during a session in course, my presence constitutes important guidance for participants, and this is so mainly because my relationship with them is not merely that of a therapist to his patients or clients, but of a spiritual guide.

In behavioral terms, the distinction between the role of a psychotherapist called "transpersonal" (and in virtue of which makes use of techniques from the traditional spiritual schools) and a "spiritual guide" may seem arguable; but in practice—and especially on an inner level, beyond his or her role or behavior—the phenomenon of devotion is different from that of simple "positive transference." Or, at least, that is how those who take part in living spiritual schools such as Buddhism, Sufism, Hindu Tantrism, Taoism, or Shamanism understand it. In all of them it is acknowledged that a "teacher" is not merely one who teaches and guides, but one who has reached developmental maturity, and who has come to know what he or she teaches by his or her own experience. Of such teachers, it is said that they convey something by their presence—something that they are sufficiently prepared or receptive to receive; and it is also said that devotion is appropriate for that mysterious transformative contact that entails the transmission of a spiritual energy—whether it is called baraka or blessing—even though such statements are treated with suspicion in our post-Christian (or pseudo-Christian) Western world, particularly in the psychotherapy profession. It is suspected specifically that the gurus of the East are a vestige of an authoritarianism that is incompatible with a democratic society and that the pretension of a spiritual leadership is necessarily a form of charlatanism, and seekers are recommended to beware of the childishness of relating to the spiritual guide as if he or she were a parental figure, etc. Such warnings, undoubtedly, reveal a half-truth, but the false coin only exists because the true coin exists, and of all things—including truth, love, goodness, and justice—there is a true form and a degraded and fraudulent form.

This is the reason I have needed these introductory paragraphs and the explanation that I am one who has been a disciple of several spiritual teachers and, having through a progressive maturation, come to know how to transmit what I received; for a long time I have myself had "disciples" rather than "students" or "patients," and in spite of the fact that I present myself to the world as a therapist who, as well as training therapists, teaches Buddhism, I have been receiving from those who are closer to me a veneration that reflects a deeper influence than that of an instructor who sometimes gives advice or uses therapeutic techniques. Therefore, if I were to describe the way I operate in a psychedelic group, I would have to mention the subtle authority I exert in spite of my non-authoritarian language—an authority that becomes manifest especially in the possibility (which is given to me by being so respected) to sometimes speak harsh truths.

It can be understood, following what I have explained about my own development, that I agree with the practice of indigenous populations that leave the task of handling psychedelics to the shamans, and that I do not agree with the supposedly democratic opinion that anyone can carry out the role of a psychedelic guide—as is beginning to occur with ayahuasca following the recent international conference in Ibiza.

At the same time, however, it seems to me that it would not be difficult to train people who, without even the need for a degree in medicine or psychology, are able to accompany others in their initiation to the world of psychedelics, or on a "healing journey" at some critical stage in life. For this purpose, the description of training procedures will not be as important as a recognition of sufficient psycho-spiritual maturity or integrity.

Having said this, I shall begin to share my ideas regarding a training for accompaniers of the healing and enlightening journey of psychedelics.

If we want to train future professionals, as necessarily will have to be done if we want to overcome the repressive policy and begin to use the healing potential of these substances (that have been recognized by all the great cultures and that are so related to the origin of religions), would we say that especially well prepared for this will be those who have devoted much time to understanding the skeleton, the muscles, the digestive phenomena, the functioning and illnesses of the eyes, the nose, and the ears? Until some time ago, only doctors were able (following a specialization in psychiatry) to use drugs, or even practice psychotherapy. However, following the time of psychoanalytical monopoly, psychologists were also able to practice psychotherapy.

Nevertheless, should it be a requisite that before using psychedelics, people study medicine or psychology? It seems to me that we ought to move beyond this prejudice of the profession. Or more precisely: although the training of a psychologist would be of help in this purpose, the schools of psychology would constitute a costly and barely justifiable academic demand when considering what is most appropriate for professional training and also for the community in the case of young people with a talent for experiential guidance, whether it is therapeutic, spiritual, or specifically psychedelic guidance. It seems to me that given a talent and a minimum of mental health, a person that handles psychedelics may need less training time, and perhaps a more complex training than what is offered now by universities; and not so much academic, but experiential, and very committed. Such a person could very well spare himself or herself the relation to general psychology, experimental psychology, the history of psychology, statistics, industrial psychology, and much more. On the other hand, what is limited of the training of psychologists for the requirement of a person preparing to accompany psychedelic experiences can be understood in view that, practically speaking, the universities do not even train expert psychotherapists. Or, in other words: people competent in psychotherapy have had to, following their psychology studies, attend a specialized institute, whether of Gestalt therapy, psychoanalysis, transactional therapy, psychodrama, etc., which has taken them practically nine years (five of university and four of specialization).

Perhaps I ought to interject here that I am known in the therapeutic world not only as one of Fritz Perls's successors, but also as a therapist with a Buddhist training and as an interpreter of the psychology of the enneatypes, and mainly as the founder of a program for training therapists and educators, which I called SAT and that I have been refining for about forty years with great success. My work took, a long time ago, the form of an association called SAT Institute (a nonprofit organization, with a special interest in education), and my initial work during the sixties in California closely followed the great transition in my life during a retreat in the desert close to Arica. In its inception, this work was more of an improvisation than a program, and already in my letter of invitation to participants I explained that there was no program as such, but there were certain ingredients, just as to make shoes one needs soles, nails, glue, and scissors, or to make bread not only flour is needed, but also salt, yeast, water, and fire.

I discontinued the SAT school in the United States after a few years, at a time in which my journey of ascension to spirit had become the descent de rigueur, and it seemed to me for a time that this activity could have been something like a meteor crashing down on my life; but my work flourished again a few years later in Europe, and now it was announced as a "program" that was called *Personal and professional development program for therapists, educators, and agents of change*. My commitment in creating this training and transformation process was that, without dealing with therapeutic theories or techniques, but with simply providing participants with a transformative experience, I could contribute to the improvement and evolution of their professional practice.

The SAT became well known from its inception, with the convergence in my group of disciples of the most charismatic therapist in the Basque Country (Antonio Asín), disciples of the most prestigious Paco Peñarrubia (with his CIPARH institute) and Juanjo Albert, a well-known Gestaltist and Reichian from Alicante. As well as the followers of the gurus, there were the gurus themselves and some foreign colleagues of theirs, like Paolo Quattrini, form Florence, Riccardo Zerbetto, from Siena, Antonio Ferrara, from Naples. . . . I had the privilege, then, of witnessing the development not only of trainees, but of Europe's most prestigious therapists.

Among the trainees not only were the followers of the leaders of the most renowned schools, but also, as the SAT became known, more and more people came who had finished their psychology courses and now sought to practice psychotherapy. Beyond the sphere of professionals, I would say that the SAT has always been open to the natural talent of therapy "enthusiasts," who turn out to be more or less the "seekers." I have related with special sympathy to these seekers, some of whom will be the shamans of tomorrow.

Naturally, in designing a condensed form of therapeutic training independent of the official cannons, I returned to what had most helped me in my own training. There were many Gestaltists in my audience from the beginning, moreover, and therefore it was natural that there was a considerable gestalt component in what I was offering them. However, in view of my early psychoanalytical training, it was also natural that I include in my program a significant Freudian element, particularly in the systematic use and refinement of the technique of free association of ideas, as well as in conveying a good psychodynamic culture. The psychology of the enneatypes, which could be said is part of dynamic psychology and which constitutes a discipline of insight on the personality, has also converged in the psychological consciousness that I transmit.

Another strong therapeutic element in the SAT program was one that did not have its origin in the academic world or in other cultures, but in a medium: the method that Robert Hoffman introduced in the seventies in his individual therapy, and the ideas of which I adapted to guided groups in a context of mutual help. It is a method to reelaborate childhood where a strong catharsis of pain and anger takes place, and that allows people to forgive their angered inner child, and through this gain the ability to understand and feel compassion for one's parents. I have many times recommended the Hoffman Process, which many institutes offer throughout the world, to acquaintances, telling them that it is one of the best opportunities to achieve profoundly transformative results in a brief period of time. In the SAT, what we offer is a condensed form of the Hoffman Process,* but it seems to me that as an element of a broader program, it contributes significantly to its almost never before seen and perhaps incomparable results.

The SAT program also includes, with a view to the personal training of participants as well as their future therapeutic ability, a good component of meditation, and more specifically of Buddhist meditation (through the three yanas, in which they learn to observe the mind, to still it, and to know it). Another dimension of the program is what I have called "spontaneous movement" (already mentioned in the previous chapter), an approximation of both Mary Whitehouse's and Janet Adler's "authentic movement," and Subud's latihan. It is a kind of discipline of indiscipline, or more precisely, a *discipline of giving up control*. A paradoxical *discipline of surrender*, that already Patañjali in his yoga sutras mentions as an alternative to the practice of stilling the mind.

Additionally, other components of the SAT program have arisen in

---

*In truth, the Hoffman Process was born as an elaboration and extension of the original group process, which is still done as part of the SAT program.

our activity, such as the therapeutic use of music, a particular form of "rebirthing," and the supervised mutual therapy workshop. I will also mention the use of music as a support to devotion, compassion, and joy, which has constituted one of my original specialties, and will especially interest those who intend to accompany psychedelic journeys.

It seemed relevant to me to describe here the main components of the SAT program because I cannot help but feel that, if the practice of psychotherapy has been so well taught to both psychologists and high-level professionals, it could also constitute the basis of a future psychedelic training, alternative to the one developed in psychology schools or psychiatric clinics. Very soon the need for a relatively economical, efficient, and brief method for training psychonaut healers will be felt, and I can imagine no better solution to this new need than this program that has interested both beginners and experts and even nonprofessionals, and that is offered in the form of only three modules lasting ten days, following a brief introductory course.

Although it is presented simply as a list of subject areas, the SAT program might seem somewhat arbitrary, what makes it highly recommended (apart from its notable results) is what might be called its "deep structure": a program less evident than the one described so far, that can be summarized in the aim of developing three forms of love, three aspects of self-knowledge, and detachment. To this set of abilities, I have given the name *existential competences,* and in my book *The Revolution We Expected* I have explained its nature in detail, as well as its relationship to the aspects of the program. For now, I list them:

1. Love, or more specifically Christian love—that is maternal, empathic, compassionate, and supportive love, which in Greek is called *agape.* "Love for one's neighbor."
2. Eros. The divine Eros, so criminalized—that must be returned to innocence and even made sacred again.
3. Appreciative love or *philia,* that creates values from its enthusiastic impulse. Appreciative love goes from respect to

admiration and, beyond, to devotion and even adoration, and is not only aimed at people, but also at values, divine beings, and life itself.

In addition to these three loves, I have listed as part of the existential competences, three forms of self-knowledge, to which we will add a fourth:

1. Becoming aware of what happens to us moment to moment.
2. Self-knowledge, both on the psychodynamic level and that which concerns our personality traits, our personal relationships, and our life itself.
3. Metaphysical self-knowledge, wisdom or gnosis. The self-recognition of the mind itself, or of consciousness itself—beyond sensations, emotions, perceptions, concepts, and other mental states. This wisdom is not easily separable from a preparation of the mind through meditation, but fundamentally it requires:
4. Detachment, a seventh existential competence, scarcely cultivated in the secular world, but without which the "death to world" that is the springboard for awakening is not possible. Detachment is cultivated through meditation, but also through the experience of confronting loss throughout life, as well as unfulfilled wishes. We can, in the face of frustration, become more avid and irritated, or learn detachment, and this is the case of better guided people.

Returning to the issue of what training to recommend to an aspiring psychonaut healer, I shall reiterate that more important than the theories of psychotherapy the academic world focuses on, what seems necessary to me is (1) a good ability to love oneself, to be able to thus love one's neighbor and be able to admire the higher things. A person who has not yet reached erotic freedom will not be a good guide, for one who is lacking in such a fundamental aspect of the psyche is not able to go with the flow of life. (2) Neither will a person be a good companion without the empathy that is a natural part of the maternal feeling. (3) Nor will a person who does not have "altruistic interests," that is to say, an altruistic or as is often said, an "idealistic" impulse, and who through his or her own aspirations inspires a movement forward in the great journey to be a good companion. If it is true that a person is needed who is erotically healthy, healthy in their affections, and healthy in their devotion, it is also necessary that the aspiring psychonaut healer be a person that is able to be in the here and now, that knows himself or herself quite well, and that has taken some steps on the path toward wisdom. Detachment, especially, is part of the repertoire of abilities necessary for living well and also for being able to help others well. Firstly, because *without detachment there is no navigating*. It is precisely attachment that keeps us stuck in problematic situations, and the more attached we are to our ways of seeing, feeling, and doing, the less are we able to surrender to the healing current that the psychedelic flow represents. However, detachment is, on the one hand, freedom from fixed positions and the ability to let go of the past, and on the other hand, surrender, just as in the complementary aspects of meditation there is detachment in both non-doing and in surrendering to the flow of life, as the Hindu god Shiva is represented sometimes as a hermit covered in ashes and others as an erect phallus, or as the union of the male and female genitals at the center of the temples. It is the complementarity between the Apollonian and the Dionysian, which in Gestalt therapy is expressed as the complementarity between "creative indifference" and "organismic intelligence." All these matters may seem to us exotic and perhaps esoteric or even far-fetched and are not part of the habitual lexicon of psychology (and even less so of education). Some months ago, however, I promoted a gathering of educators in Spain about the importance of the Apollonian and the Dionysian in education, during which my standpoint that we are unable to love due to the absence of such complementary qualities, was very well received.

I believe I have finished saying what I had set out to in response to what could be a future training of people competent in the use of hallucinogenic drugs and associated medicines, but I shall summarize here the essential points by way of a recommendation to the pertinent authorities so that they make haste in creating a training for specialists in the use of psychedelics both in universities and therapeutic training institutes, and also in new centers to attract those more specifically talented or that feel a calling to this service that requires a psycho-spiritual training rather than a traditional professional training. For this, the SAT program seems to me highly recommendable, for its level of depth, when it comes to the future preparation for psychedelic assistance of people with the necessary talent and life experience, for I am convinced that what is most useful in this situation is a live transference of the consciousness and health comparable to that which occurs in shamanism and in spiritual schools, although the psycho-spiritual development of people up until now has been more disregarded than favored by universities.

Only when I started this chapter did I begin to see how my work of decades, originally inspired by the desire to help seekers like myself, which then became predominantly a training for therapists and which more recently has interested me for what it contributes to the training of educators, is also a contribution to the psychedelic world that I believed I had left behind to a large extent, but which it seems to me I have been serving without intending to while I have been dedicated to perfecting my integrative psycho-spiritual school. Having said this now, I wonder if it might not sound like propaganda to pretend to have the solution to a great problem, so to speak, in the basement. My specialty in life seems to have been training people—not only to be better therapists, educators, entrepreneurs, or whatever, but to be better people for themselves and for the world we live in. I have always regretted that what we still anachronistically call university has become a set of professional schools that do not integrate the human being. I hope that one day the SAT program may serve as a human and humanizing complement to current professions, and especially to that of psychotherapy and education.

8

The Role of Psychedelics in a Policy for Consciousness

PSYCHEDELIC POLICY

One could say that since psychedelic substances were banned in the sixties up until the present, a cold war has been established between the spirit of prohibitionism and that of libertarians, and the impasse between these two forces does not seem to have served much purpose.

Perhaps the main problem with prohibitionism has been how the "war on drugs" has served as a political pretext for a war against youth consciousness and xenophobia directed at African Americans, Latinos, Chinese, and the poor. During an era in which the most significant problems in the world have been the perversion of politics by the intrusion of the interests of big business, a questionable preference for exercising charity toward the rich, inequality, ecological crisis, and conflict in the Middle East, many politicians have insisted that the most pressing problem is that of drugs—in part because the vehement accusation of alleged culprits incites the masses as much as the sight of the guillotine, and also because provocative political candidates have achieved electoral success through such a maneuver.

One of the problems with the "war on drugs" has been that its results have been much worse than the alleged harmful effects of prohibited drugs. For, although it is certainly true that the phenomenon of addiction exists (which in the case of certain drugs, like alcohol, destroys lives), such a destructive effect cannot be measured, for example, with the immense damage caused by the persecution of people caught with small amounts of marijuana. Imprisonment in the United States has reached four times the number in Saudi Arabia and China, climbing to 2.3 million prisoners. In an interesting documentary of 2012 entitled *The House I Live In*, it is reported that since 1971 the "war on drugs" has cost more than a trillion dollars and caused 45 million arrests. Tragically, however, such costs and damages have not succeeded in solving the alleged problem of drugs or even that of drug trafficking.

However, not only have the costs of this useless and inhumane war been a problem, but so is its motivational basis, explains the director and narrator of the documentary, Eugene Jarecki. For it is clear that the criminalization of marijuana was at the service of the persecution of African Americans, and that opium-based products could be bought in pharmacies before the political idea of criminalizing the Chinese arose. If we want to personify the aggressor behind the war on drugs, he appears to us as a villain not only full of hatred but also shameless in his deceitful spirit, by expecting that people should be "protected" from drugs, and the country from those who use them.

Prominent among political lies has been that the war on drugs is a medical matter that concerns the World Health Organization (WHO), when in reality the most significant trigger of prohibitionist policies was the so-called Revolution of Consciousness, which was hailed too optimistically in the sixties as the dawn of a new era. This moment of history was epitomized by a spiritual renaissance, a vigorous flourishing in the world of psychotherapy, feminism, ecology, movements supporting civil liberties, and a keen interest in spiritual things—such as Eastern traditions. Yet the defenders of the established order were frightened by a population of young people who were beginning to dare to invalidate their elders in their families and institutions, and even went so far as to claim that the pervasive aberration of the "system" required us to embrace a "counterculture." The threat of such a counterculture thus formed the basis for what has now been described as a "slow-moving holocaust."

I must confess that in spite of my sympathy with those who have been interested in the use of psychedelics, I have not agreed with their libertarian proposals, and I imagine that this was what prompted the American psychedelic community to have excluded me from their meetings.

When a group of forty or so MDMA therapists and myself were summoned to a series of lectures at the Esalen Institute in the mideighties, it was proposed that this drug (which had already been included in the Schedule I list of substances prohibited by the authorities) be moved into the category of those which, like aspirin, could be sold in pharmacies without a prescription, and I was the only one during those meetings to disagree—with the exception of the White House psychiatrist, with whom (though our agreement would lead to a loss of reputation in this circle) I agreed that "empathogens" should be classified as being similar to amphetamines, the use of which is permitted through medical prescription, albeit in a controlled way. Although I understand those who question that doctors should have greater authority than clinical psychologists or spiritual directors, I do not think it reasonable that such an argument should result in the freezing of a process of gradual acceptance of the authorities of this new resource.

I would say that the psychedelic movement, under the impact of repressive forces, exaggerated its understandable desire for freedom to such a degree that in its excess it became counterproductive. In this respect, I quote a letter from Antonin Artaud that I take from the prologue to Esteban's book, which translates as, "The right to inebriation: libertarian manifesto against prohibition."*

Mr. Legislator, you are a fool.

Your law serves only to irritate global pharmaceutics with no benefit to the level of drug addicts of the nation because:

---

*Javier Esteban, *El derecho a la ebriedad* (Madrid: Ediciones Amargord, 2007), 21–24.

1. The number of drug addicts that procure their drugs from pharmacies is minimal.
2. True drug addicts do not get their supplies from pharmacies.
3. Drug addicts who procure their drugs from pharmacies are all sick.
4. The number of sick drug addicts is minimal compared to that of drug addicts for pleasure.
5. Pharmaceutical restrictions of drugs will never bother well-organized drug addicts given to pleasure.
6. There will always be drug addicts out of a passion.
7. Sick drug addicts have an imperishable right over society to be left in peace. It is, above all, a matter of conscience.

The law on drugs places in the hands of the inspector-usurper of public health the right to dispose of the pain of men; it is a singular pretension of modern medicine to want to dictate its rules to the conscience of each. All the bleating of formal letters has no power of action against this act of conscience: even more than death, I am the owner of my pain. Every man is the judge, and the sole judge of the amount of physical pain and mental emptiness he can honestly withstand.

Lucidity or lack of lucidity, there is a lucidity that no illness can rob me of, it is the one that dictates to me the feeling of my physical life. Hence, if I have lost my lucidity, medicine has nothing else to do but give me the substances that allow me to recover the use of that lucidity.

Gentlemen dictators of the pharmaceutical school of France, you are miserly snobs; there is one thing that should be better measured: that opium is the indispensable and imperious substance that brings back to life the soul of those who suffered the misfortune of losing it.

There is an evil against which opium is sovereign, and that evil is called Anguish, in its mental, medical, psychological, logical, or pharmaceutical form, as you wish.

The Anguish that breeds crazy people.

The Anguish that results in suicides.

The Anguish that gives rise to the condemned.

The Anguish unknown to medicine.

The Anguish your doctor does not understand.

The Anguish that harms life.

The Anguish that severs the umbilical cord of life.

By your iniquitous law you put into the hands of irresponsible persons, cretins in medicine, filthy pharmacists, fraudulent judges, doctors, midwives, doctoral inspectors, the right to dispose of my anguish that is as acute as the needles of all the compasses of hell.

Tremors of the body or the soul, there is no human seismograph that allows to arrive at an evaluation of my pain with precision, but the instant one of my spirit.

All the haphazard science of men is not superior to the immediate knowledge that I can have of my being: I am the only judge of what is in me.

Go back to your barns, stinking doctors, and you, too, Mr. Legislator Moutonnier. You are not raving for love of men, but for a tradition of imbecility. Your ignorance of what a man is only equals your stupidity in trying to limit him. I hope that your law falls upon your father, your mother, your wife, and your children, and all your future generations. And now I swallow your law.

Many of those who would like to live in a world favorable to the wise use of psychedelics have regretted that Tim Leary, in exaggerating his insulting stance before the authorities, delayed the advent of his own dream, and the same can be said of so many others that became spokesmen of its unfettered liberationism. I myself admired him as one who spoke with the freedom of children or the intoxicated, but are not narcissism and anti-authoritarianism phenomena comparable ultimately to prejudicial anger and lies?

I once heard Gordon Wasson say (at a lunch that was my first meeting with him during the LSD conference organized by the University of California in 1966) that his wife was very fond of mushrooms, and that people can be divided into the mycophilic and the mycophobic. He meant that his wife, being a Russian, was very fond of foraging for mushrooms in the woods, and he, for equally cultural reasons, would never have thought to become enthused about such a thing. We know that he allowed himself to be influenced by her, and we already know what came of it, but I suppose that in speaking of this alternative between love or repulsion for mushrooms, Wasson was evidencing an analogous contrast between those who are attracted or repelled by psychedelic experiences: two types of people that came to be called *beat* and *square* in the sixties. I understand that the term *beat* (applied to the literary movement of Kerouac and others and to which the *San Francisco Chronicle* reporter Herb Caen added the term *nik* to characterize the pre-hippies) derived from the taste for jazz, and the term *square* seems to me a good metaphor for the overstructured mentality of conventional people, for whom there is no greater threat than giving up control of themselves. It is a fact that in any human group there are those who are interested in the adventure of moving beyond their own boundaries and others that are not in the least interested in a search that could change them. In pre-Columbian cultures the number of people wishing to become shamans can rise to a considerable percentage of the population, and this was the case in the 1960s with the "seekers." However, there are not only seekers or mystics and indifferent people in the world; there are also antimystics, and antiseekers: people who are unknowingly prejudiced toward seekers similarly to how nationalists think badly of foreigners and simple provincials of strangers. This phenomenon of antagonism toward seekers—which we could also call the proto-mystics and potential shamans—is something that has been an omnipresent factor in an implicit war, not only on drugs and on certain minorities, but *on consciousness.*

FOR A POLICY FOR CONSCIOUSNESS

Not only do we have today an "antipsychedelic policy," which is present in an explicit "war on drugs," but also an implicit war on the expanded mind that has given psychedelics its name.* Just as in the Middle Ages there was a fight to prevent people learning to read books, nowadays there is still a war on consciousness, only we have become sufficiently unconscious to not notice. R. D. Laing, the father of antipsychiatry, addressed an aspect of this theme in his book *The Politics of Experience*,† and it should be apparent to mothers how social adaptation requires that their children be taught not to say inconvenient things about what they perceive in their environment and not even ask embarrassing questions. This has also been stressed by the great psychoanalyst Alice Miller who, based on her vast experience in the formation of the child's mind, even eloquently entitled one of her books *Thou Shalt Not Be Aware*.‡

The antagonism of our society toward consciousness has been expressed in many ways, besides the domestication of early childhood that we exalt as "socialization," during which the pathology of society is passed on to children, especially through a mandate to the condemnation of their natural instinctual drives. Freud described this process as a subordination of the "pleasure principle" to the "reality principle," but with today's perspective one could question what he called "reality principle," which in fact is only a principle of adaptation to a patriarchal reality; that is to say, a socialization through which we renounce some of our psychic reality by internalizing the rejection of the instinctive spontaneity shared by all civilizations (which in this way differ from pre-Columbian indigenous cultures).

Psychedelia is a neologism coined by Humphry Osmond from the Greek words ψυχή "soul," and δῆλος "manifest": "that the soul manifests."

†R. D. Laing, *The Politics of Experience and the Bird of Paradise* (Barcelona: Crítica, 1983).

‡Alice Miller, *Thou Shalt Not Be Aware: Society's Betrayal of the Child* (New York: Meridan Printing, 1984).

In addition to parenting, the antagonism of patriarchal society is transmitted to the development of individual consciousness through the perversion of education, which not only continues the process of socialization through which conformity to a dysfunctional culture is imposed, but also inhibits the development of interiority by keeping the minds of children excessively occupied in memorizing information and neglecting the ethical aspect of psychological development (by accepting, in a purely rhetorical manner, UNESCO's statement that education should address the need to learn to live together and the need to be). However, I will not dwell here on this subject to which I have dedicated an entire book and I continue to dedicate much of my efforts through a series of foundations and associations in Spain, Italy, Chile, Brazil, and Russia.

Independently of the war on the development of consciousness that is covertly being carried out in educational establishments on the pretext of doing just the opposite, a repression of youth culture, which is feared by the authorities as a threat to the established order, is also practiced in many countries. Wherever this happens, this war is complicated by the dissent of young people through the criminalization of psychedelics, which have been a special interest of youth and whose effect (by giving back to people independent thinking and awareness of their emotions) is contrary to the pressure of conformity.

Much has also been said and written about how media control militates against truth and culture, which not only masks reality through the selection that is made among news items and through conventional and manipulative interpretations of current events, but through distraction of the essential by means of the trivial but "entertaining." Huge sums are spent today on political lies, which by implicating us all in automatic complicity makes us not only unconscious of what happens in our environment but also, depriving us of the possibility of a socially responsible existence, operates as an implicit castration in our participation in solidarity with the common good, which is characteristic of our nature as "political animals."

The dire problem in all this, it seems to me, is that it is a grave error to try to solve our problems through collective robotization; for there is reason to believe that consciousness, rather than a problem, entails precisely the promise of bringing us the indispensable answers to our serious and increasingly critical problems.

As Einstein said, "the problems we face will not be solved by the minds that created them." By what minds, then? More conscious, healthy, integrated, evolved minds, obviously. Even though the opinion has been imposed that drugs destroy the mind and entail a danger of madness, it has been denied and hidden that the right use of drugs constitutes a powerful healing and enlightening resource; and if the preceding chapters of this book have not proved this, it will only mean that the measure of prevailing prejudice requires more than mere communication of the truth. I have argued in favor of the importance of our choosing to have "an education for consciousness," instead of the traditional and patriarchal education (authoritarian and repressive and incomplete) that perpetuates our problematic way of life and our degraded consciousness. How is it possible that the name *education* is fraudulently applied to a system of education that is mainly concerned with preparing students to pass tests in view of their selection in the employment market? How is it not perceived that the neglect of human development by education is responsible for the psychologically ignorant and immoral society we have? Perhaps predominantly because "among the blind the one-eyed man is king"; that is to say: among those who have been dumbed down by education, educators are kings—who in reality have no alternative to prostituting themselves to a perverse system (in a comparable way, perhaps, to small drug dealers, who cannot find other jobs).

I cannot overlook, however, that such a strong criticism of the established order can put my credibility at risk, since the perception of such things, which are not obvious to the majorities, has taken years of reflection and experience; therefore, I will at least say that a thick book entitled *The Dumbing Down of America* documents step by step the legislation with which it was intended from the beginning of the industrial age to create an education primarily aimed at the training of a workforce, and that very insightful books such as George Leonard's (*Education and Ecstasy*) suggest that to militate against the development of consciousness is not a mere neglect of education, but an efficient performance at the service of an undeclared purpose of creating a society easily manipulated and *adapted* to conventions.

It is not necessary to contemplate the absurdity of education to think that the power that prevails in the world is either ignorant or ruthless; it is sufficient to consider what could be done in view of the general suffering of our species in the light of what is known about its causes, to understand that it would seem as if the different needs of the people were to be met only with the expectation of money, while conspiring for a progressive impoverishment of the poor and for their growing helplessness.

Is it not something like madness that we have created an economic system that does not serve us humans to live in peace and to be happy, but only serves an unwise and unkind minority that is making the world an increasingly problematic place?

Has it been perhaps the lack of a spirit of solidarity or a poverty of ideals on the part of the people with the most power that, allowing the free play of their greed, has sustained our troubled collective situation? Or the blindness of the masses, who do not know how to choose their leaders? Or a systemic evil that makes those who participate in the group spirit of corporations, bureaucracies, oligarchies, and mafias feel impotent? The degree of complexity of the phenomenon, in any case, leads to such a complication of the analyses and proposed solutions as to have generated an impotent passivity—and for that reason it seems to me that we can only see hope in a broad awakening of the mind of the majorities to another level of consciousness.

I have dwelled on the matter of a need for a change in education as a fulcrum for the more specific idea of this chapter and this book that, regardless of what is chosen to be done in favor of the development of people's consciousness through education, culture, mental health, parenting, and the economy itself, it is also crucial that we take into account a "policy of consciousness" or "policy for consciousness" when it comes to psychedelics.

I believe, moreover, that the option of making use of the drugs we know for enhancing the emotional and spiritual awareness of those who are interested in their own psycho-spiritual development should not only be limited to putting an end to the "war on drugs," but it should also aim for a creative effort toward the best possible use of the psychedelic healing potential.

Without wasting time or effort in putting forward new evidence about the clinical usefulness of psychedelics (beyond what I have already done, albeit in a somewhat impressionistic way, since it should have been made evident to broad-minded people even though such usefulness continues to be unprovable to prejudiced minds or institutions), I must at least devote a few lines to the idea that *opting for consciousness should imply a very serious reconsideration of the conventional antipsychedelic prejudice that has dominated in culture so far.*

In the case of the political authorities, the antipsychedelic tendency is understandable since political success depends on elections and the manipulated masses have so far been rather conventional. In the case of the medical authorities, which until now have been as repressive in relation to "entheogenic" drugs as churches toward their mystics, I have witnessed for many years not only how the arrogance of the scientific profession in relation to what it has not sufficiently understood reveals narrow-mindedness, competitive interests of the profession, and other evil passions, but that the fundamental problem has been that *health care agencies have given their authority to a political maneuver: it has not been in any way a concern that people may throw themselves out of windows onto the street under the effects of LSD or that their babies suffer from chromosome damage, or even that some become addicted (or, as in the case of alcoholism, bring suffering to their spouses or increase traffic accidents) that has motivated the prohibitionists,* but all this has served as a pretext for a repressive policy inspired in truth by the fear that young people will rediscover what they proclaimed during the years when they crowded into the streets of San Francisco condemning the Vietnam War or when they sang the call to a counterculture that despised the blindness of their forefathers.

An important role in the phenomenon of prohibition in the United States (and then, by extension, in the world) was due to Reagan's maneuver when he was elected governor of California in the sixties, when he developed a political alliance with the paterfamilias of that entire libertarian generation, so inspired by their experiences of inner liberation through marijuana and LSD. It was said that the generation gap had never been so dramatic as in those years when the young intellectuals of the best universities (notably Harvard and the University of Berkeley), encouraged by a new clarity about the destructive dysfunction of the violent and exploitative sociopolitical system that now wanted to send them to Vietnam, had become contemptuous of their own parents, rulers, and traditional values. Obviously, Reagan won the sympathy and votes of these parents when he proposed that these problematic and disrespectful youths were the great prevailing problem, just as Hitler once managed to persuade the German people that the economic problems of that time were due to the presence of the Jews and their power.

The case of the religious authorities has not been fundamentally different from that of the medical or political authorities, for once the word *drug* was associated with the idea of "crime," it was undesirable that its disrepute should contaminate the sacred prestige of life and religious institutions. As such, despite the capital importance of "magic plants" in the history of religions, beginning with the Iranians and India of the Vedic times and including the tantric traditions, Taoism, and the mysteries that preceded Christianity in Greece, the poor popular use of drugs in recent times has been an argument for their loss of respect—hence talking about the old sacramental drinks as "drugs" has come to seem natural.

Given the discredit of "drugs" instilled in culture by the authorities, it is not surprising that groups of people who protect their own spiritual prestige should be condemning. Since all authoritarian systems imply a dogmatic tendency and a limiting orthodoxy, just as the medical profession wanted to discredit the miracle-working shamans (some of whom continue to do inconceivable things), also doctors of the law in the modern churches are suspicious of those who navigate the seas of experience firsthand in the world of consciousness. Even though we now understand the enormous significance psychedelics have had in the history of religions, the opinion still dominates among the leaders of the Christian world that these are an invalid channel, or a gateway to experiences that, being artificially induced, should not be permitted. Yet, has not this been influenced by something similar to the case of political leaders, who are greatly concerned about public image and who are unaware of the destructive outcome of their conservative choice? No less limiting has been the questionable conventional culture of the majorities, who thrive on the scandals reported in the tabloid newspapers.

The spirit of our xenophobic culture, which treats those who take drugs as monsters or criminals (in a manner comparable to how, over the centuries, it has criminalized the Jews and now persecutes the poor), being as it is, how can one conceive that the day will come when a humanizing policy that opens the door to the therapeutic and spiritualizing potential of drugs in culture, medicine, and even a new way of educating educators is adopted?

THE PSYCHEDELIC REFLECTION OF A POLICY FOR CONSCIOUSNESS

In truth, such a "psychedelic policy" can hardly be conceived within a culture that practices (indeed, unwittingly) a war on consciousness. However, the moment it comes to light that such a war has been sustained against consciousness and against humanity itself, it is possible that, at least in an experimental way, the desire arises to explore an alternative policy that puts its hopes in the development of human potential itself, which lies not in technology but in the wisdom and recovery of the heart, and not least in the recovery of the healthy animal instinct we have tamed for thousands of years, since we began to arrogantly beat our chests in an attitude of *"Homo sapiens triumphant."* A "psychedelic policy" would simply be a willingness to make use of psychedelics for human development—whether in the sphere of public health, culture, spirituality, religion, or the training of leaders—and it is easy to imagine that this will arise when the community understands that it is time to commit to the Revolution of Consciousness imagined by Aurobindo and Krishnamurti. The latter says in *Life Ahead:*

> Political, economic or social revolutions are not the answer either, for they have produced appalling tyrannies, or the mere transfer of power and authority into the hands of a different group. Such revolutions are not at any time the way out of our confusion and conflict.
>
> But there is a revolution which is entirely different and which *must* take place if we are to emerge from the endless series of anxieties, conflicts, and frustrations in which we are caught. This revolution has to begin, not with theory and ideation, which eventually prove worthless, but with a radical transformation in the mind itself. Such a transformation can be brought about only through right education and the total development of the human being. (Emphasis in original.)

Although acceptance of psychedelic mysticism in ancient spiritual organizations is unlikely in view of the antagonism between classical spirituality and the Dionysian spirit, and of the patriarchal commitment of repressive religious institutions, it can be said that appreciation for the Dionysian spirit—which has been expressed in the enthusiasm for the books of Castaneda, in the interest of the last decades in shamanism, and in the spirit of humanistic psychology—is a favorable factor. It is in the world of psychotherapy that it is easiest for us to think that the time has come to *train professionals with the necessary preparation to accompany the many who are interested in the experience of "magic plants"* or their modern synthetic equivalents.

Of course, once one or more governments approve this intention, a series of questions will be raised, starting with what would be the nature of such a training of future psychedelic guides, who should it be open to, and what preparation should be expected of the candidates for this new, yet at the same time very old discipline?

I offer next my own opinion in the hope that it can sidestep endless discussions, to thus contribute to the healing effect of psychedelics being made effective as soon as possible.

For a long time, I cherished the hope that somewhere in the world a school for such a training of expert psychonauts would be founded, to which would be invited both people trained in the psychotherapeutic world (such as Grof, Gabor Maté, and others) and in the shamanic traditions, and in which an integrative psychotherapeutic training would also be given. More recently, however, it seems to me that it will be simpler for the psychedelic specialty to be permitted in university centers of therapy training, and perhaps also in authorized out-of-university centers—since psychotherapy is being learned in such centers or specialized institutes (in Gestalt, Rogerian therapy, psychoanalysis, etc.) more than in the faculties of medicine and psychology. Such a pluralist formula would be simpler than the creation of a model school, and would be better suited to serve local communities, where the inexperienced use of psychoactive drugs has so far been the fundamental cause of abuse.

In the event that one of the existing universities would like to create a new center for the training of therapists who are experts in the use of psychedelics, however, I would like to propose in what remains of this chapter that what may be more appropriate than the therapeutic training approach offered by existing universities, is the training I have created through more than forty years of experimentation and which is widely known throughout the world as the SAT program for personal and professional training of therapists, educators, and agents of change.

It is a very concise program, more experiential than theoretical in content, but with the theoretical content appropriate to an integrative practice of psychotherapy, which includes a theoretical-practical laboratory of psychotherapy with the necessary supervision and, above all, a work on the difficulties encountered in the relationship of helping others.

The SAT program has profoundly helped many people in many countries over decades through a combination of resources that includes not only subjects originating from academic psychology, but also Eastern elements such as Buddhist meditation and the psychology of enneatypes—as well as original elements such as the therapeutic use of theater and the practice of surrender to organismic intelligence through spontaneous movement.

I believe that the combination of the three modules of the SAT program with a psychedelic program that gradually includes the main possible experiences would be a very powerful resource—not only for the training of specialists but also for the awakening of society. Although it is still difficult to imagine (given the repressive nature of traditional education and the level of conventionalism in bureaucracies) the use of consciousness enhancers in the training of the educators of the future, I believe that just as the SAT program has been useful not only for seekers and therapists but especially for educators, the day will come when also the conventional and ignorant field of education will come to understand that nothing can be so helpful for true educators to find themselves, and to become wise and kind.

APPENDICES

The following articles highlight Dr. Naranjo's contributions to the field in the 1960s and beyond. The first three articles, written by others, detail his work and discoveries. The fourth, "Chilean Theories Are Applauded in California: From the Amazon to the Depths of the Self," has been translated into English from Spanish. The research articles of Naranjo, Sargent, and Shulgin are presented in the pages that follow.

Amazon Drug

From Page 1

type some scientists call "hallucinogenic" and others call "mind manifesting."

Whatever you call it, it has monumental effects on all persons who take it. One man even reported believing his viscera were removed and replaced by new viscera — and likewise his brain.

Yage has been used by Indians in the Amazon area, apparently for centuries, especially to train Shamans (tribal medicine men) who swallow it frequently to acquire the knowledge they feel they need.

Yage was given orally to 32 Chilean volunteers last year by Dr. Claudio Naranjo, a psychiatrist at the University of Chile School of Medicine, and currently a visiting Guggenheim Fellow at UC's Institute of Personality Assessment and Research.

He reported at a meeting in Berkeley yesterday that Yage from the standpoint of psycholherapy "seems to be more promising in some ways than LSD" — a compound invented by a Swiss chemist and currently used in the United States under strict medical supervision except when it is obtained on the black market, perhaps its most common source.

FINDINGS

Dr. Harner and Dr. Naranjo reported on their findings during the ninth annual meeting of the Kroeber Anthropological Society in the Claremont Hotel.

The distinguished anthropologist said the vine used for Yage is known as "the vine of the dead." His reports about the effects of the compound jibed amazingly with those reported by Dr. Naranjo when it was given to 32 persons of European or Chilean birth who had never been near a jungle.

One weird fact here is that seven of these urbane Chileans had vivid visions of tigers, jaguars and leopards that coincided with a characteristic effect of the brew when it was taken by Indians in the Amazon.

In a number of other respects, the two scientists reported, the effects on primitive persons and civilized persons in Santiago were, in general, identical.

Dr. Harner reported that during a total of two years in Ecuador and Peru he found Yage produced these effects in those who ingested it:

● S h a r p e r vision in the dark.

● The hearing of singing or sounds like rushing water.

● The seeing of cities as from a great height.

● T h e feeling of flying, sometimes of being a great bird.

● A sense of precognition —looking into the future.

● The experience of one's own death, sometimes of seeing one's own skeleton or c o r p s e—and contacts with spirits of the dead.

● Encounters with predatory animals, especially in the big cat family.

● The effect of the world being a merry-go-round.

●The sense that the soul has been separated from the body.

"In some cases," said Dr.

Harner, "the soul got away and the shaman had to chase it and bring it back."

SOUL

He said that when he himself ingested the brew "I likewise had the feeling that the soul was leaving my chest— which was rather a surprise —I am not a student of theology."

He commented that this was "very interesting" to him.

Dr. Naranjo, in reporting on what Yage did to his volunteers in Santiago, cited a number of astonishingly similar experiences.

DEATH

Eight of the 32 volunteers, he reported, "had visions of death." About 11 of them, he said, felt they were "suspended in space or flying," most of them experienced "the merry-go-round movement," most of them were deeply concerned about the

and City Souls

meaning of life," and the soul had been separated from the body."

None of them, Dr. Naranjo said, had been told beforehand that the brew came from the Amazon and checking of their histories showed that none had ever been near a jungle where big feline beasts live.

He said that when the Yage was given by mouth it took its peak effect within 45 minutes. When it was injected it took effect in five minutes, sending the subject flying into a fantastic world like that inhabited by the Greek or Babylonian gods.

He observed that many of the effects produced in Santiago were very similar to those reported in Hindu yoga experiences.

The psychiatrist said he got his supply of the elixir by going into the jungle in olombia, armed with a atch of LSD.

"I told them I was a shaman—which I am," he said, rinning, "and suggested we ade secrets. With LSD I as able to show them my owers."

Yage, he reported, acts uite differently from LSD hich, he said, is more inlved with the personal conhts of the unconscious; and from mescaline, which usu ly attracts great interest outer objects.

He said the Amazon bre induces the subject to clo his eyes, but—amazingly— be astonishingly concentra ed. Electroencephalograp of the brain waves at th time, he said, show the alpl waves have disappeare which means the brain is e tremely alert.

SF. Examiner June 16, 1967

African Drug Aid to Insight, UC Panel Told

By WILLAM BOQUIST
Examiner Science Writer

Folklore come to life might well be the title of the story told to the University of California's week-long SLD symposium by a slightly-built Chilean psychiatrist.

Dr. Claudio Naranjo, a Guggenheim Fellow at UC's Institute of Personaltiy Assessment and Research in Berkeley, told in yesterday's chapter of startling experimental success with biogine, derived from the root of an African plant.

The drug is said to be used to fight fatigue by West African and Congo natives, producing excitement, drunkenness and mental confusion, and is the latest in a long string of chemical agents used in psychotherapy by Doctor Naranjo.

HE TOLD theUC Extension forum he has used LSD, psilocybin, mescaline and other psychedelic or mind-altering drugs as aid to psychotherapy for several years.

In the last year he has tried ibogaine with 15 volunterr neurotic patients in his Snatiago office, and is "very much impressed with the success of these 15 applications."

The drug, he said, is "valuable," particularly in producing a state of mind where the individual, under the influence of the drug and the therapist, can analyze himself and his situation with great new clarity, and in producing long-lasting changes.

The new intellectual insights offered by ibogaine, he said, are the opposite of LSD's effect of "surrender" feelings."

LSD Special On Channel 9 Tonight

Tonight's regular "Profile: Pay Area" show on Channel 9 will be extended to 90 minutes to study the subject of "LSD: The D and the Law."

Four participants from the University of California Extension program will join moderator Caspar Weinberger in a discussion of the hallucinogenic drug family.

Weinberger's guest will be Timothy Leary, former Harvard psychologist; Rolf Von Eckartsberg, Duquesne University psychologist; Dr. Abraham Hoffer, University of Saskatchewan psychiatrist ; and Paul Lee , Massachusetts Institute of Technology philosopher.

Tonight's KQED program, presented with the financial assistance of The Examiner, will be repeated at 7:30 p.m. Sunday.

DOCTOR Naranjo's patients were young adults treated before he took leave from his post at the University of Chile. His experiments would not be permitted under present U.S. regulations.

For the first hour after swallowing ibogaine, patients were instructed to do whatever they wanted to do, with no demands that they try to discuss personal problems.

Frequently the patients would enter into fantasies, imagining themselves to be a snake or a tiger, or watching a parental quarrel.

THE FANTASIES were guided by the therapist, who might tell the patient, at a crucial point, to "become" another person, bird or animal, to try to imagine how that creature felt.

The results of the guided mental flights, in conjunction with the drug, Doctor Naranjo claimed, were frequently startling.

One patient, a 30 year old writer, described his childhood before the drug session began, as magical. He was, he said, a boy liked by everybody romping through the fields and streams, "an innocent savage uncorrupted by civilization," whose civilized, balanced mother gave him "unforgettable Christmas."

Directly after the session, he wrote:

"As a boy I was always hiding behind mother's skirts. I went from one woman to another. My father seems so nonexistent. Maybe he was nottnere already."

HE FURTHER described himself as timid, fearful, prone to crying wishing his mother would die. He once tried suicide to punish his parents, who hated each other, he said.

The difference in the two accounts, Doctor Narnjo said, illustrates the drug's ability to produce a "radical change . . . in the person's conceptual understanding of his life situation.

"In contrast with the outcome of LSD experiences which are so often purely experiential and can hardly be translated into words, ibogaine seems to lend itself better to the development of intellectual insight," he said.

"LSD, mescaline and psilocybin frequently precipitate an overwhelming experience in which there is little place for intetnional procedures, and even in low dosages stimulate a great desire to surrender in a passive way to sensations and feelings.

"IN CONTRAST with these ibogaine leads to a state of mind more compatible with the analytical attitude and with the exercise of choice," he said.

Only one drug—MMDA—allows more manipulation of therapy, Doctor Naranjo said.

Also a psychedelic, MMDA is useful in brobing the "here and now" aspects of mental behavior and attitudes, while ibogaine is better in analyzing the "there and then,"—past family or personal events and their meanings.

The two drugs may complement each other in psychotherapy, he suggested, and may in turn complement the "often impersonal experience of LSD."

Chilean Study Yields Hallucinogen That May Give Clues to Psychosis

Medical Tribune—World Wide Report

SAN FRANCISCO—"The first demonstration of an endogenous hallucinogen," some 20 years after investigators of schizophrenia raised the notion of a psychotoxic metabolite, was reported by a Chilean research psychiatrist at a symposium on the Ethnopharmacologic Search for Psycho-Active Drugs, held at the University of California San Francisco Medical Center.

The hallucinogen, 6-methoxytetrahydroharman, is formed in vivo from 5-methoxytryptamine and acetaldehyde, is chemically identical with adrenoglomerulotripine, a pineal gland hormone in animals, and invites speculation on its possible role in psychosis, Dr. Claudio Naranjo, of the Department of Anthropological Medicine, University of Chile, Santiago, said in a report on the psychotropic properties of the harmala alkaloids.

He said that it induces a mild effect in the human subject at an oral dosage level of 1.5 mg./Kg. This effect is "of a less hallucinogenic nature in the strict sense of the word [and] more akin to a state of inspiration and heightened introspection."

Dr. Naranjo cited a relationship between pineal gland activity and still another hallucinogenic 6-methoxy compound. The substance, 6-methoxyharmalan, which he has found to be more active than the endogenous chemical, is derived in vitro from melatonin. The latter substance is obtained from methylation of acetylserotonin, a reaction made possible by an enzyme present only in the pineal gland, h... oxyindole O-methyl transferase (HIOMT).

May Help Regulate Attention

Noting that increased HIOMT activity occurs in the pineal gland of rats that are kept in constant darkness for six days, he commented that "one may wonder whether the [human] pineal body, associated by Tibetan traditions with higher states of consciousness, may not actually play a part in the regulation of attention or the rhythm of sleep and wakefulness."

In order to assess the hallucinogenic effects of the 6-methoxy compounds, Dr. Naranjo compared them to a related hallucinogen, a 7-methoxy compound known as harmaline. This substance, which he administered to 30 human volunteers, is one of ...up of naturally occurring harmala a... ds, obtained from the seeds of Peganum harmala.

Harmaline proved to be a more powerful hallucinogen than either of the 6-methoxy substances, inducing phenomena in the order of LSD-25 and mescaline but without their emotionally disrupting quality, he said. A benefit from harmaline was the amelioration of neurotic symptoms in eight of the 30 subjects.

Dr. Naranjo described these effects of harmaline:

● With eyes open, the subjects commonly experienced superposition of images but rarely confused them with reality, so that the formal and esthetic qualities of the environment remained essentially unchanged, in contrast to the typical effects of LSD.

● With eyes closed, imagery was abundant, vivid, and colorful, and long dreamlike sequences were more frequent than with mescaline.

● Objects appeared to have multiple contours when they were in actual motion, and there was persistence of afterimages. These facts suggested a retinal effect of the drug, a possibility confirmed by recordings of electroretinograms in cats. The drug increased the alpha wave and decreased the beta wave of the electroretinogram before any change was observed in the brain cortex.

● Although other persons are felt to be part of the external world, desire of the subject to communicate is slight and contact usually avoided. Extreme physical passivity might be related to this withdrawal. Most subjects lay down for four to eight hours and reported a state of relaxation in which they did not feel inclined to move a muscle, even to talk.

● Some subjects felt that certain scenes that they saw had really happened and that they had been disembodied witnesses of them in a different time and place.

● Concern with religious or philosophic problems was frequent but without the aesthetic or empathetic quality of the mescaline experience. "Thus, the typical reaction to harmaline is a closed-eye contemplation of vivid imagery without much further effect than wonder and interest in its significance, which is in contrast to the ecstatic heavens or dreadful hells of other hallucinogens."

Called Purer Hallucinogen

Dr. Naranjo consequently believes that harmaline is "more of a pure hallucinogen than other substances whose characteristic phenomena are an enhancement of feelings, aesthetic experiences, or psychotomimetic qualities, such as paranoid delusions, depersonalization, or cognitive disturbances."

Combining the results of the human studies and various electrophysiologic experiments in animals, he said that "the neurophysiological picture matches well that of traditional yagé 'dreaming,' in that the state we have described involves lethargy, immobility, closed eyes, and generalized withdrawal from the environment but at the same time an alertness to mental processes and an activation of fantasy."

Del Amazonas al Fondo del Ser

Por CARLOS ALBERTO CORNEJO

EN EL AIRE PARECEN retumbar los gritos de los papagayos mecánicos de "La Isla", la última novela de Aldous Huxley, con su monocorde advertencia:
"Todo ocurre aquí y ahora... ¡Aquí y ahora, muchachos! ¡Atención, atención!"

(¿Atención a qué?, pregunta alguien. Atención a la atención, le responden, para que todo ocurra realmente aquí —en el lugar del tiempo y el espacio que estamos pisando— y podamos gozarlo verdaderamente ahora: evitemos que los acontecimientos nos sorprendan sumergidos en recuerdos del pasado o sueños del futuro; debemos vivir este momento porque es lo único que poseemos de seguro.)

La Universidad de California en Berkeley se yergue como una isla real y temporal, de vida latente, en medio del océano de una civilización automatizada y simplista. Los estudiantes y profesores no se ocupan, como esos universitarios de los films norteamericanos, exclusivamente del partido de fútbol del domingo, o el baile de la noche del sábado. Las conversaciones triviales, los "pololeos" infantiles han sido reemplazados por una actitud vital e iracunda. El patio de la Casa Central parece una réplica del Hyde Park londinense. Sobre tarimas improvisadas los muchachos gritan, discuten y reparten volantes:

● Queremos la integración racial: los negros son nuestros hermanos.

● ¡No somos culpables! ¿Por qué nos obligan a marchar a morir en Vietnam?

● Los cubanos son también nuestros hermanos. ¡Acojámoslos!

● Queremos que se retiren las tropas de Santo Domingo.

● Queremos legalizar el aborto.

Otros, menos idealistas, proclaman:
● ¡Queremos sexo!

Selvas en la ciudad

Hasta hace algunas semanas, por entre aquel barullo y polémica se paseaba un siquiatra chileno del Centro de Antropología Médica de la Universidad de Chile, Claudio Naranjo Cohen (32 años, un hijo). Alto, delgado, de rasgos filudos y aspecto extraordinariamente juvenil, ganador de una beca Guggenheim, había ido a estudiar y experimentar, pero a poco de llegar su figura comenzó a destacarse dentro de la Universidad de California. Entrevistas de radio, prensa y TV. Charlas y encuentros. El "San Francisco Sunday Chronicle", con un titular a seis columnas ("Droga del Amazonas libera almas de la Ciudad") informó sobre sus experiencias relativas al YAGE, un zumo levemente amargo extraído de vides y raíces de las riberas del Amazonas, que parece tener propiedades alucinógenas más potentes que las de la mescalina y el LSD (dietilamida del ácido licérgico). El yagé, al igual que esas drogas (conocidas actualmente con el nombre de siquedélicas, "liberadoras de la siquis") produce en quienes lo ingieren fascinantes irrupciones del subconsciente dormido en el campo despierto de la conciencia, manifestaciones de contacto con lo sobrenatural y esclarecedoras manifestaciones que podrían ayudar a explorar el fondo del "self" (el "sí mismo").

Aunque sólo en los últimos años la ciencia ha comenzado a considerar las profundas posibilidades que el empleo de dichas drogas abre en el conocimiento de la sicología, éstas han sido usadas desde hace siglos por los "chamanes o magos" de las tribus salvajes del Amazonas. En 1957, el antropólogo californiano Michael J. Harner, mientras estudiaba las costumbres de una tribu jíbara del Ecuador, fue el primero en anotar que aquella substancia que ingerían los na-

tivos durante sus ritos sagrados podría ser bastante más que mera superchería de médico-brujo. Cuatro años más tarde, Claudio Naranjo descubrió similares prácticas en tribus del sur de Colombia. Se había internado en la selva armado de una buena dosis del químico y refinado LSD y al toparse con los salvajes les dijo que él también era un "chamán ("Lo cual no deja de ser cierto, en el fondo", comenta.) Cuando entregó a los indios tabletas que produjeron en ellos análogas visiones, éstos quedaron absolutamente convencidos; el chamán de la tribu, haciéndose amigo de él, no tuvo inconveniente en intercambiar "secretos".

Volviendo a Santiago, el doctor Naranjo experimentó esta droga (ahora en forma de cápsulas) en 32 voluntarios y fue el reportaje sobre estas experiencias, presentado en una tesis conjunta con el propio descubridor Harner, el que revolucionó a Berkeley en mayo recién pasado.

Harner, basándose en pruebas efectuadas durante dos años en Ecuador y Perú, llegó a la conclusión de que el yagé producía en los indios efectos como:

● Intensificación de la vista en la oscuridad.

● El escuchar cantos o sonidos de aguas corrientes.

● La visión de ciudades como desde una terraza muy elevada.

● La sensación de vuelo, a veces acompañada de la idea de haberse transformado en ave.

● La sensación de precognición: visión del futuro.

● La imagen de encuentros con animales gigantescos, especialmente de la familia de los felinos.

● La sensación de la propia muerte, a veces viendo el paciente su propio esqueleto o cadáver y sintiendo trabar contacto con los desaparecidos.

● La visión del mundo y las acciones humanas como si fuesen un carrusel de repeticiones cíclicas.

● La sensación de que el alma se ha separado del cuerpo.

Cuando el propio doctor Harner probó el yagé, relata haber sentido igual que como le confiara un chamán, que el pecho se le partía en dos, dejando escapar el alma: "Esto en realidad me sorprendió, porque yo no soy ningún estudiante de teología."

Misticismo en tabletas

Al compararse sus estadísticas con las del doctor Naranjo (no las extrajo de nativos incivilizados sino de chilenos y europeos residentes, de un nivel cultural bastante alto), las similitudes resultaron sorprendentes.

Once de los 32 voluntarios experimentaron sensaciones de estar en vuelo; ocho tuvieron visiones de muerte; la mayoría captó el girar de carrusel de las acciones humanas; casi todos declararon haberse preocupado profundamente durante la experiencia "del significado último de nuestras existencias". Pero lo más sorprendente fue la aparición en sus visiones de gigantescos tigres, leones, o parajes selváticos; a ninguno de ellos se le había comunicado que la droga provenía del Amazonas y, de acuerdo a sus fichas personales, ninguno había visi-

Dr. Naranjo: trabajo con drogas alucinógenas.

tado jamás la jungla. También fueron sugerentes las persistentes referencias (siendo todas las experiencias aisladas) a visiones mitológicas, a símbolos religiosos o emisión de conceptos de un misticismo con grandes puntos de contacto con los yogas hindúes.

—Hay algo de "junguiano" en esta droga: parece comprobar la existencia de los arquetipos del inconsciente colectivo que teorizara el sicólogo Carl Gustav Jung. A pesar de sus diferencias culturales, geográficas y de edad, los voluntarios mostraron igual tendencia a repetir imágenes y símbolos que se encuentran en el génesis de las religiones, de todos los pueblos y costumbres. Así, la religión no sería un conocimiento adquirido externamente, sino que brotaría del fondo de nuestro inconsciente colectivo. En el caso de visiones de tigres, serpientes o murciélagos —símbolos de criaturas potencialmente hostiles— éstas parecieron depender del grado de integración personal del paciente. El encuentro con tigres que podían atacarlo, significaría una división mental en que el paciente cree tener una mitad de su ser separada de él, cuya existencia rehúsa aceptar visualizándola en la forma de esta mitad del sí mismo que lo asusta. Mientras más integrada está la persona, mientras es más "ella misma", torna a concebir que ELLA MISMA es el tigre.

Al igual que los demás siquedélicos,

el yagé comienza a hacer efecto alrededor de una hora de ingerido y rante tres o cuatro. No hay posibilidad de adicción, de tomarse muy seguido se neutraliza su efecto perdiendo potencia, las imágenes que produce no se logran al cerrar los ojos, pero como han demostrado encefalogramas, si una mente vuela por el espacio imaginario, físicamente mantiene concentración extrema. No obstante surge una radical diferencia con demás alucinógenos: mientras producen un estado de alerta y de tacto con el medio, el yagé, en causa una suerte de trance más donde el medio deja de preocupar do reemplazado por problemas del y la religión latentes en el interior mano.

—Aún queda mucho terreno por correr, pero el yagé ya presenta características más promisorias que el para usos sicoterapéuticos.

Y entonces ¡click!

Pero no fue sólo la Universidad California la que descubrió al d Naranjo, sino que también auto reves. Los vociferantes muchac patios escolares, aparte de pre parse del mundo exterior, han zado a incorporar a su vida dia nicas orientales que les abren las

n mundo interno. No conten-
sólo experimentar diversos si-
as, han adoptado prácticas res-
e, gimnásticas y han comen-
estudiar el Budismo Zen. Uno
leres de este movimiento es el
Frederick Perls, autor de la
'Therapy", que colaboró con
Freud en sus estudios ato-
a durante la década del 20.
iose más tarde del maestro,
Japón donde elaboró toda una
ersonal sobre la importancia
nciencia de nuestras actitudes
Siquiatra existencial, partida-
, toma de contacto con el pre-
a métodos de educación de la
dad son múltiples. Sema-
e reúne grupos de 15 personas,
en íntimo contacto durante 6
día, llegan a asombrosos gra-
comunicación humana produ-
violentas crisis de amor e ira,
s, parejas de novios y desco-
se reúnen en torno a Perls
sala y comienza la acción. De
mientras conversa sobre cual-
ma, el médico chasquea sus

ok!
ige a uno de los estudiantes y
omar conciencia de su ser por
e inquisidoras preguntas:
nde está su mano izquierda?
e la tiene usted en el bolsillo?
á masca la punta del lápiz?
por siente usted en la boca al
¿Cómo siente la lengua?
bstancia rozan sus dientes?
e se pasa la mano por el ca-
Por qué enrojece? ¿Qué sien-
rojecer? Tiene usted las meji-
radas, esto lo ha producido un
agregado de sangre en esa zo-
te usted un vago escozor...,
yo..., cuente algo, declare al-

mno lo hace. Entonces el pro-
pide a otro alumno que decla-
camente qué piensa sobre lo
dicho el alumno: si es cierto,
es demostración de fatuidad,
lez. Luego los hace enfrentar-
pronto, nuevamente:
ok!
ace recalcar lo que están halo que están diciendo, les mar-
osición de sus cuerpos, de sus
iades, sus gestos.
método es el Triángulo de la
cia. De acuerdo a éste, nues-
akos, percepciones y recuerdos
izan en tres sentidos: el mundo
estamos, el cuerpo que posee-
nuestra fantasía. Sin tema al-
mente, un alumno debe ir ha-
una asociación libre de decla-
r mientras un inductor le mar-
esté específicamente haciendo
stante. Las frases del alumno
mienzan con el ritornello "Es-
ciente de que..."
a contar algo que me suce-
. Mientras iba hacia mi ca-

á consciente de lo que hace?
está narrando un hecho que
o ayer, eso es lo que está ha-
en ESTE MOMENTO, no está
lo el pasado, está sólo mar-
¿por qué lo hace?
yo, yo..., yo...
vuelto a convulgarse. Su cuerpo
ostrando que usted está ínti-
o parece. ¿Por qué se ha sonríe-
Tiene haber procedido mal?
no haber comprendido lo que
tía? ¿Siente sobre usted la mi-
sus compañeros?

ando las palabras no
sirven

én se relatan sueños. Pero no
a somera, como tema coloquial.
izan, se hurgan sus símbolos,
parados, desentrañados. Es en-
ando los alumnos toman con-
la la inutilidad de sus palabras,
cesidad de aquella otra con-
ibrid: la transmisión no
sueño es una sensación, un
in estado, un frío, un temor,
de una historia. Mas a veces
ólo expresarse con gestos, bai-
dos; en los sueños las palabras
erto.

estos ejercicios, a veces vio-
torturantes, similares a tera-
grupo, sean aplicadas no a cr-
considerados enfermos sino
aparentemente normales, sue-
var en violentas crisis, ataques
erismo, convulsiones o shocks,
inada la tempestad, en medio
elaz multitudinario, en medio
comprensión mutua, los quin-
riduos que han convivido du-
días han aprendido a cono-
a conocer a los demás prolija-
No es sólo la conciencia del "si
sino también de la forma en
llega al resto de quienes nos

El Dr. Naranjo durante un foro sobre "chamanismo" televisado en California.

Pág. 15

rodean. Es la ruptura de las vallas o,
como dice Perls, el golpe que ayen-
ta los fantasmas dejando limpia nuestra caverna interior, poniendo orden
en nuestra vida.

La ira no es ocultada con sentimien-
to de culpabilidad, la cólera es una ne-
cesidad física del mismo cariz del amor.
Generalmente los no iniciados en estas teorías, tratan de reprimir sus
arrebatos los que terminan por co-
rroerlos al punto de destrozar su ser.
El Dr. George Bach, con su ayudante
Shana Alexander, autores del libro
"Íntimos Enemigos", han promovido un
nuevo trato de la furia, en sus explo-
siones entre parejas. Según la revista
LIFE, al escribir sobre su trabajo,
Bach "está haciendo con la furia, lo
que Freud hizo con el sexo": remover
la vergüenza de su existencia". No es
la represión la respuesta, sino el ma-
nejo de nuestra agresividad, proclama.
Y junto con Alexander organiza fe-
roces encuentros entre parejas a quienes se enseña a discutir, pero a discutir sabiamente hasta llegar al fondo,
a la verdadera razón del choque.
—No es una llegada tarde, ni una
posición política lo que separa a los
esposos. Son problemas mucho más
profundos los que se manifiestan en
formas tan fútiles.

El hombre completo

Otra rama es la sicosíntesis: la educación para llegar a producir el hombre integral. Las teorías al respecto del
doctor Robert Gerald establecen que
el ser humano sólo logrará un cabal
equilibrio cuando consiga la armónica
expresión de la totalidad de su natu-
raleza humana: física, emocional,
mental y espiritual. "Este Y es muy
importante. Debemos saber reconocer
cuál de nuestras cuatro fuentes de mo-
tivaciones, y cuándo son todas ellas
juntas, las que pesan sobre nuestros
actos."
Aunque aparentemente resulten manifestaciones aisladas el Budismo Zen,
los siquedélicos, las batallas reguladas
y la sicosíntesis tienden a lograr la
realización de una única premisa:
"Todo ocurre aquí y ahora".
Somos nosotros, conscientes de nosotros mismos, los que actuamos en un
medio que también conocemos y sa-
bemos en qué forma nos conoce. El 27
de agosto próximo, con esta premisa
abrirá sus puertas el ESALEN INSTI-
TUTE, el primer centro mundial de
adecuación del ser y del medio, ubi-
cado junto a las olas y el mar, en la
cálida región del Big Sur de California. En calidad experimental, sus cur-
sos durarán sólo un año y a él podrán
ingresar postgraduados de cualquier

especialidad: el estudio esta vez no
aparecerá en libros, los propios alumnos serán la materia. El tema a tra-
tar, las fronteras del desarrollo humano: la interacción, la creación y la
autosuficiencia.
—Allí se estudiará —dice el Dr. Naranjo— lo que Huxley llamó las Hu-
manidades No Verbales: se enseñará a
percibir, a moverse, a sentir, a pensar
y amar, todas funciones que aprendi-
mos en forma autodidacta y generalmente tan mal.

Realmente aquí

A través de sus contactos Claudio
Naranjo espera lograr un intercambio

entre el Esalen Institute y nuestro
Centro de Antropología chileno; los
fundamentos de este centro son los
mismos: un trozo de humanidad, de
conciencia humana, paralelo al estudio
universitario.
—No bastan los conocimientos para
recibirse de hombre.
De cundir esta idea, de obtener el
apoyo necesario, en diciembre de este
año, nos visitaría el propio Dr. Perls,
el colaborador de Freud, para organi-
zar seminarios entre estudiantes chilenos. Grandes son los planes. Es posible que lo
que ocurre actualmente en California
ocurra también aquí. Aquí..., y dentro
de poco. ∎

DISPARATARIO

El Recato Conyugal

*Una señora de unos treinta y cinco
años que se encontraba en una reu-
nión, se puso muy sofocada y notable-
mente enrojecida ante las palabras
de su marido, un sastre borracho, que
con desenfado digno de mejor causa
contaba ciertos detalles íntimos de su
vida.*

*Todas las señoras que se hallaban
presentes se miraron entre sí, sor-
prendidas, un niño dijo una imperti-
nencia y también se puso colorado. Se
abrieron las balcones en par en par y
una criadita entró ofreciendo
refrescos.*

*Las señoras, tosiendo, dijeron que en
ese momento no les apetecía nada. Los
señores encendieron sus pipas, con
lo que inmediatamente adquirieron el
aspecto de tontos, tímidamente expre-
saron su preferencia por alguna bebi-
da alcohólica.*

*Entró un perrito de lanas y todas
las miradas se volvieron a él como si
se tratase de un verdadero Paráclito
o salvador. Un espejo ovalado refleja-
ba la escena y, como el azogue de su
luna, temblaban las conciencias y los
corazones de las mujeres honradas.*

*—Cuando Josefina se despierta por
la noche—. —decía el sastre.*

*—¡Serafín! ¡Pone fin! —exclamó
Josefina en tono de reproche.*

*—Después de suspirar y quejarse
como si se estuviese muriendo...
continuaba el sastre implacablemente.*

Entonces comenzó a oírse un rumor.

*Era que un caballero que se hallaba
presente, trataba de azuzar al perrito
para que ladrase e interrumpiese tan
enojosa conversación. El perrito no so-
lamente ladró, sino que orinó al sastre en una pierna.*

*Ante la protesta furiosa de éste, otro
caballero airado le dijo:*

*—¡Señor mío, todos los procedimien-
tos son lícitos para defender el reca-
to conyugal, al que usted, en su em-
briaguez, tan imprudentemente ha
faltado, desasosegándonos a todos y
desordenando al pueblo!*

BERNARDO HERMANN

Translation of article on pages 364-65

CHILEAN THEORIES ARE APPLAUDED IN CALIFORNIA
FROM THE AMAZON TO
THE DEPTHS OF THE SELF

By Carlos Alberto Cornejo

In the air, the cries of the mechanical birds of Aldous Huxley's last novel *Island,* with their monotonous warning, seem to echo:

> "Everything happens here and now . . . Here and now, boys! Attention, attention!"
>
> (Attention, to what? someone asks. Attention to attention, comes the reply, so that everything really happens here—in the time and space that we are treading—and so that we can truly enjoy it now: let us avoid events catching us by surprise immersed in memories of the past or dreams of the future, we must live this moment because it is the only thing we truly possess.)

The University of California in Berkeley stands as a real and temporary island of vibrant life, in the middle of the ocean of an automated and simplistic civilization. The students and teachers there are not exclusively concerned about, like the university students we see in North American films, Sunday's football match, or Saturday night's dance. Trivial conversations, childish "flirting" has been replaced by a vital and angry attitude. The courtyard of the Central House looks like a replica of London's Hyde Park. On improvised platforms the youth shout, debate, and hand out flyers:

- We want racial integration: black people are our brothers.
- We are not guilty! Why are we being forced to go and die in Vietnam?
- Cubans are also our brothers. Let's welcome them!

- We want the troops to be withdrawn from Santo Domingo.
- We want to legalize abortion.

Others, less realistic, proclaim:
- We want sex!

Jungles in the City

Until a few weeks ago, a Chilean psychiatrist from the Center for Medical Anthropology of the University of Chile, Claudio Naranjo Cohen (thirty-two years old, one son), was amid all that noise and controversy. Tall, thin, with even features and an extraordinarily youthful appearance, winner of a Guggenheim scholarship, he had gone to study and experiment, but shortly after arriving his figure began to stand out in the University of California. Radio, press, and TV interviews. Talks and meetings. The *San Francisco Sunday Chronicle,* with a six-column headline ("Amazon Drug Frees City Souls") reported on his experiences with yagé, a slightly bitter concoction extracted from vines and roots of the banks of the Amazon, which seems to have more potent hallucinogenic properties than those of mescaline and LSD (lysergic acid diethylamide). Yagé, like those drugs (known nowadays as psychedelics, "liberators of the psyche") produces in those who ingest it fascinating irruptions of the sleeping subconscious in the awake field of consciousness, visions of contact with the supernatural, and enlightening manifestations that could help explore the depths of the "self."

Although only in recent years has science begun to consider the profound possibilities that the use of such drugs opens up in the study of psychology, these have been used for centuries by the "shamans" of the wild tribes of the Amazon. In 1957, the Californian anthropologist Michael J. Harner, while studying the customs of a Jivaro tribe of Ecuador, was the first to note that the substance that the natives ingested during their sacred rites could be more than mere witch-doctor superstition. Four years later, Claudio Naranjo discovered similar practices in tribes in southern Colombia. He had gone into the jungle armed with a good dose of chemical and refined LSD and when he ran into the savages, he told them that he was also a "shaman" ("Which holds true, ultimately," he says). When he gave the Indians tablets that produced in them similar visions, they were absolutely convinced; the shaman of the tribe, making friends with him, had no problem in exchanging "secrets."

Returning to Santiago, Dr. Naranjo experimented with this drug (now in the form of capsules) on thirty-two volunteers and it was the report on these experiences, presented in a joint thesis with the discoverer Harner himself, that revolutionized Berkeley last May.

Harner, based on trials carried out during two years in Ecuador and Peru, reached the conclusion that yagé produced in the Indians effects such as:

- Enhancement of sight in the dark
- Hearing songs or sounds of running water
- The vision of cities as from a very high terrace
- The sensation of flight—sometimes accompanied by the idea of having turned into a bird
- The feeling of precognition: vision of the future
- The image of encounters with giant animals, especially of the feline family
- The sensation of one's own death, sometimes seeing their own skeleton or corpse and feeling they contacted the disappeared
- The vision of the world and human actions as if they were a carousel of cyclic repetitions
- The feeling that the soul has separated from the body

When Dr. Harner himself tried yagé, he relates having felt the same way as a shaman had confided to him, that his chest was torn apart, letting his soul escape: "This really surprised me, because I am no student of theology."

Mysticism in Tablets

When his statistics were compared with those of Dr. Naranjo, who did not derive them from uncivilized natives but from Chilean and European residents, of a fairly high cultural level, the similarities were astounding.

Eleven of the thirty-two volunteers experienced sensations of being in flight; eight had visions of death; most glimpsed the spinning carousel of human actions; almost all declared to have been deeply concerned during the experience about the "ultimate meaning of our existences." But the most surprising element was the appearance in their visions of gigantic tigers, lions, or jungle surroundings; none of them had been told that the drug came from the Amazon and, according to their personal files, none had ever visited the jungle. Also suggestive were persistent references (all the experiences being isolated) to mythological visions, religious symbols, or the transmission of mystical concepts with great points of contact with the Hindu yogas.

There is an element of the "Jungian" in this drug: it seems to verify the existence of the archetypes of the collective unconscious that the psychologist Carl Gustav Jung theorized. Despite their cultural, geographical, and age differences, the volunteers showed an equal tendency to repeat images and symbols that are found in the genesis of all religions, of all peoples and customs. Thus, religion would not be an externally acquired knowledge, but rather it would spring from the depths of our collective unconscious. In the case of visions of tigers, snakes, or bats—symbols of potentially hostile creatures—these seemed to depend on the degree of personal integration of the patient. Encountering a tiger that could attack him, would signify a mental division in which the patient believes to have one half of his being separated from him, whose existence he refuses to accept, visualizing it in the form of this half of the self that attacks him. The more integrated the person is, the more "himself" he is, the more he perceives that HE HIMSELF is the tiger.

Like other psychedelics, yagé begins to take effect around an hour after ingestion and the effects continue for three or four hours. There is no possibility of addiction, if taken very often its effect is neutralized or weakened. The images it produces are absolutely voluntary, the patient tends to close his eyes, but as encephalograms have shown, although his mind flies through space and imagery, physically it maintains extreme concentration. However, there is a radical difference with the other hallucinogens: while these produce a state of alertness and contact with the environment, yagé, on the other hand, causes a kind of mystical trance, where the environment ceases to be a concern and is replaced by problems of the self and religion latent in the inner world of humans.

There is still a lot of ground to be covered, but yagé is already showing more promising characteristics than LSD for psychotherapeutic uses.

And Then, Snap!

However, it was not only the University of California that discovered Dr. Naranjo, but also vice versa. The clamorous youths of the schoolyards, besides being concerned about the outside world, have begun to incorporate oriental techniques into their daily lives that open the doors to an inner world. Not content with just experiencing various psychedelics, they have adopted respiratory and gymnastic practices and have begun to study Zen Buddhism. One of the leaders of this movement is Professor Frederick [Fritz] Perls, author of *Gestalt Therapy*, who collaborated with Sigmund Freud in his psychoanalytic studies during the 1920s. Turning away from his mentor, he traveled to Japan where he developed a personal theory about the importance of awareness of our physical attitudes. Existential psychiatrist, favoring contact with the present, his methods for educating the personality are multiple. Weekly, he gathers groups of fifteen people, who, in intimate contact for six hours a day, reach astonishing degrees of human communication producing violent crises of love and anger.

Friends, couples, and strangers, gather around Perls in a room and the action begins. Suddenly, while talking about any topic, the doctor snaps his fingers:

Snap!

He addresses one of the students and makes her aware of her being by means of inquisitive questions:

Where is your left hand? Why is it in your pocket? Why are you chewing the tip of the pencil? What taste do you feel in your mouth when you do this? How does your tongue feel? What substance is brushing against your teeth? Why are you running your hand through your hair? Why are you blushing? What do you feel when you blush? You have red cheeks, this is the result of an exaggerated blood flow in that area, you feel a vague stinging . . . Say something . . . tell us something, state something . . .

The student does as she is requested. Then the teacher asks another student to declare frankly what he thinks about what the student has said: if it is true, false, if it is a demonstration of fatuity, of shyness. Then he makes them sit face to face and suddenly, again:

Snap!

He makes them emphasize what they are doing, what they are saying, he points out the posture of their bodies, their extremities, their gestures.

Another method is the Triangle of Consciousness. According to this, our stories, perceptions, and memories are polarized in three senses: the environment we find ourselves in, the body we possess, and our fantasy. Without any subject in mind, a student is invited to make a free association of statements always around these three topics, while an inductor reminds the student what he or she is specifically doing in the moment. The student's sentences must begin with the recurring "I am aware that . . ."

"I'm going to tell you something that happened to me yesterday. While I was on my way home . . ."

"Are you aware of what you are doing? You are narrating a fact that happened yesterday, that is what you are doing at THIS MOMENT, you are not reliving the past, you are just recounting it, why are you doing this?"

"Well, I . . . yesterday . . ."

"You are blushing again. Your body is showing that you are feeling self-conscious. At least, that is what I think. Why are you blushing? Are you afraid you have done something wrong? Are you afraid that you did not understand what was being asked of you? Do you feel your colleagues looking at you?"

When Words Are of No Use

Dreams are also described. However, not superficially, as a topic of conversation. They are analyzed, their symbols are delved into, they are compared, unraveled. This is when students become aware of the uselessness of their words, of the need for that other Hindu conception: nonverbal transmission. A dream is a sensation, a taste, a state, a chill, a fear, as well as a story. So sometimes it can only be expressed with gestures, dances, sounds; in dreams words have died.

All these exercises, sometimes violent, torturous, similar to group therapies, applied however not to organisms considered sick, but to apparently normal beings, usually result in violent crises, fits of hysteria, convulsions, or shocks. Yet after the storm, in the midst of a shared moment of relaxation, of a mutual understanding, the fifteen individuals who have lived together for seven days have learned to know themselves and to know each other thoroughly. It is not only awareness of the "self," but also of the way in which it touches those around us. It is the breaking of the barriers or, as Perls says, the blow that drives away the phantoms leaving our inner cavern clean, putting order in our lives.

Anger is not covered up with feelings of guilt, rage is a physical need just as love is. Generally, those not initiated in our theories try to repress their outbursts, which ends up corroding them to the point of destroying their being. Dr. George Bach and his assistant Shana Alexander, authors of the book *The Intimate Enemy,* have promoted a new approach to dealing with fury, in their explorations with couples. According to *LIFE* magazine when writing about his work, Bach "is doing with anger what Freud did with sex: removing the shame of its existence." Repression is not the answer, but managing our aggressiveness, he proclaims. Together with Alexander, they organize fierce encounters between couples, and teach them how to have a discussion, but to argue wisely until they get to the core of the issue, to the real reason for the clash.

It is not a late arrival, nor a political position that separates couples. They are much deeper problems that manifest in such futile ways.

The Whole Man

Another branch is psychosynthesis: education to produce the whole human being. Dr. Robert Gerald's theories on this establish that human beings will only attain a perfect balance when they achieve the harmonious expression of the totality of their human nature: the physical, emotional, mental, and spiritual domains. "This *AND* is very important. We must know how to recognize which of our four sources of motivation, and when it is all four of them together, that bear on our actions."

Although they appear to be isolated manifestations of Zen Buddhism, psychedelics, regulated battles, and psychosynthesis tend to achieve the realization of a single premise:

"Everything happens here and now."

It is us, conscious of ourselves, who act in an environment that we also know and know in what way it knows us. On the twenty-seventh of August, with this premise, the Esalen Institute will open its doors, the first global center for the adaptation of human beings and the environment, located next to the waves and the sea, in the warm region of Big Sur in California. The experimental courses will last only one year and will be open to postgraduates of any specialty: the object of study will not be found in books this time, the students themselves will be the subject. The theme addressed will be the frontiers of human development: interaction, creation, and self-sufficiency.

"This will be a place to study," says Dr. Naranjo, what Huxley called the Nonverbal Humanities: students will be taught to perceive, to move, to feel, to think, and to love, all functions that were self-taught, and generally, poorly.

Really Here

Through his contacts Claudio Naranjo hopes to achieve an exchange between the Esalen Institute and our Chilean Center for Anthropology; the foundations of this center are the same: a part of humanity, of human consciousness, parallel to university studies.

Knowledge is not enough to graduate as a man.

If this idea bears fruit, if the necessary funding is obtained, in December this year we will be visited by Dr. Perls, Freud's collaborator, to organize seminars among Chilean students. Great are the prospects, and great are the plans. It is possible that what is currently happening in California also happens here. Here . . . and soon.

Research Articles

Evaluation of 3,4-Methylenedioxyamphetamine (MDA) as an Adjunct to Psychotherapy

By C. Naranjo, A. T. Shulgin and T. Sargent

From the Center for Studies of Anthropological Medicine, School of Medicine, University of Chile, Santiago.

The alkaloid mescaline (Ia), the principal active component of the cactus Peyotl *(Lophophora williamsii)*, is one of the oldest, simplest, and best studied of all the known psychotomimetic chemicals. Its close resemblance to the natural neurotransmitter norepinephrine (II) has suggested that the mechanism of function of these two materials may have some points in common in their action upon the human nervous system. A chemical of intermediate structure, 3,4-dimethoxyphenethylamine (DMPEA, Ib), lacks one of methoxyl groups of mescaline. Interest in his base was kindled by the observation of its presence in the urine of schizophrenic patients, but not in that of normal subjects *(Friedhoff and Van Winkle* [6]. This chemical is most probably not an endogenous psychotogen, for evaluation of it in human subjects by *Hollister* and *Friedhoff* [8] and *Shulgin et al.* [16] revealed neither psychotropic nor sympathomimetic properties.

Ia R = OCH$_3$
b R = H

II

The addition of an α-methyl group to the side chain (to provide a structure analogous to amphetamine) has been shown in a number of experiments to influence both qualitatively and quan-

Med. Pharmacol. exp. *17*: 359–364 (1967).
Received: September 21, 1967.

titatively the psychotropic properties observed. The α-methyl homolog of mescaline is TMA (IIIa); it displays psychotomimetic properties much like those of mescaline but is approximately twice as potent (*Peretz et al.* [12]; *Shulgin et al.* [13]). The analogous two-methoxy counterpart (IIIb) has been reported to have produced 'mescaline-like' effects at levels of 10 mg/kg in one of two psychiatric patients (*Fairchild* [4]). Investigations by *Alles* (*Fairchild* [5]) at a lower level of 1.4 mg/kg showed only minor autonomic changes and no subjective phenomena or perceptual alterations.

IIIa R = OCH₃
 b R = H

IVa R = OCH₃
 b R = H

The replacement of two vicinal methoxyl groups by a methylenedioxy ring reasonably followed from the frequent concomitancy of these systems in the plant world. The methylenedioxy analog of TMA (i.e., MMDA, IVa) was shown to elicit a syndrome comparable to mescaline in the production of imagery (*Shulgin* [14]), but different in the absence of depersonalization or of perceptual distortions. It has been shown to be useful in the facilitation of certain psychotherapeutic procedures (*Naranjo* [11]). The two-oxygen analog, 3,4-methylenedioxyamphetamine (MDA, IVb) would, on the basis of the above analogies, be expected both to lack the potency by weight of its three-oxygen counterpart, and not to evoke as intense a psychotomimetic response. In biochemical (*Mann* and *Quastel* [10]) and pharmacological (*Gunn et al.* [7]; *Benington et al.* [2]; *Alles* [1]) studies in various animal species, MDA has been compared with amphetamine. At high dose levels in cats, effects were observed that suggested psychotomimetic properties.

Only three reports are available that refer to the investigation of MDA in human subjects. One has described the production of increased rigidity through an unspecified dosage in one case of Parkinson's disease (*Loman et al.* [9]). A study was made of the *levo*-isomer of MDA as an anorexigenic agent (*Cook* and *Fellows* [3]), and it was noted in clinical trials with obese patients that levels up to 120 mg/day produced unpleasant CNS effects (*Shulgin* [15]). The report of *Alles* [1] is the first study in which an attempt at subjective evaluation of psychotropic properties was made. Here direct comparisons of MDA were made with amphetamine at oral levels between 60 and 120 mg. The threshold for a 'real subjective central effect' was about 60 mg total dose, although there was neither the change of mood nor the sleeplessness that was found characteristic for some one-fourth this amount of amphetamine. At higher levels (maximum 126 mg) there were observed distinct visual and related sensory changes (peripheral field changes and possibly auditory hyperacuity), although there were no color or hallucinogenic effects, and only minor autonomic symptoms.

These preliminary studies suggested that this compound had a potential for producing changes in affective mood and mild depersonalization; i.e., a psychotropic effect free of the visual and auditory distortions which regularly occur with other hallucinogens. An evaluation of this material in a selection of normal human volunteers is the subject of this report.

Method

MDA was administered orally, as the hydrochloride salt, to eight volunteers who had on previous occasions experienced the effects of LSD under conditions comparable to those in the present experiment. It was explained to them that MDA might well have the effects of a hallucinogen, and that records would be made of their subjective experiences and of their comments upon how this experience compared to that under LSD. All of the subjects were interviewed on their life histories and on their interest in experimentation with psychotomimetic compounds. Close observation was maintained during the complete time of the drug's effect, and thus a sympathetic audience was available if a subject wanted to discuss personal or symptomatic problems; otherwise the experimental situation was left largely unstructured. There were six MDA sessions in all: four of these involved one person only, the other two were with married couples. At one point or another in all sessions the volunteers were asked to look at objects, at their hands, at a mirror and at other people in order to detect perceptual distortions. They were also asked to close their eyes and attend to possible imagery and to report their ongoing feelings and body sensations. For the rest of the time, they were encouraged to relax, to be at ease, and to spend the time as they wished.

The dose of MDA was 150 mg in the last five sessions. In the first session, involving one of the couples, each received 40 mg, and one partner was given an additional 40 mg after the first hour.

Results

In spite of the expectation that MDA would be a hallucinogen, none of the subjects reported hallucinations, perceptual distortions, or eye-closed imagery within the dosages employed. Yet a similarity was pointed out by all participants between MDA and their previous experience with LSD. It was stated that both drugs had brought about an intensification of feelings, a facilitation of self-insight, a heightened empathy or aesthetic enjoyment at some point during the intoxication. The effects of MDA were noted by all subjects between 40 and 60 minutes after ingestion. The subjective effect of the drug reached its peak within thirty minutes of the beginning of symptoms, and lasted for approximately eight hours. These symptoms were clearly and unequivocally recognized by the subjects on the basis of their previous experiences with similar drugs. The only conspicuous physical symptom was moderate mydriasis, and this was constant.

Of the four single subjects, one spent much time writing on certain aspects of his life history, which he now wanted to understand better. Each of the remaining three interacted very actively within his experimental situation, and reported waves of euphoria and of depression or guilt throughout his session. In either state most of their concern was with their own life and personality.

For both of the married couples the session was a fruitful one in terms of achieving better communications and mutual acceptance, and much time was spent in the discussions of common difficulties. For seven of the eight subjects, music was perceived with 'three-dimensionality' as is often reported with the hallucinogens.

There was amnesia for some episodes in the sessions of both married women. This is remarkable in that neither of them is aware of amnesia in other circumstances (including three LSD sessions); they appear to be healthy psychologically and for one of them the MDA intoxication must be held as being subjectively slight, with a total dose of only 40 mg. The amnesia appeared to be temporary, however; a few days later, most of the session could be recalled with the assistance of the therapist.

Discussion

On the whole, judging from the previous reports and from the results of the studies here, the effects of MDA appear to be *sui generis:* it affects the feelings in a way which is comparable to that observed with hallucinogens, but it does not bring about the perceptual phenomena, depersonalization, or disturbances of thought which characterize those substances. Further, there is little evidence of the peripheral sympathomimetic effects of amphetamine. It is suggested therefore that this compound may be of value in the facilitation of psychotherapy, by virtue of its ability to enhance access to feelings and emotions without the distractions of sensory distortion. In instances of such usage, attention must be directed to the occasional possibility of amnesia, and constant attendance during psychotherapy is advised.

Summary

Consideration of structure-activity relationships of known hallucinogens suggested that 3,4-methylenedioxyamphetamine (MDA) might produce psychotomimetic effects in humans. In a series of trials in eight subjects, doses of 150 mg of MDA produced none of the perceptual alterations or the depersonalization which had been anticipated, but it did cause heightened affect, emotional empathy and access to feelings which suggested that MDA may be a useful drug if utilized as an adjunct to psychotherapy.

References

1. *Alles, G. A.:* Neuropharmacology. Trans. 4th Conf. (J. Macy Jr., New York 1957).
2. *Benington, F.; Morin, R. D.; Clark, L. C.,* Jr. and *Fox, R. P.:* Psychopharmacological activity of ring- and side chain-substituted β-phenethylamines. J. org. Chem. *23:* 1979 (1958).
3. *Cook, L.* and *Fellows, E. J.:* Anorexigenic preparation and a method of curbing the appetite. U.S. Patent 2 974 148 (1961).
4. *Fairchild, M. D.:* Thesis: Some central nervous system effects of four phenyl-substituted amphetamine derivatives, p. 23; personal communication from the U.S. Army Chemical Center, Edgewood, Maryland (1963).
5. *Fairchild, M. D.:* Personal communication from *Alles, G. A.* (1963).
6. *Friedhoff, A. J.* and *Winkle, E. van:* Isolation and characterization of a compound from the urine of schizophrenics. Nature, Lond. *194:* 897 (1962).

7. *Gunn, J. A.; Gurd, M. R.* and *Sachs, I.:* The action of some amines related to adrenaline: methoxy-phenylisopropyl-amines. J. Physiol., Lond. *95:* 485 (1939).
8. *Hollister, L. E.* and *Friedhoff, A. J.:* Effects of 3,4-dimethoxyphenylethylamine in man. Nature, Lond. *210:* 1377 (1966).
9. *Loman, J.; Myerson, P. G.* and *Myerson, A.:* Experimental pharmacology of postencephalitic Parkinson's disease. Trans. amer. Neur. Ass. *67:* 201 (1941).
10. *Mann, P. J. G.* and *Quastel, J. H.:* Benzedrine (*β*-phenethylisopropylamine) and brain metabolism. Biochem. J. *34:* 414 (1940).
11. *Naranjo, C.:* The Employment of Drugs in Psychotherapeutic Procedures (in press) (Berkeley, University of California Press).
12. *Peretz, D. I.; Smythies, J. R.* and *Gibson, W. C.:* A new hallucinogen: 3,4,5-trimethoxyphenyl-*β*-aminopropane, with notes on the stroboscopic phenomenon. J. ment. Sci. *101:* 317 (1955).
13. *Shulgin, A. T.:* The psychotomimetic properties of 3,4,5-trimethoxyamphetamine. Nature, Lond. *189:* 1011 (1961).
14. *Shulgin, A. T.:* 3-Methoxy-4,5-methylenedioxy amphetamine, a new psychotomimetic agent. Nature, Lond. *201:* 1120 (1964).
15. *Shulgin, A. T.; Bunnell, S.* and *Sargent, T.:* Personal communication from R. B. Doughty, Smith, Klein and French Laboratories, Philadelphia, Pa. (1964).
16. *Shulgin, A. T.; Sargent, T.* and *Naranjo, C.:* Role of 3,4-dimethoxyphenethylamine in schizophrenia. Nature, Lond. *212:* 1606 (1966).

Animal Pharmacology and Human Psychopharmacology of 3-Methoxy-4,5-Methylenedioxyphenylisopropylamine (MMDA)

A.T. Shulgin, T. Sargent and C. Naranjo

Abstract. A rationale is presented for the investigation of the synthesis and pharmacology of 3-methoxy-4,5-methylenedioxyphenylisopropylamine (MMDA) as a potential psychodysleptic compound; these experiments are reported. The chemical synthesis and physical properties of this compound are described. The pharmacologic effects of MMDA in several animal species are presented, as are its clinical effects in man. The animal pharmacology was generally unremarkable, except for a hypotensive effect in the dog, and the therapeutic index (LD_{50} rat/MED_{50} human) was 85. The subjective effects of MMDA in man include an enhancement of feeling and of eyes-closed visual imagery, but no hallucinogenesis or other disturbance of the sensorium. Reality testing and environmental contact are not affected except for a tendency to withdraw into a state of drowsiness, or into a world of fantasy and visual imagery. The induced state of increased availability of emotion was easily manipulated in the psychotherapeutic setting used, and appeared to lead to an enhanced insight into subconscious content.

Key Words
Hallucinogen
Psychodysleptic
Psychotherapy
Psychotomimetic

The psychopharmacologic activity of mescaline (I) has prompted the synthesis and pharmacologic evaluation of a large number of analogs. The structure-activity relationships of these analogs, and the chemical relationship of mescaline to the neurohumoral catecholamines have led to the proposal of some structural relatives as potential endogenous psychotoxins and causative agents in mental illness (18). This report describes the chemistry and pharmacology of one of these analogs, 3-methoxy-4,5-methylenedioxyphenylisopropylamine (MMDA).

The first mescaline analog with demonstrated psychotomimetic activity was 3,4,5-trimethoxyphenylisopropylamine (TMA, II). This homolog of mescaline contains the phenyl ring and side chain of the sympathomimetic stimulant, amphetamine. The synthetic details were first described by *Hey* (4) and details of human pharmacology have been reported by *Peretz et al.* (9) and *Shulgin et al.* (12). It was found to produce changes in sensory perception (of color, perspective and time) at half the dosage required of mescaline, although the qualitative nature of the intoxication was somewhat different. Homologs of TMA

Pharmacology *10:* 12−18 (1973)
Received: August 7, 1972.

have been prepared by progressive extension of the α-alkyl chain (*Shulgin*, 13) but the absence of any quantitative increase in psychotropic potency has led to the conclusion that the amphetamine-like three carbon chain represents an optimum structural feature. The replacement of two of the adjacent methoxyl groups of TMA with the heterocyclic methylenedioxy counterpart, leading to the title compound 3-methoxy-4,5-methylenedioxyphenylisopropylamine (MMDA, III), was a logical step suggested by three separate lines of research.

Mescaline (I)   TMA (II)   MMDA (III)

The first suggestion came from the alkaloids found to accompany mescaline in the peyotl cactus *Lophophora williamsii*. Although many of the tetrahydro-isoquinolines present are clearly related to mescaline in that they are tri-methoxy derivatives, a number of these isolates have a methylenedioxy bridge in place of adjacent methoxyl groups (11). There seems to be a roughly equal representation of these two chemical families (dimethoxy versus methylene-dioxy) in the cactus.

A second clue was found in the reports of the psychotropic activity of 3,4-methylenedioxyphenylisopropylamine (MDA) in humans (1, 8). This compound, although lacking a methoxyl group of the title compound, does have the methylenedioxy ring structure. The analogous dimethoxy counterpart (3,4-dimethoxyphenylisopropylamine) apparently does not produce perceptual alterations or other related subjective phenomena in subjects who did experience such changes with MDA (3). It seemed clear that the replacement of two vicinal methoxyl groups with a methylenedioxy ring leads to an increase of potency.

A third argument came from studies of the essential oils. As we have pointed out in a previous report (17), there are a number of natural essential oils with various combinations of methoxyl and methylenedioxy substituents on the ring. At the time the work reported here was begun, two compounds (MDA and TMA) with ring structures identical to two of the essential oils (safrole and elemicin) but with a phenylisopropylamino side chain, were known to have psychopharmacologic activity in humans (1, 9). Since elemicin is readily convertible to TMA *in vitro*, it seemed a reasonable projection that myristicin might be similarly converted to MMDA. This conversion was successful and this procedure proved to be generally applicable to the essential oils (18). A preliminary report (*Shulgin*, 14), has described MMDA as being active in humans as a psychotomimetic, and an outline of the synthesis, as well as the supporting animal and human pharmacology, are presented here in detail.

Materials and Methods

Myristicin serves as the most convenient starting material for the synthesis of MMDA. The details of its isomerization to *trans*-isomyristicin, to myristicinaldehyde, and to the β-nitromyristicin precursor of MMDA have been described (*Shulgin,* 16). The lithium aluminium hydride reduction of this nitrostyrene (*Ramirez and Burger,* 10), yielded a base easily isolated as the hydrochloride salt, recrystallizable from isopropyl alcohol, m.p. 190–191.

A number of preliminary animal studies were conducted. In mouse experiments, male albinos weighing approximately 25 g were injected either intravenously or intraperitoneally with solutions of MMDA·HCl. Solutions were approximately 1-percent MMDA at the highest level made up in physiological saline. In rats, behavioral and toxicologic data were obtained by oral administration (stomach tube) of MMDA·HCl in a 10-percent solution in distilled water. Male albino rats (Holtzman strain) of approximately 250 g weight were employed. Respiratory and cardiovascular effects of MMDA were observed in the anaesthetized dog (beagle, average weight 8.6 kg). Phenobarbital was administered intravenously at a dose of 30 mg/kg with supplements necessary to maintain satisfactory anaesthesia. The vagi were sectioned, the tracheae were cannulated, and polyethylene catheters were inserted into the femoral artery and vein. All injections (either 1.3 or 4.3 ml per dose, in physiological saline, and at levels of 0.3, 1, 3, 10, 30 and 100 mg/kg) were given through the venous cannula, and femoral arterial pressure was measured via a Statham transducer. The EKG was recorded using standard limb leads. Respiratory expirations were recorded kymographically with a tambour connected to the tracheal cannula side arm.

The human pharmacology was studied at dosages that did not exceed those required to achieve psychotropic symptoms, the effective levels having been previously determined as being approximately 2 mg/kg (*Shulgin,* 15). The doses employed varied between 100 and 350 mg, but most of the subjects received 120–150 mg. MMDA was administered orally, as the hydrochloride salt, to 13 male and 7 female volunteers ranging from 24 to 50 years of age, in a psychiatric clinic setting. Eight of the subjects were at the time receiving therapy for various neurotic complaints, and two more were interested in the experience mainly in terms of the benefit that might be expected from experimentation, during the session, with certain psychotherapeutic procedures. Fifteen of the subjects had had one or more sessions with either LSD or mescaline, either for experimental or for therapeutic purposes. Thus, it was possible to compare the effects of these latter psychotropic materials directly with those of MMDA.

Results

The LD_{50} in mice was 150 mg/kg i.p. and 55 mg/kg i.v. The minimal effective doses (MED_{50}) were also dependent upon the manner of administration; the MED_{50} i.p. was 30 mg/kg and the MED_{50} i.v. was 5 mg/kg. With allowance for the dose differences as defined by the route employed, the qualitative nature of the behavioral changes was quite consistent. At 30 mg/kg i.v. an increase of locomotor activity was almost immediately evident, and persisted for several hours. There was a mild increase in respiratory rate, distinct mydriasis, and an increased sensitivity to sounds. The initial decrease in the sensitivity to touch (noted only at this high level) was replaced by hypersensitivity within an hour, and this lasted for an additional 6 or 8 h. At lower levels, (10 mg/kg i.v.) only this latter hypersensitivity was noted and both the respiratory and locomotor changes were still evident. Similar reactive signs resulted from the i.p. administration of MMDA, but the dosage requirements were several-fold higher.

The LD_{50} in rats was 170 mg/kg orally. Gross autopsies performed on the rats that died generally showed hemorrhagic lungs, dark liver, and congestion both in the adrenals and the kidneys. Death occurred within the first 3 h following administration. The MED_{50} of orally administered MMDA was 20 mg/kg. As with the mouse studies above, hyperactivity was noted within 10 min of ingestion of doses representing 100 mg/kg (increased respiration rate, piloerection, and tremors) but these signs were lost completely at 4 h. All rats, including those surviving the acute trials at levels of the LD_{50}, showed normal weight gain during the following 2 weeks, and showed no significant gross pathology at autopsy after this period.

In the dog, no heart-rate changes were noted up to the level that achieved complete cardiac arrest (100 mg/kg) except that at lower levels there were T-wave changes in the EKG, from inverted to upright. Only minimal depressor responses appeared at the lowest doses (1 mg/kg). Maximum hypotensive effects (at 10 mg/kg) decreased the blood pressure from 200/142 to 60/50. Although the rate of respiration was substantially unaltered over the entire dosage spectrum, changes in the character were noted beginning at 1 mg/kg. Whereas in the control periods, inspiration was slow and expiration rapid and forceful, in periods of drug administration, inspiration was prolonged and deep, followed by slow passive expirations. Arterial depressor and respiratory effects were rapid in onset (10–20 sec). The effects of the 30 mg/kg dose indicated tachyphylaxis with a more rapid return to normal of both arterial pressure and abnormal respiration than after the 10 mg/kg dose. The duration of the arterial depressor response at 10 mg/kg was approximately 45 min; and the altered respiration persisted for 10–15 min.

In human subjects, the first symptoms appeared within 30–60 min following administration. Moderate mydriasis was constant, and slight to moderate dizziness was noticed by most of the subjects. Frequent somatic sensations were those of heat and cold, or trembling. The latter corresponded to actual trembling of the arms or lower jaw in five subjects. On one occasion under the effects of 250 mg, a pendular nystagmus was observed in all directions of gaze, and on two occasions a difficulty in focusing was reported. Nausea was present in three subjects during a brief interval, and in one it led to active vomiting.

The psychological effects were mild, so long as the experience was allowed to develop spontaneously. In general, whenever psychotherapeutic techniques were attempted, responses were exaggerated beyond those expected from similar procedures under normal circumstances. Under the effects of MMDA, intense feelings could be aroused, and emotional insight seemed to be facilitated. The spontaneous phenomena most frequently reported were the accentuation of feelings (anxiety, euphoria, loneliness, loving warmth), the visualization of images (with eyes closed), a state of drowsiness and muscular relaxation, and an overestimation of elapsed time. The imagery was generally realistic and related to everyday perception of people, landscapes, or objects. When no spontaneous imagery was reported, it was generally possible to elicit it by calling to mind some scene (for example, a dream episode). The effects usually reached a peak after the first hour following the initial symptoms, diminished during the second hour, and had disappeared by the end of the fifth hour.

Discussion

The therapeutic index of MMDA (LD_{50}/MED_{50}) varied somewhat; in mice it was 5 i.p. and 11 i.v., and in rats 8.5 orally. In humans, however, undoubtedly due to the greater sensitivity of measurement of the psychoactive dose level, a therapeutic index based on LD_{50} rat oral/MED_{50} human oral yields a value of 85, a satisfactory margin of safety.

The rather striking hypotensive effect of MMDA in the dog is worthy of some note. Possibly analogs of MMDA could be synthesized which would be free of psychoactive effects, and which might be useful as hypotensive drugs. This depressor effect is in contrast to the marked pressor action of amphetamine, and indicates that the amphetamine-like isopropylamine side chain in the case of MMDA does not produce the autonomic effects of amphetamine.

This series of pilot clinical trials was not designed for a detailed study of perceptual and emotional effects in human subjects. It does appear that this compound is an effective psychodysleptic drug. It has characteristic effects which were not anticipated and are distinctly different from the effects of mescaline or LSD as observed by other authors and by one of us (C.N.) in many years of clinical experience. A brief discussion of these differences follows.

(1) The effects were of shorter duration, about 4 h compared to 8–10 h for LSD (7) or mescaline (2).

(2) The subjects' experiences were more 'familiar', i.e. closer to the quality of everyday experience. Both the 'transcendental' and 'psychotic' aspects that are frequently described as part of drug experiences with hallucinogens (5, 2), were here observed only rarely. True depersonalization was not observed at all.

(3) The content of the eyes-closed imagery was in general realistic, and was only occasionally mythical or 'archetypal' as has often been observed with LSD or mescaline (5, 2).

(4) The experience of MMDA intoxication was easy to control by the subject himself, even at the highest dosages employed here. He feels that he has the choice of giving in to a feeling of fantasy or of withdrawing his attention from it; thus, the experience is not spontaneously overwhelming, as it often is with LSD.

As a result of this the subject's contact with the environment and his cognitive processes are not disrupted. The subject may feel that he is under the influence of a drug only when his eyes are closed and he is attending to the images available. On other occasions, the subject might feel that the effects have subsided, or in other cases not even yet begun, until he volunteers some expression that reveals his feelings; the experience can then reach a peak of intensity through deliberate concentration and guidance by the therapist.

(5) Visual phenomena with open eyes, such as enhancement of color or distortion of facial expressions or objects, were observed with MMDA in only three instances, in all three cases at the large dosages. Phenomena such as imagery filling the visual world, illusions or hallucinations frequently reported with LSD (5) were not observed here.

(6) Anxiety has been a more prominent feature with MMDA than with LSD or mescaline. *Hollister* (6), for instance, found unusual tension or anxiety in only 40 % of his subjects with LSD or mescaline. Most of the subjects studied here expressed anxiety, but it invariably led the subject to deal with some personal situation by virtue of the therapeutic setting used. Muscular tremor occurred in only 25 % of the cases reported here, but it was very intense when it did appear. It could not always be related to subjective anxiety, but was suggestive of some alternate expression of feeling. *Hollister* (6) found 'trembling inside' in 65 % of his LSD and mescaline subjects.

MMDA appears to share the properties of mood-intensification, feeling-enhancement and minimal sensory distortion previously described for MDA (8) and 4-bromo-2,5-dimethoxyphenylisopropylamine (19). We suggest that these compounds represent a new class of psychopharmacologic agents, distinct from the psychotomimetics, which deserve further investigation as useful drugs in treatment of neuroses.

Summary

The pharmacologic effects of MMDA in animals appear to be relatively mild until near-lethal levels are reached, but the therapeutic index (LD_{50} rat/MED_{50} human) is large. The psychodysleptic effects in human subjects seem to be concentrated in the areas of feeling enhancement and eyes-closed visual imagery, in marked contrast to the profound distortions of the sensorium found with LSD or mescaline. The differences are sufficiently great that it would be inaccurate to refer to MMDA as a psychotomimetic or hallucinogenic drug. With MMDA, reality testing and environmental contact are not affected except for a tendency to withdraw into a state of slumber or into a world of fantasy. This state of increased availability of feelings has been shown to be easily stimulated and manipulated in a therapeutic setting, where it appears to lead to an enhanced insight into subconscious content.

References

1 *Alles, G.A.:* Neuropharmacology. Transactions of the Fourth Conference (1957), pp. 196–204, New York Josiah Macy Jr. Foundation, N.Y. (1959).
2 *Beringer, K.:* Der Meskalinrausch. pp. 1–315 (Springer, Berlin 1927).
3 *Fairchild, M.D.:* Thesis: some central nervous system effects of four phenyl-substituted amphetamine derivatives, pp. 23–24 (Univ. of Calif., Los Angeles 1963).
4 *Hey, P.:* The synthesis of a new homologue of mescaline. Quart. J. Pharm. Pharmacol. *20:* 129–134 (1947).
5 *Hoffer, A. and Osmond, H.:* The hallucinogens, pp. 110–128 (Academic Press, New York 1967).
6 *Hollister, L.E.:* Drug-induced psychoses and schizophrenic reactions; a critical comparison. Ann. N.Y. Acad. Sci. *96:* 80–92 (1962).
7 *Hollister, L.E.:* Chemical psychoses; LSD and related drugs, pp. 32–74 (Thomas, Springfield 1968).
8 *Naranjo, C.; Shulgin, A.T., and Sargent, T.:* Evaluation of 3,4-methylenedioxy-amphetamine (MDA) as an adjunct to psychotherapy. Med. Pharmacol. exp. *17:* 359–364 (1967).
9 *Peretz, D.I.; Smythies, J.R., and Gibson, W.C.:* A new hallucinogen: 3,4,5-tri-methoxyphenyl-β-aminopropane, with notes on the stroboscopic phenomenon. J. ment. Sci. *101:* 317–329 (1955).
10 *Ramirez, F.A. and Burger, A.:* Reduction of phenolic β-nitrostyrenes by LiAlH₄. J. amer. chem. Soc. *72:* 2782 (1950).
11 *Reti, L.:* Chapter; in *Manske and Holmes* The alkaloids, vol. IV, pp. 7–20 (Acad. Press, 1954).
12 *Shulgin, A.T.; Bunnell, S., and Sargent, T.:* The psychotomimetic properties of 3,4,5-trimethoxyamphetamine. Nature, Lond. *189:* 1011–1012 (1961).
13 *Shulgin, A.T.:* Psychotomimetic agents related to mescaline. Experientia *19:* 127–129 (1963).
14 *Shulgin, A.T.:* 3-methoxy-4,5-methylenedioxy amphetamine, a new psychotomimetic agent. Nature, Lond. *201:* 1120–1121 (1964).
15 *Shulgin, A.T.:* Psychotomimetic amphetamines: methoxy 3,4-dialkoxyamphetamines. Experientia *20:* 366–369 (1964).
16 *Shulgin, A.T.:* A convenient synthesis of myristicinaldehyde. Canad. J. Chem. *46:* 75–77 (1968).
17 *Shulgin, A.T.; Sargent, T., and Naranjo, C.:* The chemistry and pharmacology of nutmeg and of several related phenylisopropylamines; in *Efron* Symposium: Ethno-pharmacologic search for psychoactive drugs, pp. 202–214 (U.S. Governm. Print. Office, 1967).
18 *Shulgin, A.T.; Sargent, T., and Naranjo, C.:* Structure-activity relationships of one-ring psychotomimetics. Nature, Lond. *221:* 537–541 (1969).
19 *Shulgin, A.T.; Sargent, T., and Naranjo, C.:* 4-bromo-2,5-dimethoxyphenylisopropyl-amine, a new centrally active amphetamine analog. Pharmacology *5:* 103–107 (1971).

More on MMDA

By Claudio Naranjo, M.D.

MMDA (3-methoxy-4,5-methylenedioxyphenylisopropylamine) is a synthetic compound obtained from the amination of myristicin, the main component of the aromatic fraction in oil of nutmeg. Nutmeg itself—*mada shaunda,* "narcotic fruit" in the Indian Ayurveda—is psychoactive, and its popular use for such an effect had been growing in the United States in the sixties.* The effects of nutmeg can be attributed to transformation products of several related essential oils,† and this may be one reason for the differences between its action and that of MMDA. From the accounts of nutmeg poisoning since the Middle Ages,‡ it is clear that the spice as such is of far greater toxicity than MMDA, one to three nutmegs being enough to precipitate agitation, delirium, unconsciousness, gastrointestinal or respiratory symptoms, and obvious circulatory disturbances.

The effective dosage of MMDA, orally, is approximately 2 mg/kg (150 mg for a person of average weight, corresponding to the myristicin in one-and-a-half nutmegs) and elicits few physical symptoms, if any. Such a dosage may be estimated to be one-eightieth of the lethal dosage level, as determined in dogs and mice.§ As to the character of the psychological syndrome resulting from the ingestion of nutmeg, this also differs from that described in this chapter on account of its definite hallucinatory quality. This may be attributed to elemicin and

---

*This was written in 1966.

†A. Shulgin, T. Sargent, and C. Naranjo, "The Chemistry and Psychopharmacology of Nutmeg and of Several Related Phenylisopropylamines," (proceedings of the symposium on "The Ethnopharmacologic Search for Psychoactive Drugs," University of California, San Francisco Medical Center, 1967).

‡A. Weil, "Nutmeg as a Psychoactive Drug," *Journal of Psychedelic Drugs* 3, no. 2 (1971): 72–80.

§C. Naranjo, T. Sargent, A. Shulgin "The Chemistry and Pharmacology of 3 methoxy-4,5 methylenedioxyamphetamine (MMDA)" (a monograph in preparation).

probably its derivative TMA,* known to elicit form distortion and colored effects resembling those of mescaline. MMDA might be called a borderline hallucinogen, in that it shares some of the effects of those substances on the emotions and thinking, but rarely causes visual symptoms other than mental imagery in some persons. It also does not elicit the transcendental or the psychotomimetic reactions so typical of the hallucinogens.

The following account of the psychological effects of the drug is based on the experiences of thirty subjects, to fifteen of whom it was administered in a therapeutic setting. For the remaining fifteen, the purpose of ingestion was the investigation of the spontaneous effects of the substance, and sessions were conducted with a relaxed attitude and atmosphere in a private house.

The effects of MMDA generally begin to be felt at about 45–60 minutes after ingestion and reach a peak within the first hour after the initial symptoms. These usually subside after five hours, though some persons (10 percent) have reported aftereffects up to twenty-four hours: insomnia, sleepiness, or an uneasy stomach.

Intensity Variability

In speaking of the intensity of the drug's effects, it is essential to point out the degree of decisiveness in the situation at the time of ingestion and the activity in which the subject may be engaged. This is definitely more true in the case of MMDA than in that of the hallucinogens. Thus, persons taking a dosage of 150 mg who have chosen to give in passively to the experience or who are not engaged in a therapeutic interaction compare their symptoms (disregarding qualitative differences) to those produced by about 50 micrograms of LSD-25. Yet, in spite of this mild effect, there is a potential for very powerful experiences, which only become apparent when the situation is manipulated to arouse feelings.

---

*A. Shulgin, S. Bunnell, and T. Sargent, "The Psychotomimetic Properties of 3,4,5-trimethoxyamphetamine," *Nature* 189 (1961): 1011–12.

This is obvious from the fact that persons who have taken this dosage of MMDA for a therapeutic session compare the drug's intensity of effect to that of 200 or even 300 micrograms of LSD-25.

This variability in the drug's manifest potency according to situation or attitude can also be observed in the course of the experience of a given individual. Thus a patient may be left in silence during some minutes in the midst of a therapeutic session, and he may feel that since all his symptoms are gone, the drug's effect has ceased. When therapy is resumed, however, feelings, images, or body sensations will reappear, or the person may not be aware of any initial manifestation of the drug's effect until he is about to state this, only to discover that he is feeling different in the act of breaking silence. Yet of greater importance than the alternative between talking or not seems to be the distinction between engaging in deep communication or in superficial and stereotyped interaction. Many persons who have taken MMDA in a nontherapeutic setting and felt only mild effects engage in relatively superficial conversation and social interaction in general. And alternatively, in the course of therapy it could be observed that there would be a sudden wave of intense feeling or sensations at the point where conversation reached a delicate point, when the therapist challenged the patient by bringing him to a conflict, after which new insight was attained, etc. Generally the subject feels he can control the drug's effect, in that he can choose to let go to it or adhere to a well-defined social role or course of action. In one instance, a person alternated between writing and participating in his family life, and found that he only felt under the influence of the drug when writing, where he gave in to his essential concerns, while he did not notice a difference between his state at teatime this day and any other day while at the table, except for a desire to withdraw and resume his writing. This contrast between the intensity of the inward manner of experiencing and the flatness of normality of the contact with the external world has been to some persons the same as the difference between keeping their eyes closed or open: "I open my eyes and nothing happens. The drug has no effect on me. I feel as I feel

every day. I close my eyes and the mental pictures are there, like a film."
Yet such a clear-cut distinction is the exception, marking a type of person who reacts to MMDA purely in terms of visual imagery.

Not only does the MMDA experience lend itself to manipulation, in the sense that the individual feels free to go in and out of it to a greater extent than is possible under the effects of the mescaline-like hallucinogens, there is also in a more general sense a possibility of "administrating" the experience, by turning one's mind from one to another concern, activity, or stimulus. In contrast to the overpowering type of LSD experience, where there is a tendency to reject all initiative that interrupts the spontaneous flow of thought or feeling at the moment, it is easy here to adopt a more task-oriented attitude. This is how activities such as writing, systematic exploration of a dream, or acting, are quite possible and do not appear unspontaneous.

Variability of Pleasant Experiences

Most of the effects of MMDA are in the sphere of feeling, visual perception, and bodily sensations, but the extent to which these are apparent in a given domain varies according to the individual and perhaps the occasion. Compare, for instance, the following illustrations taken from the subjects' own descriptions of their experiences:

1. (Woman, twenty-five years old) "As I described a dream, the material seemed to affect me suddenly—an extremely pleasant feeling of warmth, tingling, and light-headedness that made me want to lie down. I did so and for quite a long while (a few hours?) was completely absorbed in a nonthinking, nonvisual, nonhallucinatory feeling of my body, which became more than my body by a melting sensation; a deeply moving experience—I felt so good—the sensations of my body were lovely, warm, fluid. Having a body was truly a joyful experience."

2. (Man, forty years old) "Usual feeling (under a drug) of having hollow teeth and uneasy stomach right into the night, with traces of

the hollow teeth next morning. Imagery was active, fast succession of faces, seascapes, a sudden flash of a campfire, irregular designs, and dozens of scenes not remembered. The one below was the most significant, especially since Claudio questioned me about them within five minutes of its appearance.

"An Idiot Boy with a very wide nose at the top, consequently very small eyes at the sides. His mouth opened, and I could see at the root of the tongue a scene like a lunette in the Library of Congress in the United States, only this one was jeweled and alive. On the top of the center of a rounded hill, there was a huge cross of onyx, on which were imbedded diamonds easily the size of a human head. The cross was turning slowly like a revolving door, and dancing around it was a tall blonde nymph in a long diaphanous gown, her long hair pulled nicely together at the neck. The top of the hill seemed to be the top of the world, the black onyx, the concentrated black of the heavens, the diamonds, the concentrated essence of stars . . ."

3. (Man, forty-five years old) "He (the therapist) has received the gift of Grace, and that is all that I need to say about him. And through him, today, I have received the gift, at last. As I wrote this word *received* there came a moment so holy that I can only lower my eyes. Through the holiness that I saw in his gently and nakedly open face, I have touched now once more deeply into the Mystery, in which the spirit and the flesh cannot be separated. And this is called Love.

"This was really what would happen on deathbed, where there is no longer any pretense, and any emotion may be expressed so long as it is worthy or good, and so long as it is in accord with the finest traditions of human history . . ."

Though different in terms of the psychological domain in which the experiences find expression (physical sensations, visual images, or feelings in the interpersonal relationship), the three share the trait of "good" experiences, or even peak experiences. It could be conceived that there is an underlying common experiential ground in them, a common source from which there flows, according to the individual and the specific occasion, the ecstatic awareness of immediacy and physical existence, the mandala-like imagery of the center of the world and the top of the mountain, or the "gift of Grace" in the feeling of love.

Not all experiences are of the kind illustrated so far, however, and the alternation of pleasant and unpleasant stages in a given session is of frequent occurrence.

Variability of Unpleasant Experiences: Imagery

Unpleasant emotions have never been as intense as they can be under LSD, but were of greater frequency. As with that drug, they can be present for periods of variable duration in the course of a session, and can alternate with feelings of well-being or else dominate the scene. Unpleasant emotions, just like pleasant ones, either may be experienced as such, translated into visual symbols, or converted into somatic manifestations.

The following is an illustration in which imagery predominates:

"I saw people coming from out of space toward me, and then, but not at first, recoiling from me and becoming lifeless, ugly doll creatures. This seemed to represent much of my relationship with people. In the imaging, the people, who were very beautiful and healthy looking, would come up to me and look me right in the eyes. Then things changed, and they began to recoil from me and to look like stuffed things, dwarflike."

Not only is this episode far from the horror of ferocious visions reported with other drugs, but this is one of the only three instances of any "negative" visual content in notes from thirty sessions. Recalled imagery is generally either beautiful or it does not arouse emotions, so that it might be suggested that psychic contents that are unacceptable to the individual do not tend to become manifested through such an understandable medium as visual representation. As it will be shown toward the end of this chapter, a state of drowsiness is typically associated with the less pleasant experiences, so it may well be that there is a selective recall of the less threatening images from the state of restricted awareness. Subjects often do report that they have been visualizing, but they cannot remember what, since the content of the image disappears from consciousness as soon as the mind turns to a different one. In these instances only the last and ongoing visualization is reported upon questioning.

Remembered images are prone to unfold some significance without any attempt at analysis, either at the time of occurrence or in the following hours and days. In the case of the image quoted above, the subject had the insight, at the time of the vision, of a pattern in his relationship to people in general, and later he comments:

> "It is like meeting someone. They come up to you and look into your eyes to see if they are acceptable to you. They smile at anyone—my little girl says, 'Daddy, you never smile.' I can think of nothing to say to people and can't tell interesting anecdotes. It is as though I do not want to captivate or reach out to them. People must reach out and capture me. But I do nothing, and they recoil. At work among 'higher-ups' I do not know what to say and thereby defeat my purpose, although I feel as capable as many. In actuality I am only able to open up around uneducated people. When I do, I tend to speak in their vernacular, make the same grammatical errors, mispronounce as they do . . ."

The therapeutic implication of such readiness to probe into the symbolism of the reverie is obvious, but since this is frequently of spontaneous occurrence, it may be mentioned as a cognitive aspect in the description of the MMDA experience. It might be suspected that it is precisely this proximity between visual and conceptual understanding that accounts for the tendency of some individuals to prevent the unaccepted aspects of their inner life from becoming expressed in conscious images.

It would be misleading to present these examples of imagery without stating that dreamlike sequences are by no means the most typical occurrence. Isolated scenes are perhaps reported more often, and these may at times appear to be both rather indifferent in terms of affective-aesthetic content and empty of meaning. What seems characteristic of MMDA visions in general terms, when contrasted to those of LSD or mescaline, is their realism and everyday-like quality: landscapes and people are the most usual themes, while abstract patterns, mythical beings, or distorted forms are less frequent.

"I began experiencing fascinating visions, very rapid, very clear, of many, many people who seemed real to me—not phantom figures, but men, women, and children of all ages simply going about their business. The fact that they were doing nothing unusual and the fact that they were such ordinary individual people, combined with the enormous number of them, made me feel that I was somehow witnessing actual people who either were or had been alive."

Psychosomatic Manifestations

Physical sensations—probably originating in vascular and muscular phenomena—are the most frequent trait of unpleasant experiences. These might occasionally be regarded as purely pharmacological effects of MMDA on a given individual, but they are often spontaneously recognized by the subjects as an outward manifestation of a feeling, and therapeutic experience suggests that this may well always be the case.

The most frequent physical effects of MMDA aside from the state of heightened well-being already mentioned—are dizziness (80 percent), nausea (12 percent), extremes of temperature (15 percent), and trembling of arms or jaw (18 percent). Both a pleasant state of muscular relaxation and the desire to stretch, contract, twitch, and squeeze seem rather characteristic of MMDA. Aside from these frequent symptoms, any specific psychosomatic reactions of the individual tend to be triggered by the drug: low backache, abdominal pain, headache, or ocular pain, etc. All such symptoms, as feelings in general or images, may be fleeting or may develop into a different kind of feeling and symptom, either spontaneously or as a result of therapeutic manipulation.

The following excerpts illustrate typical sequences:

1. *"My first reaction to the drug was a chilled feeling. I put on my sweatshirt. Then I felt clammy, especially my face. It was feverish. Soon after this I felt a greater awareness of the room visually: the rug, the drapes, and the flowers suddenly became three-dimensional.*

   "I felt good, content, smiling. Friendly. I wanted the others in the room to feel the same way. Very soon after this I felt nauseous. C. (the therapist) and I went to the bathroom together. C. suggested that I feel into the nausea, addressing it and asking it what it wants. Speak to it rather than necessarily giving in to it. I know what the nausea is. It is the same feeling of self-hate that I experienced in the yagé session. In the process of reflection I found out that the nausea went away."

2. *"I began feeling something uneasy-easy, dizzy-not-dizzy, and the light from the window began to hurt my eyes. I got up to close the shade. My stomach was very touchy. I sat down, lay down, and told C. that I felt like sleeping. ('What do you have against sleeping?') I suppose what I had against it was that I didn't want to withdraw from conscious drama or to remove myself from the group.*

   "When I walked to the bathroom I knew I had an alternative— to throw up or not to—and perhaps could follow either course. But to throw up is even pleasant under those circumstances, and I did not feel I would thereby avoid any of the experience. So I did—my stomach was empty—stomach acids came up, and I heaved with enthusiasm. But not very long. I washed my mouth out and returned to the room. There the flowers were fragrant and beautiful and the carpet was very warm-colored—light yellow gold—the people in the room—I liked them all— which was not new to me." (Pleasant, beautiful imagery follows.)

Anxiety and Emptiness

Anxiety frequently leads to a stimulation of the urge toward psychological healing, not only in patients, but in volunteers. Since the emotion is typically a familiar one to the subject and associated with his personal troubles, he soon finds himself wanting to do something about some issue in his life or personality. This was even true for two subjects who were left alone in the room with no specific assignment: one turned to yoga exercises and the other to a written self-examination. The latter process ended in a state of peacefulness, with the following insight:

"Everything falls into place when I decide to respect what is, what I feel, and what I want—to respect it as something given. There is no place for judgment—only for desire that something may change, or decision to take action. No place for condemnation, since it just is, everything converged to make it as it is. Respect toward necessity. All is in that necessity—needfulness. The whole calling toward life. The holy flame. Holy wish to keep R. in my life. Holy impulse to go out into the wind and rejoice with B. Holy desire to live."

A therapeutic urge is not the only response to anxiety that can be observed in the course of MMDA sessions. A characteristic of the drug (when compared to the familiar hallucinogens) has been the frequency of evasive responses toward the ongoing experience. This happened especially when there was only slight acquaintance between the person and the therapist, as was the case of some volunteers or patients who were referred by a colleague for the session and had only one preparatory interview. The reaction in these instances was frequently one of withdrawal into a state of drowsiness, lack of desire to communicate, and only slight recall of the images that seemed to occur during periods of silence. Typically, therefore, these experiences are of slight productivity, in that little is reported aside from a few physical symptoms, sleepiness, and a vague feeling of being "hung up."

"Nothing seems to happen. I don't know where to go from here. And yet I don't feel like not doing anything. My whole life is like this, limbolike. And yet this is a more intense limbo. Intense in its vagueness, in its lack

of feeling or purpose. I wish I could open up to tragedy. I feel tragically incapable of seeing my tragedy, and I suspect it is there. I am not alive, and that is tragedy enough."

Avoidance is not always expressed in a dimming of consciousness ("being half-alseep") or in the interruption of communication, but it can also manifest itself in what is apparently the opposite. A few persons, at the same point in the session, wanted to avoid closing their eyes and witnessing the display of emotionally meaningful imagery, and chose to move about, talking about anything impersonal or taking refuge in abstract reasoning.

The following illustration is from a session with a scientist whose main concern in the experience was that of speculating on the neurophysiology of the phenomena involved.

The effects of the drug begin while the scientist is alone in the room, and he feels very afraid, so he has to call me. As soon as I come in, he feels euphoric, and enjoys physical movements. He engages in what he calls "pseudo-calisthenics"—gymnastics executed with no strength or effort, as in a dance. On several opportunities I ask him about the fear he recently experienced or about his feelings at the moment, and every time he is about to answer, he gets somewhat anxious and evasive. If not pressed, he becomes euphoric as soon as he disposes of the question. I ask him whether he has experienced any visual phenomena. He reports no alteration of the external world, and he has not noticed any imagery, but he has not tried closing his eyes and at first does not agree to try. Ten minutes later, quite reluctantly since the thought makes him anxious, he accepts closing his eyes just to find out how the experience feels. He reports seeing insectlike forms, but more important than this is a very unpleasant and indescribable feeling that culminates in panic. During the following half hour he experiences the same anxiety every time we remain silent or I lead him to an introspective attitude. He does not want to close his eyes during the remaining hours of the drug's effect, but enjoys looking at paintings.

It may seem paradoxical to say that the effects of MMDA at the cognitive level are, on the one hand, an increased flow of insights of a personal nature, and on the other, limited conceptual activity. While rational thought and reading comprehension are available, there is usually no inclination to seek intellectual answers. Insights of an abstract and impersonal nature, which are so typical of LSD-25, together with a concern about understanding, are substituted here with emotional insights that may be described as a "feeling of one's feelings," rather than as interpretations. As in the case of one person who saw himself as an Englishman awkwardly driving the camel of his spontaneous being, one who understood his life as a limbo or passionlessness, or one who discovered his buried self-hate, most persons came out of the experience with an increased awareness of some facet of their personality that was contacted through feelings or images while in the session.

Perception of the external world is not often affected by MMDA. Visual illusions or distortions are exceptional at the usual dosage level. With larger doses, fleeting visualization of nonexistent objects (pseudo-hallucinations) seems to occur more often than distortions in the objective environment. One person, for instance, "had the impression" that a cat walked several times into the house at the periphery of his visual field. In another instance a subject saw, suddenly and fleetingly, a bowl of fruit before her.

The most common visual transformation in the environment is one that takes place during states of contentedness, warmth, and serenity that are characteristic of episodes in the sessions, and this is described as a greater awareness of volume, color, or relationships, while everything appears beautiful.

MMDA Effects Compared with Hallucinogens

In summation of the preceding description of MMDA effects, it can be seen that this substance shares with the hallucinogens the feature of arousing feelings or imagery, but that it differs from substances like

LSD-25 or mescaline in several ways: on the whole this experience is of a more personal, particular, and physical kind, with less emphasis on impersonal abstraction or symbolism. Contact with the environment is not usually affected except for a tendency to withdraw into a slumber in the less pleasant experiences or moments, and there usually is a remarkable readiness to manipulate the experience by turning one's attention at will toward or away from different topics, stimulating imaginary situations, or activities.

Since Huxley's characterization of psychedelic experiences in terms of "heaven and hell," these terms have become widely used in referring to some of the states of mind induced by hallucinogens, and in fact such archetypal images or ideas seem most adequate to describe the unfamiliar states of consciousness precipitated by LSD or mescaline. Yet this is not quite the case with MMDA.

Even though it is true that experiences with this drug tend to be of a pleasant or unpleasant kind, the quality of both extremes of feeling is different from the otherworldly ones so often reported from the use of the better-known hallucinogens. Even when the "heavenly" or "hellish" qualities happen to be present in MMDA experiences, they appear to be superimposed on or particularized in more familiar emotions, such as sympathy or anxiety. And the contents of the mind to which these feelings are related are in the nature of personal concerns rather than universal entities. On the positive side of the feeling range, rarely does MMDA bring about experiences of a definitive mystical nature as LSD or psilocybin frequently do (and have done for several of the experimental subjects), or of a mythical, highly symbolic, and archetypal kind, as with yagé.

MMDA, like such hallucinogens, can lead to "peak experiences," but they tend to differ from the ones induced by the latter in the same way that MMDA experiences differ on the whole. Thus, in place of the mystical quality of the LSD peak experience, the aesthetic peak of mescaline, and the mythical one of yagé, there is with MMDA an emphasis on the experiences of love and self-acceptance. Here are typical illustrations:

"It was lovely to feel the irritation slip away and to feel open and loving."

"My state in about two hours seemed to be one of empathy and passivity, compassion of an impersonal sort."

Any psychotherapist who works with hallucinogens understands that a patient may feel more closely related to him after a session in which the depth of his being was exposed to an unusual degree and many meaningful experiences were shared. Not only can MMDA sessions be an instance of such increased relatedness, but I find that there is a greater tendency for this relatedness to be based on feelings of warmth and empathy. As it has been pointed out, the mystical and religious elements are not characteristic of the MMDA experience. In the single instance in which a religious language was dominant in the expression of the experience (that of a very religious man), that quality of it seemed to stem from or lead to the personal relationship with the therapist at the moment. Here is a fragment of this patient's diary, written four days after the session:

"I suddenly see what a man is. Romero is not a man; Rojas is not a man. Tonio Gonzalez isn't quite. Tito Soler isn't. A man is an unusual event, in the definition I require. C. is a man. It is terribly difficult, and all history measures you in this struggle; you either make it, or you give up, or you kill yourself. So many did just that, trying very hard for manhood. I can see that I can avoid that, God willing, (and tonight I say 'God' with tears in my eyes and my head bowed truly). Ah, here is the inner secret of manhood: <u>to dare to serve God</u>. To dare to follow the lonely way, as necessary, on the mountaintop and in the valleys; to dare to turn your back on society's nagging "should," in order to pray and cut wood and make love and write and sing and whittle and sleep in <u>your own way</u>. That is what manhood is about.

". . . I love him and will enjoy being with him under any circumstances. Love is the greatest force of all, and I dare to say simply, 'I love him,' is, in itself, <u>standing free in the place of bondage.</u>"

The person who wrote this is one of the few who had experienced the effects of LSD and yagé in addition to MMDA, and his comments below are of value in understanding the uniqueness of each of the drugs and how the three may act in complementary ways in the promotion of a coherent process.

The following summary of the three experiences was written at my request six months after the MMDA session:

"In my first experience with 350 micrograms of LSD on May 1, the central area was experienced as religious, in which I departed from a gyrating, whizzing, clicking cosmic system, of some terribleness, to enter a sort of nave of utmost richness, formed in lovely lights that were also hard, like jewels, with the quality of good stained-glass windows. It was a sort of clearing surrounded by richness and beauty beyond comprehension, but not quite beyond experience, and without sound. Yet there was music, and the last piece, an old Dutch Thanksgiving hymn, carried this value into the post-LSD world for me in the succeeding weeks. The recollection is of an almost too painful intimacy with . . . God? Family? Mankind? I said aloud on May 1, with great joy, 'Now we are all together.' I felt this meant my unfortunate, disjointed, and never-unified family, as well as all of us on the earth who have been and are disjointed, one from the other. I felt this was an elite place, and recalled the statement, 'Many are called, but few are chosen,' quoted by Jung in his writing about the unconditional call of Vocation. On the tape I say, 'I knew we'd make it . . . one's little family.' This combines the urgency of unification of the family parts with the relative unimportance of this little group, when measured against Man and God. The May 1 experience was potent dynamite, revealing so much sorrow and the enormity of unlivedness in my past.

"The next experience was yagé-LSD, on August 7. This picked up two themes from the May 1 experience: the religious reality and an extremely strong sexual interest in Hindu women, or parts of them, this only partially perceived.

"On August 7, the sexual theme appeared mainly in a scene in which many delicious animals were kept by men in a part of a huge tropical river . . . for the use of other men with elegant, erotic tastes, or for the use of fastidious felines like tigers. I wrote two days later, 'I must have somehow overlaid human beings with nonanimal qualities. Perhaps because my mother's (old) body disgusted me.'

"The religious theme was introduced here in a new version of 'Now we are all together': all of the folks of my young boyhood in Switzerland got together on a Sunday afternoon; all was peaceful, and somehow very erotic in a most quiet way. This combination of religious sexual movements came to a stunning climax when pilgrimages began: vigorous, rather young Protestant ministers, each carrying a cross and each struggling upward continually, laboring and laboring, not complaining, but not heroic either . . . just busy at the task of founding churches. (I recall Christopher Fry, The Boy with a Cart.) Amid all this struggle to build, I saw Roman Catholics, women as well as men, and children sometimes. They worshipped too, in another way. By being so near them I understood at last the marvel of the Catholic's belief in the Virgin, his profoundly spiritual and emotional and almost physical love of the Mother of God. Somewhere or sometime, the Catholics and the Protestants had a union . . . a solid moment of good understanding, resulting in quiet celebration. A miracle took place when the Catholics had their service in a new place, not the usual church, but amid the Protestant movements. A young Irish priest was brought near to the holy place, where the Mother of God was invoked or even present, where the ultimate Mystery could be approached, a very feminine and sensitive thing, so ripe and rich and forbidden, so different from our Protestant way. The young man was led toward this, his penis exposed and erect, young flesh very eager, almost compulsively anxious to have a union with this feminine Mystery. . . . The young penis was taken in, but apparently not in the physical act of love, but otherwise. It is an act too holy to look at as it takes place behind the screen.

"October 15: MMDA. The religious experiences cited herein moved into a completely new phase, here (seemingly), because the godhead that had been so remote and mysterious suddenly flowed strictly from C. Perhaps my first group experience also helped to effect this social turn in the road. First I absolutely saw C. as God, or one most intimately connected with God, and his gazing at me was an ecstatic experience, not in the sense of losing myself, but in seeing how a human face . . . including my face . . . could become such a divine instrument. It was a definitive statement of Love . . . Gentle Love; and a deeply religious experience, deeper than I have ever known before . . . a completely new dimension, showing me for the first time, somehow, that any deeply questioning man can get into that meadow where 'Now we are all together'; and that there is a way to relate those once-remote inner experiences as the one on May 1 to the ongoing, tactual experiences. This is the revolutionary aspect of the MMDA thing for me: it built, at last, the much longed-for bridge between the depth of the 'archetypal world' and the usual conceptual world that most people seem to be limited to. It was glorious to feel I was no longer alone on this journey: others were there, ahead of me, and behind me, and abreast of me, for here was Claudio, proving it. At the same time, he proposed by his face and actions a new world for me: I saw his face as the Devil's, and his hair as red; and looking into his eyes in an intimate moment, I saw that God and the Devil coexisted there, and that Claudio somehow was able to house them both comfortably, or at least without disasters."

The process has continued in that the feeling experienced under MMDA also appeared to greater or lesser extent in other relationships of this man and influenced his life. Thus he believes that MMDA was valuable to him in that "the estrangement between the perceived inner truths and the application of them was lessened."

This particular experience with MMDA is of exceptional importance ("It was the central experience of my life") because the dimension of personal awareness and love was blended in it to the spiritual dimension discovered in the previous experiences of the typical "psychedelic" sort. The MMDA quality was here that of an "incarnation" and immanence of a deity that had only been experienced as transcendent and outside of human beings.

Sometime in the sixties I wrote a book on the use of Gestalt therapy under the effects of MMDA. I thought that I might call it "Gestalt Therapy Revisited," and this so infuriated Fritz Perls that our friendship came to an end. Later, I was satisfied with my chapter on MMDA in *The Healing Journey,* and never came to show my psychedelic Gestalt book to a publisher, but I will still include here a passage on the suitability of MMDA as a reinforcement of Gestalt therapy and the effects of MMDA.

Having been engaged in research and therapy with various hallucinogens for several years, I have felt strongly, on one hand, the enormous potential of these substances for the therapy of neuroses and, on the other, the decisive importance of what is tackled and how, in the state of mental functioning that they can induce. In this connection I have become aware of the need for a therapeutic guide and an approach to use in working with the drugs if lasting healing is to be the goal. Yet the best-known verbal and interpretational forms of therapy have not seemed to apply ideally to the regressive, prerational, and nonverbal quality of the experience with the hallucinogens. Some nonverbal devices that have been developed by therapists dealing with this specific context (such as the use of a mirror or the discharge of hostility) were helpful, but not a comprehensive approach to the situation.

Gestalt therapy, a specific and not very widely known system of psychotherapy, with its emphasis on "awareness" rather than interpretation, "coming to the senses" rather than translating into words, "enacting" rather than "thinking about," seemed to be the ideal tool to use in dealing with the hallucinogen-induced state of mind, at least among the existing approaches. Yet some shortcomings were to be anticipated in using this approach with the hallucinogenic drugs, principally because the "psychedelic" is difficult to manipulate, since impairment of communication often occurs when a conflict-laden area is approached, as well as sometimes an overwhelming desire to give in passively to the experience—which does not lend itself well to activities such as taking sides with the alternatives in a conflict or enacting a dream.

Moreover, the aesthetic or mystical aspects of a mescaline or LSD-25 experience, when present, seem to be somewhat independent of the therapeutic aspect, valuable as they can be. While they last, they constitute an experience of sanity, but once they are over, the person may find he is again unable to elicit them, trapped in personal (and principally unconscious) conflicts that were not dealt with at the time. It seems that it is sometimes possible with the better-known hallucinogens to short-circuit or circumvent the domain of conflict and "go directly to heaven." When this happens, a detached and unobstructed view of reality, an opening of "the doors of perception," is gained at the expense of leaving aside for a moment the very obstruction that is to be contemplated and eventually dissolved through awareness. Commonly during such an experience, the person infatuated with the glorious vision will turn away from the matters that would lead him to one of the well-known "hellish" states. And if he does not, the result may be the same, in that fragments of the habitual response to an issue seem to be absent and cannot be dealt with: "There is not a problem." And yet the problem will be there the next day, as usual. Resistances, neurotic pride, hurt feelings, disgust—all these will be there to deal with. In fact, if this situation is not manipulated in some way, it would be more advantageous to use therapy without drugs.

These reservations were the reason for my interest in the properties of MMDA (3-methoxy-4,5-methylenedioxyphenylisopropylamine), together with the belief that these would lend themselves better to an active psychotherapy than mescaline, LSD-25, psilocybin, or combinations of these. The properties of MMDA are essentially those of a stimulant to the awareness of feelings and body sensations and a facilitator of the visualization of imagery (generally with the eyes closed). Thinking and contact with the environment are not impaired, the experience is easy to manipulate (in that attention can be directed at will to a given issue), and specific images can be called to mind. As it will be shown in the next chapter, there is what might be called an MMDA *peak experience,** which is more like what Maslow has designated by the term than the *psychedelic experience*† is. Such peak experiences are rarely spontaneous, but more often come as a result of coming to terms with an internal problem that has claimed attention and has been worked through. Unpleasant feelings, such as anxiety or depression, are the most frequent at the beginning of a session, and these generally lead to the spontaneous need to give attention to a life problem.

In this book then, I propose to deal with the situations encountered in the practice of Gestalt therapy in conjunction with MMDA. Gestalt therapy is a psychiatric approach and relevant procedures developed by Dr. Frederick [Fritz] Perls. This approach, practiced by his trainees all over the United States, is fragmentarily described in his books.‡ Essentially a form of existential psychiatry, it is also characterized by the relevance of the holistic and gestaltist conceptions, as well as ideas derived from psychoanalytic theory. My personal training in this form of therapy took place in group settings, with Drs. Perls and James Simkin conducting therapy and discussion either singly or in collaboration. I found that in each of the several week-long intensive workshops

---

*The term *peak experience* has been introduced by Maslow to denote states of exceptional value that are experienced by many persons spontaneously at one time or another in their lives. In this book I am borrowing the expression to designate drug-induced states of similar quality, such as mystical, aesthetic, or loving experiences, without necessarily assuring more than an analogy between Maslow's concept of a peak experience and such pharmacologically induced states.

†The notion of a *psychedelic experience* was introduced by Osmond (1), and more insistently put forward by A. Hoffer (2) to designate the ecstatic, ego-dissolving type of reaction to LSD-325 and similar drugs.

‡*Ego Hunger and Aggression* and *Gestalt Therapy*.

that I attended, at least one-half of the participants experienced a major crisis, followed by what promised to remain as a definitive personality change. My personal experience from about one hundred hours of exposure to the procedures has had greater bearing on my life—both as a person and a therapist—than some three hundred hours of orthodox psychoanalysis. At the time of this writing I have witnessed the reactions of forty-five persons to MMDA, twenty-eight of them being psychoneurotic patients who had experienced psychotherapy (analysis or Gestalt) and most of whom (twenty-five) had taken LSD-25 in a therapeutic setting. The outcome for each of the twenty-eight cases has invariably been a greater step in understanding or change than what might have been expected from a similar number of hours of psychotherapy not facilitated by the drug, and for eight of the subjects this amounted to a critical point in their lives. I therefore believe that a single psychotherapeutic session of four or five hours using MMDA—adequately prepared by the establishment of goals—may be useful even where other methods have failed, either in terms of self-understanding or subjective improvement.

About the Author

Claudio Naranjo, M.D. (1932–2019), Chilean psychiatrist, writer, teacher, and lecturer of international renown, is considered a pioneer in his experimental and theoretical work as an integrator of psychotherapy and spiritual traditions. One of the first researchers of psychoactive plants and psychedelic therapy and one of the three successors of Fritz Perls (founder of Gestalt therapy) at the Esalen Institute, he later developed the psychology of enneatypes from Ichazo's Protoanalysis and founded the SAT Institute (Seekers After Truth), which offers a program of psycho-spiritual integration. When he was not writing, he traveled throughout the world, devoting his life to help others in their quest for transformation and trying to influence public opinion and authorities regarding the idea that only a radical transformation of education can change the catastrophic course of history.

CAREER

Claudio Naranjo was born on November 24, 1932, in Valparaiso, Chile. He grew up in a musical environment and, after an early start at the piano, he studied musical composition. Shortly after entering medical school, however, he stopped composing and devoted himself to his philosophical interests. Important influences of that time were the visionary Chilean poet and sculptor Tótila Albert, the poet David Rosenman Taub, and the Polish philosopher Bogumil Jasinowski.

After graduating as a medical doctor in 1959, he was hired by the University of Chile medical school to form part of a pioneering studies center in medical anthropology (CEAM), founded by Professor Franz Hoffman. At the same time, he served his psychiatry residency at the Psychiatric Clinic of the University of Chile under the direction of Ignacio Matte-Blanco.

Interested in research on the effects of the dehumanization of traditional medical education, he traveled briefly to the United States, on a mission assigned by the University of Chile, to explore the field of perceptual learning, and at that time became acquainted with the work of Dr. Samuel Renshaw and Hoyt Sherman at the Ohio State University.

In 1962, he was at Harvard as a visiting professor with a Fulbright scholarship at the Center for Studies of Personality and at Emerson Hall, where he was a participant in Gordon Allport's Social Psychology Seminar. He also studied with Paul Tillich. Prior to his return to Chile in 1963, he became Dr. Raymond Cattell's associate at the Institute of Personality and Ability Testing (IPAT) in Champaign, Illinois, and was invited to the University of Berkeley, California, to participate in the activities of the Institute of Personality Assessment and Research (IPAR). After another period at the University of Chile Medical School's Center of Medical Anthropology Studies, Dr. Naranjo returned once again to Berkeley and to IPAR, where he continued his activities as a research associate until 1970. During that time, he became a student of Fritz Perls and part of the first Gestalt therapy community, and then began to give workshops at the Esalen Institute.

In the years that led up to his becoming a key figure at Esalen, Dr. Naranjo also received additional training and supervision from Jim Simkin in Los Angeles and attended sensory awareness workshops with Charlotte Selver. He became Carlos Castaneda's close friend and also took part in Leo Zeff's pioneering psychedelic therapy group (1965–66). These meetings resulted in Dr. Naranjo's contribution of the use of harmaline, MDA, ibogaine, and other phenylisopropyl-amines in the field of psychotherapy, partially described in his book *The Healing Journey*.

In 1969, he was sought out as a consultant for the Education Policy Research Center created by Willis Harman at Stanford Research Institute. His report as to what in the domain of psycho-logical and spiritual techniques in vogue was applicable to education later became his first book, *The One Quest*. During this same period, he coauthored a book with Dr. Robert Ornstein on meditation (*On the Psychology of Meditation*), and also received an invitation from Dr. Ravenna Helson to examine the qualitative differences between books representative of matriarchy and patriarchy from his facto-rial analysis of children's fiction writers, which led him to write *The Divine Child and the Hero,* which was published at a much later time.

The accidental death of his only son in 1970 marked a turning point in his life that led him to set off on a long pilgrimage, under the guidance of Oscar Ichazo, which included a spiritual retreat in the desert near Arica, Chile. He considers this is the true beginning of his spiritual experience, contemplative life, and inner guidance.

After leaving Arica, he began teaching a group in Chile that included his mother, Gestalt trainees, and friends. This group, which began as an improvisation, took shape as a program in Berkeley dur-ing the 1970s, and originated a nonprofit corporation called the SAT Institute. The early SAT programs were implemented by a series of guest teachers, including Zalman Schachter, Dhiravamsa, Ch'u Fang Chu, Sri Harish Johari, and Bob Hoffman.

In 1976, Dr. Naranjo was a visiting professor at the Santa Cruz campus of the University of California for two semesters, and later, intermittently, at the California Institute of Asian Studies. At the same time, he also began to offer workshops discontinuously in Europe, refining certain aspects of the mosaic of approaches in the SAT program.

In 1987, he launched a redesigned SAT Institute for personal and professional development in Spain. Since then, the SAT program has been very successfully extended to Italy, Brazil, Chile, Mexico, Colombia, Argentina, France, and Germany, and, more recently, to England and South Korea.

Dr. Naranjo has taught at the Tibetan Nyingma Institute in Berkeley, was a professor of comparative religion at the California Institute of Asian Studies (now the California Institute of Integral Studies), is a member of the North American branch of the Club of Rome and the Institute for Cultural Research in London, as well as honorary president of the Madrid School of Gestalt Therapy and the Gestalt Institute of Santiago de Chile, among many others.

Since the late 1980s, Dr. Naranjo has divided each year between his activities abroad and his writing at his home in Berkeley. His numerous publications of that time include the revised version of an early book on Gestalt therapy, as well as three new titles on this subject. He also wrote three books on the application of the Enneagram to personality (*Character and Neurosis, Enneagram of Society,* and *Transformative Self-Knowledge*), a new book on meditation (*The Interface between Meditation and Psychotherapy*) and *Songs of Enlightenment,* an interpretation of the great books of the West as expressions of the inner journey and variations of the tale of the hero. In his book *The End of Patriarchy* (the forerunner of *Healing Civilisation* and *The Patriarchal Mind*), he first offered his interpretation of the world crisis as an expression of a psycho-cultural phenomenon intrinsic to civilization itself—that is, our warrior culture's devaluation of feminine parenting and the child's instinct—and offered a possible solution to this situation in the harmonious development of our three brains. In recent times, he has coordinated the works *27 Characters in Search of Being* and *Character in the Helping Relationship,* where, together with a team of collaborators in the field of psychotherapy, he writes about the unpublished subject of the subtypes of the psychology of enneatypes; in addition, he was preparing a new series of works on the Enneagram and other diverse subjects, the fruit of which are the recent books *Dionysian Buddhism* and *The Inner Music,* on musical hermeneutics. Recently he has also published, in Spanish, *Ayahuasca, the Vine of the Celestial River,* which gathers fifty years of his research work in psychotherapy with this Amazonian drink, and *The Revolution We Expected,* for a policy of consciousness that would be an antidote to our world in crisis.

Since the late 1990s, Dr. Naranjo has given many lectures on education and has sought to influence the transformation of the educational system in different countries. It is his conviction that "nothing is more hopeful, in terms of social evolution, than the collective furthering of wisdom, compassion, and individual freedom." Through his book *Changing Education to Change the World,* published in 2004, he has sought to stimulate the efforts of teachers among SAT graduates who are beginning to be involved in the project of SAT education, which offers the staff of schools and the students in schools of education a supplementary curriculum in self-knowledge, repair of parental relationships, and spiritual culture. Due to these contributions, he was presented with a Doctorate Honoris Causa in Education by the University of Udine in 2005.

In 2006, the Claudio Naranjo Foundation was created to apply Dr. Naranjo's proposals concerning the transformation of traditional education into an education that does not neglect human development, which, in his opinion, depends on our social evolution.

LINKS

Personal website:
www.claudionaranjo.net

Claudio Naranjo Foundation (in Spanish):
www.fundacionclaudionaranjo.com

OTHER BOOKS
BY CLAUDIO NARANJO IN ENGLISH

Changing Education to Change the World:
A New Vision of Schooling

Character and Neurosis: An Integrative View

Dionysian Buddhism, to be published by Synergetic Press

The Divine Child and the Hero:
Inner Meaning in Children's Literature

The End of Patriarchy:
And the Dawning of a Tri-une Society

The Enneagram of Society:
Healing the Soul to Heal the World

Enneatypes in Psychotherapy:
Selected Transcripts of the First International Symposium
on the Personality Enneagrams

Ennea-type Structures:
Self-Analysis for the Seeker

Gestalt Therapy:
The Attitude and Practice of an Atheoretical Experientialism

Healing Civilization

The Healing Journey: New Approaches to Consciousness

How to Be:
Meditation in Spirit and Practice

The One Quest: A Map of the Ways of Transformation

On the Psychology of Meditation (with Robert E. Ornstein)

Transformation through Insight:
Enneatypes in Life, Literature, and Clinical Practice

The Way of Silence and the Talking Cure:
On Meditation and Psychotherapy

OTHER BOOKS
BY CLAUDIO NARANJO IN SPANISH

La vieja y novísima gestalt: Actitud y práctica

La agonía del patriarcado

La única búsqueda

Carácter y neurosis*

Entre meditación y psicoterapia*

El eneagrama de la sociedad. Males del mundo, males del alma*

Cambiar la educación para cambiar el mundo*

Cantos del despertar*

Gestalt de vanguardia*

Cosas que vengo diciendo*

El niño divino y el héroe

Por una gestalt viva*

La mente patriarcal

Sanar la civilización*

Auto-conocimiento transformador*

27 personajes en busca del ser*

Ayahuasca, la enredadera del río celestial*

La revolución que esperábamos*

El viaje interior en los clásicos de Oriente*

Psicología de los eneatipos—Vanidad*

Gestalt sin fronteras*

Budismo dionisiaco*

La música interior*

---

*Titles published by Ediciones La Llave

Index